Polish Literature ir

Polonistik im Kontext

herausgegeben von

Prof. Dr. Alfred Gall
(Universität Mainz)

Prof. Dr. Michał Kuziak
(Universität Warschau)

Prof. Dr. Izabela Surynt
(Universität Wrocław)

Prof. Dr. Dirk Uffelmann
(Universität Passau)

Band 2

LIT

Polish Literature in Transformation

Edited by
Ursula Phillips

with the assistance of
Knut Andreas Grimstad and Kris Van Heuckelom

LIT

This book is printed on acid-free paper.

Bibliographic information published by the Deutsche Nationalbibliothek
The Deutsche Nationalbibliothek lists this publication in the Deutsche Nationalbibliografie; detailed bibliographic data are available in the Internet at http://dnb.d-nb.de.

ISBN 978-3-643-90289-4

A catalogue record for this book is available from the British Library

Klosbachstr. 107
CH-8032 Zürich
Tel. +41 (0) 44-251 75 05
Fax +41 (0) 44-251 75 06
E-Mail: zuerich@lit-verlag.ch
http://www.lit-verlag.ch

LIT VERLAG Dr. W. Hopf
Berlin 2013
Fresnostr. 2
D-48159 Münster
Tel. +49 (0) 2 51-62 03 20
Fax +49 (0) 2 51-23 19 72
E-Mail: lit@lit-verlag.de
http://www.lit-verlag.de

Distribution:
In Germany: LIT Verlag Fresnostr. 2, D-48159 Münster
Tel. +49 (0) 2 51-620 32 22, Fax +49 (0) 2 51-922 60 99, E-mail: vertrieb@lit-verlag.de
In Austria: Medienlogistik Pichler-ÖBZ, e-mail: mlo@medien-logistik.at
In Switzerland: B + M Buch- und Medienvertrieb, e-mail: order@buch-medien.ch
In the UK: Global Book Marketing, e-mail: mo@centralbooks.com
In North America: International Specialized Book Services, e-mail: orders@isbs.com
e-books are available at www.litwebshop.de

Contents

Acknowledgments

First and foremost, I should thank my two assistants, Knut Andreas Grimstad and Kris Van Heuckelom, who between them reviewed the contributions to the volume and offered their expert advice. I would like to express my gratitude also to Przemysław Czapliński and to Jacek Dehnel, who generously gave up their time to discuss with me some of the issues raised by our research. I am most grateful to Dirk Uffelmann for suggesting *Polonistik im Kontext,* the series he edits with Alfred Gall, Michał Kuziak and Izabela Surynt, as a suitable venue for its publication, and to both Dirk Uffelmann and Alfred Gall for reviewing the completed volume.

Thanks are likewise due to Roland Chojnacki and Magda Raczyńska of the Polish Cultural Institute, London, who provided the bulk of the funding, as well as to Richard Butterwick of UCL SSEES for providing additional financial support from the Centre for the Study of Central Europe.

Unless otherwise stated, all translations from Polish in the volume are by the authors of the individual chapters in which they appear, or by the editor. We would like to thank Urszula Chowaniec who translated the chapter by Jerzy Jarzębski, Marta Natalia Wróblewska the chapter by Agnieszka Mrozik, and Soren Gauger the chapter by Grzegorz Niziołek. Adjustments to English style throughout the volume are solely the responsibility of the editor.

Ursula Phillips

Introduction

Ursula PHILLIPS

This volume attempts to capture, account for and analyse some of the developments that have taken place in literary production in the Polish language since the fundamental change to Poland's political and economic system in 1989—the transition from communism and a centrally planned economy, to Western-style parliamentary democracy and a capitalist market economy, which in turn had the effect of pluralizing and commercializing all aspects of the book publishing industry and distribution networks. It is intended to be a useful, albeit introductory guide to students and researchers working in the fields of Polish literary and cultural studies, Slavic studies generally, comparative literature, postcolonial and/or post-communist studies, and the study of political and social transformation. It is designed to be accessible to recipients who are not native or fluent speakers of Polish, although it does assume a certain basic awareness of Polish history and political change. Care has been taken to provide each chapter with a substantial bibliography, which in some cases records not only works specifically cited in the chapter but also scope for further reading. The current Introduction is also supported by a long—though still selective—bibliography, where key works of scholarship and criticism are included (mostly in Polish, however, as most work in the field to date has been conducted by Polish scholars and critics) that have already attempted to charter the essence of the post-1989 changes as they have affected, or been reflected in literature (Jarzębski 1997; Czapliński 1997, 2007a, 2007b and 2009; Uniłowski 1998; Nowacki 1999; Śliwiński 2002; Iwasiów 2002; Dunin 2004; Lachman 2004; Nasiłowska 2006; Wachtel 2006; Zaleski 2008). The book is intended as an initial tool, not as a final interpretation or judgment, an inspiration to further research rather than a conclusion, part of a process, a witness to changes that are still ongoing and constantly in flux—although a few tentative and provisional general conclusions will be offered at the end of this Introduction.

The general critical approach of the volume is one of openness and enquiry, not one of proving a point. Each of the individual authors brings to bear his or her methodology, critical apparatus and point of view—no overall constraints have been imposed by the editorial team. However, the overarching principle of openness and acceptance of change itself acts as a kind of unifying feature of the volume. Hence the position of the editor, her two assistants—and indeed the contributors—is not neutral. We regard openness to change as a positive mental, intellectual and indeed ideological attitude. Meanwhile we see plurality as a healthy development in itself, we are not seeking to discover, identify, substantiate or prove any one single dominant narrative, "great" or not so great, although some individual contributors may have a stronger sense of such a narrative than others.

Thus the emphasis of our enquiry is on what has changed since 1989, on what has become more open and socially inclusive—not so much in the sense of becoming more universal (or European) and less specifically "polonocentric"—whatever that term actually means (I use it here to suggest a matrix of nationalistically-orientated, exclusive cultural identity markers, stemming from the 19th-century Polish Romantic heritage but still used indiscriminately in the rhetoric of present-day politicians and partisan cultural commentators)—but rather in the sense of what aspects of Polish reality have been allowed to come to the fore since 1989, and in some cases, what aspects repressed between 1945 and 1989 have been restored (for example, the Jewish identity of many writers). In some chapters, the contributors also look at negative reactions within post-1989 Polish society, as reflected in literary texts, precisely to social change, and to the inclusion of hitherto excluded elements (such as gays and lesbians). Here, a distinct conflict often emerges between generations as represented in literature—not an absolute or across-the-board one, but one that is nevertheless tangible, as Jerzy Jarzębski observes in his analysis in this volume of a large variety of novels that portray conflict between parents and children (a universal theme, but one which in the post-1989 Polish context nevertheless acquires specific characteristics).

The separate chapters of the book also have a generational aspect since they are written by Polish scholars of three different generations: those prominent and established in Polish literary studies before 1989, those who studied and published already in the 1980s but whose careers have flourished mainly subsequently, and those who have no direct personal experience of communism; and, on the other hand, by non-Polish authors—German, Belgian, Scandinavian and British (Scottish and English)—also representing at least two generations, i.e. those who were already involved in Polish literary studies before 1989, and those who have emerged in the 1990s and 2000s. The volume should be regarded meanwhile not only as the work of individuals, each with her or his separate perspective (cultural, academic, ideological) writing on their chosen topic, but as part of a team, where the individual authors share the above-mentioned common feature: openness to change.

The immediate context that inspired the volume was the conference on post-1989 Polish literature held at University College London School of Slavonic and East European Studies, 10-11 November 2011.[1] However, the volume is not a

---

1 The conference was made possible by the generous funding received from the Polish Cultural Institute, London, and from the Zdanowicz Fund, University of Cambridge. The conference opened on 9 November with an evening devoted to the centenary year of Czesław Miłosz funded

reflection of the conference proceedings but a collection of papers (now chapters) that a self-selecting group of the conference speakers have reworked following the conference and its discussions (not all conference participants chose to contribute to the book), for the purpose of creating a well-considered and useful lasting tool for other scholars and students. It should therefore be disconnected from any direct association with the conference itself.

The reasons why the conference actually arose, however, and one why it was considered important to appraise the post-1989 developments in a similar forum, are connected with an earlier conference also held at SSEES (then one of the Senate institutes of the University of London) back in 1993, when the conference delegates not only discussed Polish literary production of the 1970s and 80s (the headline topic of the conference) but also speculated about what might happen next: how the new conditions created by the fledgling democracy and new capitalist economy would affect literature, and what was likely to—and even ought to—emerge. Among the participants were many eminent scholars and critics of Polish literature mostly based in Polish universities who only after 1989 could travel freely to the West and publish without potential interventions from censors—including, among others, Jan Józef Szczepański, Tadeusz Nyczek, Aleksander Fiut, Małgorzata Czermińska, Włodzimierz Bolecki, Zdzisław Łapiński, Edward Balcerzan, Leonard Neuger, Jerzy Jarzębski and Ryszard Nycz.[2] Whilst no clear developments could be signalled let alone prophesied, the questions that arose in discussion were remarkably similar to those posed in a recent (January-March 2010) debate on the contemporary state and future direction of Polish literature published in the weekly cultural newspaper *Tygodnik Powszechny* (numbers 2, 4, 5, 6, 8, 11).

It began with Anna Nasiłowska's piece (10 January), concerned about the effects of the commercialization of literary production in free market conditions, and the fact that (in her view) writers seemed to have lost any sense of "engagement" with society, with collective values, and were no longer driven by concerns surrounding "freedom," which was arguably once again under threat from other, commercially driven forces. In the debate that ensued, the premises of such complaints were challenged—by, among others, commentators who had a more posi-

by the Book Institute, Kraków. The current volume is based on the main two-day conference; no articles are included on Miłosz.

2 The conference entitled "From the New Wave to Cultural Pluralism? Polish Literature 1970-1993" took place on 22-25 March 1993, and was organized by Stanisław Eile, Radojka Miljević, Ursula Phillips, Włodzimierz Bolecki and Jerzy Jarzębski. It was attended by Wisława Szymborska. The papers were never published as a volume, although individual authors may have published their papers subsequently. Apart from the editor, the following contributors to the present volume attended this earlier event: Jerzy Jarzębski, Knut Andreas Grimstad, Joanna Michlic, Anthony Kemp-Welch.

tive view of the literary pluralism that had evolved since 1989 (Inga Iwasiów, 24 January), or by those who questioned whether pre-1989 (oppositionist) writers had in fact been so monolithically concerned with "freedom" in the first place (Stefan Chwin, 7 February), or by those who questioned whether literature should be expected to fulfil any social obligations at all (Dariusz Nowacki, 31 January). The following writers and critics, representing at least two generations, participated and presented different takes—perhaps not surprisingly—on where Polish literature now stood: Anna Nasiłowska, Inga Iwasiów, Piotr Wojciechowski, Dariusz Nowacki, Stefan Chwin, Krzysztof Biedrzycki, Tadeusz Lipski and Piotr Śliwiński. There is no space here to discuss the intricacies of the debate. However, the three driving questions (reprinted each time a new contribution appeared, under the heading "On the Condition of Literature"), are worth quoting, because they are an interesting re-articulation seventeen years later of the concluding questions left hanging in the air after the 1993 SSEES conference, suggesting that to some people they are still the crucial questions:

– What role does a writer fulfil in society today?
– Has Polish literature—which had previously defined its tasks within the context of the Cause (struggle with the system, with ideological constraints)—reformulated its aesthetic, social and political obligations, after regaining freedom in 1989?
– Have writers succeeded in thinking through the most important problems of the past and working out ways of dealing with the new—market—conditions?

Our book does not provide any conclusive answers to these questions, but it is worthwhile noting that among certain critics of contemporary literature they still have relevance. Rather, our book suggests that literary production has been diverse and pluralist, and has given voice to a vast range of different individual voices writing in different genres and linguistic styles, and reflecting many aspects of contemporary reality—and that it has not settled, and most likely will not settle into any fixed collective pattern along any shared ideological lines, assuming conditions of market-driven democracy continue. In other words, literature has become "normalized," according to the political and economic order that now pertains: capitalism. Our book cannot cover all aspects of this literary production, but it at least captures several features of both production and scholarship that have emerged or become more visible since 1989.

A few further remarks about the choice of 1989 as our point of departure and its significance as a turning point in Polish cultural development are in order. It is by now a well-known fact, repeated with the insistence of a mantra, that the date of the removal of the Berlin Wall, heralding fundamental systemic change across most of the former Soviet bloc, initiated reforms in Poland. Discussion in the volume will not be directly about politics, but as another link to the 1993 conference and the questions it raised, we are including an "Afterword" by political historian and writer on the Communist Party (PZPR) Anthony Kemp-Welch (2008), who led a discussion at the 1993 event following Norman Davies's introductory lecture ("The Polish Road to Cultural Freedom"). Kemp-Welch's current text is not intended to be a conclusive summary of political developments in Poland since 1989, but to provide a point of reference for the rest of the book, which is about literature.

During 2009-2010 there was much discussion inspired by the twenty-year anniversary of the political changes in Eastern and Central Europe, including at another conference organized by UCL SSEES and held in June 2010 entitled "Children of the Revolution." In addition, when planning the 2011 conference, which formed the basis of the current volume, comparisons were frequently being made by historians and cultural commentators between the twenty-year period of the Second Republic (1918-1939), when a Polish state enjoyed independence from foreign domination for the first time in 123 years, and the so-called "new twenty years" or "nowe dwudziestolecie" (1989-2009), including the implications of new independence for literature (see, for example, Gosk 2010; Nowacki and Uniłowski 2010-2011). Both periods could be said to represent a time of struggle with the new-found responsibilities of self-governance and economic reconstruction (when national identity could no longer be uniformly or collectively defined *against* an external oppressor), including a reckoning with the recent past (hence the tasks that the new "post-dependency" studies have set themselves, addressing and comparing—incidentally—the post-1918 period, see Nycz 2011 and below). But, at the same time, these two periods could be perceived as having provided the opportunity for culture, including literature, to flourish in relatively unhampered ways (e.g. free of official state censorship), and where individual artistic projects have been just as significant as collective ones. None of our contributors deals directly with this comparison, but it nevertheless sits in the background to their discussions along with the consciousness of the profound systemic and societal changes provoked by 1989.

We should also ask, however, whether, despite these profound changes, developments in the arts—here, specifically literature, poetry, drama—can be said to map precisely onto political events. Do not artistic developments take place according to a somewhat different time-scale? Prompted, for instance, rather by the publication of some crucial philosophical work or the emergence of some original new artistic style or artistic manifesto? This is always a problem with the periodization of literature, where literary historians tend to find a convenient hook, onto which they can hang changes in literature—although political events, of course, are not without their influence. Yet new developments are often afoot ahead of such "revolutionary" events, while older patterns persist despite them.

The years 1863-1864 (the date of the January Insurrection), for example, are regularly cited as the end of Romanticism in Polish literary culture and the beginning of Positivism, but no such clear-cut change took place precisely then; it was more gradual. Similarly, can we honestly say that 1918 alone and of itself prompted new literary developments? Hence, to use 1989 as a categorical starting point for our discussions is not entirely satisfactory, and can be challenged, as our final contributor, translator Elżbieta Wójcik-Leese, implies between the lines in her discussion of post-1989 English-language anthologies of Polish poetry. This questioning of the 1989 watershed in politics as the sole indicator of change, is also imminent in certain retrospective compilations, compendiums and critical studies undertaken in recent years by Polish literary historians (see Czapliński et al. 2003; Nasiłowska 2006, both of which contain extensive and extremely useful chronological tabulations of literary publications alongside political events). These are driven partly by the need to explain what came before, in order to describe what is current or contemporary, but they also indicate that new trends already evident in the 1980s, or even late 1970s, were to some extent what were to find eventual expression post-1989. Likewise, Jerzy Jarzębski (1997) sees Paweł Huelle's novel *Weiser Dawidek* (1987) as already heralding fresh thematic content, not just a Polish variation on magic realism: the suppressed Jewish past, the German city underlying the present-day Polish one—i.e. the "lost others" discussed in prose of the 1990s and 2000s by Uilleam Blacker in this current volume. We wish to register therefore that we are fully conscious of the reservations that can be raised from the literary or aesthetic point of view against the choice of 1989 as our point of departure. However, the changes were so fundamental we believe that it can be justified irrespective of these reservations.

A single volume such as this meanwhile cannot hope to cover all literary activity in Polish since 1989, which has been overwhelming prolific, as well as diverse. The focus of the book is therefore on what has changed since 1989, not what has obviously continued. Hence it is important to state clearly what this book is *not* about as well as what it *is* about. It is not an attempt to comprehensively chronicle everything that has happened since 1989. Likewise, it is not so much about stardom—sensational individual texts, exceptional talents and big names—as about texts as markers of change (although we do highlight certain individuals whose contributions to literary production we regard as having been crucial or symptomatic, as representing, as it were, a "sea change"—as in the cases of Izabela Filipiak, Michał Głowiński or Piotr Paziński, discussed in the chapters by Monika Świerkosz, Urszula Chowaniec, Joanna Michlic and Knut Andreas Grimstad respectively). We do not discuss, for example, the work of well-known figures continuing to write and publish after 1989, such as Czesław Miłosz (1911-2004), Zbigniew Herbert (1924-1998), Wisława Szymborska (1923-2012) and Tadeusz

Różewicz (b. 1921), even though Miłosz, for example, published several major collections of poetry post-1989 as well as collections of essays; similarly Szymborska, winner of the Nobel Prize for Literature in 1996. These writers have been the subjects of a relatively large body of scholarship already both in Polish and in other languages, have been copiously translated into English (by Adam Czerniawski, Stanisław Barańczak and Clare Cavanagh, among others) and continue to be translated (Joanna Trzeciak received the Found in Translation Award 2012 for her translation of Różewicz's *Sobbing Superpower*). Likewise, a large number of other poets of the same generation or the next—to name only Julia Hartwig (b. 1921), Ewa Lipska (b. 1945) or Adam Zagajewski (b. 1945) among the most prominent—have continued to publish since 1989 and be discussed in the media and/or researched by scholars.

Similarly in prose, to mention here only the twice winner of the Nike Award (established 1997 and funded by leading newspaper *Gazeta Wyborcza*, a prize equivalent in status to the Man Booker Prize), novelist Wiesław Myśliwski (b. 1932), for his novels *Horizon* (*Widnokrąg*) and *Treatise on Podding Peas* (*Traktat o łuskaniu fasoli*) in 1997 and 2007 respectively; in 2012, meanwhile, this writer gained even greater prominence with Bill Johnston being awarded two international prizes for his 2011 translation of an earlier novel *Stone upon Stone* (*Kamień na kamieniu,* 1984). Another writer of this generation, and like Myśliwski formerly associated with the "countryside" or "peasant" trend in Polish literature, and likewise published officially in the former People's Republic, not in the underground or dissident "second" circulation, Marian Pilot (b. 1936), won the Nike in 2011.

The continued prolific activity, success and recognition of such writers begs questions about the relationship (if there is one) between literary production (in terms of universal human or artistic values) and political dissidence: were certain opposition writers, but not those honoured here, artificially promoted pre-1989 by émigré milieus or by scholars sympathetic to the opposition for the content rather than the literary value of their work? Meanwhile, such prestigious awards are interspersed in the Nike role of honour with recognition for younger generations. The prize has been not awarded in any chronological order of generation, over the last ten years: Jarosław Marek Rymkiewicz (2003), Wojciech Kuczok (2004), Andrzej Stasiuk (2005), Dorota Masłowska (2006), Wiesław Myśliwski (2007), Olga Tokarczuk (2008), Eugeniusz Tkaczyszyn-Dycki (2009), Tadeusz Słobodzianek (2010), Marian Pilot (2011), Marek Bieńczyk (2012). Other nominated texts that reached the final seven include those by the newest generation of published writers (Jacek Dehnel in 2010, Justyna Bargielska in 2011).

One could go on listing. The point here, however, is that many writers established both within pre-1989 literature in Poland itself or in emigration (the changed perceptions of which will be addressed below), continued to publish after 1989 alongside new generations of fresh talent (naturally, why shouldn't they?)—but these will not be the topic(s) of the current book. At the same time, however, it should give pause for thought that certain remarkable, radically inventive texts published post-1989, or even post-2000, do not always fall into *either* the category of "previously established" (i.e. sanctioned *either* by the communist authorities *or* by émigré or dissident circles) *or* "younger" writers—viz. Bożena Keff's *Song on Mother and the Fatherland* (*Utwór o Matce i Ojczyźnie,* 2008). The Holocaust theme of this text, as well as its feminist framework, already suggest something about change: Keff was born in 1948, but such a text saw the light of day only in 2008, when the author was sixty. Therefore, whilst recognizing "generation" as being a key factor in literary change (Jerzy Jarzębski), the focus here will always be on published texts and when they appeared, rather than on the actual age of particular authors (in other words: the ages of authors discussed will be given, but this should not be understood as suggesting that all authors born at roughly the same time necessarily write in a similar way or share identical views *just because* they are of the same generation).

It is also important to make clear what, for the purposes of this book, we understand by literature and therefore what kind of works the reader should expect to find discussed by our contributors. By "literature," we broadly understand the traditional genres of prose fiction (novels, short stories), drama and poetry. In this book, rightly or wrongly—but this is the choice of our contributors on this occasion—we treat "literature" as printed literature in most cases, as "words on a page": we do not discuss internet publishing or significant changes in "verbal" production provoked by new technologies and practices (Wilk and Górska-Olesińska 2011). This implies that we refrain from discussing forms of digital literature such as Sławomir Shuty's hypertext novel *Blok* (*The Block*, 2002), examples of so called "liberatura" ("liberature") such as Zenon Fajfer and Katarzyna Bazarnik's *Oka-leczenie* (*Eyes-sore*, 2000) or new cross-media projects such as Szczepan Kopyt's *buch* (2011). This does not represent any deliberate value judgment on our part, rather the fact that our own experience and research has been within the more traditional forms of literature. That said, however, several contributors introduce "short-form" works that could be said to be of a hybrid or mixed-genre nature, such as the mini-prose of Justyna Bargielska or "poetical" notebook of Wioletta Grzegorzewska, both discussed by Urszula Chowaniec. Hybrid, disjointed, "non-epic" forms are one of the most distinctive formal features of recent literature, and might be said to have replaced the "realistic" novel (Czapliński 2007a, 39-43, 55); one only has to think of the structure, for example, of Olga Tokarczuk's *House of Day, House of Night* (*Dom dzienny, dom nocny,*

1998) or *Runners* (*Bieguni,* 2007). But the focus of the current contributors is not form or style, but the content of literary texts.

Because of the topical choices made by the individual contributors, the majority of the chapters have turned out to be in fact on prose. However, the "prose" itself is generically diverse and extends the boundaries of what we understand by "fiction" or "autobiography" or "family chronicle," for example, as well as blurs the once clearer distinction between "highbrow" ("artistic"?) so-called belles-lettres and popular works. "Popular" elements are visible in many of the texts discussed (see Lachman 2004). This is very clear in the wide range of novels analysed, for instance, by Dirk Uffelmann and Kris Van Heuckelom, who examine aspects of Polish sexual and national identity as evidenced in texts by Polish authors who are themselves part of the recent economic emigration to other EU countries, and do not represent any scholarly or literary milieu. Uilleam Blacker's discussion of how texts of contemporary fiction remember the "lost others" in specific locations of contemporary Poland, which were either part of Germany, and/or had a substantial German or Jewish population before World War II, includes works from what is generally termed "crime fiction." Meanwhile, the women's autobiographical texts discussed by Agnieszka Mrozik—from the perspective of female identity politics—and by Katarzyna Zechenter—from the perspective of a comparison between Polish and Jewish Mother stereotypes—form part of a similarly fluid type of literature that seems to combine aspects of family memoir, Holocaust memoir and autobiographically-inspired fiction. Joanna Michlic's contribution concentrates specifically on works by Michał Głowiński, "fictional" and "autobiographical," where the genre status of both becomes somewhat fluid. However, the current book is not a discussion of genres as such. At the same time, the vast range of titles included by the contributors in their various discussions—from different genres, and sub-genres—as well as the various thematic issues they cover, raises questions about the canon (I shall return to this point).

Also, as already indicated, we tend to treat literary texts as sources of information about society and how literary authors perceive the world around them. We do not totally ignore the aesthetic or linguistic aspects, but we examine the texts predominantly as reflections of social reality—although, let it be said, the aesthetic and linguistic choices of writers are themselves indicative of aspects of social reality and of attitudes either to traditionalist viewpoints or indeed to change itself, as may be seen in the linguistic styles of Dorota Masłowska or Michał Witkowski, for example, or in the language use of many poets discussed in the "reconnaissance" of developments in post-1989 poetry by Wioletta Grzegorzewska and Marek Kazmierski. Following the approach of Kinga Dunin (2004) and Przemysław Czapliński (2007b; 2009), we look at literature as reflecting aspects of a wider phenomenon of social and cultural change.

Summarized briefly and in general terms, the areas which the contributors to the current volume have identified as "new" or "transforming" between the systemic changes of 1989-1990 and 2011-2012 are as follows:

First, the "boom" in the publication of female authors, especially in the first decade, accompanied by the absorption by academic literary studies of Western feminism and feminist literary theory, then of gender and queer studies—not always sympathetically received however by vocal critics in the national media and sometimes in academe (see the chapters by Chowaniec, Świerkosz and Mrozik). There was initially a more direct assimilation of Western approaches in the 1990s—see, for example, the pioneering collections of critical articles and translations of key French and Anglo-American feminist texts published in 1993 by the journal *Teksty drugie* (numbers 4-6 under the collective title "The Laugh of the Feminists," a reference to Hélène Cixous' famous 1975 article "The Laugh of the Medusa," which is one of the texts included) or in the volume *Body and Text* (*Ciało i tekst,* 2001), both edited by Anna Nasiłowska (see also Gajewska 2008; and Phillips 2008, where I provide a bibliography of works published up until that date). These were later supplemented by full translations (in most cases long overdue), as opposed to excerpts, of key texts, such as Virginia Woolf *A Room of One's Own* (1929, translated 1997 by Agnieszka Graff), Betty Friedan *The Feminine Mystique* (1963, translated 2012 by Anna Wysokińska), Germaine Greer *The Female Eunuch* (1970, translated 2001 by Joanna Gołyś and Bożena Umińska), Adrienne Rich *Of Woman Born* (1976, translated 2000 by Joanna Mizielińska), Judith Butler *Gender Trouble* (1990, translated 2008 by Karolina Krasuska), to be followed by a distinct desire evident in the first decade of the new century among Polish scholars, and indeed writers, to adapt these ideas to specifically Polish conditions—in other words: there has been a movement away from a new form of intellectual "colonization" in search of a more home-grown feminism (Iwasiów 2002; Dunin 2004; Kraskowska 2012). Western theory should therefore be regarded as an inspiration that enabled Poles to think critically afresh about their own historical and psycho-cultural situation, but not as an infallible authority in itself. At the same time, especially as regards feminism and women's studies, a backlash in the 2000s is clearly discernible, not only because of a lack of adequate funding in academic institutions to support such studies, but because of the continuing male-centred and anti-feminist, conservative character of Polish mainstream culture (Iwasiów 2006; Kłosińska 2010; Chowaniec 2012). Meanwhile, in scholarship, doubts have sometimes been raised by feminists themselves about the actual practice of feminist literary studies in Poland (Filipowicz 2009), about Polish misunderstandings of feminist practice in the West as well as about the evident confusion in the minds of certain anthologists, for example, in their arbitrary understandings of "women's" and "feminist" writing (Kałuża 2009).

Yet despite such critical setbacks, Polish feminism, in its more radical as well as academic form(s) is up and running, albeit it in limited milieus, publishing a range of journals and magazines (Darska 2008). The first feminist journal to appear was *With Full Voice* (*Pełnym Głosem*) in 1993, published by the feminist eFKa foundation in Kraków, succeeded in 1999 (and still publishing) by *Splinter* (*Zadra*). Today another major source of feminist materials is the publishing foundation and website *Feminoteka* (www.feminoteka.pl/news.php). It should go without saying that Polish feminists have done much to deconstruct stereotypical and monolithic myths, also perpetuated in literary texts, about Polish womanhood (Hryciuk and Korolczuk 2012; Mrozik 2012).

The 1990s were thus marked by an upsurge in published texts by women and hence by women authors' greater public visibility as a group than heretofore, introducing new styles of writing and new subject matter that undermined the dominant "great narratives"; negative androcentric criticism and pejorative designations such as "menstrual literature," however, ensured its eventual return to the margins, despite the successes of individual writers (Filipiak 1999; Czapliński 2007b, 100-105 and 2009, 297-303; Chowaniec 2010 and 2012; Mrozik 2013, 42-49). Several of these female authors (born in 1950s and 1960s) had emerged from the 1980s underground milieu associated with the second-circulation literary magazine *bruLion*, including Natasza Goerke, Izabela Filipiak, and Manuela Gretkowska. The early to mid-1990s also saw the debuts of, among others, Magdalena Tulli and Olga Tokarczuk, two of the most artistically acclaimed and popular contemporary Polish writers of either sex, at home and in translation—but whose "feminism" is perhaps more implied in their fiction than directly expressed. The most symptomatic work was Filipiak's novel *Total Amnesia* (*Absolutna amnezja,* 1995)—part *Bildungsroman* and part feminist polemic against the father's power. Inspired by many intricate references to Polish, classical and European literary precedents, this book more than any other articulated the sociocultural restraints on female personal development (in the years of late communism) as well as on the female author's freedom to write and be fairly received in patriarchal society. Although initial responses to the novel were generally positive, the novel's reception sparked a crucial debate among critics about the so-called "menstrual" literature, as well as Filipiak's response to this "monstrous" accusation (1999). Filipiak's portrayal of the female author's dilemma, symbolized in the novel by the analogy with Bluebeard's bloody chamber, is analysed in the current volume in the chapter by Monika Świerkosz.

Second, the emergence of gay and lesbian texts—in particular, the "coming-out" stories discussed in the current volume by Błażej Warkocki, inspired here by the theoretical approach of Eve Kosofsky Sedgwick, especially post-2000 and especially since the publication of Krzysztof Tomasik's crucial book *Homobiogra-*

phies (*Homobiografie,* 2008), and the greater public awareness and discussion of this topic since then, despite the resistance of negatively-disposed elements in Polish social and political life (such as Lech Kaczyński's attitude as mayor of Warsaw to the Equality marches). The development of queer and LGBT studies owe a great deal to the recent work of Joanna Mizielińska (2004, 2006 and 2011), Robert Kulpa and Anna Gruszczyńska, cultural critic and Kristevan Tomasz Kitliński and art historian Paweł Leszkowicz (2005), and in the literary field, most importantly the publications of Swiss literary historian German Ritz, which have had a significant impact on foregrounding and legitimizing the field, even though most of his work has been on pre-1989, interwar and even 19th-century Polish writers (1999, 2002 and 2011). Another work of Western scholarship that is ground-breaking in terms of the application of queer theory to Polish literary figures is Joanna Niżyńska's very recent publication on Miron Białoszewski (2013), though this again is not directly about post-1989 literature (Białoszewski died in 1983). But we should confess here to an omission, which must be corrected by future research: the emphasis in Warkocki's article is on gay texts, and we do not include discussions of lesbians—although Warkocki himself has addressed issues of lesbianism and literary representation in his own separate book (2007) in relation to Izabela Filipiak's novel *Total Amnesia* (1995). Filipiak is the first openly lesbian writer publishing in Polish, her 2002 collection *Madame Intuita* challenging by its very title the male ethos embodied in Zbigniew Herbert's famous *Pan Cogito.* Research into lesbian writing is as yet underdeveloped, whereas several writers, to mention here only novelist Ewa Schilling (b. 1971) and poet and short-story writer Agnieszka Kłos, deserve our proper critical analysis.

Third, the enormous revival of Jewish-related topics—from questions of Polish-Jewish identity and interrelations, to Holocaust memoir, to aspects of pre- and post-World War II antisemitism (as well as Polish reactions to antisemitism), to rediscovery of elements of the former Jewish presence in the Polish-speaking lands and in Polish literary history (see, for example, Janion 2000 and 2009, Michlic 2006, and in the current volume, the chapters by Michlic, Grimstad, Zechenter, Vickers and Blacker in particular, but also mentions in others). Here we cannot overestimate the value to the field and especially to research outside Poland of the journal *Polin,* published annually since 1986 by the Institute for Polish-Jewish Studies (Oxford), edited by Antony Polonsky and others. In Poland itself, of special note is the monthly cultural journal *Midrasz,* founded in 1997 by Konstanty Gebert and currently edited by Piotr Paziński, author of *The Boarding-House* (*Pensjonat,* 2009)—a novel discussed in the present volume by Knut Andreas Grimstad. Of immediate impact to Polish literature and drama was Jan Gross's book *Neighbors* (2001) about the Jedwabne massacre (July 1941), which prompted not only controversy in Poland but references both direct and oblique in many diverse literary texts, from Tadeusz Słobodzianek's play *Our Class* (2008/2009, the two versions of which are discussed in the current volume by Paul Vickers) to Joanna Bator's novels *Sandy Hill* (*Piaskowa Góra,* 2009) and *Cloudalia* (*Chmurdalia,* 2010), especially the concluding scenes of the latter. Katarzyna Zechenter's chapter meanwhile discusses Jewish elements in some of the many memoir-cum-autobiographies by women published since the late 1990s.

Fourth, questions surrounding the functioning of memory, and its interconnections with both individual and collective identity, and/or trauma, especially as theorized by Marianne Hirsch, Paul Ricœur or Jan Assmann, and as applied to the specifically Polish cultural context, for example, by Ewa Thompson, form the starting point not only to the chapters primarily devoted to Jewish interest but also to the wide range of post-1989 literary figures (mostly writers of fiction, in this case) discussed by Uilleam Blacker in search of the "lost others" of the regions they inhabit—i.e. the geographical peripheries of present-day Poland. Here the mainly pre-World War II German or Jewish communities of Gdańsk, Wrocław, Łódź, Szczecin and other cities, "lost" as a result of the shifted national-state borders and vast population resettlements in the immediate post-war period, are—albeit partially, imperfectly—resurrected in fictional works by Henryk Grynberg, Paweł Huelle, Stefan Chwin, Olga Tokarczuk, Jarosław Marek Rymkiewicz, Piotr Paziński, Marek Krajewski, Andrzej Bart and others, as well as in the autobiographical essay *Two Cities* (*Dwa miasta,* 1991) by poet Adam Zagajewski.

The fascination with memory, its functions and uses, however, prompts the admittance of another omission of our volume, which would be a chapter devoted specifically to memory and/or representation of the Polish People's Republic, that is the immediate pre-1989 period (1945-1989) in texts of post-1989 literature, in the works, for example, of Izabela Filipiak, Andrzej Stasiuk, Antoni Libera, Joanna Bator, Inga Iwasiów, and many others. This is an area begging for further research; current readers are referred, however, to the recent collection of essays on this topic entitled *Relating the People's Republic* (*Opowiedzieć PRL,* Chmielowska and Wołowiec, 2011). The present editor, agreeing with Katarzyna Chmielowska's view that literary texts (she refers specifically to Iwasiów and Bator) addressing questions of traumatic memory, regional experience and the way these have affected several generations of Poles are ahead of scholarly historical works in this respect, has also analysed novels by these particular authors in two separate recent publications (Phillips 2012; 2013). That said, the current book does testify to the consciousness among many contemporary Polish literary voices of the continuing psychological impact of World War II, the post-war political settlements, and the imposition of a totalitarian regime—and perhaps above all to the fact that people's true and very painful experiences were not only repressed during the forty-five years of communism and rarely discussed openly, but were also manipulated by the authorities in ways that played on people's festering unresolved *ressentiments.*

Furthermore, these popular ressentiments appear not to have been sufficiently appreciated by liberal-minded politicians and cultural leaders since the advent of democracy in 1989, wishing to draw a "thick line" under the past, and have burst forth with resentful new vigour in the last decade, in the demands of less cosmopolitan and more nationalistically-minded groups demanding, for example, "lustration" of former communist collaborators. This shift in perception from a more cosmopolitan, universalist and morally uncommitted artistic stance, to one of renewed engagement in issues of national identity and political ethics, can be seen to be reflected in developments over the past twenty years in Polish dramatic performances and dramatic texts, as Grzegorz Niziołek demonstrates in his analysis of "ressentiment as experiment" in Polish theatre. Certainly this chapter of our book, as well as others, in particular Paul Vickers's analysis of the two versions of Tadeusz Słobodzianek's play *Our Class* and Jerzy Jarzębski's of changes in inter-generational perceptions of Polish reality as reflected in novels, bear out Przemysław Czapliński's contention that the conservative backlash in both Polish politics and culture in the last decade—in contrast to the liberal, open-minded tendency in the first half of the 1990s—was in part due to the much greater visibility of liberal, Western-leaning cultural figures' rejection of hermetic or parochial Polishness outright, representing themselves as culturally superior, and thus erecting a barrier in communication between this rarefied sphere and the disaffected rest of society; this, he suggests, provoked the resurgence of popular conservative feeling a few years later (Czapliński 2007a, 50).

Fifth, we look at the present state of some émigré writing, or writing inspired by exilic experience, prompted by the recent waves of economic migration to Britain, Ireland, Scandinavia and Germany, which in turn begs a fundamental redefinition of what we understand by the designation "émigré," or even the total abandonment of the term in favour of another one, such as "migrant" or simply "traveller"—while some contemporary writers living outside Poland (e.g. in London, Stockholm or Brussels), such as novelist Grażyna Plebanek, regard themselves as precisely and only as that; they do not regard themselves as "émigrés" in the pre-1989 understanding of the word or as economic migrants (another much-travelled female author, Joanna Bator, calls herself a "nomad"). And this, of course, takes further the debate about whether, when speaking of "Polish literature," we are talking about a single literature or two (or several) distinct literatures (Filipowicz 1989), and indeed whether any talk of a separate exilic literature is now redundant, as Eva Hoffman wonders in her article in *Tygodnik Powszechny* (2011). Exile or "migration" or simply living abroad is no longer connected with political (i.e. anti-communist) dissidence or with underground opposition in Poland itself and/or with activist anti-communist milieus in foreign centres such as London or Paris, but with personal choice, with economic necessity or preference—yet, in most cases (at least as portrayed in literature), the writing outside Poland somehow remains connected in less or more subtle ways with the home country and with what it means to be Polish or, indeed, "foreign" at home (Gosk 2012). Dirk Uffelmann, Kris Van Heuckelom, Urszula Chowaniec—and also Elwira Grossman in her comparison of language use in two dramatic productions performed outside Poland—consider different aspects of this issue: in terms of personal identity as a woman and the psychological-emotional condition of melancholy (Chowaniec, who discusses contemporary poet Wioletta Grzegorzewska, currently resident in the UK, as well as prose texts by Filipiak and others, which reflect women's "alienation" from full citizenship within Poland itself); masculinity in relation to the Polish migrant experience (Uffelmann); and—also in relation to migrant experience—issues of national identity, and of what can still or now be said to constitute "Polishness" (Van Heuckelom).

All these themes, however, are interconnected: traditional, stereotypical national identity traits, questions of sexuality and emancipation, are made all the more pertinent in the situation outside the home country, in confrontation with Europeanism (especially after Poland joined the European Union in 2004, which made such large-scale migration possible in the first place) and with local British or Irish, for example, values and indeed prejudices (see also Rostek and Uffelmann 2011). The whole experience begs the fundamental question: Who am I? Often provoking at the same time feelings of melancholy, insecurity, frustration, resentment and disorientation. One question, however, which remains unexamined, is whether Polish emigrant experience is essentially or qualitatively any different from that of other national groups.

Here, it is worth emphasizing the general interconnected nature of the chapters of the book, because in most cases these five identified features overlap in some way, indicating that the contributors are sensitive to all spheres at once: for example, discussions of sexuality (masculinity, homosexuality) or specifically female identity may interconnect with the "emigrant" experience, or with recovery of Jewish identity, while enquiries into the functioning of memory not only relate to the current non-presence of Jews but to other suppressed areas of experience, such as the uprooting and forced migration of whole populations. In this sense, although the individual contributions concentrate on specific topics, these topics are not isolated but form parts of a coherent multi-voiced discussion. All topics feed into each other.

As indicated above in relation to Grzegorz Niziołek's discussion, the book also demonstrates the general observation, made in various publications by Przemysław Czapliński (2007a; 2007b; 2009), that the last two decades may be roughly divided into two distinct periods: an initial liberal, open, almost anti-national period lasting until at least 1996-1997, celebrating inter alia "otherness" or "marginalization" or the "local/ regional," and expressing itself as an innovative "pluralism" and heteroglossia marked, for example, by such tendencies as the so-called literature of "small homelands" or the sudden "invasion" of women writers, and perceived in the mid-late 1990s by, inter alia, Jerzy Jarzębski as indicative of an "appetite for change" or by Maria Janion, as the end of the Romantic paradigm, and then, from the early 2000s, a return to engagement (from many different, and sometimes highly conflictive points of view) with specifically Polish national and societal collectivist concerns, in response to populist reactions. Referring to Janusz Sławiński's description of cultural change in the first half of the 1990s as the "disintegration of the centre," Czapliński observes the centre's "return." Symptomatic of the reverse swing in Polish reception, he notes the reactions of the Polish media to the two Nobel prize winners: the demands for Szymborska's "communist" past to be revealed and publically vilified after she was awarded the prize in 1996, and the accusations made against Miłosz (as anti-Catholic, anti-Polish etc) following his death in 2004 and the arguments about whether or not he should be buried in the pantheon reserved for other national writers (2007a, 54-55). A similarly polarized debate erupted in the Polish media in April 2010 in response to Olga Tokarczuk's remarks to the *New York Times* about reactions to the Smolensk disaster, where she criticized Poles' national tendency to regard themselves as perpetual victims, a polarization constantly evident however in reactions to the subsequent investigation into the tragedy's causes.

Czapliński's "return to the centre" and the division, however nebulously defined, into two periods before and after 2000, are sweeping generalizations, of course, and do not perhaps do justice to many representatives of the youngest generation of published authors, born in the late 1970s and early 1980s (such talented individuals as Jacek Dehnel or Justyna Bargielska, or many other young writers mentioned by Grzegorzewska and Kazmierski in their "reconnaissance"), yet it has nevertheless been a perceivable trend which raises interesting questions as to the role of literature and writers in post-communist societies (see Wachtel 2006), or, quite simply, in capitalist market economies, which Poland has now joined, where the role of literature (if it has any socially significant role at all?) has now been "normalized"—by which I mean taken down from the "Romantic" pedestal, as defender of a collective national culture and its ideological or cultural freedom, claiming to speak in the name of all Poles—to its "normal" or "natural" place according to market forces, i.e. to the financial interests of publishers and the buying power—and tastes—of "ordinary" readers, namely readers with undemanding popular tastes, as well as intellectuals. Nevertheless, the tangible shift "back to the centre" in the reception of literary texts should not be dismissed merely as the fault of backward-looking academics or politically-inspired media critics, because it does pose more profound and longstanding questions about the purpose of so-called "serious" literature and its role in any particular society and culture. Is it not—or should it not be?—more (or other) than simply a source of intellectual or aesthetic pleasure for a limited group of that society's members—even though this is the very thing that some contemporary critics find particularly lacking in Polish literary production since 1989—if not exactly looking for "great" works ("arcydzieła"), then at least those which would exceed their place, language and culture of origin, as opposed to commercial "bestsellers" (Zaleski 2008, 49-50)? Isn't literature more than mere "words on a page" (Czapliński 2007a)? We literary historians and critics may like to think so, but maybe it's not.

One interesting development in Polish literary scholarship, meanwhile, since about 2008, has been the emergence of the so-called "post-dependency" studies ("studia postzależniościowe"), represented by their own research body: Centrum Badań Dyskursów Postzależnościowych, Warsaw University. These studies, while not in themselves representing at all a socially conservative or chauvinist outlook, nor any ideological "return to the centre," reflect a kind of reaction to the application of "Western" postcolonial or post-communist theory to Polish conditions without due attention to the specifics, to what is unique to the Polish situation. These studies have been developed largely within literary studies, the leading scholars being Ryszard Nycz and Hanna Gosk. Inspired by Western postcolonial theory (Michel Foucault, Edward Said, Gayatri Spivak, Homi K. Bhabha and others), with which Polish scholars have been familiar for at least ten years—see issues of *Teksty drugie* devoted to postcolonialism, especially Cavanagh 2003, and also *Teksty drugie* 2003 (6), 2007 (4) and 2010 (5)—they try to identify ways in which it can be adapted not only to analysing specifically Polish contemporary reality (the condition of "post-communist" understood here as "postcolonial" in terms of Soviet communist ideological "occupation") but also those complex and contentious elements of past reality that remain active in the present-day, like the "ressentiments" discussed by Grzegorz Niziołek. Hence a similar desire to create their own analytical space to accommodate specifically Polish experience has emerged among Poland's "postcolonialists" as that noted above among feminists.

Our endorsement—even if only in very broad terms of Czapliński's analysis—is one of the few tentative conclusions we can draw from the research undertaken by our contributors. Another is perhaps the implication of the great variety of literature produced since 1989, serious and popular, by several generations publishing at the same time, in many genres (no longer even identifiable as recognizable, traditional genres anyway), in different aesthetic styles with varying degrees of linguistic experiment, for the *canon*. Again this is not a topic specifically addressed by any single contributor, but the overwhelming evidence of change, openness and pluralism would seem to imply it. Connected, naturally, with the shift away from a "central" collective narrative into pluralism and individuality, the task of identifying which literary works represent some post-1989 collective experience to which all Poles might sign up, has become impossible. What then is the basis for selecting a canon? Aesthetic, formal criteria? Universality, and addressing human existential problems? International acclaim (which depends itself on recognition by foreign translators, publishers, critics and promotional networks)? Or should we worry at all about defining a canon; has the concept itself become redundant—either for the curriculum studied by Polish school children, or for academic commentators like ourselves? The chapters of this book suggest that renegotiation of the canon is now central, and that—at least as far as works published in the 1990s and 2000s are concerned, new criteria need to be become clear for assessing what makes "good" literature and what is likely to last. Which writers, for example, will be studied in twenty or fifty years from now as being in some way representative of Polish literary excellence, and according to what criteria?

Literature itself meanwhile, i.e. the accumulated body of fiction, poetry, plays, memoirs, autobiographies, as well as more "popular" forms, written in the Polish language and produced by a plethora of individual voices, has proved more resilient than transitory political imperatives or constructed conceptions of "Polishness"—in which I include, perhaps above all, the (specifically Polish) Romantic heritage of victimhood and martyrdom dating from the time of political partition, along with its adopted standard icons such as the Polish Mother, now defunct in the minds of Poland's feminists (Hryciuk 2012). Polish literary "tradition" or (perhaps better expressed) "practice" stretches far back before this particular cultural strain emerged, which was prompted by the specific conditions of Polish cultural repression under occupying powers in the 19th century, and re-actualized in the communist years when Poles were subject again to ideological colonization. Clinging to the stereotype by certain milieus ten, fifteen, twenty, twenty-five years after Poland regained self-determination and independence from Soviet domination, bespeaks a sense of insecurity and resistance to change in those very milieus, not to say cultural immaturity (*pace* Gombrowicz): insisting on exclusivity and uniqueness, defining oneself *against* someone else—even against European identity post-2004, consolidating one's own identity as *the* collective one by which all members of a community should be bound (defining and hence controlling those who do not conform, as Foucault might have argued), in effect does the very things supposedly toppled by the revolution of 1989.

The findings of the current volume, based on an examination of a wide spectrum of literary texts, suggest, however, that such an exclusive interpretation of Polishness is a thing of the past. Literary production in Polish, variegated but also universal in its cultural and spiritual inspirations, went on for at least four centuries before the final partition of the Polish political state in 1795. Meanwhile the twenty years of political independence between the world wars (1918-1939) represent a period of diverse cultural development that was nipped in the bud by the war and subsequent communist censorship and repression. The editor of this volume, at least, sees the current situation as something of a resumption of the pre- and post-Partition continuity, a continuity that has only one unifying factor—that of the Polish language.

Bibliography

Cavanagh, Clare. 2003. "Postkolonialna Polska. Biała plama na mapie współczesnej teorii," translated by Tomasz Kunz. *Teksty drugie* 2-3: 60-71.

Chowaniec, Urszula. 2010. "Intimately Social": The Experience of Menstruation in Polish Women's Writing." In *Mapping Experience in Polish and Russian Women's Writing,* edited by Marja Rytkönen et al., 150-170. Newcastle upon Tyne: Cambridge Scholars Publishing.

—. 2012. "Listening to Women's Voices: Historical Overview of Women's Right to Write in Poland." In *Women's Voices and Feminism in Polish Cultural Memory,* edited by Urszula Chowaniec and Ursula Phillips, 26-46. Newcastle upon Tyne: Cambridge Scholars Publishing.

Czapliński, Przemysław. 1997. *Ślady przełomu. O prozie polskiej 1976-1996.* Kraków: Wydawnictwo Literackie.

—. 2007a. "Przesilenie nowoczesności. Proza polska 1989-2005 wobec Wielkich Narracji." In *Narracje po końcu (wielkich) narracji. Kolekcje, obiekty, symulakra,* edited by Hanna Gosk and Andrzej Zieniewicz, 34-55. Warsaw: Elipsa.

—. 2007b. *Powrót centrali. Literatura w nowej rzeczywistości.* Kraków: Wydawnictwo Literackie.

—. 2009. *Polska do wymiany. Późna nowoczesność i nasze wielkie narracje.* Warsaw: W.A.B.

Czapliński, Przemysław et al., eds. 2003. *Kalendarium życia literackiego 1976-2000. Wydarzenia, dyskusje, bilanse.* Kraków: Wydawnictwo Literackie.

Darska, Bernadetta. 2008. *Czas Fem. Przewodnik po prasie feministycznej i tematach kobiecych w czasopismach kulturalnych po 1989 roku.* Olsztyn: Portret.

Dunin, Kinga. 2004. *Czytając Polskę. Literatura polska po roku 1989 wobec dylematów nowoczesności.* Warsaw: W.A.B.

Filipiak, Izabela. 1999. "Literatura monstrualna." *Biuletyn OŚKi* 1: 1-3.

Filipowicz, Halina. 1989. "Fission and Fusion: Polish Émigré Literature." *Slavic and East European Journal* 33(2): 157-172.

—. 2009. "Pułapki, paradoksy i wyzwania *Gender Studies.*" *Ruch Literacki* 50(2): 101-108.

Gajewska, Agnieszka. 2008. *Hasło: Feminizm.* Poznań: Wydawnictwo Poznańskie.

Gosk, Hanna, ed. 2010. *Nowe dwudziestolecie (1989-2009). Rozpoznania, hierarchie, perspektywy.* Warsaw: Elipsa.

Gosk, Hanna, ed. 2012. *Narracje migracyjne w literaturze polskiej XX i XXI wieku.* Kraków: Universitas.

Gross, Jan Tomasz. 2001. *Neighbors: The Destruction of the Jewish Community in Jedwabne.* Princeton, NJ and Oxford: Oxford University Press.

Hoffman, Eva. 2011. "Poza obczyzną." *Tygodnik Powszechny* 39, *Magazyn Literacki* (25 September): 5-6.

Hryciuk, Renata E. and Elżbieta Korolczuk, eds. 2012. *Pożegnanie z Matką Polką? Dyskursy, praktyki i reprezentacje macierzyństwa we współczesnej Polsce.* Warsaw: Wydawnictwo Uniwersytetu Warszawskiego.

Iwasiów, Inga. 2002. *Rewindykacje. Kobieta czytająca dzisiaj.* Kraków: Wydawnictwo Literackie.

—. 2005. "Blaski i cienie krytyki feministycznej w Polsce." In *Literatury słowiańskie po roku 1989. Tom II: Feminizm,* edited by Ewa Kraskowska, 26-45. Warsaw: Kolor Plus.

Janion, Maria. 1996. *Kobiety i duch inności.* Warsaw: Sic!

—. 2000. *Do Europy tak, ale razem z naszymi umarłymi.* Warsaw: Sic!

—. 2009. *Bohater, spisek, śmierć. Wykłady żydowskie.* Warsaw: W.A.B.

Jarzębski, Jerzy. 1997. *Apetyt na Przemianę. Notatki o prozie współczesnej.* Kraków: Znak.

Kałuża, Anna. 2009. "Stracone złudzenia." *Tygodnik Powszechny*, 8 December. Accessed 8 February, 2013. http://tygodnik.onet.pl/1,37701,druk.html

Kemp-Welch, Anthony. 2008. *Poland under Communism: A Cold War History.* Cambridge: Cambridge University Press.

Kłosińska, Krystyna. 2010. *Feministyczna krytyka literacka.* Katowice: Wydawnictwo Uniwersytetu Śląskiego.

Kraskowska, Ewa, ed. 2005. *Literatury słowiańskie po roku 1989. Nowe zjawiska, tendencje, perspektywy. Tom II: Feminizm.* Warsaw: Kolor Plus.

—. 2012. "Feminism Polish Style: Our Tradition or a Borrowed One?" In *Women's Voices and Feminism in Polish Cultural Memory,* edited by Urszula Chowaniec and Ursula Phillips, 67-75. Newcastle upon Tyne: Cambridge Scholars Publishing.

Lachman, Magdalena. 2004. *Gry z "tandetą" w prozie polskiej po roku 1989 roku.* Modernizm w Polsce 7. Kraków: Universitas.

Leszkowicz, Paweł and Tomasz Kitliński. 2005. *Miłość i demokracja. Rozważania o kwestii homoseksualnej w Polsce.* Kraków: Aureus.

Michlic, Joanna. 2006. *Poland's Threatening Other: Images of the Jew from 1880 to the Present.* Lincoln, NE: University of Nebraska Press.

Mizielińska, Joanna. 2004. *(De)Konstrukcja kobiecości. Podmiot feminizmu a problem wykluczenia.* Gdańsk: słowo/obraz terytoria.

—. 2006. *Płeć, ciało, seksualność. Od feminizmu do teorii queer.* Kraków: Universitas.

Mizielińska, Joanna and Robert Kulpa, eds. 2011. *De-Centring Western Sexualities: Central and Eastern European Perspectives.* Farnham, Surrey: Ashgate.

Mrozik, Agnieszka. 2012. "'The Time of Visionary Artists Has Come to an End?' Manuela Gretkowska's Literary and Political Activity." In *Women's Voices and Fem-*

inism in Polish Cultural Memory, edited by Urszula Chowaniec and Ursula Phillips, 112-126. Newcastle upon Tyne: Cambridge Scholars Publishing.

—. 2012. *Akuszerki transformacji. Kobiety, literatura i władza w Polsce po 1989 roku.* Warsaw: Instytut Badań Literackich PAN.

Nalewajk, Żaneta. 2011. *Podmiot w literaturze polskiej po 1989 roku. Antropologiczne aspekty konstrukcji.* Warsaw: Elipsa.

Nasiłowska, Anna, ed. 1993. "Śmiech feministek." *Teksty drugie* 4-6.

—. 2001. *Ciało i tekst. Feminizm w literaturoznawstwie—antologia szkiców.* Warsaw: Instytut Badań Literackich PAN.

—. 2006. *Literatua okresu przejściowego 1975-1996.* Warsaw: Wydawnictwo Naukowe PWN.

Niżyńska, Joanna. 2013. *The Kingdom of Insignificance: the Traumatic, the Quotidian, and the Queer in the Prose of Miron Białoszewski.* Evanston, IL: Northwestern University Press.

Nowacki, Dariusz. 1999. *Zawód: czytelnik. Notatki o prozie polskiej lat 90.* Kraków: Znak.

Nowacki, Dariusz and Krzysztof Uniłowski, eds. 2010-2011. *Dwadzieścia lat literatury polskiej 1989-2009.* 2 vols. Katowice: Wydawnictwo Uniwersytetu Śląskiego.

Nycz, Ryszard, ed. 2011. *Kultura po przejśiach, osoby z przeszłością. Polski dyskurs postzależnościowy. Konteksty i perspektywy badawcze.* Kraków: Universitas.

Phillips, Ursula. 2008. "Polish Women Writers: Research and Publications." In *Masquerade and Femininity: Essays on Russian and Polish Women Writers,* edited by Urszula Chowaniec, Ursula Phillips and Marja Rytkönen, 16-27 and 36-39. Newcastle upon Tyne: Cambridge Scholars Publishing.

—. 2012a. "Generation, Transformation and Place in Inga Iwasiów's Novels *Bambino* (2008) and *Ku słońcu* (2010)". In *Philosophy and Literature: Generation and Transformation in Gender and Postdependency Discourse,* edited by Urszula Chowaniec and Marzenna Jakubczak. [Special issue of] *Argument: Biannual Philosophical Journal* 2(1): 17-35.

—. 2012b. "Problems of Feminism and Postfeminism in Novels by Inga Iwasiów and Joanna Bator." In *Women's Voices and Feminism in Polish Cultural Memory,* edited by Urszula Chowaniec and Ursula Phillips, 127-154. Newcastle upon Tyne: Cambridge Scholars Publishing.

Ritz, German. 1999. *Jarosław Iwaszkiewicz. Pogranicza nowoczesności,* translated [from German] by Andrzej Kopacki. Kraków: Universitas.

—. 2002. *Nić w labyrincie pożądania. Gender i płeć w literaturze polskiej od romantyzmu do postmodernizmu,* translated [from German] by Bronisław Drąg, Andrzej Kopacki and Małgorzata Łukasiewicz. Warsaw: Wiedza Powszechna.

—. 2011. *Poeta romantyczny i nieromantyczne czasy. Juliusz Słowacki na drodze do Europy. Pamiętniki polskie na tropach narodowej tożsamości,* translated [from German] by Małgorzata Łukasiewicz. Kraków: Universitas.

Rostek, Joanna and Dirk Uffelmann, eds. 2011. *Contemporary Polish Migrant Culture and Literature in Germany, Ireland, and the UK.* Frankfurt am Main: Peter Lang.

Śliwiński, Piotr. 2002. *Przygody z wolnością. Uwagi o poezji współczesnej.* Kraków: Znak.

Tomasik, Krzysztof. 2008. *Homobiografie*. Warsaw: Krytyka Polityczna.

Uniłowski, Krzysztof. 1998. *Skądinąd. Zapiski krytyczne*. Bytom: FA-art.

Wachtel, Andrew Baruch. 2006. *Remaining Relevant after Communism: The Role of the Writer in Eastern Europe*. Chicago, IL and London: University of Chicago Press.

Walczewska, Sławomira. 1999. *Damy, rycerze, feministki*. Kraków: eFKa.

Warkocki, Błażej. 2007. *Homo niewiadomo. Polska proza wobec odmienności*. Warsaw: Sic!

Wilk, Eugeniusz and Monika Górska-Olesińska, eds. 2011. *Od liberatury do e-literatury*. Opole: Wydawnictwo Uniwersytetu Opolskiego.

Zaleski, Marek. 2008. "Co dalej?" In *Co dalej, literaturo? Jak zmienia się współcześnie pojęcie i sytuacja literatury*, edited by Alina Brodzka-Wald, Hanna Gosk and Andrzej Werner, 82-99. Warsaw: Instytut Badań Literackich PAN.

The Conflict of Generations in Contemporary Polish Prose

Jerzy JARZĘBSKI

Conflict between generations is an eternal theme of literature so it is hard to claim that young Polish prose writers have come up with anything radically new in this respect in the last twenty years. Yet, the frequent occurrence of this theme and its prominent position within many individual works makes one wonder. What is more, writers who made their debut in recent years tend to take an analytical approach to the problem. They inquire into the main reasons underlying misunderstandings between the generations and search for causes in the fields of psychology, sociology, economics or politics. It would seem that the contrast between the generations is a multi-dimensional phenomenon, while diagnoses that fall within the domain of literary prose are linked to the overall socio-cultural phenomena that have shaped images of Polish society at the turn of the century.

Let us start, however, from the relatively idyllic and harmonious visions of inter-generational relationships portrayed in a number works of the 1990s and early 2000s. When we read the early novels of Stefan Chwin (b. 1949) or Paweł Huelle (b. 1957), we are struck by the affirmative attitude of the main characters towards their parents and towards tradition in general. Images of the protagonists' immediate families found in Chwin's *Hanemann* (1995; translated as *Death in Danzig*, 2005) and *Esther* (1999), Huelle's *Who was David Weiser?* (*Weiser Dawidek*, 1987), *Moving House and Other Stories* (*Opowiadania na czas przeprowadzki,* 1991) and *Mercedes-Benz* (2002), or in other early works by both authors, are invariably positive, tinged at times with a warm irony, but basically affirmative. The family in these novels or short stories is a bearer of traditional values, which successive communist governments tried but failed to destroy. This is particularly vivid in *Mercedes-Benz*—constructed both as an apotheosis of both the fathers' and grandfathers' generations, and of the good pre-World War II days when everything was "normal." From today's perspective, this trend in Polish literature has not quite disappeared, but is less apparent. We might mention prose works written in a rather traditional style, such as *Lala* (2006) by Jacek Dehnel (b. 1980) and *Reisefieber* (2006) by Mikołaj Łoziński (b. 1980), where both the grandmother (in Dehnel) or the mother (in Łoziński) are sources of great fascination for the main protagonists, even though it is not easy to communicate with them. Similarly, with reference to generations of fathers, Jerzy Pilch (b. 1952), in the novels *His Current Woman* (*Inne rozkosze*, 1995; trans. 2002) and *A Thousand Peaceful Cities* (*Tysiąc spokojnych miast*, 1997; trans. 2009) draws a humorous and melancholic portrait of a large traditional Protestant family from the small town of Wisła in the Polish Beskid mountains (where Pilch grew up), where respect for elders is inscribed in the customs of the region.

Furthermore, generational conflicts do not appear in the works of older writers, born before World War II, such as those of Wiesław Myśliwski (b. 1932), where parents—especially in his novel *Horizon* (*Widnokrąg*, 1996)—are treated positively, even if we sense a component of indulgent irony in this affection.

A sign of trouble in this inter-generational relationship is the three-part novel by Olga Tokarczuk (b. 1962), entitled *Final Stories* (*Ostatnie historie,* 2004). True, there are no specific animosities or direct conflicts depicted as such in the relationships between mother, daughter and granddaughter, yet there is a far-reaching incomparability and dichotomy in their life-stories—so much so the reader is surprised by information about the family connection between the three heroines. They are so very dissimilar and therefore lonely, unable to create a family extending into three generations.

Following this line in prose we encounter other interesting examples, such as *Snow White and Russian Red (Wojna polsko-ruska pod flagą biało-czerwoną,* 2002) by Dorota Masłowska (b. 1983), where one of the characters—known as Silny (literally: the Powerful), king of the youth subculture described in the novel—respects his mother and is even a little afraid of her. She is the patron of a particular thread in the cacophonic tapestry of Silny's soul that eventually triggers his unexpectedly middle-class behaviour. Silny presumably does not realize to what extent he is a conformist. He does not see his mother for a long time, just as she, in turn, does not understand the hellish language he speaks in his peer milieu, a sort of mixture of youth slang and the language of the media, contemporary politics, and even school textbooks. Silny's life goes on elsewhere—among his peers formed by the same youth jargon which they all speak.

The breakdown of consensus between old and young has a strong linguistic aspect, because it is language that creates the new environment—an environment which has to accommodate the separate generations, but the idea of a common language has exploded and fallen apart and with it any chance for real communication between users of different generations.

Perhaps the first symptom of serious dissonance in inter-generational harmony was Izabela Filipiak's (b. 1961) novel *Total Amnesia* (*Absolutna amnezja*, 1995), in which the teenage heroine rebels against her despotic father. Her father is a despot in terms of family, gender (the author of the novel was one of the first feminists of this generation), and politics—because the heroine's father is also secretary of the Communist Party committee in his district and wields unlimited power over his subordinates. Filipiak brings together all three kinds of tyranny in her novel: the father dominates completely over a good but submissive wife; he mistreats his daughter (raising her like a man—because he would rather have a son), and finally realizes his bloated ego as a political activist, accustomed to the unconditional obedience of people who are dependent upon him. Filipiak moulds the figure of the father according to the conservative mores of a past era, which valued the independence of women only in theory. Consequently, the rebellion of the heroine is, on the one hand, the rebellion of a woman fighting for her rights and, on the other—the rebellion of a representative of a younger generation, who completely rejects the rules and principles prevailing in the era when her parents grew up.[1]

Filipiak aptly captures one of the main reasons why a strong generational conflict appeared at this time: the parents of the protagonists (who were in their adolescence at the end of the 1980s) were shaped by the communist system. Even if they did not tolerate or support the regime, the parents bore its stigma, which manifested itself in a propensity for violence against those weaker than themselves, combined with an involuntary servility towards power, as well as hypocrisy and cowardice, and yet they had very relaxed moral principles, which primarily meant they consented to dishonest actions profitable to their own interests. The elders, then, were depicted by Filipiak in a contradictory manner: either they were brave, heroic fighters struggling against slavery (as also in Chwin's or Huelle's texts), or they were demoralized and hypocritical (as in many other subsequent writers), while the actual nature of their corruption varied widely. It is worth noting that Filipiak also alludes in her novel to numerous texts of culture and literature, creating a multilayered palimpsest, while the patron of her tormented teenage heroine Marianna is not Antigone—as it used to be during more repressive political times—but Iphigenia: the victim of her father's ambition, who has no choice but to surrender to his intentions and die on the sacrificial altar.[2]

Later, novels and memoirs would appear which revealed that writers from the generation *preceding* Filipiak's, i.e. the so-called "March 1968" generation, already had trouble with their parents—i.e. where the parents of these 1968-generation writers had been engaged in building communist society in the late 1940s and 1950s, actually believing in that system, but where their children (born in second half of the 40s) then opposed it. Powerful portrayals of such conflicts may be found in texts by Bronisław Świderski (b. 1946), Henryk Dasko (b. 1947),

---

1 See also the chapter on *Total Amnesia* by Monika Świerkosz in the current volume.

2 The significance of the replacement of Antigone by Iphigenia is discussed by Maria Janion in her detailed analysis of the novel in *Women and the Spirit of Otherness* (*Kobieta i duch inności*: Janion 1996, 319-344). I am also grateful to Justyna Jaworska for her valuable inspiration regarding this and other topics.

Eli Barbur (b. 1948) and Viola Wein (b. 1946), in particular Świderski's *The Assistant of Death* (*Asystent śmierci,* 2007), Dasko's *Gdańsk Station: An Unfinished Story (Dworzec Gdański. Niedokończona historia,* 2008), Barbur's *Groups in the Free Air* (*Grupy na wolnym powietrzu,* 1995) or Wein's volume of seven short stories entitled *Rachmunes* (2005), especially the first story. Significantly, all the above mentioned books were written by writers of Jewish origin and often deal (especially in Świderski's case) with difficult relations between Jews and Poles. However, my focus here will be on the inter-generational conflicts.[3]

Another distinctive character is the father in Wojciech Kuczok's novel *Muck: An Antibiography* (*Gnój. Antybiografia,* 2003). This book is not only the portrait of a parent-tyrant but of an entire family, in which individual members are bound by ties of a peculiar interdependence. The most dominant member is the grandfather, who was a successful man: he builds a house before the war, where his children and their families continue to live throughout the years of political upheaval and social change. The monumental figure of the grandfather is a burden to the protagonist's father who wants to emulate his achievements, but finds it impossible simply because the new economic (i.e. communist) order after 1945 does not allow him the chance. Thus, the father turns out to be a petty and insignificant individual in society, but still tries to establish his supremacy within his family. He despises his neighbours, tyrannizes his wife, and above all, his son, whom he educates in an extremely authoritarian way, tormenting him with commands and prohibitions and humiliating him in various ways—all supposedly for his own good. The father creates for himself a vision of a "perfect son" and imposes it on a boy who cannot possibly fit into it, just as his own father was unable to fit the vision of the "ideal father," passed on by the monumental grandfather.

On the one hand, Kuczok performs a kind of ritual murder on the father-monster, while, on the other, he shows how the political and economic climate did not allow him to take over the inheritance of the grandfather. I have here in mind not so much material wealth as the formation of personality, the fate of the "inner" rather than external loser, who is incapable of even bringing up his son properly, no matter how much he tries.

As can be seen, the first or initial diagnosis of reasons for the conflict between generations in Polish prose after 1989 was a *political diagnosis*: fathers were violent and intolerable as a result of the communist reality that had shaped them. This diagnosis was later expanded, however, deepened and made more nuanced through psychological or psychoanalytic interpretation, due in part to the renewed popularity of Freudian psychoanalysis during the past two decades in Poland.

[3] On relations between Poles and Jews and the restoration of Jewish themes to literature written in Polish after 1989, see the Editor's Introduction to the current volume, as well as the contributions by Blacker, Grimstad, Michlic, Vickers and Zechenter.

There are more father-tyrants like the one in Kuczok's *Muck*; it suffices to mention the father of the main protagonist in Jerzy Franczak's (b. 1978) novel *Da capo* (2010) or the stepfather in *Queen of Tiramisu* (*Królowa tiramisu,* 2008) by Bohdan Sławiński (b. 1977). Both are authoritarian personalities who embody nothing that might be interesting or enriching for their young victims. Hence, a fairly stereotypical spectacle of naked violence is enacted in their family homes, although in both cases it has a different psychological base. The father in Franczak's novel instils in his son various fears and anxieties, moulds him into a man who cannot cope with life, condemned to successive failures and humiliations. This causes the son—an eternal loser—to eventually land back in the family home, where he is nevertheless welcomed and understood. The novel ends, paradoxically, with an act of reconciliation between father and son and the affirmation of that very same patriarchal order which had previously led to the protagonist's psychological and personality disturbances.

The situation in *Queen of Tiramisu* is different: the hero's stepfather is a surrogate father, a somewhat insincere and untrustworthy rival to the boy's Oedipal passion for his mother. The protagonist of the novel, repressed in real life, transfers his psychological complexes onto his personal relationships, and eventually plays out these complexes in the fairy-tale world of his imagination, where the characters in his drama perform symbolic roles.

In the novels mentioned above, the figures of the father-tyrants lack sophistication: they are usually full of complexes and act like primitive losers who compensate for their defeats at home. The scenes of domestic violence are not too sophisticated either, even when depicting petty bourgeois, narrow-minded parents trying to deal with a child's different sexual orientation, as in the case of *Rust* (*Rdza*, 2008) by Ewa Berent (b. 1985). Here the female protagonist, who is victimized for her lesbianism and sent by her parents to the country to separate her from her partner, throws herself instead into a totally unrestrained sexual relationship with a village boy, and organizes a gang carrying out theft and robbery. In other words, she actively protests against a social order that interferes with her true sexual identity.

Another type of rebellion is the hero's behaviour in the debut novel *Boiduda* (2012) by Jakub Lubelski (b. 1984). Here the son, brought up by the mother—abandoned by his father when he started a second family, takes a specific kind of revenge. He describes the blunders of his father, who tries to fulfil his paternal responsibilities towards his first-born child, even though he inadvertently underlines by his each and every deed that the boy doesn't really interest him. Yet his final separation from his father happens on a different level: the novel's protagonist chooses a right-wing ideology, alien to his father's sympathies, as his own. On the other hand, he promises respect for the rules of traditional family life which his father had violated.

Much more intriguing, however, is the example of the mother in the drama, or dramatic poem *Song on Mother and the Fatherland* (*Utwór o Matce i Ojczyźnie*, 2008) by Bożena Keff (b. 1948). The fundamental conflict between mother and daughter in this book has both political and gender dimensions. The daughter cannot forgive her mother for constantly evaluating her situation falsely. Her received education causes the mother to take the side of her oppressors and situate herself against her own daughter, who should be her natural ally. The mother is Jewish, but a Polish patriot, irrespective of the presence of antisemitism in Poland. At the same time she refuses to acknowledge that throughout her life she was exploited as a woman. The drama in this relatively short work lies in the fact that the conflict between mother and daughter stems from events and phenomena that should, ideally, consolidate their alliance. Stereotypes, however, are stronger than solidarity: the mother, behaving in harmony with them, does nothing but complain—when trying to raise her daughter—about the daughter's attitudes and beliefs. She speaks—as some feminists would put it—from the phallocentric and patriarchal position, since the ideals of manly and fatherly patriotism are so firmly rooted in her mentality she takes them to be universally valid and fair, and does not regard them as motivated by the interests of one sex.

Agreement between the generations becomes impossible, it would seem, because the young have simply had a completely different education, and understand the mechanisms of social exclusion and oppression much better than their mothers and fathers. Both sides seem to be prisoners of their own language and rhetoric, which are so different they form cocoons enveloping both sides and obstructing the access of one to the other.

The inter-generational conflict that is taking place at the turn of millennia seems to be much deeper and more radical than generational conflicts known from previous decades. The reason for this is that there is no common ground between parents and children, and if it does exist (as in Franczak's novel, for example), it would seem to derive—paradoxically—from the quite specific, traumatic relationship between tormentor and victim, as in the notorious "Stockholm syndrome."

There are no other types of relationship between parents and offspring portrayed in these texts; nor is there a shared historical fate, resulting either from a continuing political story, in which both parties might be similarly involved, or consisting of parallels in the personal situations of parents and their children. The parents portrayed in these novels—in so far as they achieve success in life—are deemed worthy of hatred; if they fail—they are despised. Any empathy in this situation seems impossible to achieve, unless it has a specifically gendered character and is driven by the solidarity of women and their fates: sometimes, we have a case of a mother and daughter, as in *Total Amnesia*, but more often it happens between single women from different generations not related by family bonds—as again in *Total Amnesia,* as well as in more recent feminist works such as *Pocket Atlas for Women* (*Kieszonkowy atlas kobiet,* 2008) by Sylvia Chutnik (b. 1979).

Where it is shown to be possible to rebuild an emotional relationship between the generations—at least for a short time as, for example, before a parent's death, as in *Gestures* (*Gesty,* 2008) by Ignacy Karpowicz (b. 1976)—the reader tends to treat it as exceptional and sensational, not as a regular thing. Insensitivity towards parents is inscribed into the successful life-model of young (professional) people, just as cruelty towards children was previously a feature of the prevalent model of authoritarian fatherhood.

In *Rebellion* (*Rebelia,* 2008) by Mariusz Sieniewicz (b. 1972) older people are excluded from a society in which youth becomes the most important feature of an individual. The elders are banished to some kind of penal colony, while any rebellion they might organize to challenge the authorities, such as the birth of a child and then hiding it from the supervisors, becomes a rebellion precisely because the normal loving relationship between parents and children has become disrupted, and the thing that is most strongly repressed. Following the political diagnosis, this is the second principal defect identified by literary writers in relations between the generations. Another version of this same syndrome—for example, in *Weep, O God!* (*Bóg zapłacz!,* 2000) by Włodzimierz Kowalewski (b. 1956)—is the gentle urging of the sick and infirm to accept euthanasia. Relationships between parents and children are therefore saturated with violence (real and symbolic), which appears to compensate for their frustrated lust for power and domination. In the inverse relationship, in the striving for a kind of "rationalization," there is thus a tendency to remove older "redundant" individuals, perceived as having become a burden to younger generations, or who simply spoil the optimistic image the youngsters wish to portray of society.

Are such phenomena opposed in any constructive way? Do the writers of these texts expect any social response to, or remedy for the evil tendencies they describe? There is nothing to indicate that this is the case. Experiences which representatives of different generations went through in recent decades seem to be untranslatable in ways that make sense to people beyond their own generation. Perhaps this is the source of the persistent loneliness experienced by the protagonists of literary texts, irrespective of generation, for example, in the novel *Final Report* (*Ostatni raport*, 2009) by Zbigniew Kruszyński (b. 1957) or *All the Time* (*Cały czas*, 2006) by Janusz Anderman (b. 1949)—protagonists who are ambivalently involved in opposition activities, and/or espionage. Since their experiences cannot be passed on, i.e. to a younger generation, in any coherent and sensible way devoid of the self-compromising element, these protagonists do not have children (despite their many superficial relationships with women).

To summarize then, perhaps it is this loneliness that constitutes the major defect of the heroes of recent, post-1989 Polish prose: loneliness resulting from the untranslatability of life experiences between the generations, and from the life failures of the fathers and mothers—failures which are likewise related to their generational situation, and which younger people are no longer able to understand, much less forgive. In the case of fathers especially, there is nothing left but to impose their authority on their children by force, even by violence. In response, sons and daughters can only hate or ignore their parents. The family idyll as portrayed in the novels by Huelle and Chwin is thus destroyed.

Agreement between the generations—generally portrayed as broken—may occasionally be rebuilt for brief interludes, caused, for example, by a momentary attraction—as in the conversations between the main protagonist and a housewife in *Taksim* (2009) by Andrzej Stasiuk (b. 1960) or in the surprising romance between a young hoodie and an older woman in *Balladyny i romanse* (2010) by Karpowicz. Every time, however, it is a specific, isolated instance. The mythical situation, where the elders tell of their lives surrounded by a circle of attentive young listeners, belongs decidedly to the literary past. And I mean "literary" past! Because I do not describe here the real lives of contemporary Poles, but only their images as created by writers for the purposes of literature. In these images, conflict and mutual misunderstanding between generations play a significant role. To what extent this theme really reflects the actual situation of society in Poland (whether the new generations of Poles, who do not recall communism, are necessarily different or not from their parents, or whether their parents actually hinder them in gaining a distinct identity)—is a question for sociologists and scholars of culture, rather than for literary specialists.

Bibliography

Anderman, Janusz. 2006. *Cały czas*. Kraków: Wydawnictwo Literackie.

Barbur, Eli. 1995. *Grupy na wolnym powietrzu*. Izabelin: Świat Literacki.

Berent, Ewa. 2008. *Rdza*. Olsztyn: Stowarzyszenie Artystyczno-Kulturalne "Portret."

Chutnik, Sylwia. 2008. *Kieszonkowy atlas kobiet*. Kraków: Ha!art.

Chwin, Stefan. 1995. *Hanemann*. Gdańsk: Marabut.

—. 2005. *Death in Danzig,* translated by Philip Boehm. London: Secker and Warburg.

—. 1999. *Esther*. Gdańsk: Tytuł.

Dasko, Henryk. 2008. *Dworzec Gdański. Niedokończona historia*. Kraków: Wydawnictwo Literackie.

Dehnel, Jacek. 2006. *Lala*. Warsaw: W.A.B.

Filipiak, Izabela. 1995. *Absolutna amnezja*. Poznań: Obserwator.

Franczak, Jerzy. 2010. *Da capo*. Kraków: Wydawnictwo Literackie.
Huelle, Paweł. 1987. *Weiser Dawidek*. Gdańsk: Wydawnictwo Morskie.
—. 1991. *Who was David Weiser?* translated by Antonia Lloyd-Jones. London: Bloomsbury.
—. 1991. *Opowiadania na czas przeprowadzki*. London: Puls.
—. 1996. *Moving House and Other Stories,* translated by Antonia Lloyd-Jones. London: Bloomsbury.
—. 2001. *Mercedes-Benz. Z listów do Hrabala*. Kraków: Znak.
—. 2005. *Mercedes-Benz: From Letters to Hrabal,* translated by Antonia Lloyd-Jones. London: Serpent's Tail.
Janion, Maria. 1996. *Kobiety i duch inności*. Warsaw: Sic!
Karpowicz, Ignacy. 2008. *Gesty*. Kraków: Wydawnictwo Literackie.
—. 2010. *Balladyny i romanse*. Kraków: Wydawnictwo Literackie.
Keff, Bożena. 2008. *Utwór o Matce i Ojczyźnie*. Kraków: Ha!art.
Kowalewski, Włodzimierz. 2000. *Bóg zapłacz!* Warsaw: W.A.B.
Kruszyński, Zbigniew. 2009. *Ostatni raport*. Kraków: Wydawnictwo Literackie.
Kuczok, Wojciech. 2003. *Gnój. Antybiografia*. Warsaw: W.A.B.
Lubelski, Jakub. 2012. *Boiduda*. Warsaw: Fronda.
Łoziński, Michał. 2006. *Reisefieber*. Kraków: Znak.
Masłowska, Dorota. 2002. *Wojna polsko-ruska pod flagą biało-czerwoną*. Warsaw: Lampa i Iskra Boża.
—. 2005. *White and Red,* translated by Ben Paloff. London: Atlantic Books; as *Snow White and Russian Red*. New York: Grove Press.
Myśliwski, Wiesław. 1997. *Widnokrąg*. Warsaw: Warszawskie Wydawnictwo Literackie MUZA SA.
Pilch, Jerzy. 1995. *Inne rozkosze*. Poznań: Wydawnictwo a5.
—. 2002. *His Current Woman*, translated by Bill Johnston. Evanston, IL: Northwestern University Press (Hydra Books).
—. 1997. *Tysiąc spokojnych miast*. London: Puls.
—. 2009. *A Thousand Peaceful Cities,* translated by David Frick. Rochester, NY: Open Letter.
Sieniewicz, Mariusz. 2008. *Rebelia*. Warsaw: W.A.B.
Sławiński, Bohdan. 2008. *Królowa Tiramisu*. Warsaw: Jacek Santorski.
Stasiuk, Andrzej. 2009. *Taksim*. Gładyszów: Czarne.
Świderski, Bronisław. 2007. *Asystent śmierci*. Warsaw: W.A.B.
Tokarczuk, Olga. 2004. *Ostatnie historie*. Kraków: Wydawnictwo Literackie.
Wein, Viola. 2005. *Rachmunes*. Warsaw: Sic!

Polish Urban Literature and the Memory of Lost Others

Uilleam BLACKER

Remembering lost others: place, text and image

The literature of "small homelands," from its origins in the post-war period to its variants and transformations through the 1990s and 2000s, has received much attention from Polish critics. As Przemysław Czapliński points out, the "small homeland" aesthetic, which mourned the passing of the Arcadian spaces of Poland's former eastern borderlands, the *kresy*, has evolved in various innovative directions in recent decades (Czapliński 2001, 105-128). What unites all of these writings, from the small homelands to the more recent, invented, individualized homelands, is an attention to memory and loss. This chapter will focus on a particular element of the problem of memory, place and loss in recent Polish literature: the memory of lost others. In many Polish cities and towns, the question of those who inhabited these spaces "before us" is one that inspires variously anxiety and fascination. In my discussion I refer mainly to the Germans who inhabited the so-called "reclaimed lands" and were deported after World War II and the Jews who were murdered in the Holocaust. While these are the most numerous groups to have disappeared from Polish territory, they are not the only ones, and one could also extend this idea to, for example, the Ukrainians who were deported from south-eastern areas of Poland after the War. What I understand by the phrase "memory of lost others" is not only how "we" remember "them," but, in my view more interestingly, how "their" memories, and "their" past, are accessed or internalized by "us."

Memory is normally understood as existing within individual or collective subjects. However, as Jan Assmann has shown, "cultural memory" transcends the immediate memories of individuals, or the "communicative memories" of groups that exists only across a limited span of generations. Cultural memory is a vast archive of texts, artefacts, rituals, customs and places which retain stories of a given group's past that go far beyond living memory (Assmann and Czaplicka 1995, 130). Urban space, with its memorials, monuments, landmark buildings and place names, is one of the key bearers of cultural memory identified by Assmann (Assmann 2006, 7-8). Memories abide within places themselves, existing in the fabric of cities and towns, ready to be deciphered. The idea of the city as a text, or body of texts is, as Czapliński points out, a common trope in writing on urban space. Writers imagine the city as a palimpsest, a multi-levelled surface containing many, overlapping narratives:

> [...] to be an inhabitant of any space today is to be aware that we exist on the pages of a palimpsest, that we walk in the footsteps of those who lived here before us, we write down our narrative in their narratives, we erase the signs of their existence, we add our own motifs to their motifs. (Czapliński 2001, 127)

Each inhabitant of a city or town must confront the narratives inscribed by those who made those places—their buildings, their monuments, their place names, their objects. These constitute physical "lieux de mémoire" by which communities anchor themselves to a particular place and a particular past. These texts do not necessarily disappear even if the group in question does, but remain as ghostly reminders of those who are no longer there. Recent Polish literature has repeatedly asked how those who come to occupy the abandoned streets and homes of vanished others deal with the proliferation of memories that surround them. During the communist period, the German or Jewish pasts of Polish cities and towns were silenced or erased in favour of a purely Polish narrative. This involved extensive renaming of streets and squares, the destruction of monuments and installation of new ones, and attempts to literally erase traces of the previous culture from the face of the city's buildings (see for example the case of Wrocław as discussed by Thum, 2009). In the decades since the collapse of communism, these latent pasts have begun to resurface, and be celebrated and valued for their historical or simply human interest, but also for the cultural capital that they afford. Poland's major cities now celebrate the pasts of those groups who have vanished from them in exhibitions, festivals and investment in tourist attractions. This process was in many ways anticipated by literature, which began to rediscover and explore these pasts in the 1980s or earlier.

If we treat the city as text, then we assume it to be a chain of signifiers. The question thus arises as to what its signified is. The signified, I would suggest, are those who built the city, their identity, their aspirations, their culture, their past. If we understand the process of signification in this way, then it transpires that, at least initially, the urban signifier contains within it its own referent—its inhabitants. Signifier and signified are one, or at least locked together in a symbiotic, and not just semiotic, relationship. In this sense, the city functions in a way similar to Roland Barthes' characterization of the photograph, which at one and the same time both signifies and contains its signified. In order for the photograph to exist, Barthes points out, there must be an actual referent. The semiotic relationship is thus not purely arbitrary (Barthes 1982, 5). Cities and towns are built on this same principle: they both refer to and contain their referents. It is for this reason the phenomena of dislocation, deportation and resettlement are so epistemologically traumatic. Those who were signified become homeless and unrepresented, are condemned to the muteness of immigrants. Those who come to inhabit strange places are not the referent of the text that surrounds them, and are thus alienated, unrepresented within the very space in which they exist. The main challenge faced by new inhabitants is to become signified. One way of approaching this problem is to forge a new sign system and to erase the previous one, which was the dominant strategy in the post-war period. Another strategy is to somehow become the signified of the existing, unfamiliar town or city. This means not forcing space to signify a new referent, but modifying identity in order to become a referent suited to the existing sign system. This involves a movement of internalizing the sign system of the given city, and thus, of internalizing the memories of others found inscribed there. The latter option has been explored, if not always acknowledged as possible, by many Polish writers.

Coming to terms with the ghosts of others

There are numerous tactics by which Polish writers go about exploring the possibility of growing into a new space and dealing with the memories that linger there. One of the earliest engagements with this problem, in relation to Poland's lost Jewish communities, can be found in the work of Henryk Grynberg (b. 1936). As Marek Zaleski points out, Grynberg is preoccupied with the "image and symbolics of the empty place, the empty space that is left after the murdered and deceased, and which—and this is no less important—demands to be filled" (Zaleski 2004, 153). In 1993, Grynberg's documentary work *Heritage* (*Dziedzictwo*) returned to those empty places, and attempted to refill them with memory. It did so not through the author's own narrative as such, as a representative of the community that was annihilated, but through the narratives of those who remained in those villages that are now riddled with memory-holes. Grynberg's approach encouraged Poles to narrate that absence. His technique is powerful in its simplicity: it is a documentary form of writing that aims at a direct "reminding" of the Polish reader of those who have vanished. This project finds a continuation of sorts in Hanna Krall's (b. 1935) work, for example in *Proof of Existence* (*Dowody na istnienie*, 1995), which takes a similar, sparse, documentary approach, and in which the narrator/author directly approaches inhabitants of places previously inhabited by Jews and elicits memory from them. These texts at once remind us of those who have vanished and yet also affirm their absence, pointing to emptiness. They reinforce the relationship between spatial signifiers and their vanished referent, and also the absence of that referent, but do not necessarily attempt to negotiate a place in this relationship for those now inhabiting the empty spaces.

These texts perform the crucial task of archiving and preserving memories of Jewish communities. Yet towns and cities are not archives, but are inhabited by living communities, and the acknowledgment of absence is only the beginning of the process of establishing a meaningful mnemonic connection with space. One of the earliest works to tackle this problem directly is Jarosław Marek Rymkiewicz's (b. 1935) partly documentary novel *Umschlagplatz* (1988; translated as *The Final Station: Umschlagplatz*, 1994), which explores the specific past of the *Umschlagplatz* in Warsaw's ghetto, the point from which Jews were transferred to the death camps. For Rymkiewicz, it is not the recognition of absence that is most important, but rather the question: "What does Umschlagplatz signify in Polish life and Polish spirituality, and what does it portend for posterity? We live within the orbit of their death." (Rymkiewicz 1988, 11; 1994, 8) Following Rymkiewicz, numerous other writers have set about exploring how present urban communities may begin to actively appropriate and internalize the memories they find around them.

Reconstructing other places

In texts that attempt to negotiate the relationship between the self, place, and others' memory, there are three basic ways of situating the narrative in time. The first and perhaps most obvious approach is the situating of the narrative in the past, before the population shift. This approach is found in parts of Rymkiewicz's novel or in the work of Stefan Chwin (b. 1949)—at the beginning of *Hanemann* (1995; translated as *Death in Danzig*, 2004), for example, or in works such as *Esther* (1999) or *Miss Ferbelin* (*Panna Ferbelin*, 2011), as well as in the work of writers of "retro-detective fiction" such as Marcin Wroński's (b. 1972) novels about interwar Lublin or, most famously, Marek Krajewski's (b. 1966) novels set in German Breslau. In these types of narrative, the authors wish to regain the memory of the city through painstaking reconstruction—of a past that they themselves, being of a later generation, did not directly experience. They return the memory of others to the reader, educating through historical verisimilitude and engaging the imagination through entertaining, dynamic plots, often through the use of popular fiction conventions such as those of crime fiction. Details are important: the details of everyday life, what people wore, what they ate, what they read, what shows they saw in the theatre. We must know what the streets were called then, what the buildings on them looked like, what kind of people lived in them. The reader is made familiar with what Paul Connerton calls the "rhetoric" of place. It is not enough, according to Connerton, to know *about* a place, one must *know* a place directly in order to be able to inscribe memories in it, and in order that the memories inscribed in it can be comprehended (Connerton 2009, 32).

At the centre of the process of learning the rhetoric of place is topographical knowledge, which Connerton relates to the classical art of committing certain rhetorical tropes to memory by locating them in space (Connerton 2009, 4). Thus, Krajewski's first novel, *Death in Breslau* (*Śmierć w Breslau*, 1999), features a footnote giving the contemporary name for any street or square mentioned (and there are many), while later novels feature a glossary. Chwin employs the same technique in *Hanemann*, for example, not only giving the Polish equivalents, but adding important historical details into his index. The idea of the topographical glossary is taken to another level by Szczecin (pre-war German Stettin) author Artur Liskowacki (b. 1956), whose collection of essays *Streets of Szczecin* (*Ulice Szczecina*, 1995) guides the reader through the city's streets, cross-referencing them with their German equivalents, and inscribing their German past into them. These works are an exercise in the art of memory through reference to topography: just as one can associate ideas with places in order to remember them, the readers of these works take part in an exercise in associating the German place names with their Polish equivalents, and associating the "ideas" of the German cities—episodes or characters from its history, or its general atmosphere and appearance—with the topographical loci of the contemporary Polish cities. Through this the contemporary Polish reader commits the lost German city to memory.

Historical reconstruction is not purely about educating readers about the past of a place (as Grynberg and Krall also do, for example); it must also engage their imaginations, their emotions, and crucially, their senses. To this end authors try to reproduce a sense of eidetic memory. Smells, sounds, sensations, tastes and sights are all central to the reconstructive process. Krajewski, for example, appeals to all the senses in his novels: the plentiful scenes of eating and drinking, with specific foods and drink, usually alcohol, carefully named and described, allow us to taste and smell the city of Breslau; the careful descriptions of people's appearances allow us to see them vividly; snippets of popular songs let us hear the sounds the former inhabitants of the city would have heard; even the tactility of the city is evoked through, on the one hand, plentiful scenes of seedy urban sexuality, and, on the other, violent contact with the physical city itself—falling onto pavements, being injured by collapsing buildings or by fires. Such physical contact may not overtly evoke any particular memory, but it does afford the reader a visceral physical encounter with the city that goes beyond merely knowing *about* it. This immediate and multi-levelled engagement with the city, engaging the intellect, the imagination, the emotions and the senses vividly simulates many of the elements of genuine place-based memory. The sheer popularity of Krajewski's novels tells us something about the effectiveness of this approach, and also about the demand for such recovery of memory among Polish readers: granted, many of their readers will be interested mainly in the thrill of the plot, but it is beyond doubt that a large part of their appeal lies in the past they so vividly reconstruct. Similar tactics are employed by, and also explain the success of, writers such as Chwin or Wroński.

Inhabiting other places: childhood, phantoms and material traces

Another repeated approach to the memory of others is to assume the view of the unfamiliar place from shortly after the war, through the eyes of a child narrator. This approach occurs, for example, in Stefan Chwin's (b. 1949) *Hanemann* (in the second part), Paweł Huelle's (b. 1957) *Moving House and Other Stories* (*Opowiadania na czas przeprowadzki*, 1991), Adam Zagajewski's (b. 1945) essay "Two Cities" ("Dwa miasta," 1991) and Julian Kornhauser's (b. 1946) autobiographical novella *House, Dream and Children's Games: A Sentimental Story* (*Dom, sen i gry dziecięce: opowieść sentymentalna*, 1995). The reason for the choice of narrative temporality is often related to the wish to explore private, biographical memory, and not to express space-memory disjunctions, yet in all of these texts the process of coming to know the world experienced by the child narrator is mirrored by the experience of a whole community coming to know a new space. What comes through strongly in these narratives is the bewilderment felt in inhabiting a space that signifies a referent that has been driven out, a space that seems to stubbornly ignore its new inhabitants. The new inhabitants are disorientated, as Zagajewski writes, "looking with amazement at the Prussian bricks of the tenements" and "absorbed with dying and taken aback by the place in which they were to die" (Zagajewski 1991, 15; 1995, 15-16). They cope by returning in their minds to the city they have left:

> Paradoxically, by losing their memories they recovered them, because it is clear that the loss of memory in old age means loss of control over the most recent layers of memories and a return to old memories, which nothing is capable of eradicating. They returned to Lwów. (Zagajewski 1991, 15; 1995, 16, translation slightly adjusted—Ed.)

Adults and especially older people refuse to move in their minds, but the children show more curiosity. In Huelle's *Moving House and Other Stories,* the young narrator is fascinated by maps of pre-war Gdańsk, and by the discovery that the Polish place names are only recent impositions. His discovery of the map of the pre-war city, and the knowledge that it affords, provides a degree of identification: he realizes that the German city, which seems so distant, unreal and inaccessible, is in fact only just under the surface of the "new" city—although they masquerade as Polish, the new names are often simply translations of the German ones, are phonetically very similar or even exactly the same (Huelle 1991, 34). The young narrator and his father wander the city, discovering the past inscribed in this space as they go, the boy "clumsily" pronouncing the German names. Here the reader is not submerged in reconstruction, but sees place through the eyes of a child as a fragmented, distorted landscape from which he must garner what he can from the scraps of evidence available to him. The effect is not of alienation, but of learning to inhabit and identify with a dual system of spatial signs. Zagajewski describes a similar double spatial consciousness in reference to his own childhood. Here he walks through the city with his grandfather:

I was a sober young boy with a memory as small as a hazelnut, and I was absolutely certain that in walking through Gliwice, among the Prussian secessionist tenements decorated with heavy granite caryatids, I was where I really was. My grandfather, however, despite his walking right next to me, was in Lwów. I walked through the streets of Gliwice, he the streets of Lwów. I was on a long street that would certainly have been named Main Street in America, but here bore the sneering name Victory Street (after so many defeats!) and joined the small square with an equally small railway station. At the same time my grandfather was strolling down Sapieha Street in Lwów. (Zagajewski 1991, 15; 1995, 16-17, slightly adjusted—Ed.)

Despite being taught to regard the new city as inferior, as incomparable to the lost city, Zagajewski describes how, as a young boy, he grew to love the city. He compares the presence of the two cities in his childhood to two intertwining musical motifs, motifs that are "different, but destined for a difficult love affair." It is precisely the interaction of the motifs, their "dance," that constitutes the piece of music, just as it is the "difficult love" of two cities that defines the young Zagajewski as a person and a poet (Zagajewski 1991, 46; 1995, 68).

More direct links to the other past persist in the few people who have remained from the pre-war cities. In Huelle's collection, the most powerful figure in this sense is the neighbour of the narrator's family, an elderly German woman who had occupied the large house before the war, but is now confined to a small section of it, where she keeps herself hidden away, the object of suspicion and speculation from her new Polish neighbours. The narrator's access to the woman's apartment is a point of access to the past, but one, again, that is characterized by both fascination and lack of comprehension—the boy cannot understand her German, while her Polish is poor, and the objects in her home seem alien to him: their "contours [...] were blurred, and their shaped merged together, as if through an out-of-focus lens." (Huelle 1991, 43; 1994, 82) Another obvious example is the reclusive figure of Hanemann himself in Chwin's novel, who refuses to leave with other German evacuees, and persists like a ghost in the Polish city. These figures provide a direct, living link to the communities that have vanished, yet they are, as in the case of both Hanemann and the German woman, hidden away, through their own choice but also because of the wish of their neighbours not to see them.

One of the most striking tropes in this type of narrative is the proliferation of objects left behind by those who have disappeared. Chwin's *Hanemann* contains a chapter devoted entirely to objects (Chwin 1995, 25-29). The objects fall into several categories: those that will be taken and remind the displaced of their home, those that will be destroyed—and here objects belonging to Jews are particularly prominent, such as the synagogue candlesticks that will be melted down to decorate a Nazi officer's sword—and those that remain to speak of the old inhabitants to the new ones. Chwin is careful to attach specific objects to specific people or specific stories. The description of these objects is an inventory of the city, its citizens, and their everyday existence; the destruction or dispersal of these objects testifies to the shattering of the old city, and the memories it contains, into many fragments. Jerzy Jarzębski has noted the preponderance of objects in recent Polish prose, describing the phenomenon as "history written in things" (Jarzębski 2006, 153), while Przemysław Czapliński suggests these objects "can be read like the book of time, like a palimpsest of private histories" (Czapliński 213-14). This book of objects is, however, one that is often incomprehensible to those who now possess those objects. Sometimes objects can literally be read, although not necessarily understood, as in Olga Tokarczuk's *House of Day, House of Night* (*Dom dzienny, dom nocny,* 1998) where the words inscribed in domestic objects speak to their new owners in a foreign language. Not only is the actual language inscribed on them incomprehensible, but the function of the objects themselves is sometimes not understood, such as the indoor taps in the German houses in the same novel (Tokarczuk 1998, 221-225). The otherness of these objects reflects the otherness of those of whom they remind us. This is also underlined when objects that are explicitly intended to preserve personal and family past are discovered in the attics or cupboards of the German houses—locks of hair, photographs, children's teeth (Tokarczuk 1998, 261).

Objects are particularly resonant as signifiers of lost others in that they are constantly present in the most intimate spheres of life of the new inhabitants—when they cook and eat, next to their skin as clothes. Yet while they are so physically intimate with their new owners, they undeniably bear the direct, physical traces of their real referent, the original owners. Thus the women of Nowa Ruda in *House of Day, House of Night* discover to their surprise the used handkerchiefs in the pockets of the jackets they have appropriated. An illustration of the disturbing, haunting nature of this persistence is Huelle's story of the German table appropriated by the narrator's family. The table is described as being awkward, somehow too big, with one leg too short, it refuses to fit into the family's everyday life, and at night insects can be heard devouring it from inside. The narrator's mother cannot rest for the memory of the Germans attached to the table, the Germans whom she so detests, and she forces her husband to destroy it.

In the context of a conversation with friends on the sudden renaming of the places in her region, the narrator of Olga Tokarczuk's *House of Day, House of Night* reflects:

> But then words and things do form a symbiotic relationship, like mushrooms and birch trees. Words grow on things, and only then are they ripe in meaning, ready to be spoken aloud, when they grow into the landscape. [...] People are like words in this way too—they cannot live without being attached to a place. So people are words. Only then do they become real. (Tokarczuk 1998, 168; 2002, 176-177, translation slightly adjusted—Ed.)

Tokarczuk expresses here the sense of disjunction from place felt by those who live surrounded by the material traces of others specifically in terms of language and signification. The language used by the newcomers, the system of signs they use to describe the places they inhabit and the objects in those places, does not seem to comply with reality, has not "grown into the landscape" or "on things." Neither, subsequently, have those people.

Sifting through the fragments: the impossibility of return

Tokarczuk's *House of Day, House of Night* represents a third kind of narrative temporality used by Polish writers to approach the memories of others. These narratives may contain elements of reconstruction or shifts in temporality, but they always return to the subjective seeking of the past in the present moment, and thus are always self-reflexive, sometimes self-ironic. The main thrust of such narratives is to reflect on the possibility or, as is often the case, impossibility of recovering a sense of memory in other places. These narratives seem to be spoken from the persona of the author herself, and from this very immediate, autobiographical point of view guide the reader into fantastical experiments in accessing other pasts. Thus Tokarczuk's novel, which is set partly in the present, presents various, fragmented and surprising approaches to the past that is inscribed in the microcosmic spaces she describes. While in many ways a very different novel, Andrzej Bart's *Flypaper Factory* (*Fabryka muchołapek*, 2009) also assumes a narrative pose of identity with the author himself in the present moment, yet its fantastical exploration of pre-war Łódź, particularly its Jewish past, and its wartime ghetto, are highly experimental.

A similar, quasi-autobiographical approach is taken by Inga Iwasiów in her novels *Bambino* (2008) and *Ku słoncu* (*Towards the Sun*, 2010), which, from the point of view of the present, employ multiple characters and shifts in time to explore the experience of displacement and melancholy of inhabiting post-war Szczecin (Phillips, 2012). Piotr Paziński's *The Boarding House* (*Pensjonat,* 2009) likewise features a present-day, first-person narrator, but weaves the story of Jewish Warsaw—both pre-war and post-war—into his subjective narrative in a way that blurs the boundaries between his own memories and the memories of those he remembers. While Paziński's narrator is Jewish himself, and explores his own family past, the city that he recalls is nevertheless one that is irretrievably lost, and in many ways strange to him.[1]

The narrators in Tokarczuk's, Bart's and Iwasiów's novels, and to a certain degree in Paziński's, represent the position of many inhabitants of present-day Polish cities and towns: they feel at once a fascination with their surroundings, and with the past they read in those surroundings, yet they are haunted by a feeling of distance, disjunction, of not knowing, not being able to see that past clearly. The narrator of *Flypaper Factory* is a writer who goes to great lengths to come to "know" his city. He is quite open in his discussion of his extensive, not say obsessive, research; at the same time the novel's centrepiece, the description of the imagined posthumous trial of Chaim Rumkowski (1877-1944), the bitterly controversial Nazi-appointed leader of the Jewish Council in the Łódź ghetto, with its detailed discussion of the ghetto's historical reality, shows the implementation of the same kind of meticulous research by the author himself. Yet while factual historical knowledge is openly paraded, the access to the past built up by the narrator is consistently framed as an illness or dream (he is not sure which), and the reader is constantly reminded of things the narrator has been unable to find out. No matter how much information he retrieves about the past of his city, there are always gaps, and the resulting construct is always an illusion.

Bart's novel is above all a reflection on the desire to know the past of a city. Renata Plaice contends that, for Bart's protagonist, "the landscape presents a network of signifying traces and fragments which consolidate memory" (Plaice 2012, 41). At the same time, however, the effort to "consolidate memory" and the various strategies by which this may be achieved are continually undermined and questioned. As Bartosz Dąbrowski aptly notes, Bart's narrator's explorations "reveal history to be an opaque ruin, reconstructed with fictional additions and amended with *ex-post* inventions." (Dąbrowski, 2011, 262) Thus, in an ironic echo of the sensory reconstruction of place described above in relation to Krajewski, the narrator relates how a friend of his, another local history enthusiast, met a woman who could remember much about pre-war Lódź, and who knew a Jewish architect whose life the narrator has been researching. "She could even remember what they ate then!" the friend exclaims. Yet the friend breaks off his story and we never find out "what they ate," and the life of the architect becomes another unfinished fragment of the past (Bart 2009, 39). Symbolic of the difficulty of the

---

1 See the detailed analysis of Paziński's *The Boarding House* by Knut Andreas Grimstad in the current volume.

entire process of recovering the past of others is a pen that the narrator is left by a young Jewish woman from Prague whom he meets when he is taken into the fantasy world of the imagined trial. The pen is presented as a clichéd conceit of the object in the dream that persists after waking, uncannily suggesting that the dream was real. The narrator seems to have recovered from his strange hallucinations at the end of the novel, yet the pen troubles him:

> I feel fine, it's time to forget the hallucinations and put a full-stop to the whole story. Yet that green tortoiseshell pen bothers me, in its velvet-lined box, with the golden inscription "Pramen & Sohn" on its lid. I look at it, a few times I've tried even to write a word with it, yet it is not mine. I did not buy, nor was I given this pen, the like of which there are only a few in the world. I read that it was meant to be the first Czech fountain pen, and Mr Pramen wanted to make his firm into a stationery Koh-I-Noor. He didn't manage it, because before he was able, he was sent to Theresienstadt with his son. What his pen is doing in my house, I'm afraid to even think. (Bart 2009, 275-276)

This trope ironically comments on the obsession with significant objects that link us to the past, and yet, as a pen, also comments on the desire to know and to speak the memory of others, to re-inscribe them into the present—something which ultimately proves impossible. The narrator has this pen in his possession, just as he inhabits the city once inhabited by many Jews, and yet he is frightened to think what the implications of this are, and cannot feel that it is truly his. Bart's novel at once strives to reconstruct the past, and yet constantly reminds the reader that the semiotic disjunction between *that* city and its current inhabitants will never quite be bridged.

A similar attitude to memory emerges in *House of Day, House of Night*. Despite the various vivid forays into the past, from the reconstruction of the life of a medieval German saint to the post-war process of deportation and resettlement itself, which are doubtless based on extensive research, the narrator remains an outsider to the place, and her various attempts at accessing the past remain disparate fragments. This is symbolized in her relationship with an elderly neighbour, Marta, a Polish woman who remembers the pre-war past. The narrator can never quite understand Marta, or feel comfortable with her, partly because Marta seems to hide her own memories from her. The narrator complains that Marta "likes to invent things" when asked about the past, and "simply has nothing to say about herself" (Tokarczuk 1998, 10; 2002, 4-5). Marta, who is deeply rooted in place and memory, represents the exact opposite of the narrator, who is uprooted and must work hard to recover memory. Like the place, Marta will not fully reveal her true knowledge to the narrator, giving her only enigmatic fragments.

Photographs and the postmemory of others

The opening of *House of Day, House of Night* is telling in this respect. The narrator dreams that she is "purely vision" (or: "pure looking"—"jestem czystym patrzeniem") expressing a desire to be able to see everything in the small space that is the focus of the novel; yet at the same time she experiences the sensation that nothing here belongs to her (Tokarczuk 1998, 7-8; 2002, 1-2). This is the tension between the desire to know and to reconstruct, and the feeling of distance from the strange place. Marek Zaleski points out how Polish authors use seeing, vision, the "snapshot" image, or indeed photography itself in order to overcome the temporality that produces loss and thereby recover memory. Seeing, fixing reality into an image makes that image eternal, outside of time, and thus recoverable (Zaleski 2004, 60). Correspondingly, the idea of "pure seeing" in Tokarczuk's opening lines evolves in the novel into an attempt to make all times present in the eye of the narrator's imagination. By learning to see her surroundings, she aims to recover the memory of times past to which neither she, nor the community she belongs to has any direct link. The project does not succeed in completely reconciling the contemporary Polish subject to the past inscribed in her surroundings. It does not establish a correspondence between the spatial signifiers and its inhabitants. What it does manage to do is reconfigure the relationship between them, and the same can be said of Bart's novel: these authors open up possible strategies for accessing the pasts signified in space, and at the same time problematize this very process, exposing it to discussion and examination, and often to irony and doubt.

The question of vision and memory brings us back to the question of the semiotic similarities between place and the photograph discussed at the beginning of this chapter. Both of these are central elements in Marianne Hirsch's theory of postmemory, which posits that the overwhelmingly traumatic memories of the generation who experienced the Holocaust are internalized by the generations that come after them as their own memory. Memories of the trauma itself are internalized, but so also are memories of life before the trauma, specifically, of places (Hirsch 1997, 243-244). The generation of postmemory remembers places in prewar Eastern Europe that they have never visited. Postmemory of these places is accessed not through "recall," but through what Hirsch calls "imaginative investment, projection, and creation" (Hirsch 2008, 107). It is as much the result of overbearing inherited narrative as it is of active, creative, seeking of memory that is not one's own. Photographs assist in this search in that they "enable us, in the present, not only to see and touch that past but also to try to reanimate it by undoing the finality of the photographic 'take'" (Hirsch 2008, 115). Hirsch also states how photographs, in their fragmentary nature as split seconds of the past, are "open to narrative elaboration and embroidery and to symbolization" (Hirsch 2008, 117).

The experience of viewing photographs for the generation of postmemory is in many ways similar to the experience of inhabiting spaces whose signifiers refer to others. Indeed it is testament to the similar processes involved in both that in the work of many contemporary Polish writers place, photographs and memory are closely linked: photographs play an important role in *House of Day, House of Night* and in Huelle's *Moving House and Other Stories*, while Marek Krajewski explicitly cites his wish to "enter old photographs" as an inspiration for starting to write about Breslau (Szczerba, 2006). Another well-known example is Piotr Szewc's 1987 novel *Annihilation* (*Zagłada*), which opens by narrating the past of the city of Zamość by looking through an album of photographs. Jarosław Marek Rymkiewicz's narrator in *Umschlagplatz* is disturbed by his own wartime childhood photographs, taken in Warsaw and nearby Otwock, which provide troubling hints as to the destruction of the Jewish community that was taking place at the time, while the narrator of Piotr Paziński's *The Boarding House* recovers the memory of Jewish Warsaw through a pile of old photographs he is given, and provides lengthy descriptions of them in the text. The photograph at once affords a direct route to the past, to its referent, and at the same time, in its fragmentary nature, provides space for the work of the imagination. The same applies to cities and towns. Buildings, streets, monuments, cemeteries not only tell of the past, but physically connect those who encounter them directly to their referents—the cultures that created and previously inhabited them. These remnants are invariably in a state of degradation, fragmentation, and thus are "open to narrative elaboration." Hence writers such as Chwin and Tokarczuk are inspired by some small object—as is Huelle's child narrator in *Who was David Weiser?* (*Weiser Dawidek*, 1987), by the half-erased German inscription on a gravestone—to extrapolate larger stories, to delve further into the past. In our direct contact with these fragmented spatial signifiers, we have physical access to the past, we touch what "they" touched, we are where "they" were; yet what is ultimately underlined in this experience is absence, rather than presence. As Hirsch also says of photographs, "the retrospective irony of every photograph, made all the more poignant if violent death separates its two presents, consists precisely in the simultaneity of this effort and the consciousness of its impossibility." (Hirsch 2008, 115) Ironically, it is as we uncover the traces of those vanished others that the consciousness of the distance between us and them appears, as Tokarczuk and Bart's narrators, for example, both become painfully aware. The creation of postmemory serves to underline the lack of real memory. As Dąbrowski points out in reference to Bart and Paziński, the reversion to photographs and other media of postmemory serves to illustrate the necessary limits of literary representation of the past (Dąbrowski 2001, 261).

Hirsch also describes how the very experience of viewing the family photographs of victims of the Holocaust gives access to a postmemory of those people and the tragedy they suffered, because we are all, regardless of our family backgrounds, able to identify with the process of looking at family photographs (Hirsch 1997, 255). Hirsch calls this "affiliative postmemory" (Hirsch 2008, 117). Similarly, through inhabiting the same spaces as those who came before us, through that common experience of walking the same streets and sleeping in the same rooms, we are able to develop a vivid postmemory of them and the past that they represent. The development of this kind of postmemory, which is based partly on the narrative possibilities afforded by fragmented spatial signifiers, and partly on a feeling of "affiliation" with lost others through the experience of inhabiting the same space, is precisely what underlies the varying projects of recovering other memory described in this chapter. This connection to the past allows the contemporary Polish subject to begin to participate in the semiotic structure of the place she inhabits, to access, in a mediated way, the memories that are signified in it. This is not an intervention in that semiotic process, not a direct assumption of the position of referent. The postmemory aesthetic acknowledges loss, ironically reflects on the impossibility of return and of the recovery of the broken semiotic whole. Instead it creates a memory-effect that follows the arc of the original memory-place relation, but is always a mnemonic simile, rather than a memory as such.

While acknowledging the impossibility of assuming the position of referent is important here, it does not imply a status of eternal "outsider" for the contemporary Polish subject. The process of shaping place is always occurring, and the inhabitants of every city and town continually shape their connection to place through the new spatial signifiers they create. What many Polish literary texts have demonstrated is that those spatial signifiers do not always have to be new, original, national, or "ours." Existing, hidden or even reconstructed spatial signifiers can also be incorporated into this process. The process of developing a hybrid system of spatial signifiers that incorporates both "our" and "others'" signs must have a formative effect on the signified. As Huelle's child narrator or Zagajewski's autobiographical reflections show, it is possible to study and learn two sets of place names, to listen to the music of two cities, and to allow two memories of one place to shape who we are.

Bibliography

Primary sources

Bart, Andrzej. 2009. *Fabryka muchołapek*. Warsaw: W.A.B.
Chwin, Stefan. 1995. *Hanemann*. Gdańsk: Marabut.
—. 2004. *Death in Danzig,* translated by Philip Boehm. Orlando, FL: Harcourt.
—. 1999. *Esther.* Gdańsk: Tytuł.
—. 2011. *Panna Ferbelin.* Gdańsk: Tytuł.
Grynberg, Henryk. 1975. *Życie ideologiczne*. London: Polska Fundacja Kulturalna.
—. 1993. *Dziedzictwo*. London: Aneks.
Huelle, Paweł. 1991. *Opowiadania na czas przeprowadzki*. London: Puls.
—. 1994. *Moving House and Other Stories,* translated by Antonia Lloyd-Jones. London: Bloomsbury.
—. 1991. *Who was David Weiser?* translated by Antonia Lloyd-Jones. London: Bloomsbury.
—. 2001. *Weiser Dawidek.* Gdańsk: słowo/obraz terytoria.
Iwasiów, Inga. 2008. *Bambino.* Warsaw: Świat Książki.
—. 2010. *Ku słońcu.* Warsaw: Świat Książki.
Kornhauser, Julian. 1995. *Dom, sen i gry dziecięce: opowieść sentymentalna.* Kraków: Znak.
Krall, Hanna. 1995. *Dowody na istnienie.* Poznań: a5.
Krajewski, Marek. 1999. *Śmierć w Breslau.* Wrocław: Wydawnictwo Dolnośląskie.
—. 2008. *Death in Breslau,* translated by Danuta Stok. London: MacLehose Press.
Liskowacki, Artur Daniel. 1995. *Ulice Szczina*. Szczecin: Albatros.
Rymkiewicz, Jarosław Marek. 1988. *Umschlagplatz.* Paris: Instytut Literacki.
—. *The Final Station: Umschlagplatz,* translated by Nina Taylor. New York: Farrar, Straus, Giroux.
Szewc, Piotr. 1987. *Zagłada*. Warsaw: Czytelnik.
Tokarczuk, Olga. 1998. *Dom dzienny, dom nocny.* Wałbrzych: Ruta.
—. 2002. *House of Day, House of Night,* translated by Antonia Lloyd-Jones. London: Granta.
Zagajewski, Adam. 1991. *Dwa miasta*. Paris: Zeszyty Literackie.
—. 1995. *Two Cities: On Exile, History and Imagination,* translated by Lillian Vallee. New York: Farrar, Straus, Giroux.

Secondary sources

Assmann, Jan and John Czaplicka. 1995. "Collective Memory and Cultural Identity." *New German Critique* 65:125-133.
Assmann, Jan 2006. *Religion and Cultural Memory: Ten Studies*, translated by Rodney Livingstone. Stanford, CA: Stanford University Press.
Barthes, Roland. 1982. *Camera Lucida: Reflections on Photography*. London: Jonathan Cape.
Connerton, Paul. 2009. *How Modernity Forgets.* Cambridge: Cambridge University Press.

Czapliński, Przemysław. 2001. *Wzniosłe tęsknoty. Nostalgie w prozie lat dziewięćdziesiątych*. Kraków: Wydawnictwo Literackie.

Dąbrowski, Bartosz. 2011. "Postpamięć, zależność, trauma." In *Kultura po przejściach, osoby z przeszłością. Polski dyskurs postzależościowy – konteksty i perspektywy badawcze,* edited by Ryszard Nycz, 257-270. Kraków: Universitas.

Hirsch, Marianne. 1997. *Family Frames: Photography, Narrative and Postmemory*. Cambridge, MA, and London: Harvard University Press.

—. 2008. "The Generation of Postmemory." *Poetics Today* 29(1): 103-128.

Jarzębski, Jerzy. 2006. "Historia zapisana w rzeczach." In *Terazniejszość i pamięć przeszłości. Rozumienie historii w literaturze polskiej XX i XXI wieku,* edited by Hanna Gosk and Andrzej Zieniewicz, 153-165. Warsaw: Elipsa.

Phillips, Ursula. 2012. "Generation, Transformation and Place in Inga Iwasiów's Novels *Bambino* (2008) and *Ku słońcu* (2010)." In *Philosophy and Literature: Generation and Transformation in Gender and Postdependency Discourse,* edited by Urszula Chowaniec and Marzenna Jakubczak. [Special issue of] *Argument* 2(1): 17-35. Accessed 22 January, 2013. http://www.argument-journal.eu/back-\mbox{issue}s/vol-2-no-1?lang=en

Plaice, Renata. 2012. "Holocaust Memory in Recent Polish Literature: Andrzej Bart's *Fabryka muchołapek* and Piotr Paziński's *Pensjonat*." *Journal of European Studies* 42(1): 34-49.

Szczerba, Jacek. 2006. "Chcę wejść w stare fotografie. Rozmowa z Markiem Krajewskim." *Gazeta Wyborcza*, 21 August. Accessed 23 January, 2013. http://wyborcza.pl/1,75517,3563752.html?as=1startsz=0#ixzz1AjKcYZuM

Thum, Gregor. 2009. "Wrocław's Search for a New Historical Narrative: From Polonocentrism to Postmodernism." In *Cities after the Fall of Communism: Reshaping Cultural Landscapes and European Identity,* edited by John Czaplicka, Nida Gelazis and Blair A. Ruble, 75-101. Washington DC: Woodrow Wilson Center Press; and Baltimore, MD: John Hopkins University Press.

Zaleski, Marek. 2004. *Formy pamięci.* Gdańsk: słowo/obraz terytoria.

Polishness in Crisis? Migration and Inter-Ethnic Coupling

Kris VAN HEUCKELOM

A Pole arrives at a police station and says: "My fiancée wants to kill me." "How do you know?" asks the policeman, "did she threaten you?" "No," the Pole replies, "but I found this in her bathroom." He hands the officer a bottle with the label "Polish Remover."
Polish joke told by a Dublin taxi driver (Brzezińska 2010, 247)

Migration and inter-ethnic coupling

Following the disintegration of the communist regime in 1989 and the gradual disappearance of exilic institutions and networks, the traditional paradigm of Polish émigré literature has undoubtedly come to an end. In the mean time, old ideas of emigration, such as the notion of a stable identity and a fixed homeland, have made way for new conceptions of identity and nationhood. Within contemporary Polish culture, the shift toward a more postmodern understanding of the (e)migrant condition has often been linked to the nomadic or bohemian-type lifestyle of the female protagonists in the early novels of Manuela Gretkowska. Along with Gretkowska, authors such as Janusz Rudnicki, Krzysztof Maria Załuski, Izabela Filipiak and Bronisław Świderski have put much effort into coming to terms with the traditional commitments and expectations imposed upon Polish émigré authors, and into outlining the existential dilemmas and universal challenges faced by Poles living and working abroad in the post-1989 era. The literary protagonists (and authors) embodying this new literary paradigm receive manifold names: stipend-holders, cosmopolites, semi-emigrants, transnationals, globetrotters, transmigrants (Czapliński 1997; Gasyna 2003; Błędowska 2003; Pasterska 2008).

New westbound migration waves in the years preceding and following Poland's accession to the European Union seem to have consolidated and reinforced the topicality of migration-related issues in Polish literary and cultural discourses. The past few years have seen a considerable outburst of creativity on the part of fresh authors providing fictional—and less fictional—accounts of their recent expat experiences.[1] Interestingly, whereas traditional émigré literature used to privilege elements of either nostalgia or mockery with respect to the homeland (Pasterska 2008), a significant number of these recent books seem to revolve around the need for self-realization, featuring narrators or protagonists in their twenties, for whom the stay abroad takes on the form of a rite of passage (Rostek 2009; Uffelmann 2010 and 2011; Chowaniec 2011; Gall 2011; Olszewska 2011). In a variety of ways, these migration books relate to the tradition of the *Bildungsroman* and its contemporary manifestations, ranging from explicit (and sometimes touchingly naive) cravings for self-realization to more self-reflexive and ironic approaches.[2]

This chapter deals with recent fictional responses to Poland's accession to the European Union, focusing in particular on the literary treatment of out-group relationships in the diasporic space. If in 19th- and early 20th-century émigré literature "marriage to a properly Polish mate was shown to bring not just domestic happiness but generational continuity, national and family honor, and a sustained relationship with the (Polish) homeland" (Majewski 2003, 125), then one might have suspected that Poland's new political and economic situation had made the taboo formerly surrounding intermarriage plainly irrelevant. Remarkably, however, quite the opposite seems to be true. A case in point is offered by the script of the Polish TV serial *Londoners* (*Londyńczycy*, 2008-2010)—about a group of Polish immigrants who seek their fortune in the British capital in the post-accession period. Instead of creating fantasies of transnational redemption and conciliation through inter-ethnic coupling (a narrative device that often returns in European feature films dealing with Polish labour migration), the high-budget Polish serial envisions the beneficial potential of immigrant characters who succeed in becoming successful entrepreneurs on British soil but remain attached—at least in matrimonial terms—to their Polish roots and their fellow migrants (Van Heuckelom 2011 and 2013).

If the device of intermarriage (or exogamy) may be said to establish an intimate bond between the migrant and the host country, then the migrant's persistent attachment to his or her country of origin can be embodied by a marital alliance

---

1 See the books listed in the first section of the Bibliography.

2 While the body of recent migration-related fiction is massive, the artistic quality of these texts is sometimes rather precarious. As Dariusz Nowacki (2009) aptly remarks in one of his reviews: "Why does it seem to me that the emigration theme in Polish prose is on the decline? [. . .] The works that belong to the new load of emigration prose are dominated by epic naivety combined with a similarly naive form of interventionism." Compare also Wach 2010.

between the traveller and a partner who stayed behind. Undoubtedly, one of the most prototypical and powerful narratives expressing the close bond between the male traveller and his fatherland is the story of Odysseus and Penelope. Interestingly, apart from exposing the neat link between patriotic and marital virtues, the story of the Greek hero and his faithful wife also indicates that our cultural constructions of travel are essentially gendered and have tended to privilege travelling as a typically masculine activity. As Karin Sarsenov rightly asserts, "[a]lthough a myriad of women have indeed set out on dangerous and distant journeys, few stories have been told about them. In the grand narratives of Western culture, beginning with the *Odyssey*, male heroes explore and conquer space, in order to return to a home that in every aspect is coded feminine: as motherland; as maternal, fertile soil; as inhabited by the custodian of the hearth. The image of the waiting, passive Penelope and her repetitious, fruitless labour at the loom has moulded the conception of proper women's work for centuries." (2006, 2)

Although these constructions of women's immobility and passivity have long been superseded in practice, the story of Odysseus and Penelope remains a powerful metaphor for conceptualizing the migrant condition, especially with regard to the Polish migration narratives under discussion. For some of the authors involved (especially the male ones), references to the Homeric narrative allow them to describe the deplorable condition of contemporary male migrants in terms of a tension between the patriarchal order and its (post)modern rivals. Its most typical manifestation is the recurring representation of contemporary female Polish migrants as "Penelopes on the loose": instead of remaining beside the domestic hearth in the ancestral Ithaca, these women leave the home country, thereby endangering the generational continuity of the nation. Moreover, in accord with the idea that "geographical 'looseness' in women is assumed to be a universal marker of sexual wantonness—or at least cause for concern about their respectability" (Domosh and Seager 2001, 130), the representational practices that will be discussed here tend to identify— at least in part—the increasing mobility of Polish women with promiscuity.

Male migrants on the hunt

As Karen Lawrence has indicated with respect to gendered constructions of mobility, there has been a strong cultural tendency to "encode the traveler as a male who crosses boundaries and penetrates spaces; the female is mapped as a place on the itinerary of the male journey." (1994, 2) This "sexual mapping" of travel as a typically masculine activity comes to the surface in some of the migration narratives under scrutiny (i.e. those written—and narrated—by males). In Łukasz

Suskiewicz's novel *egri bikaver* (2009),[3] the autodiegetic narrator articulates his high expectations and fantasies about moving to Ireland in the following way: "I expected that some nice adventure would immediately fall to our share. Preferably an erotic one. A crowd of merry girls taking us along for some pleasure. Wrapping us up with their reddish braids." (Suskiewicz 2009, 10) In a similar vein, one of the male protagonists in Adam Miklasz's *The Polish Boxing School* (*Polska szkoła boksu,* 2009) overtly conceives of his trip to the UK in terms of sexual hunting: "I will show these bastards how Poles handle things. I will run off with all the lassies, no shit! I will leave you nothing, you will see. Fucking hedonism is my motto! I am not coming back to Poland, I will become the king of the isle." (Miklasz 2009, 13) In neither case, however, does the feminine soil of the Isles turn out to be susceptible to the aspirations of the Polish male protagonists. In Suskiewicz's case, the protagonist's immediately added remark that "unfortunately, nothing of the kind took place" (Suskiewicz 2009, 10) could be said to anticipate the failure of his migration project as a whole: the author's *alter ego* (who is sometimes referred to as Łukasz) is hardly able to find decent accommodation in Dublin, experiences difficulties in overcoming the language barrier and fails to find a job that is up to his intellectual capabilities. Moreover, while his fantasies about red-haired Irish girls are immediately superseded by reality, the Polish girls that cross his path in Ireland do not meet his expectations either. As it transpires, the only erotic adventure he experiences in Dublin results from an unexpected encounter with a well-known painting by Jacek Malczewski—*The Polish Hamlet: A Portrait of Aleksander Wielopolski*, which is on temporary display in the Irish National Gallery:

> Wandering through the National Gallery in Dublin, I stood face to face with Hamlet. I was stunned because even though I knew this picture so well, I had never seen it live. It had to be stuck somewhere in the subconscious, because it made an immense impression. I stood there open-mouthed and followed the veins on the shoulders of the Young and the Old Poland. I especially stared at the naked breast. Strangely enough, the breast seemed familiar, while the breasts on the works of foreign painters resembled abstract vegetables. [. . .] In the folder I read that it was part of an exhibition of art made in countries that were about to join the Union. While I thought it had come after me." (Suskiewicz 2007, 56)

The protagonist's profound fascination with this particular painting—combining eroticism with elements of Polish national martyrdom and resurrection—seems to be indicative of his inability to leave behind the cultural mindset, complexes and sentiments he grew up with in Poland and to fully adapt to the foreign environment he now finds himself in. Interestingly, the atavistic Polish traits the protagonist

3 The title refers to the Hungarian wine Bull's Blood.

ascribes to himself are not limited to the mental and emotional sphere, but have also left a genetically encoded impression on his face. In a telling conversation with “M” (a Polish friend who joins him on his trip to Dublin) the first-person narrator is given the following explanation of his unfortunate condition as an immigrant in the Irish capital: “Nothing will change your physiognomy, which is full of genetically determined suffering. You cannot change history.” (Suskiewicz 2009, 30)

The condition of the male Polish migrants described in Adam Miklasz’s *The Polish Boxing School* is very similar. The book tells the story of four Polish friends who depart from Kraków for the UK immediately after Poland’s accession to the European Union. All of them eventually end up in a small provincial town called Buckby where they try to make a living by collecting garbage and doing cleaning and gardening jobs. The highly marginal position of these Polish men in the host society acquires a particular expression in the way they conceive of their relationships with the opposite sex.[4] First of all, unlike immigrants from other countries, these Polish migrants prove to be very unsuccessful in matters of love and sexual intimacy. What is more, their inability to establish amorous bonds with locals also sets them apart from their female compatriots. The first-person narrator comments upon this issue in the following characteristic way:

> Polish women also had a great time, adopting with chameleon-like speed the rules governing this new and better world, the trends and the appropriate way of existence in a society of Übermenschen. They towered above their lady friends from all over the world—they were not as cheap and submissive as some girls from behind the eastern border, they were more refined and fastidious than English women, they did not aim at instantaneous pleasure, they reasoned like outstanding strategists—tactically and on the long run. They were looking for stability, preferably in the shape of a charming young man who could guarantee them a better life, cheaper housing, a ride to their workplace and some money to preserve their outer beauty. Hoping that a better model would turn up indeed. Along with them, Russian nouveaux riches, hot Spaniards and impudent Turks and Greeks wonderfully immersed themselves in the magical aura of the Friday night. Everyone but the Polish males. Tired of working all week, meticulously counting their pounds, often not very attractive physically and intellectually, burdened by complexes and a huge language barrier, completely unadjusted, forgotten by history, the media and God, without any friends, despised even by their female compatriots, they used to drink vodka and gnaw sausages in their bungalows, barracks or kitchens just like the one we have. (Miklasz 2009, 87)

By way of compensation, these male “Untermenschen” from Poland strongly focus on the bonds that link them to their home country, especially alliances of a marital nature. While doing so, these outcasts strongly draw on typical patriarchal discourse—in accordance with which males are allowed to chart foreign territory,

---

4 See also the chapter by Dirk Uffelmann in the current volume.

whereas the female element is to be kept in the place of origin. Characteristically, a frequently heard mantra among these men is that the only objective of their stay abroad is to save money for their marriage and honeymoon in Poland. The most emblematic description of the male protagonists' attachment to the patriarchal code of yore is offered by the following fragment:

> "When I get back to Poland, my sweet Grażyna will make me Polish meat stew, make up the bed, pour out tea... She is better than a thousand English women!" We totally agreed with our friend and drank a toast to our fatherland, to all these decent Grażynkas, Bożenkas and Helenkas living in places such as Pcim, Sieradz and Ostrołęka, these true reflections of the mythical woman from Sienkiewicz's prose, a woman who—just like Penelope—faithfully waits for us to return home, us decent Ulysseses effectively avoiding all sorts of temptations. (Miklasz 2009, 96)

In more ways than one, the (caricaturized) drama of these male protagonists revolves around the clash between their idealization of the home country (the domestic hearth) and the underlying awareness that this patriarchal way of thinking has long been superseded by reality. On the one hand, this contrast rises to the surface in their own ambivalent attitude toward inter-ethnic relationships: if they were only able to gain the love and sympathy of local women, they would undoubtedly surrender willfully to "all sorts of temptations." This ambiguity reveals itself in a characteristic way at the very end of the appraisal of the Polish "Penelopes" quoted above: when a local beauty suddenly passes by, one of the Polish protagonists immediately alerts his compatriots by saying "Look! Look at that nice bit of skirt!" (Miklasz 2009, 97) On the other hand, their attachment to the outdated patriarchal order is put under pressure as a result of the persistent doubts they have about the trustworthiness and good intentions of the women they have left behind. Quite typically, the reliability of Polish women is ultimately revealed as spurious when it transpires that the Polish fiancée, to whom one of the male protagonists was planning to return, is a cheat who had entered into amorous relationships with several returning emigrants at one and the same time.

Similar narrative threads are deployed in Daniel Koziarski's novel *A Sociopath in London* (*Socjopata w Londynie,* 2007). Written as a sequel to his debut novel *Troubles Are My Specialty, or the Chronicles of a Sociopath* (*Kłopoty to moja specjalność, czyli kroniki socjopaty,* 2007), Koziarski's second book revolves around the London adventures of a young Polish migrant named Tomasz Płachta. Endowed with a chronic lack of awareness and disregard for other people's feelings, the novel's protagonist usually says the wrong things at the wrong time, demonstrating meanwhile an unwittingly offensive attitude toward ethnic minorities, women and disabled people. Significantly, the main character shares his London apartment with two compatriots whose migrant condition may be directly linked to the aforementioned patriarchal discourse. The fate of his flatmate Alex

(Olek), on the one hand, is quite similar to that of the male protagonists featured in *The Polish Boxing School*. Having left behind his fiancée in Poland, this romantic soul cannot stop talking about his beloved Jarosława and keeps worrying about her faithfulness. Tomasz derives in turn a particular satisfaction from intensifying and magnifying his doubts. The third Polish tenant (Kasia), on the other hand, represents the prototypical self-conscious and career-driven female immigrant from Poland (Rostek 2009, 190-193). Endowed—in her own words—with a particular "power of perseverance" (Koziarski 2007, 19), the girl firmly dissociates herself from her male compatriots and leads a turbulent love life (for instance by dating a guy from Bangladesh). The harsh and unsympathetic words she usually addresses to her Polish flatmates are indicative of the marginalization to which the male immigrant characters are subject. In addition to calling her flatmates "Fucking Polish arseholes!" (Koziarski 2007, 18), she assures them that she would never ever consider having a Polish boyfriend: "Let me tell you something—neither you nor Alex would ever cross my mind. Even if I were captured with the two of you on a desert island . . . " (Koziarski 2007, 219) Perhaps the most characteristic expression of her aversion to Polish men occurs when she refers to the terrorist attacks that took place on the London Underground in July 2005. While discussing the unfortunate fate of the three Polish women who fell victim to these attacks, Kasia says to her flatmate Tomasz: "May I ask you why these primitive clowns driving in pairs did not die in their place—you know, all these Mieteks and Zdzichs, these workmen?" (Koziarski 2007, 187)

A similar ironic dismantling of the old patriarchal code is at stake in Piotr Czerwiński's *Résuméum Lifae or the Cardboard Web* (*Przebiegum życiae czyli kartonowa sieć,* 2009).[5] The novel tells the story of a forty-year-old Polish economist (Gustaw), whose personal and professional life goes from bad to worse after he loses his well-paid job in a reputable Warsaw company. Abandoned by his wife and their two daughters and bereft of most of his belongings, he eventually ends up in Dublin where he lands a job as a dustman in a local factory. Gustaw's unfortunate life story is narrated by "Mister Konrad Hubalczyk," a young sociologist from Warsaw who bought a one-way ticket to Ireland soon after graduating from university. Once again, the marginalization of Polish males seeking their fortune abroad is accompanied by ironic descriptions of their outdated patriotic reflexes and sentiments.[6] The most emblematic scene takes place in an Irish pub

---

[5] We have preferred here the translation of the title suggested by Dirk Uffelmann. See also Marek Kazmierski's alternative suggestion: *Kurrviculum Eire,* the title used for Kazmierski's "test" translation of short extracts from the book; all translated passages in the current chapter, however, are those of the author—Ed. Accessed 6 November, 2012. http://off-press.org/main/wp-content/uploads/2010/02/OFF_Czerwinski-KURRVICULUM-EIRE_test.pdf

[6] See also the chapter by Dirk Uffelmann.

where Gustaw and his company are spending their Saturday night. While Gustaw is having an in-depth conversation with an Irish girl he fancies (Siobhan or "She-Von"), his Polish friends Konrad and Robek get involved in a patriotically inspired fight that takes place outside the pub. Triggered by an assault on a Polish woman by a couple of Irish adolescents, the Polish-Irish conflict gains momentum, when a shriek in Polish ("They are beating ours!") reaches the interior of the pub. The first-person narrator Konrad and his friend Robek immediately interrupt their drinking activities:

> "Sorry, honey," he [Robek] said to the girl. "The fatherland is calling." [. . .] I looked at Gustaw who sat as if frozen. His face did not move. He and She-Von behaved as if time had stood still. Robek and I ran out, to the very centre of the disturbance. Oh man, what confusion, I can't even describe it! There were kinda five of us Poles, while the girl stood leaning against the wall, stemming the blood from her nose. And a whole bunch of Irish kids." (Czerwiński 2009, 285)

Self-evidently, the conduct of the Polish protagonists is closely connected with the romantic dispositions of their Mickiewiczian namesakes. What is more, when asked by Konrad why he refused to take part in the Polish-Irish fight, Gustaw boldly states: "This is not my fatherland anymore. [. . .] And this is none of my business. To get into a fight on behalf of a country which I don't care about anymore." (Czerwiński 2009, 287) In the case of Gustaw, rejected by his wife and daughters and bereft of his fatherland, the collapse of the patriarchal order has taken on absolute proportions, both on the private and the collective level. Not unlike other male protagonists in the books under discussion, however, Czerwiński's protagonist is not in a position to accept the host country as his new home. Moreover, although his relationship with the Irish Siobhan (a former artist who had grown addicted to drugs and come down in life) takes on the form of a short-term romance, he finally ends up committing suicide.

Perhaps the only non-problematic inter-ethnic romance is offered by Grzegorz Kopaczewski's *Global Nation: Snapshots from the Time of Pop Culture* (*Global Nation. Obrazki z czasów popkultury,* 2004). Its main character, Daniel Berski, is a young Polish economist who shares a cosy flat near the Arsenal with a couple of other foreigners (among whom there are, significantly, no other Poles). Central to Kopaczewski's novel is the idea that immigrants from different countries can easily feel at home in a foreign metropolis such as London because of the very fact that they participate in a global culture (embodied, for instance, by pop music, film and TV fiction). As the title of the book indicates, the "nation" to which these young protagonists belong is "global" by nature, which does not mean, however, that they renounce their roots and family bonds (in accordance with the often repeated mantra "think global, act local"). Being in daily contact with other

"Others," who have come from elsewhere, but share similar values and interests, the Polish first-person narrator does not experience his Polish roots as a particular burden, although he does not refrain from criticizing at the same time his country's preoccupation with history and martyrology. Characteristically, whenever the word "losers" appears on the pages of Kopaczewski's book, it does not function as an invective directed against Polish male migrants, but rather as a way of expressing the state of mind of a new generation trying to postpone its entrance into adulthood and deeply concerned about the ruthless economic system in which it will have to work and live. Moreover, the romance Daniel Berski experiences (with a Canadian girl temporarily working in London) is strongly affected by the "auberge espagnole" atmosphere that permeates the entire novel and forms part of his coming-of-age process (at the end of which he decides—bearing in mind the principle "think global, act local"—to go back to Poland and financially support his younger sister).

At least some of these fictional accounts deploy literary strategies of identity construction (such as self-orientalization) which seem to be typical of male Polish migrant narratives (Uffelmann 2010 and 2011). Therefore, compared to the early works of Manuela Gretkowska who "creates artificial, caricatured epitomes of postmodern cosmopolitans (a provocative move against the conventionally understood émigré narrative)" (Chowaniec 2011, 140-141), these male authors might be said to create "artificial, caricatured epitomes" of male anti-heroes who have missed the boat of postmodern cosmopolitanism. In the mean time, however, the anxieties faced by the male protagonists in the stories under scrutiny seem to parallel certain trends and developments in the real diasporic world. First of all, as recent statistics regarding the civil status of Polish migrants in the UK indicate (Farago 2011, 14), not only is there a considerable difference between the percentage of married females and married males (62% versus 40%), even more significant is the statistical disproportion relating to the spread of intermarriage (28% versus 3%). What is more, the "policing" of transgressional behaviour such as mixed relationships seems to play a prominent role in the diasporic public discourse, not the least in the Polonia press in the UK (Berdak 2008).

Female perspectives on inter-ethnic coupling

In general, whereas most of the aforementioned "male" novels draw ironically on age-old gendered constructions of travel and mobility (as part of an all-encompassing patriarchal order, on the level of family and community life alike) and simultaneously depict the current migrant condition as a state of neglect, obscurity and downfall, women writers focus on migration rather as a means of upward social mobility. If the texts discussed above refer ironically to the Homeric narrative of Odysseus and Penelope, then the latter conceive of the migration project in terms rather of a Cinderella story. In other words: instead of portraying unfortunate and marginalized migrant characters living on the fringes of the host society, they focus on women who aspire to climb up the ladder (if need be, with the assistance of a local Prince Charming).

The most straightforward—and artistically the least subtle—manifestation of this approach is to be found in Ada Martynowska's novel *Carps, Swans and Big Ben* (*Karpie, łabędzie i Big Ben*, 2009). A highly conventional and schematically written romance novel, Martynowska's debut displays certain characteristics of chick lit, in the sense that it features a young and ambitious, career-driven female protagonist in her twenties (Beata Martynek). Compared with the naturalistic approaches to migrant life in some of the previously discussed novels, Martynowska's book offers a more escapist and glamorous perspective on the fate of the Polish migrant in the UK. Influenced by the advice of two Polish friends who have landed rich foreigners, the main character dreams of living in Notting Hill and of gaining access to the exclusive life of the British financial and intellectual elite. The prey she decides to hunt down is one of her British colleagues, a wealthy aristocrat named Richard Bellingham. In the mean time, the author puts much effort into showing that the lead character is an independent and self-confident woman who does not want to be dictated to by men. This reveals itself most obviously in Beata's conversations with her Polish cleaning lady Sabina, whom she tries to convince to set up her own business once she gets back to Poland. The inevitable clash between Beata's progressiveness and Sabina's conservatism takes on quite predictable narrative forms: instead of opening a boutique with the money she earned in London, Sabina and her partner Dariusz decide to invest their savings in a car service station as soon as they return to Poland.

Similar narrative threads make their appearance in the more recent detective novel *The Club of Matchmaking Mothers: Mission London* (*Klub matek swatek. Operacja: Londyn*, 2011) by Ewa Stec. Written as a follow-up to Stec's 2010 book *The Club of Matchmaking Mothers* (*Klub matek swatek*), the novel revolves around the attempts of a group of professional matchmakers to couple a young Polish emigrant (Alicja Karolak) with a rich British aristocrat (Archibald Nelson). Not surprisingly, these plans meet with the resistance of the young man's parents. In a similar vein, the novel abounds in explicit and less explicit references to the Cinderella story. Characteristically, one of the male characters comments on the matchmaking business in the following way: "You women are all the same. Sentimental and stupid. Every woman buys a Cinderella fairy tale, it is like a dream come true." (Stec 2011, 262)

The issue of inter-ethnic coupling also rises to the surface in Gosia Brzezińska's debut novel *Irish Cocktail* (*Irlandzki koktajl*, 2010). In essence, by focusing on the stay abroad of a female protagonist (Kasia Przybylska), who has left behind her Polish boyfriend, the book offers a reversal of the traditional Odysseus and Penelope narrative. On the one hand, the girl's unaccompanied stay abroad is perceived in terms of a quest for self-realization. On the other hand, however, the female protagonist does not want to give up the relationship with her Polish partner either. As such, the novel seeks to investigate the question as to whether long-distance relationships are able to endure or not. Interestingly, while the female lead character tries to be a faithful Penelope (which restrains her from falling in love with her Irish friend Eamon) she soon finds out that her Polish partner in Warsaw observes the idea of fidelity less scrupulously and has started dating someone else. Typically, whereas the first-person narrator Kasia characterizes herself as a "real bitch" (Brzezińska 2010, 225) after her first flirtation with Eamon, other female Polish characters treat more freely the bonds that link them to their home country. The most prototypical example is Kasia's acquaintance Magda, who explicitly describes herself as a "hunter" (Brzezińska 2010, 172) and does not refrain from expressing her profound depreciation of Polish men ("Poles are good in Poland," Brzezińska 2010, 172).

Compared with the main character of Ada Martynowska's *Carps, Swans and Big Ben*, Brzezińska's lead protagonist undoubtedly displays a more traditional and less mercantilist mindset. Yet, apart from the central focus on the issue of inter-ethnic coupling, both novels share a series of additional narrative threads. First of all, they both focus on young and ambitious successful migrant Polish women who live in a highly international environment and perform jobs that are appropriate to their educational qualifications (which rarely, if ever, happens to their male counterparts).[7] Moreover, in addition to the amorous vicissitudes and professional challenges faced by these women abroad, the only "danger" that crosses their paths is embodied by a local character with xenophobic feelings trying to thwart the career prospects of the female Polish migrant.

Not all women writers, however, focus on self-confident Polish Penelopes who try to realize their own version of the Cinderella story. The most interesting case is offered by the character of Przystupa in the eponymous novel by Grażyna Plebanek (2007).[8] On the one hand, the remarkable life story of Przystupa inevitably evokes associations with the Cinderella narrative, not only because of the prominent stepmother motif, but also because of the protagonist's upbringing in a lower social environment (i.e. a poor peasant family living in the eastern part of

7 See also Uffelmann.

8 Other female narratives that favour a more nuanced and multi-faceted perspective on the issue of migration include Magdalena Orzeł's *Dublin: My Polish karma* (*Dublin. Moja polska karma*, 2007) and Iwona Słabuszewska-Krauze's *Hotel Ireland* (*Hotel Irlandia*, 2006), both of which have received considerable academic attention (see Rostek 2009; Gall 2011; Olszewska 2011).

Poland). On the other hand, Plebanek clearly refrains from developing her story in a Cinderella-styled way. Instead, she uses the protagonist's mobility to create a critical and satirical image of the various milieus Przystupa passes through. While offering her services as a cleaning lady, the girl is first hired by a Polish popstar residing with her husband/manager in Warsaw. Afterwards, she moves to Sweden where she works as a cleaning lady and nanny for a couple of migrant and expat families. A silent and highly enigmatic heroine who never comments on the conduct of the people who surround her, Przystupa acquires here the role of a close witness and observer of the diasporic space.

Over the course of the novel, the issue of in- and out-group relationships within the migrant community in Sweden comes to the fore several times. The first family for whom Przystupa works in Sweden consists of a Polish couple and their adolescent son. The conversations these people conduct among themselves and with their friends expose the conservative discourse to which they adhere (replete with elements of homophobia, religious devotion and narrow-minded morality). What is more, the lady of the house takes on the traits of a contemporary Pani Dulska, the protagonist of Gabriela Zapolska's 1906 drama *The Morality of Mrs Dulska* (*Moralność Pani Dulskiej*), who—when confronted by the sexual escapades of her husband and her adolescent son—uses her Polish housemaid as an easy scapegoat by hypocritically accusing her of displaying "whorish" conduct. By so doing, the woman exploits, of course, the age-old aura of "wantonness" that surrounds the idea of single women travelling without a male companion. Interestingly, Plebanek's portrayal of a Polish-Finnish couple living in Sweden is no less critical, and helps to deconstruct the myth of Polish women gaining a fortune by marrying a foreigner.

Finally, in one of the later chapters, Przystupa herself becomes involved in a mixed marriage. In accordance, however, with the general demystifying tone of the book, this is not a fairytale-like wedding with a foreign prince, but an ordinary paper marriage with a Swedish acquaintance (which prevents her from being expelled from the country). Nevertheless, although no reward or remarkable fortune awaits Przystupa during the course of her journey, she is undoubtedly represented as a positive character. Partly inspired by the traditional notion of the "noble savage," Przystupa's role as a cleaning lady on the loose helps bring to the surface the garbage and filth slumbering in the various milieus in which she ends up. Characteristically, as soon as this narrative task has been fulfilled, she repeats her mantra "Muszem jechać" ("I gotta go") and sets out on the road again.

The (male) offspring of intermarriage

Interestingly, several of the texts under scrutiny focus on the fate of children of emigrants rather than on first-generation emigrants, namely Katarzyna Tubylewicz's *Places of One's Own* (*Własne miejsca,* 2005), Maja Wolny's *Carol* (*Kara,* 2009) and Grażyna Plebanek's *Illegal Liaisons* (*Nielegalne związki,* 2010; English translation, 2012). In each of these books, the narrative focuses on male protagonists who grew up abroad (respectively in Sweden, Belgium and the UK), within the framework of a mixed marriage. In each case, these male protagonists foster a great deal of sympathy for the home country of their Polish parent and enter into a relationship (or even marriage) with a Polish girl. In two out of three cases (Tubylewicz and Wolny), this return to the ancestral realm is explicitly conceived of in terms of compensation: it makes up for the feelings of loss, nostalgia and guilt experienced by the generation that moved away from Poland. Moreover, in both emigration narratives, the sympathy fostered for Poland grows partly out of a feeling of unease and discontentment with the country in which these male characters grow up (embodied by the bourgeois narrow-mindedness of the Belgian mother in *Carol* and the emotional coldness and down-to-earthness of the Swedish father in *Places of One's Own*). Characteristically, these male protagonists warmly and enthusiastically embrace their Polish genealogy, instead of perceiving it as a burden. What is more, unlike the male immigrant protagonists who appear in the previously discussed "male" narratives, these characters are depicted as respected figures (in Poland and in their country of birth alike), having successful careers and not experiencing any particular difficulties in finding a partner.

Although *Illegal Liaisons* shares a series of narrative threads with the two other novels, the main character in Plebanek's book (Januszek or Jonathan) differs from the second-generation male protagonists depicted by Tubylewicz and Wolny in that he is much less preoccupied with his Polish roots. Having lived in Warsaw during the first years after his marriage with the Polish jurist Magda (Megi), he and his family move to Brussels where his spouse is about to work in one of the European institutions. Of all the male characters depicted in the books under scrutiny, Jonathan is by far the most cosmopolitan and transnational, floating freely between different languages, cultural circles and countries.

Characteristically, notwithstanding the fact that the EU expat community in Brussels seems to operate in an international environment, one of Jonathan's Polish friends tries to convince him that he cannot escape from his Polishness either, implying at the same time that he should stand by his compatriots:

"But for people here, you're still one of us, a Pole, a cousin of the lad who carries bricks, the guy who can give you the number of a cheap, hardworking Polish cleaner. You've got so many advantages but aren't doing anything with them. You don't care about work or a position, you don't want to show that we Poles ... " (Plebanek 2010, 198; 2012, 171)

Remarkably, however, although Plebanek's lead protagonist certainly sympathizes with Poland, he does not give the impression that these alleged Polish "cousins" and "nieces" really concern him. Jonathan's—non-patriotic and, at the same time, non-patriarchal—viewpoint is presented by the heterodiegetic narrator in the following way: "To expect a group of people tied by blood always to stand like a wall behind them was, he believed, childish." (Plebanek 2010, 72; 2012, 57) Apart from this symbolic renunciation of consanguinity, Jonathan's fluid (or blurred) identity also reveals itself in terms of gender. Instead of being the traditional breadwinner, he takes care of the household and stays at home with his two children, while his spouse focuses on her career.[9] These partly inverted gender roles do not prevent him, however, from playing more traditional masculine roles at the same time.

As the title of the book indicates, central to the storyline of *Illegal Liaisons* is the issue of forbidden love alliances. In essence, the plot revolves around the passionate affair that unfolds between Jonathan and the partner of his spouse's British superior. This thread of marital betrayal, however, is not deployed in terms of national disloyalty. Characteristically, what mentally links Jonathan and his Czech-Swedish mistress Andrea Kunz is the fact that both of them had grown up—after spending their early childhood years behind the Iron Curtain—as migrant children in a foreign, strongly international environment. Their shared "mixed-breed" character gains particular prominence in the dog metaphor that runs like a motif through the novel. On the one hand, this thread refers to the animal instincts that seem to govern their "illegal" behaviour and the "dog law" to which they adhere (and which gains additional expression through the very fact that their affair seems to be driven by sexual motifs rather than by strong emotional or intellectual ties). On the other hand, Jonathan—who is writing a children's book about dogs while the novel unfolds—conceives of these omnipresent dogs as "mongrels" (Plebanek 2010, 299; 2012, 261), a characterization that aptly underscores the hybrid genealogy of the protagonists themselves.

When we compare the figure of Jonathan with most of the male protagonists featured in the previously discussed "male" narratives, it is difficult not to notice the immense gap that separates them. Whereas most experience serious difficulties in finding either a Polish or a non-Polish partner, Jonathan easily butters his bread on both sides. If the marginalization of these Polish male migrants (be it in terms of employment or in terms of coupling) is closely linked to the downfall of

9 Highly indicative in this regard is the following statement: "'Masculine' and 'feminine' were so flexible [for Jonathan] and kept on changing; he himself was the best example of this" (Plebanek 2010: 148; 2012, 126).

the patriarchal code, then Jonathan's hybrid identity both in terms of gender and national belonging seems to be directly proportional to his success on the diasporic love market. Although some of the previously discussed "male" narratives (such as Kopaczewski's *Global Nation*) feature male heroes who might be said to move in the same direction, it is significant that the most far-reaching portrait of a "successful" male migrant in recent Polish prose is the creation of a female author.

Conclusion: Removing Polish(ness)

Compared to a patriotically-themed TV serial such as *Londoners*—with its unambiguous renunciation of inter-ethnic coupling in the diasporic space—the books under discussion offer a less homogeneous picture and constitute a conglomeration of various narrative approaches, not only as far as the different types of coupling are concerned, but also regarding the degree to which the issue of intra-ethnic coupling and marital loyalty parallels notions of national loyalty. That being said, the most prototypical narratives provided by mainly male authors offer portrayals of marginalized Polish migrant men, who face matrimonial and other forms of rejection both in the diasporic and the domestic space. The most prototypical female figure in turn is that of a Penelope-figure on the loose, represented—depending on the point of view—either as a self-confident, career-driven individual trying to catch a foreigner or as a woman with loose morals (not to say a prostitute). Interestingly, although the mimetic dimension of these representational practices is subverted in a variety of ways, these fictional accounts seem to correspond with on-going intermarriage trends in the diasporic space (not only in statistical terms, but also in view of the topicality of the issue in public discourse).

The general patterns outlined above find apt expression in the Polish joke taken from Gosia's Brzezińska's *Irish Cocktail* quoted at the outset of this chapter. On a symbolic level, the story of the male Polish migrant who thinks his fiancée is planning to kill him neatly reflects the various anxieties and expectations associated with an ongoing dissolution of the patriarchal and patriotic order. Whereas male protagonists tend to perceive the "looseness" of Polish women—in terms of both geographic and social mobility—as a betrayal of their shared Polishness, their female counterparts tend to use the ominous "Polish Remover" as a means towards self-realization, enabling them to get rid of traditional gender roles imposed on them by their patriarchal home society. In this respect, the threat embodied by the "Polish Remover" label reveals a profound fear not so much about the possible removal of Polishness as such, as about the inevitable loss of a particular kind of Polishness: a Polishness that is male-centred and patriarchal, relegating women to a secondary and subordinate status.

Bibliography

Primary sources

Brzezińska, Gosia. 2010. *Irlandzki koktajl*. Warsaw: Bliskie.

Czerwiński, Piotr. 2009. *Przebiegum życiae czyli kartonowa sieć*. Warsaw: Świat Książki.

Helbig, Brygida. 2005. *Anioły i świnie. W Berlinie!* Szczecin: Forma Autorska.

Kępski, Piotr. 2009. *Single*. Warsaw: Jirafa Roja.

Kopaczewski, Grzegorz. 2004. *Global Nation. Obrazki z czasów popkultury*. Wołowiec: Czarne.

Koziarski, Daniel. 2007. *Kłopoty to moja specjalność, czyli kroniki socjopaty*. Warsaw: Prószyński i S-ka.

—. 2007. *Socjopata w Londynie*. Warsaw: Prószyński i S-ka.

Kropiwnicki, Aleksander. 2007. *Zajedznia Londyn*. Warsaw and Bydgoszcz: Branta.

Martynowska, Ada. 2009. *Karpie, łąbędzie i Big Ben*. Katowice: Sonia Draga.

Miklasz, Adam. 2009. *Polska szkoła boksu. Powieść emigracyjna*. Kraków: Skrzat.

Orzeł, Magdalena. 2007. *Dublin. Moja polska karma*. Kraków: Skrzat.

Plebanek, Grażyna, 2007. *Przystupa*. Warsaw: W.A.B.

—. 2010. *Nielegalne związki*. Warsaw: W.A.B.

—. 2012. *Illegal Liaisons,* translated by Danusia Stok. London: Stork Press.

Słabuszewska-Krauze, Iwona. 2006. *Hotel Irlandia*. Warsaw: Semper.

Stec, Ewa. 2011. *Klub Matek Swatek. Operacja: Londyn*. Kraków: Wydawnictwo Otwarte.

Suskiewicz, Łukasz. 2009. *egri bikaver*. Szczecin: Forma.

Tubylewicz, Katarzyna. 2005. *Własne miejsca*. Warszaw: Jacek Santorski.

Wieteska, Mariusz. 2009. *Zielona wyspa*. Warsaw: Anagram.

Wojnarowski, Marcin. 2008. *Okrutny idiota albo prywatny żart*. Poznań: Wydawnictwo EP.

Wolny, Maja. 2009. *Kara*. Warsaw: Prószyński i S-ka.

Wyzszowski, Michał. 2010. *Na lewej stronie świata*. Warsaw: Wydawnictwo MG.

Secondary sources

Berdak, Oliwia. 2008. *Gender and Ethnicity in Transnational Contexts: Policing the Boundaries of Polishness in Multicultural London*. MA diss., University College London School of Slavonic and East European Studies.

Błędowska, Magdalena. 2003. "Uchodźcy, półemigranci, kosmopolici. Doświadczenie emigracyjne w prozie lat dziewięćdziesiątych (M. Gretkowska, J. Rudnicki)." In *Literatura utracona, poszukiwana czy odzyskana. Wokół problemów emigracji*, edited by Zbigniew Andres and Jan Wolski, 369-379. Rzeszów: Wydawnictwo Uniwersytetu Rzeszowskiego.

Chowaniec, Urszula. 2011. "Displacement, Emigration, and Travel: Contemporary Polish Literature and the Notion of Émigré Literature." In *Contemporary Polish Migrant Culture and Literature in Germany, Ireland, and the UK*, edited by Joanna Rostek and Dirk Uffelmann, 133-152. Frankfurt am Main: Peter Lang.

Czapliński, Przemysław. 1997. *Ślady przełomu. O prozie polskiej 1976-1996*. Kraków: Wydawnictwo Literackie.

Domosh, Mona and Joni Seager. 2001. *Putting Women in Place: Feminist Geographers Make Sense of the World*. New York: Guilford.

Farago, Marysia. 2011. *Sytuacja poakcesyjnej emigracji Polaków w Wielkiej Brytanii i jej obraz w serialu telewizyjnym "Londyńczycy"* (unpublished MA thesis). Budapest: Uniwersytet Katolicki im. Pétera Pázmánya.

Gall, Alfred. 2011. "Migration and Global Society: The Issue of Internationality in Contemporary Polish Literature." In *Contemporary Polish Migrant Culture and Literature in Germany, Ireland, and the UK*, edited by Joanna Rostek and Dirk Uffelmann, 177-200. Frankfurt am Main: Peter Lang.

Gasyna, George. 2003. "Inscribing Otherness: Polish-American Writers after the Great Divide." In *Living in Translation: Polish Writers in America,* edited by Halina Stephan, 331-377. Amsterdam: Rodopi.

Krowiranda, Krzysztofa. 2005. "Wizerunek emigranta w prozie polskiej lat dziewięćdziesiątych XX w. Natasza Goerke, Manuela Gretkowska." In *Pisarz na emigracji. Mitologie, style, strategie przetrwania,* edited by Hanna Gosk and Andrzej Stanisław Kowalczyk, 492-502. Warsaw: Elipsa.

Lawrence, Karen. 1994. *Penelope Voyages: Women and Travel in the British Literary Tradition: Reading Women Writing*. Ithaca, NY: Cornell University Press.

Majewski, Karen. 2003. *Traitors and True Poles: Narrating a Polish-American Identity 1880-1939*. Athens, OH: Ohio University Press.

Nowacki, Dariusz. 2009. "Przebiegum życiae." *Gazeta Wyborcza*, 20 October. Accessed 31 May, 2013. http://wyborcza.pl/1,75475,7162447,Przebiegum_zyciae__Czerwinski__Piotr.html.

Olszewska, Kinga. 2011. "Dynamic Identities: Polish Migrants in Ireland." In *Contemporary Polish Migrant Culture and Literature in Germany, Ireland, and the UK*, edited by Joanna Rostek and Dirk Uffelmann, 153-176. Frankfurt am Main: Peter Lang.

Pasterska, Jolanta. 2008. *"Lepszy" Polak? Obrazy emigranta w prozie polskiej na obczyźnie po 1945 roku*. Rzeszów: Wydawnictwo Uniwersytetu Rzeszowskiego.

Rostek, Joanna. 2009. "Die Migration von (Stereo-)Typen der Weiblichkeit: Die Literatur von und über polnische Migrantinnen in Irland und Großbritannien." *Zeitschrift für Slavische Philologie* 66 (1): 181-209.

—. 2011. "Living the British Dream: Polish Migration to the UK as Depicted in the TV Series *Londynczycy* (2008-2010)." In *Contemporary Polish Migrant Culture and Literature in Germany, Ireland, and the UK*, edited by Joanna Rostek and Dirk Uffelmann, 245-276. Frankfurt am Main: Peter Lang.

Rostek, Joanna and Dirk Uffelmann, eds. 2011. *Contemporary Polish Migrant Culture and Literature in Germany, Ireland, and the UK*. Frankfurt am Main: Peter Lang.

Sarsenov, Karin. 2006. "Is it a Sin to Travel? Itinerant Women in Post-Soviet Narrative." *Eurozine*, 7 September. Accessed 31 May, 2013. http://www.eurozine.com/pdf/2006-09-07-sarsenov-en.pdf.

Uffelmann, Dirk. 2010. "Autoidentyfikacja ze Wschodem w narracjach polskich migrantów." *Rocznik komparatystyczny* 1: 253-277.

—. 2011. "Self-Orientalisation in Narratives by Polish Migrants to Germany (by Contrast to Ireland and the UK)." In *Contemporary Polish Migrant Culture and Literature in Germany, Ireland, and the UK*, edited by Joanna Rostek and Dirk Uffelmann, 103-132. Frankfurt am Main: Peter Lang.

Van Heuckelom, Kris. 2011. "Polish (Im)Potence: Shifting Representations of Polish Labour Migration in Contemporary European Cinema." In *Contemporary Polish Migrant Culture and Literature in Germany, Ireland, and the UK*, edited by Joanna Rostek and Dirk Uffelmann, 277-298. Frankfurt am Main: Peter Lang.

—. 2013. "Londoners and Outlanders: Polish Labour Migration Through the European Lens." *Slavonic and East European Review* 91(2): 210-234.

Wach, Jarosław. 2010. "Sen wariata tudzież marne losy polskich emigrantów." *Akcent* 4. Accessed 31 May, 2013. http://www.akcentpismo.pl/pliki/nr4.10/wach.html.

Wrong Sex and the City: Polish Work Migration and Subaltern Masculinity

Dirk UFFELMANN

[...] while recent years have seen increasing recognition of the role of women in the migration process, the same period has seen a growing tendency to (re)marginalize male migrants. (McIlwaine et al. 2006, 5)

Polish men who write so are desperate, they are nobody in the UK. (From an internet forum of Poles in the UK, quoted in Siara 2009, 178)

A feminist bias in Polish Gender Studies

As is well known, popular literary genres reinforce gender stereotypes. Unsurprisingly, books written about Poland from a Western (or half-Western) popular (or half-popular) perspective tend to operate with stereotypes of Polish women rather than men. The index to Stefanie Peter's *Alphabet of Polish Miracles: A Dictionary* (*Alphabet der polnischen Wunder. Ein Wörterbuch*), for example, has no entry for "men" ("Männer") but 17 for "women" ("Frauen") (Peter 2007, 323). The often chided comedian Steffen Möller provides a positive exception to this rule of ignoring Polish men and their "psycho-social conditioning"[1]: the chapter "Men and Women" ("Mann und Frau") (Möller 2008, 200-208) in his book *Viva Polonia: As a German Gastarbeiter in Poland* (*Viva Polonia. Als deutscher Gastarbeiter in Polen*) opens with "marital migration"—Polish women marrying Western men (Möller 2008, 200). On the other hand, this chapter does not mention migrating men even once.

The concentration on Polish women that we have observed in popular heterostereotyping is echoed in research focusing on Polish migrants (see for example Coyle 2007; Kwiatkowska 2010). This gives Wolverhampton's Dariusz Galasiński the right to diagnose that "men have been practically invisible"

[1] "psychisch-soziale Konditionierung" (Möller 2008, 200).

(Galasiński 2010, 247; cf. Datta 2009, 191). The investigation of female gender stereotypes (Rostek 2009) and the "female perspective on displacement" (Chowaniec 2011, 145) dominates research into literature produced by migrants as well.

This paper follows Galasiński's appeal for research into post-communist masculinities by combining two major topics in recent Polish cultural studies—gender and migration. I will focus on the neglected aspect of the gender effects of male migration, basing my investigation on material from the literary output of Polish migrants from the recent, post-socialist wave to Ireland and the UK.[2]

A similar research focus seems to be even more necessary if one considers that the nexus of migration and masculinities has also barely been explored with reference to other cultures. Marchand and Runyan's edited volume of 2000 discusses migration's effects on masculinities in the context of globalization. And yet, the *International Encyclopedia of Men and Masculinities* (Flood et al. 2007) has no entries such as "Migration" or "Immigration." The social impact of migration on male gender roles is underexplored.

McIlwaine et al. 2006 demonstrate that migration triggers renegotiations of gender practices, especially if male migrants end up working in "female" sectors such as cleaning or care (McIlwaine et al. 2006, 13). While exploitation of migrant women has been debated more intensively in recent years, the same does not apply to low-paid male migrants. According to the authors, "the position of migrant men is often *not* much better, certainly in terms of their concentration in the low-paid service sectors of the economy." (McIlwaine et al. 2006, 6, emphasis in the original)

When it comes to sociological research into Polish migration, the revealing absence of East Central Europe in Raewyn Connell's 2005 enumeration of recent publications on masculinities in particular regions of the world no longer appears so drastic (Connell 2005, xiv-xv).

Dariusz Galasiński's article "Post-communist Masculinities" (2010) described the pre-history of the crisis tendencies challenging conventional masculinity on London's building sites, arguing that, in general, post-communism, with the concomitant socio-economic problems (transformation, unemployment etc.), posed a challenge to the dominant, still guiding model of masculinity (Galasiński 2010, 254). In the same year Ayona Datta observed: "After the new Polish migrants arrive in London, their ideas of masculinity [. . .] and sense of self are continually reshaped in their new social, political, economic and spatial contexts." (Datta 2009, 193)

---

2 I have discussed works by German migrants in earlier contributions, touching also upon the implications for masculinity (Uffelmann 2009, 2011).

The facets of this reshaping are manifold: Anne White has explored the various changes in family roles for men, while Bernadetta Siara has investigated the renegotiation of gender models of masculinity on UK Polish internet forums, demonstrating that Polish men faced allegations of having "a poor level of personal hygiene and bad taste in clothes" (Siara 2009, 172) or were abused as "'blunt primitives'" (Siara 2009, 173).

Despite these observations of change, a certain continuity in experiences of marginalization can be diagnosed in men of East European origin, drinking heavily and sleeping rough on the streets of London (Garapich 2011, 314). According to Michał Garapich's recent findings, the "masculine discourse of war and struggle on the streets of London" (Garapich 2011, 322) can be traced back to the socialization of *homo sovieticus*. Thus the older problems of masculinity persist, while the traditional patriarchal dominance also faces additional challenges.

In sharp contrast to these socio-psychological findings, research into literary and filmic representations of Polish migration to Germany, Ireland and the UK has demonstrated patterns of success stories: when discussing depictions of interethnic relationships between Poles and Western Europeans in European films, Kris Van Heuckelom acknowledges that Poles "seem to have become Europe's representational labour migrants" (Van Heuckelom 2011, 278), who are often depicted in these films as being abused by their employers or landlords, the males among them reacting with actual impotence (Karol in Krzysztof Kieślowski's *White* (*Blanc*); Van Heuckelom 2011, 288). Many of the Polish protagonists, for example Karol in Ken Loach's *It's a Free World*, fulfil the role of "problem solvers" (Van Heuckelom 2011, 286). Even more positive is the pattern in the soap opera series *Londoners* (*Londyńczycy*), analysed by Joanna Rostek as a mass of success stories from the occupational "zero," a building site, to "hero" (Rostek 2011, 252-257), while the series widely ignores "the fact that migrants from Poland are for the most part employed in so-called 3D-jobs—i.e. they perform dirty, difficult, and dangerous tasks below their qualifications" (Rostek 2011, 267).

This intriguing ambivalence deserves further investigation. Is it due to traditional narrative patterns that male disorientation is often outweighed by final success? Can the theory of narration provide mediation between economics and group sociology, on the one hand, and individual psychology, on the other? I venture that there is an opportunity for Literary Studies to address a widely unexplored (if relatively narrow) research field: *Migrant Men Literary Studies.* In this area, Polish Studies can offer a productive focus which allows us to connect with several paradigms in the humanities that prevail today (migration studies, gender studies, subaltern studies). The issue with which I will try to illustrate this is whether there is a correlation between the silence *about* men in research on literary topics and the "unheardness" *of* men in literary works.

Male "unheardness" in the recent wave of migration to Germany, Ireland and the UK

The recent wave of Polish migration to West European countries combines cultural and educational aspects (students coming to Oxbridge, bankers entering the City of London) with economic reasons. I will leave aside the relatively small group of elite white-collar bankers and brilliant students, who have both the position and the linguistic skills to express themselves in English and to be heard by a British audience, and concentrate on blue-collar workers, who constitute the bulk of the wave of migrants in the 2000s (Datta 2009, 193 and 195). A particular subgroup consists of unemployed, rough-sleeping or homeless men who, more often than not, suffer from alcoholism. It is these economically degraded groups that are most dramatically confronted with specific crisis tendencies, compelling them to reconfigure their manhood in the wake of their decision to migrate. I see five main factors behind such a reconfiguration:

First, as with all migrants, Polish migrant workers from the recent wave to Ireland and the UK are more directly confronted with negative heterostereotypes about Poles as primitive workers, thieves and alcoholics (Garapich 2010, 46)—more palpably in Germany than in the British Isles—than before their migration.

Second, this cultural hardship is underscored by the socio-economic degradation of well-educated migrants who must accept employment below their qualifications. Even if, after 2004, Polish migrants in the EU live a life "much less on the margins than it used to be" (Coyle 2007, 38) and although employment below their qualifications need not automatically be perceived as degradation—thanks to better wages in the UK than in Poland and to the opportunity for cultural self-development (Trevena 2010, 153-157)—many of the 35% of Poles in Britain who work below their qualifications[3] perceive degradation (Trevena 2010, 158).

Third, among the plethora of individual reasons for perceptions of degradation, gender is a prominent factor. Migration combined with employment below their qualifications or even unemployment and homelessness makes Polish men more vulnerable to challenges to their assumed gender dominance. The male worker's "psychological mechanism of self-valorization"[4] as described by Trevena faces challenges from female fellow migrants who—at least if they are young and employed (and do not stay at home)—come into contact with alternative gender models and are likely to change their own gender habits.[5]

---

3 27% of men and 43% of women (Iglicka 2007, 9).

4 "psychologiczny mechanizm autowaloryzacji" (Trevena 2010, 157).

5 Coyle 2007, 43. The researcher even argues that female migration implies resistance to traditional gender models and gender discrimination against women at home (Coyle 2007, 39). A literary illustration of this thesis can be found in Michał Wyszowski's short story "Camille," about the lesbian coming-out of a Polish female migrant: "[...] when a Polish woman migrates

Fourth, in the urban setting of Berlin, Dublin or London, these practical "Encounters with Feminism" (Connell 2005, 128) are accompanied by confrontation with cosmopolitan big-city life, posing a possible threat at least to those male Polish migrant workers who come from rural areas in Poland B.

Fifth, even if urban communities are accustomed to people with non-native language skills, there is yet another challenge posed by the barrier of the dominant language, English. This applies to the articulation of personal needs, to the defence of individual rights at work and to private gender interactions with non-Polish women *and* men (cf. Datta 2009). Obviously literature as verbal art is predisposed to reflect the linguistic dimension of gender reconfigurations.

The conclusion drawn from the five factors listed above is that the complex "interplay of gender with other structures such as class" (Connell 2005, 80), migration culture, urbanism and language, triggers massive reconfigurations of Polish masculinities. My argument, once again in the context of legal migration from Poland to the UK and Ireland since May 2004 (and to Germany since May 2011) or of legal seasonal migration, is that the urban, economic, gender and linguistic implications have the potential to make male Polish migrant workers perceive themselves as being in a subaltern position.[6] Alluding to the New York-based, upper-class women-centred TV series, I intend to use literary material to explore how male migrant workers of Polish origin perceive themselves in a constellation of "Wrong Sex and the City," even if in this case the global "City" is London rather than New York.

My working hypothesis is that, by virtue of its linguistic structure, literature illustrates this perceived male subalternity predominantly (but not exclusively) through subaltern communicative constellations, by depicting male silence or, alternatively, logorrheic overcompensation arising out of not being listened to.[7] I am looking at male subaltern unheardness, as opposed to Gayatri Spivak's findings about silent subaltern women in South India. The thesis I am trying to defend is that, in the context of the recent wave of Polish migrants to Ireland and the UK, the silent subaltern is significantly male.[8]

As to the theoretical underpinning, let us briefly remind ourselves of one key argument in the already canonical discussion about Spivak's 1988 article "Can

to England for work and half a year later returns with a black woman on her arm and announces that she is lesbian, this must be a huge step for mankind" (Wyszowski 2010, 214).

6 Challenges to male gender roles and male subaltern silence are thus not confined to forced mobility (Burrell 2008) or illegal immigration (Osipowicz 2001). They are also not only a matter of race (Richardson 2007).

7 I am thus building on certain suggestions already made in this direction and discussed in an earlier article co-authored with Joanna Rostek (Rostek and Uffelmann 2010).

8 Marty Rogers has already demonstrated—without reference to Spivak—that even in Southern India subaltern masculinity also needs to be explored (Rogers 2008).

the Subaltern Speak?" in which Spivak doubts the possibility of the subaltern's self-representation. Her statement that the (poor, female, South Asian) "subaltern cannot speak" does not refute the capacity of people belonging to the lowest stratum to speak, but maintains the impossibility of them being heard (or translated) in order to be included in the hegemonic discourse: "So, 'the subaltern cannot speak,' means that even when the subaltern makes an effort to the death to speak, she is not able to be heard, and speaking and hearing complete the speech act." (Spivak 1996, 292; cf. Maggio 2007)

As becomes clear from Spivak's concentration on political self-representation, subaltern masculinity, as I understand it, does not coincide with subordinate masculinity in Raewyn Connell's definition of minority models, such as homosexuality in contrast to "hegemonic masculinity."[9] Used in the context of masculinity studies only occasionally and without reference to Spivak (for example Sheller 2005; Rogers 2008), subalternity should be understood in a narrower sense as the struggle, often in vain, to communicate and represent oneself, and its social (especially gender) effects. This also differs from the occasional use of the notion of subalternity in research into contemporary Polish literature in non-migratory contexts; in Hanna Gosk's "Voices of Former Subalterns" ("Głosy byłych subalternów"), for example, the subalterns' silence has already been overcome and they are able to articulate their "colonial" trauma (Gosk 2010, 197-230).

Male migrants' literature

In contrast, I am interested in literary representations of an ongoing challenge—urban migrants' gender reconfigurations. In this article, I must confine my reading to male authors, although the female (external) perspective might be no less instructive.[10]

My analysis covers the following migration novels: Piotr Czerwiński's *Résuméum Lifae or the Cardboard Web* (*Przebiegum życiae czyli kartonowa sieć,* 2009), Daniel Koziarski's *A Sociopath in London* (*Socjopata w Londynie,* 2007), Adam Miklasz's *The Polish Boxing School* (*Polska szkoła boksu,* 2009), Mariusz Wieteska's *Green Island* (*Zielona Wyspa,* 2009) and Marcin Wojnarowski's *Brutal Idiot or a Private Joke* (*Okrutny idiota albo prywatny żart,* 2008). When it comes to smaller genres, I also include "egri bikaver" from Łukasz Suskiewicz's

---

9 Connell 2005, 78–79. Whereas Connell mentions Gramsci (Connell 2005, 77) he does not draw on Spivak. For my notion of subaltern masculinity, the connection with hegemonic concepts of masculinity is less decisive than for Connell's much debated dichotomy between hegemonic and subordinate masculinity (see Connell 2005, xviii).

10 For female perspectives on the gender effects of migration on men, see the chapter by Kris Van Heuckelom in this volume.

eponymous 2009 book (7-90); three stories with male heroes titled "Bronek," "Arek" and "Roman" from Alekander Kropiwnicki's *Depot London* (*Zajezdnia Londyn,* 2007, 30-46, 62-76, 91-99); several of the short stories collected in Michał Wyszowski's *On the Left Side of the World* (*Na lewej stronie świata,* 2010); and finally two contributions to the anthology *Written on the Edge of the World* (*Napisane na końcu świata,* compiled by Polish Books UK, 2008): Jakub Bolec's "Resurrection of a Dustman" ("Zmartwychwstanie śmieciarza") and Michał Sędzikowski's "The Curse" ("Klątwa").

Both the novels and short stories are for the most part somewhat unsophisticated in literary terms. This in no way reduces, however, their productivity for analysing the gender reconfigurations of their male protagonists. Rather the opposite: the recurrence of specific social and economic motifs will allow me to treat these texts together, in a condensed way, by approaching them with a typological interest rather than by discussing their relative aesthetic values.[11] The following common features are central: the protagonists are almost exclusively men who migrate to Britain for work, alone without family, usually possess a rather poor command of English and experience class degradation, which challenges their gender roles. Both class degradation and gender challenges result mainly from the problems they face when communicating in English, which makes it hard for them to get in contact with—both British and Polish!—women. They cope with these multiple hardships through some sort of misguided overcompensation.

The primary texts in question differ in the narratological respect of heterodiegesis versus autodiegesis, which has important implications for the depiction of marginalization: whether the narrator describes problems faced by others (heterodiegesis), whether he allows himself to identify with the situation of his fellows (autodiegesis framed by heterodiegesis) or whether he writes a document of life-writing (autodiegesis).

In some cases heterodiegesis implies distance. I propose to describe depictions of subaltern masculinity by authors who are not migrants themselves *sensu stricto* but speak about and for others, as "transitive marginalization." The most striking example is Aleksander Kropiwnicki, a former press officer at the Polish Embassy in London, who draws on his autoptic experiences with labour migrants. From this detached and elitist position, Kropiwnicki depicts the lot of underdog migrants. The distance between the narrator and the protagonists is insurmountable. In these texts, to quote indirectly from Marx, the subaltern does not represent her/himself,

[11] Nevertheless, the analysis will focus on two texts more often than others—Miklasz's *The Polish Boxing School* and Czerwiński's *Résuméum Lifae*. Miklasz's novel will play a prominent role because of its confrontation of collective male migrant sociology with an individual inter-ethnic love story, whereas Czerwiński deserves attention because of his intense use of devices borrowed from high literature (see discussion below).

s/he is represented—cf. Marx's *The Eighteenth Brumaire of Louis Bonaparte* (*Der Achtzehnte Brumaire des Louis Bonaparte*, 1852).

Other authors, such as Jakub Bolec, Piotr Czerwiński, Mariusz Wieteska or Michał Wyszowski, who rely on a non-elitist migration experience, deploy a heterodiegetic narrator who is characterized as a work migrant as well. His narration frames autodiegetic parts told by his fellows, who often fall behind the main narrator when it comes to both linguistic and literary capacities, but receive his sympathy, solidarity and compassion. Even more prominent is the autodiegetic narrator in the texts by Łukasz Suskiewicz or Marcin Wojnarowski, who reflects on his own situation in Dublin. Both texts include a prominent second male hero, "M" (Suskiewicz) and Radek (Wojnarowski), whereas Koziarski's autodiegetic narrator Tomasz is the dominant point of reference in this self-centred auto-sociopathy.

Kropiwnicki's transitive marginalization from a distance remains the exception. All other narrative constellations encompass a strong element of literary "self-representation" or at least close same-sex-representation. Explicit references to masculinity such as "The Man" ("mężczyzna," Wieteska 2009, 23), "the males" ("Samce," Miklasz 2009, 86) and "'masculinity'" ("'męskość'," Wieteska 2009, 74) are frequent. The male fellow migrant of the first-person narrator of Suskiewicz's "egri bikaver" is introduced with the abbreviation "M" (Suskiewicz 2009, 11), as used in administrative contexts to distinguish between the sexes. A comparable double male configuration can be found in the case of Kuba and Daniel in Wieteska's novel and—with additional implications (see below)—in that of Gustaw and Konrad in Czerwiński's *Résuméum Lifae*. Often the immediate social environment is likewise predominantly male, and very palpably so with the group of exclusively male migrants living in a Buckby flat in Miklasz's novel, who demonstrate a strong feeling of (male) solidarity (Miklasz 2009, 61-62) and are preoccupied with stereotypical male activities such as collective drinking (Miklasz 2009, 89) and the prototypical male-proletarian-migrant sport: football.

Last but not least, migrant masculinity amounts to a concrete danger when it comes to conflicts with other migrant communities and mafia gangs, because male solidarity demands collective fights (Miklasz 2009, 251). Suskiewicz contrasts the gender behaviours expected of a Polish man with more secure female gender role models, in a situation of apparent danger: "[. . .] the men in the kitchen play with weapons while the women watch sadly at a safe distance./ For a moment I wished to change my sex."[12] (Suskiewicz 2009, 13)

[12] This particular example is located in Poland before the protagonists' emigration.

Class degradation

How do traditional expectations of male sovereignty and fearlessness interact with the situation of migration? Almost all male heroes accompany their migratory step with enormous economic, social and sometimes also explicitly erotic expectations (cf. Kropiwnicki 2007, 31; Wieteska 2009, 11; Suskiewicz 2009, 18; Wyszowski 2010, 29, 206). As a rule, these high expectations very quickly turn into disappointment (Czerwiński 2009, 58; Miklasz 2009, 13; Wyszowski 2010, 29; cf. Van Heuckelom in this volume), when the migrants are forced to "lower their standards" (Wyszowski 2010, 30). For the vast majority, migration to Britain or Ireland means social degradation, lack of emotional closeness and sexual abstinence. Emigration either directly causes these deprivations or deepens already existing challenges. Czerwiński's protagonist Gustaw, for example, earned an MBA and worked for fifteen years as an economist in Warsaw before he lost his job, and was rejected by his wife, a "bardzo successful woman" (Czerwiński 2009, 25, English in the original), with whom he has two daughters (Czerwiński 2009, 13, 18). From Dublin he cannot even contact them via email (Czerwiński 2009, 199), just like Kropiwnicki's bus driver Arek, who longs for his daughter who stayed in Poland (Kropiwnicki 2007, 72, 75-76).

For many, the immediate situation on arrival in the British Isles is characterized by pure misery. Suskiewicz's narrator diagnoses ironically: "I would describe our situation as not the best. We had neither accommodation nor work nor money." (Suskiewicz 2009, 19) Together with "M" he is forced to live in substandard conditions (2009, 20-26, 37-38), while Czerwiński's Gustaw spends three months in a hostel before moving into a substandard flat shared with six other migrant workers.

Whereas poor living conditions are reflected upon extensively only by Suskiewicz and Czerwiński, employment in the lowest segment of the labour market is a standard topic in all the texts. The typical hero is an unqualified worker, often from rural parts of Poland B (Kropiwnicki 2007, 31), who has to take up "low-paid physical labour" (Miklasz 2009, 30). In the works in question, many Polish migrants work as dustmen (Berni in Miklasz's *The Polish Boxing School* and Gustaw/Konrad in Czerwiński's *Résuméum Lifae*). Bolec's narrator cynically speaks of other unskilled migrant workers as a "veritable binmen's club" ("[i]stny klub śmieciarza," Bolec 2008, 72). Kropiwnicki's Bronek is explicitly warned about exploitation (Kropiwnicki 2007, 39), and yet still ends up being denied payment for his work (Kropiwnicki 2007, 42), an experience shared by Suskiewicz's first-person narrator (Suskiewicz 2009, 46-50), who over a long period does not even manage to find a 3D-job (2009, 29-30) and returns to Poland after two months (2009, 79).

Administrative jobs are a rare exception, such as Patryk's in *The Polish Boxing School*: "[...] as the only one among us, he [Patryk] worked in an office, which for a Pole was a decent success and distinction." (Miklasz 2009, 43) The usual experience is employment below qualification, as Suskiewicz generalizes:

> I saw many Poles looking for work. The big accession would take place in a few months and everybody hastened to make his career in the West. In practice this meant terrified couples (masters of biology or pedagogy) traipsing around from bar to bar and begging for the position of a dishwasher. (2009, 27)

Using the same generalizing trope, Suskiewicz diagnoses the unwillingness of migrants to speak about their previous (more highly qualified) employment in Poland: "You also know that asking the question 'What was your work in Poland?' is not always a good idea. It's a sensitive string which easily breaks." (2009, 30)

The precarious socio-economic circumstances have psychological consequences. In a socio-psychological reflection, Miklasz's narrator observes in himself the "anxieties typical of an emigrant—the continual fear about work, money and accommodation." (Miklasz 2009, 155; cf. also Suskiewicz 2009, 39-40) The continual fear resulting from unstable living and working conditions is accompanied by loneliness: "Apart from the new experience he gained while living in a new country, he had nobody," Wieteska says (2009, 120). The most dramatic case is described by Czerwiński: in combination with his social isolation, which had already begun back in Poland, the unease Gustaw faces in living and working in Dublin eventually leads him to suicide. Long before taking the ultimate step, Gustaw, his name recalling the vampiric hero of Adam Mickiewicz's *Forefathers' Eve* (*Dziady,* 1823-1832), appears as a vampire hovering between life and death (cf. Czerwiński 2009, 224). After his suicide he lives on in/as Konrad, who can be interpreted as Gustaw's schizophrenic imagined and sublimated better self (cf. Czerwiński 2009, 253, 268). It is Konrad who posthumously tells the story of Gustaw's social and psychic degeneration.

Unheardness

As mentioned above in the theoretical part of this chapter, literature is especially suited to illustrating socio-economic problems through verbal communication or—as in this case—failures of communication. This obviously includes both male and female protagonists. Patrycja, in Kropiwnicki's *Depot London* (*Zajezdnia Londyn,* 2007), who falls victim to rape but refuses to contact the police and thus does not speak out against her tormentors, can serve as an illustration of the fact that subaltern silence occurs in the context of female Polish migration (cf. Rostek and Uffelmann 2010, 323-324). Another example is Grażyna

Plebanek's novel *Przystupa* (2007), the "silent girl" ("milcząca dziewczyna," Plebanek 2007, 23) who migrates to Sweden, where she utters only very short, dialectically marked replies when asked, hardly ever defending her own rights, as in the following scene: "'Want more'/ [...]/ 'Will do if you pay me more.'" (Plebanek 2007, 347-348) Her usual reflex, however, is to stay silent or to eventually run away (2007, 392).

Similar a-communicative behaviour is ascribed to shy male migrants such as Felo in Miklasz's *The Polish Boxing School*, who even before his emigration was "a man of few words with complexes, silent, shy, and with few friends" (Miklasz 2009, 33) or Wafel in the same novel who was "isolated and hardly said anything" (2009, 43).

The "destructive loneliness" ("destrukcyjna samotność," Miklasz 2009, 87, cf. 89) of some of the work migrants is related to their very limited command of English. Many authors use the comic potential of failing communication in English, for example Czerwiński, who repeatedly points to the special problems Gustaw faces in trying to understand taxi and bus drivers (Czerwiński 2009, 61). The narrator's style is characterized by a macaronic mixture of languages (the novel contains a glossary of English terms for Polish readers; Czerwiński 2009, 337–351). In order to make the reader feel like a Polish migrant who does not understand English, he ridicules Irish pronunciation ("Pointaginys"; Czerwiński 2009, 67) and distorts Polish in order to illustrate the irritation effect: "Ye myst be kidding" (Żyrtujesz Pyn," 2009, 67), "Yer Poulish experince dys not count hyre" ("Pyńskie pulskie doświdczenie się tutyj nie liczy," 2009, 127), "Fook!" ("Kyrwa!" 2009, 248)

Wyszowski also diagnoses migrants suffering from chronic uncertainty when functioning in an English linguistic context (Wyszowski 2010, 154). He envies those among his fellow migrants (with higher qualifications) who make more progress in learning English (Wyszowski 2010, 157–158), because he understands the direct connection between almost non-existent English skills and work at the very end of the spectrum. Miklasz's narrator asserts:

> The least loved and least profitable job was dustman. Berni, who [...] had major problems with understanding even elementary English phrases, was indeed, together with some Poles from Taverham, some Slovaks and Czechs and English who looked like troglodytes, a dustman. (Miklasz 2009, 30-31)

Command of English in comparison to women

Of special importance is the inter-gender vector of communication. Anne White argues that in Polish migrant couples, "[...] husbands usually have a better command of spoken English because of their job and because they had been in the

UK longer than their wives, including a period alone when they had had to fend for themselves." (White 2010, 153) In such cases traditional "[g]ender roles became ever more distinct" (White 2010, 153). According to the British researcher, however, there are also other cases "[...] where the husband has poorer English, conventional gender roles can seem to be reversed, and this can create an uncomfortable situation." (White 2010, 154)

In the texts under investigation, we are dealing with men migrating alone without a female partner. For them, language becomes even more relevant, since they cannot rely on existing social bonds but must build new relationships.

Obviously, migrating women face the same challenge. But statistical data from the Population Register of the Republic of Poland concerning intermarriage show that, in 2010, "[s]imilarly to previous years, mixed marriages in Poland are contracted more often between a husband residing abroad and a wife residing in Poland (75%). [...] it is highly probable that mixed marriages contracted with a man residing in the United Kingdom, Germany, Italy, Ireland or France concerned mostly Polish emigrants." (Fihel 2011, 35) The imbalance appears even more drastic if one takes into account the fact that, after Poland's accession to the EU in May 2004, men began to dominate among Polish migrants to Great Britain: 93,185 men versus 68,763 women; 57.5% versus 42.5 % (Grabowska-Lusińska and Okólski 2008, 37–38). And yet this majority of 57.5 % engages in no more than 25% of intermarriages. These figures are obviously only a partial indicator, but they show a trend in gender differences among Poles working and/or living abroad.

The case of Miklasz's Boruta (2009, 311), with his extremely deficient command of English, which prevents him from establishing contact with local women, demonstrates the negative effects for "male pride" ("męska duma," 312). Wieteska's hero lays bare the true reason for the lack of contact a second after providing a banal heterostereotype: "Local women did not count because of their geometrically poor figures and because of the language barrier." (Wieteska 2009, 18) Boruta's fellows, who attempt to establish contact with women in discos, also fail very quickly (Miklasz 2009, 95).

Here even intellectuality does not help, as we learn from Suskiewicz:

> Sitting around in the gallery, I was also looking for young female intellectuals. I particularly hunted next to paintings with an erotic topic. But even if I saw some candidate, I did not take any action because—what could I say to her? *How are you? What's your name?* I would only stammer out these two phrases and then run away. At best I would go red in the face. (Suskiewicz 2009, 55)

Something comparable even applies to Miklasz's protagonist, who is relatively self-confident when it comes to language: "[...] nobody among the Poles I met was a linguistic eagle. In comparison to them I felt like a translator of Shakespeare and Beckett." (Miklasz 2009, 81) But he also runs into misunderstandings with his beloved Sonia when he admits complexes about communicating with native speakers in bigger groups:

> "There will be your friends, I know my place in the row... When you talk to me you are aware that I am a foreigner, you speak more slowly and in a more articulated way, for which I am grateful to you. This will be another situation. Everybody will want to talk and nobody will pay any attention whether I understand every word or not." (2009, 212, cf. 239)

The last resort is Polish women abroad, with whom male migrants can communicate on a native level. But, as we learn from the literary texts, the migrant men experience problems even with establishing contact with women from Poland. Suskiewicz's narrator suspects that Polish women deliberately avoid contact with male fellow migrants:

> I met a Polish girl who worked as a waitress there. I tried to persuade her to give me her telephone number but she weaselled out of it. She had been there for a long time, so I suspect that she avoided contact with compatriots. This, to a certain extent, is understandable. (Suskiewicz 2009, 50)

Not even an existing relationship appears to be a safe haven. Niziołek from Bolec's short story feels that in London, the good command of English of his Polish girlfriend renders him superfluous: "What can I offer her? Why does she need such a ...—[...]." (Bolec 2008, 75) This betrays the suspicion that female migrants are ready for quasi-prostitute behaviour (cf. Rostek 2009, 191, on Koziarski). Suskiewicz's protagonist remembers his first visit to London's Victoria Station in a similar way:

> It's only half the problem if one is a young woman and, *one loves this anyway*, because then one can spend one's time nicely, earn money and even get to know a cultivated gentlemen aged seventy. Such a lover will live one or two more years and bequeath his little house with a garden to his beloved wife. (Suskiewicz 2009, 60, italics in original)

Symptomatically enough, Miklasz also allows himself an abstract metathematization of the adaptation skills of female migrants:

> The Polish women also enjoyed themselves when, with a chameleon's speed, they adopted the rules which governed this new, better world, its trends and mode of existence [...]. They were looking for stability, preferably in the form of a gallant young man guaranteeing a higher standard of living. (Miklasz 2009, 87)

The literary counter-examples to Patrycja and Przystupa (see above) might convince us that the male narrators, with their heterosexual panic, exaggerate both thc real social adaptability and linguistic capacities of female migrants. What counts, however, are the literary representations that highlight a stark contrast in perception:

> Everybody [enjoyed themselves] apart from Polish males. They were tired after a full week of work, meticulously counted their pounds, were often physically and intellectually not very attractive, were full of complexes, *faced an enormous linguistic barrier and were not adapted at all* [...], had no friends and were despised even by their female compatriots. (Miklasz 2009, 87, emphasis—D.U.)

This corresponds to the way in which Galasiński sums up some women's perceptions of Polish men in the "post-communist condition": "The helpless men are juxtaposed with practical women who manage to survive in the urban jungle." (Galasiński 2010, 253)

In such an uneven constellation—amid helpless silent (in English) male Poles, unattainable British girls and female fellow migrants—the successes in inter-sex relationships which migrant writers ascribe to their male protagonists are very modest, be it an almost-kiss with an anonymous Polish woman on the coach (Wieteska 2009, 90) or the open ending of Kropiwnicki's story "Bronek," where the linguistically gifted Polish decorator meets an English woman who, as *dea ex machina* in a hardly convincing twist (from the literary point of view), offers him a private loan so that he can set up his own small business (Kropiwnicki 2007, 46).

But there remains the romantic turn in Miklasz's story towards an inter-ethnic relationship with the British girl Sonia. Temporarily, it seems to the male protagonist that he expected too much: "I was surrounded by a mass of ordinary home-grown women living in the rat world of emigrants, but I laid claim to conquer an English princess, a representative of the dominant caste." (Miklasz 2009, 231) After a while, however, he establishes intimate relations with Sonia and even receives an offer from her father, a police investigator, to move into their house (2009, 266). Mr Watkins eventually suggests that he study in the UK together with Sonia (2009, 295). In this moment the migrant worker seems to have a realistic opportunity of leaving the milieu of subaltern male migrants: "When I moved to Monksberry, I reckoned that, thanks to Sonia, I would cut myself off from the brutal world of the drunken immigrants in Buckby." (2009, 301) But the social obligations between male migrants destroy this hope. Since he cannot let down his Polish mates and thus avoid engaging in their street fight with the Albanian mafia, he eventually finds himself forced to abandon his beloved and flee from Britain (2009, 339).

This makes it clear that final success, as diagnosed by Van Heuckelom and Rostek with regard to narrative patterns in films about male migrants (see above), is absent from all the texts in question.

Mechanisms of male overcompensation

Violent conflicts with other men form a traditional outlet for male frustration. Accordingly, many of the subaltern migrant workers react with conventional patterns of (deceptive) hegemonic masculinity. In Miklasz's *The Polish Boxing School*, boxing is presented as a way out of subalternity (2009, 111) although, in street fights with mafia gangs, it rather reaffirms this subalternity (305). Similarly counterproductive, when it comes to perceived rejection by women, is the primitive physiological sexism of Miklasz's Szymek, who "in his quests for the chosen one of his heart [. . .] was [. . .] fairly desperate": he wears a shirt with an illustration of the male genitals and the inscription "HARD COCK" (Miklasz 2009, 57).

The most direct connection between negative perceptions and aggressive overcompensation can be detected in the abundance of swear words in many of the literary works where socio-economic situations and linguistic representation coincide: "[. . .] shit jobs are for shit people ("gówniane prace są dla gównianych ludzi"). /—We are the shit people, my dear colleague!" (Czerwiński 2009, 87) Miklasz's narrator spares his readers half the "five or six 'fucks' in each compound sentence and at least two in a simple sentence" (Miklasz 2009, 78) and explains that "the most appropriate synonym for 'fuck' is 'helpless'" ("najodpowiedniejszym synonymem 'kurwa' jest 'bezradność'," 2009, 314). Czerwiński's narrator recognizes a group of thieves as being Poles because they "chuck in a few 'fucks'" (Czerwiński 2009, 91), but he reproduces a similar pattern himself in his macaronic mixture of languages: "koorva" (Czerwiński 2009, 10 et passim).

Much verbal aggression is also inherent in the way a male protagonist called Roman grumbles in the short story named after him (Kropiwnicki 2007, 91-99): "Why the hell have you come? ("Czego żes tu, kurna [sic], przyszedł?") What interview? Wanna talk to me? Why bother, there's nothing to talk about." (2007, 91) The swear word bears the trace of collective hegemonic masculinity—something that Roman, following his social degradation, can only possess by quoting a vulgar gynophobic discourse. But these short quotations are clearly overshadowed by his social degradation as a rough sleeper.

If we return to linguistic subalternity—do none of the cursing men speak? They do, but with logorrhoea, for example Bolec's Dresiaty: "The words poured out of his gob like rusty cans from a dustbin." (Bolec 2008, 82-83) Victims producing such logorrheic monologues, replete with swear words and defective syntax, do not produce a revolutionary discourse that would be heard by representatives of the dominant discourse. What they have at their disposal is a solely verbal overcompensation for their marginal situation where nobody listens to them—namely, unheard logorrhoea.[13]

Daniel Koziarski's Tomasz Płachta in his *Sociopath in London* attacks women from Poland and from other countries with verbal over-aggression; he offensively disassociates himself from the older, World-War-II Polish émigrés in London and from their auto-martyrology (Koziarski 2007, 53–55). This comes close to Michał Garapich's diagnosis that representatives of the new wave tend to distance themselves from the militant, romantic self-image of the previous waves of emigration by means of what Garapich convincingly coins—"banal counter-nationalism" ("banalny kontr-nacjonalizm," 2010, 50)—drawing on Michael Billig's canonical concept of "banal nationalism." What is interesting for our heuristic question is the fact that this counter-nationalism implies a challenge to traditional émigré models of masculinity represented by "peasants and soldiers" (2010, 35).

One might argue that first comes a crisis of traditional masculinity in the wake of migration, followed by a "displacement of aggression and rage" about this fact, which then produces a compensatory reaction from men in subaltern positions (Rogers 2008, 86), who intrinsically still adhere to the traditional model of hegemonic masculinity. Joanna Rostek has demonstrated how Koziarski's narrator tries to overcompensate for the dangers which encounters between Polish female migrants and men from other cultures and continents pose to his traditional white hegemonic masculinity (Rostek 2009, 192) and concludes—correctly for Koziarski, but too statically, that: "[...] the literary production of Polish [male] migrants [forms] a part of the patriarchal system which, according to Coyle, migrating [female] Poles strive to overcome." (Rostek 2009, 207) I would rather maintain that aggressive reactions to women's emancipated behaviour are already testimony to the incompatibility of the patriarchal system with the global city.

In parallel to this, Koziarski's protagonist also makes an effort to compensate for his subalternity through his (alleged) intellectual sovereignty. Intellectual overcompensation for marginalization is clearly a more modern attempt to preserve hegemonic masculinity—via intellectual superiority and schizoid self-distancing from one's own subaltern situation. For this purpose, several of the migrant narrators use intellectual name-dropping, going beyond the obligatory (in Dublin) Joyce (Suskiewicz 2009, 32) by also including references to Sholokhov, Dostoevskii or Yeats (Suskiewicz 2009, 32, 33, 44, 50) as well as to Polish paintings (Suskiewicz 2009, 56). Bolec combines the subaltern work situation which triggers the drive for compensation with intellectual healing: his narrator tries to distinguish himself from other unskilled workers by reading Zbigniew Herbert's *Barbarian in the Garden* (*Barbarzyńca w ogrodzie,* 1962) while waiting for a job (Bolec 2008, 70; cf. Rostek and Uffelmann 2010).

---

[13] Cf. Konrad's monologue entitled *The Great Improvisation* (*Wielka Improwizacja*) in Adam Mickiewicz's *Forefather's Eve, Part III.*

In the biographical information provided for Jakub Bolec, we also find a hint about his literary endeavours: "He is 29 years old. At present he lives in London, where he works as an unskilled construction worker. Every now and then, he writes short stories." (Polish Books UK 2008, 66) The same applies to Suskiewicz's narrator (2009, 53) and to Wieteska's protagonist, who writes poetry as compensation for social frustration and boring work (Wieteska 2009, 12, 17), and as an expression of loneliness: "nobody understands when you speak/ Polish/ but you must speak/ you do not have to whom." (2009, 39, punctuation as in original) The most advanced literary project is the film scenario which Czerwiński's Gustaw creates as "the last saving plank" for his migration experience ("ostatnia deska ratunku," 2009, 151). Long excerpts are quoted in the text (Czerwiński 2009, 173-181 et passim). Both the text within the text and the intertextual play with the double name of the hero of Mickiewicz's *Forefathers' Eve* Gustaw/Konrad, make this the most sophisticated work under discussion here from a literary point of view, because the allusion to Mickiewicz not only forms a structural element in the constellation of personages in Czerwiński's novel, but also launches a thesis about migrants' schizophrenic overcompensation for their migratory hardships.

Whereas all these compensatory mechanisms draw on pre-modern or conventional modern models of physical or intellectual masculinity, the only truly new pattern of compensation in migratory circumstances is over-adaptation. This is not yet the case with the rather desperate attempts of some migrants, such as Suskiewicz's narrator, to learn English (2009, 8 and 32). A telling example, however, is the protagonist of Michał Sędzikowski's "The Curse" ("Klątwa") who tries hard to insert himself into the British discourse of labour regulations. An employee at a food store, he defends himself against the charge of illegally eating sandwiches whose best-before date had passed and which were therefore supposed to be thrown away, by arguing in a sophisticated philosophical way (Sędziowski 2008, 236). But his strategy does not work, and he guesses that the reason for this is his lack of English. He thus changes his strategy and quotes keywords from the official British discourse: "equal rights and opportunities," "health and safety" and "mobbing theory" ("teoria mobbingu," 2008, 237). Yet in the end, he loses his job anyway, which means that the discursive adaptation of a migrant demands more than the simple dropping of key notions from the political discourse of the receiving country (2008, 239).

Self-subalternization and doubly wrong sex and the city

Migratory narratives do not only lament over precarious socio-economic conditions and unheardness, but often play with the protagonist's social degradation and/or the migrant authors' own descent from the "barbarian East."

Earlier, I proposed calling the latter subject-constructing device employed in their texts: "self-orientalization." If I return to this tendency in the context of masculinity studies, this is intended to be a combination of earlier arguments made about self-orientalization and about the subaltern silence of Polish migrants to Germany, Ireland and the UK (Uffelmann 2009; Rostek and Uffelmann 2010). As a parallel to self-orientalization, the authors in question often also develop a sense of social self-degradation, which I propose to call self-subalternization. From the point of view of subaltern unheardness, the concept of an active self-silencing is even more paradoxical than self-orientalization, if one recalls the fact that Marx's optimistic belief that (German—in contrast to Slavic) proletarians *are* able to represent themselves, was implicitly corrected by Gayatri Spivak. Spivak redefined Antonio Gramsci's social category of the subaltern as a social stratum lacking self-representation (Spivak 1988). But how can a writer—who is obviously expressing himself in print—"subalternize himself"?

One might read the repeated (and repeatedly turned down) job applications through the "résuméum lifae" ("przebiegum życiae") of Czerwiński's desperate protagonist, instead of non-alienated *życie* (life) in the sense of Marx's critique of alienation. Much more ironic, however, is Czerwiński's comment "We are the self-made slaves of the twenty-first century" (2009, 192) and fake job application:

> Dear Sir/Madam, this is my twenty-seventh attempt to apply for work in the Irish media. I do not expect any answer from you, let alone employment, so have a nice day and an invigorating mug of Guinness in the evening which, I guess, you will be served by a Polish waiter whom you maybe did not employ earlier. Yours sincerely... (Czerwiński 2009, 137)

This sounds more like postmodern play than an active proletarian protest. The subaltern remains unheard and commits suicide—at least within the literary text.

The decisive question for our evaluation of subaltern masculinity as a literary device is whether playful self-subalternization does not automatically erase subalternity—on the level of the publication and reception of the novel. Indeed it does, since a self-representing, aesthetically constructed subaltern is no silent subaltern anymore and thus—in Spivak's view—no subaltern at all.

We should, however, be more sceptical when it comes to the traditional hegemonic masculinity of Miklasz's Boruta or Koziarski's Płachta. Here we clearly do not see the same mechanism of self-erasure: even a defiantly contesting primitive "bloke" does not become a cosmopolitan metrosexual, but preserves a pre-modern model of masculinity. One cannot call this pre-modern masculinity "hegemonic" anymore (this is one reason why Connell's notion of "hegemonic masculinity" is too unidirectional). It strives to present itself as physically or intellectually hegemonic, but in so doing denounces itself as subaltern in the urban setting: wrong sex and the city.

The main hypothesis I have tried to prove using material from Polish migrant literature of the recent wave is that there is a neglected male gender dimension to subaltern unheardness in the globalized world. In global cities, the least privileged people are to a significant extent unskilled males. Drawing on Spivak's concept of subaltern unheardness, but "masculinizing" it in the urban contexts of the recent wave of Polish work migration to London, Dublin and other big West European cities, we should recognize that what the texts demonstrate is not so much absolute silence as the linguistically-based failure of attempts to communicate, especially in inter-gender constellations. On the intra-textual level, the problem of being unheard is hardly ever overcome. Even the most successful example, the relationship between Miklasz's protagonist and the British girl Sonia, who really makes an effort to listen to him, ends abruptly as a result of traditional male street fights.

Separate from this is the paradoxical effect of literary self-subalternization, by means of which migrant authors—on the extra-textual level—manage to make themselves heard, at least by a limited public (and a few academic readers). Assuredly, none of them has reached canonical status, but the fact that the Verden-based Polish migrant author Artur Becker received the prestigious Adelbert von Chamisso book prize in 2009 demonstrates that, in Germany, in the case of Polish migrant authors writing in German, we can no longer speak of "unheardness." When it comes to the United Kingdom and Ireland, the literature written by Polish migrants in Polish has clearly not yet had a comparable effect of self-erasing subalternity.

One aspect I have been unable to take into account further here is the literary presentation of heteronormativity and homophobia,[14] which tends to become stronger in subaltern situations.[15] I venture to suggest something like this affects the labour contexts of subaltern Polish migrants to London. The prevalence of heteronormativity in Polish migrant communities can be illustrated through the example of Krzysztof, the protagonist of one of the short stories by Michał Wyszowski (2010, 46-54), by far the most sensitive of migrant authors when it comes to sexual taboos. Krzysztof simulates heterosexual intercourse with drunken female migrants in order not to be suspected of being gay:

---

[14] Cf. Błażej Warkocki's *Homo niewiadomo* (2007) and his contribution to this volume.

[15] As demonstrated in colonial settings (Stecopoulos 2008).

> He did not seek women, he had his club [the Polish Club]. Admittedly, every now and then he disappeared with a drunken emigrant on his back, but just so as not to give grounds for rumours to his compatriots, so instilled in tolerance. Because if someone is alone, then he can't be alone. He cannot even be an uncompromising arsehole with a huge ego, he must simply be gay. A pederast [. . .]. (Wyszowski 2010, 151)

If Wyszowski's guess about heteronormativity in migrant communities is correct, we are dealing with a double marginalization of sexual minorities among subaltern migrants through both discursive unheardness and subordinate masculinity (cf. Torres 2008) such as homosexuality. When addressing this dual otherness (subaltern *and* subordinate masculinity),[16] we probably need to speak of "doubly wrong sex and the city."

Bibliography

Primary sources

Bolec, Jakub. 2008. "Zmartwychwstanie śmieciarza." In *Na końcu świata napisane. Autoportret współczesnej polskiej emigracji. Konkurs Literacki Polish Books, Londyn 2007*, edited by Polish Books UK, 66-106. Chorzów: Videograf.
Czerwiński, Piotr. 2009. *Przebiegum życiae czyli kartonowa sieć.* Warsaw: Świat Książki.
Koziarski, Daniel. 2007. *Socjopata w Londynie*. Warsaw: Prószyński i S-ka.
Kropiwnicki, Aleksander. 2007. *Zajezdnia Londyn.* Bydgoszcz and Warsaw: Branta.
Miklasz, Adam. 2009. *Polska szkoła boksu. Powieść emigracyjna.* Kraków: Wydawnictwo Skrzat.
Plebanek, Grażyna. 2007. *Przystupa.* Warsaw: Wydawnictwo W.A.B.
Polish Books UK, ed. 2008. *Na końcu świata napisane. Autoportret współczesnej polskiej emigracji. Konkurs Literacki Polish Books, Londyn 2007*. Chorzów: Videograf.
Sędzikowski, Michał. 2008. "Klątwa." *Na końcu świata napisane. Autoportret współczesnej polskiej emigracji. Konkurs Literacki Polish Books, Londyn 2007*, edited by Polish Books UK, 231-257. Chorzów: Videograf.
Suskiewicz, Łukasz. 2009. *egri bikaver.* Szczecin: Wydawnictwo Forma.
Wieteska, Mariusz. 2009. *Zielona Wyspa.* Warsaw: Wydawnictwo Anagram.
Wojnarowski, Marcin. 2008. *Okrutny idiota albo prywatny żart*. Poznań: Euro Projekt.
Wyszowski, Michał. 2010. *Na lewej stronie świata.* Warsaw: Wydawnictwo MG.

Secondary sources

Burrell, Kathy. 2008. "Male and Female Polishness in Post-war Leicester: Gender and its Intersections in a Refugee Community." In *Gendering Migration: Masculinity, Femininity and Ethnicity in Post-War Britain,* edited by Louise Ryan and Wendy Webster, 71-87. Aldershot and Burlington, VT: Ashgate.

[16] The dimensions of class and representational silence must be added as a fourth factor to the triadic scheme of otherness as proposed by Hans Mayer (1975, 499; cf. Warkocki 2007, 31–32).

Chowaniec, Urszula. 2011. "Displacement, Emigration, and Travel: Contemporary Polish Literature and the Notion of Émigré Literature." In *Contemporary Polish Migrant Culture and Literature in Germany, Ireland, and the UK*, edited by Joanna Rostek and Dirk Uffelmann, 133-151. Frankfurt am Main: Peter Lang.

Connell, R.W. 2005. *Masculinities*. Berkeley and Los Angeles, CA: University of California Press.

Coyle, Angela. 2007. "Resistance, Regulation and Rights: The Changing Status of Polish Women's Migration and Work in the 'New' Europe." *European Journal of Women's Studies* 14 (1): 37–50.

Datta, Ayona. 2009. "'This Is Special Humour': Visual Narratives of Polish Masculinities on London's Building Sites." In *Polish Migration to the UK in the "New" European Union: After 2004,* edited by Kathy Burrell, 189-210. Aldershot and Burlington, VT: Ashgate.

Fihel, Agnieszka, ed. 2011. *Recent Trends in International Migration in Poland: The 2011 SOPEMI Report* (=CMR Working Paper 52/110). Accessed 6 May, 2012. http://www.migracje.uw.edu.pl/publikacja/rodzaj/CMR/.

Flood, Michael, Judith Kegan Gardiner, Bob Pease and Keith Pringle, eds. 2007. *International Encyclopedia of Men and Masculinities.* London and New York: Routledge.

Galasiński, Dariusz. 2010. "Post-Communist Masculinities." In *The Post-Communist Condition: Public and Private Discourses of Transformation*, edited by Aleksandra Galasińska and Dariusz Galasiński, 247-262. Amsterdam and Philadelphia, PA: John Benjamins.

Garapich, Michał P. 2010. "Chłopi i żołnierze, budowlańcy i pijacy. Dominujący dyskurs migracyjny, jego kontestacje oraz konsekwencje dla konstruowania polskiej grupy etnicznej w wielokulturowym Londynie." In *Drogi i rozdroża. Migracje Polaków w Unii Europejskiej po 1 maja 2004 roku. Analiza psychologiczno-socjologiczna*, edited by Halina Grzymała-Moszczyńska, Anna Kwiatkowska and Joanna Roszak, 35-54. Kraków: Nomos.

—. 2011. "Of Alcohol and Men – Survival, Masculinities and Anti-institutionalism of Polish Homeless Men in a Global City." *Studia Migracyjne – Przegląd Polonijny* 37(1): 309-330.

Gosk, Hanna. 2010. *Opowieści "skolonizowanego/kolonizatora". W kręgu studiów postzależnościowych nad literaturą polską XX i XXI wieku*. Kraków: Universitas.

Grabowska-Lusińska, Izabela and Marek Okólski. 2008. *Migracja z Polski po 1 maja 2004 r. Jej intensywność i kierunki geograficzne oraz alokacja na rynkach pracy krajów Unii Europejskiej* (=CMR Working Paper 33/91). Accessed 6 May, 2012. www.migracje.uw.edu.pl/download/publikacja/608/.

Iglicka, Krystyna. 2007. *Badanie nad legalnymi migracjami zarobkowymi z Polski do Wielkiej Brytanii po 1 maja 2004 roku.* Accessed 6 May, 2012. http://csm.org.pl/fileadmin/files/Biblioteka_CSM/Raporty_i_analizy/2007/KrystynaIglicka_Badanie nad legalnymi migracjami zarobk.pdf.

Kwiatkowska, Anna. 2010. "Tożsamość na emigracji: czy tożsamość emigranta ma płeć?." In *Drogi i rozdroża. Migracje Polaków w Unii Europejskiej po 1 maja 2004 roku. Analiza psychologiczno-socjologiczna*, edited by Halina Grzymała-Moszczyńska, Anna Kwiatkowska and Joanna Roszak, 209-222. Kraków: Nomos.

Maggio, J. 2007. "'Can the Subaltern Be Heard': Political Theory, Translation, Representation and Gayatri Chakravorty Spivak." *Alternatives* 32: 419-443.

Marchand, Marianne H. and Anne S. Runyan. 2000. *Gender and Global Restructuring: Sightings, Sites, and Resistances*. London et al.: Routledge.

Mayer, Hans 1975. *Außenseiter.* Frankfurt am Main: Suhrkamp.

McIlwaine, Cathy, Kavita Datta, Yara Evans, Joanna Herbert, Jon May and Jane Wills. 2006. "'Arriving on High Heels': Gender and Ethnic Identities among Low-paid Migrant Workers in London." Accessed 23 October, 2011. http://www.geog.qmul.ac.uk/globalcities/reports/docs/workingpaper4.pdf

Möller, Steffen. 2008. *Viva Polonia. Als deutscher Gastarbeiter in Polen.* Frankfurt am Main: Scherz.

Osipowicz, Dorota. 2001. "Marginalizacja społeczna migrantów." In *Ludzie na huśtawce. Migracje między peryferiami Polski i Zachodu*, edited by Ewa Jaźwińska and Marek Okólski, 382-409. Warsaw: Wydawnictwo Naukowe SCHOLAR.

Peter, Stefanie, ed. 2007. *Alphabet der polnischen Wunder. Ein Wörterbuch.* Frankfurt am Main: Suhrkamp.

Richardson, Riché. 2007. *Black Masculinity and the U.S. South: From Uncle Tom to Gangsta.* Athens, GE and London: The University of Georgia Press.

Rogers, Martyn. 2008. "Modernity, 'Authenticity', and Ambivalence: Subaltern Masculinities on a South Indian College Campus." *Journal of the Royal Anthropological Institute* N.S. 14: 79-95.

Rostek, Joanna. 2009. "Die Migration von (Stereo-)Typen der Weiblichkeit. Die Literatur von und über polnische Migrantinnen und Migranten in Irland." *Zeitschrift für Slavische Philologie* 66 (1): 181-209.

—. 2011. "Living the British Dream: Polish Migration to the UK as Depicted in the TV Series *Londyńczycy* (2008-2010)." In *Contemporary Polish Migrant Culture and Literature in Germany, Ireland, and the UK*, edited by Joanna Rostek and Dirk Uffelmann, 245-275. Frankfurt am Main: Peter Lang.

Rostek, Joanna and Dirk Uffelmann. 2010. "Can the Polish Migrant Speak? The Representation of 'Subaltern' Polish Migrants in Film, Literature and Music from Britain and Poland." In *Facing the East in the West: Images of Eastern Europe in British Literature, Film and Culture*, edited by Barbara Korte, Eva Ulrike Pirker and Sissy Helff, 311-334. Amsterdam: Rodopi.

Sheller, Mimi. 2005. "Her Majesty's Sable Subjects: Subaltern Masculinities in Post-Emancipation Jamaica." *Political Power and Social Theory* 17: 71-99.

Siara, Bernadetta. 2009. "UK Poles and the Negotiation of Gender and Ethnic Identity in Cyberspace." In *Polish Migration to the UK in the "New" European Union: After 2004,* edited by Kathy Burrell, 167-187. Aldershot and Burlington, VT: Ashgate.

Spivak, Gayatri Chakravorty. 1988. "Can the Subaltern Speak?." In *Marxism and the Interpretation of Culture*, edited by Cary Nelson and Lawrence Grossberg, 271-316. Basingstoke: Macmillan.

—. 1996. *The Spivak Reader: Selected Works*, edited by Donna Landry and Gerald MacLean. New York and London: Routledge.

Stecopoulos, Harry. 2007. "Race and Ethnicity." In *International Encyclopedia of Men and* Masculinities, edited by Michael Flood, Judith Kegan Gardiner, Bob Pease and Keith Pringlem 525-528. London and New York: Routledge.

Torres, Manuel. 2007. "Subordinate Masculinity". In *International Encyclopedia of Men and Masculinities,* edited by Michael Flood, Judith Kegan Gardiner, Bob Pease and Keith Pringle, 589-590. London and New York: Routledge.

Trevena, Paulina. 2010. "Degradacja? Koncepcje socjologiczne, percepcja społeczna a postrzeganie własnego położenia przez wykształconych migrantów pracujących za granicą poniżej kwalifikacji." In *Drogi i rozdroża. Migracje Polaków w Unii Europejskiej po 1 maja 2004 roku. Analiza psychologiczno-socjologiczna*, edited by Halina Grzymała-Moszczyńska, Anna Kwiatkowska and Joanna Roszak, 147-160. Kraków: Nomos.

Uffelmann, Dirk. 2009. "Paradoxe der jüngsten nichtslavischen Literatur slavischer Migranten." In *Die Ost-West-Problematik in den europäischen Kulturen und Literaturen. Ausgewählte Aspekte. Problematika Východ – Západ v evropských kulturách a literaturách. Vybrané aspekty*, edited by Helena Ulbrechtová and Siegfried Ulbrecht, 601-630. Práce Slovanského ústavu. Nová řada 25. Dresden: Neisse Verlag.

—. 2011. "'Self-Orientalisation' in Narratives by Polish Migrants to Germany (by Contrast to Ireland and the UK)." In *Contemporary Polish Migrant Culture and Literature in Germany, Ireland, and the UK*, edited by Joanna Rostek and Dirk Uffelmann, 103-132. Frankfurt am Main: Peter Lang.

Van Heuckelom, Kris. 2011. "Polish (Im)Potence: Shifting Representations of Polish Labour Migration in Contemporary European Cinema." In *Contemporary Polish Migrant Culture and Literature in Germany, Ireland, and the UK*, edited by Joanna Rostek and Dirk Uffelmann, 277-296. Frankfurt am Main: Peter Lang.

Warkocki, Błażej. 2007. *Homo niewiadomo. Najnowsza polska proza wobec odmienności.* Warsaw: Wydawnictwo Sic!

White, Anne. 2011. *Polish Families and Migration since EU Accession.* Bristol: The Policy Press.

(E-)Migration and Displacement: Melancholy as a Subversive Gesture in Prose by Women

Urszula CHOWANIEC

(E-)Migrating scholarship

This chapter is devoted to the theme of (e-)migration and travelling and the process of transgressing one's own language, culture, moral code, habits and worldview, which result from the experience of dislocation, as well as to its opposition—namely, the notion of citizenship. I present a selection of recent Polish literary texts by women that address precisely these motifs and problems. I claim that there is a strong presence of melancholy in all texts dealing with migration, but that this melancholy, when it appears in texts written by women, plays a significantly different role from the traditionally understood melancholy: instead of apathy and withdrawal from the world, the "melancholy of the woman's text" may be read as an impeachment of patriarchal culture and statement of dissatisfaction, behind which lies a demand to change the world. It can be seen as a kind of active, transgressive melancholy, however oxymoronic that may sound.

Much scholarly research has been undertaken on migration during the past ten years or so. It is usually conducted according to the interdisciplinary method where connections are made between social studies, politics, statistics, economics, cultural studies and also, although somewhat marginally, literary research. The migration or emigration experience is currently regarded as an important theme in understanding the contemporary world. In so-called "border studies," for example, human history is understood as the history of crossing borders: the physical borders of the tribe, polis, town, state, continent, but also the borders of one's own culture and language. Meanwhile the history of transgressing these borders becomes the history of political, social and cultural conflicts, the history of wars. Understood in this sense, a border (boundary or limit) can hardly claim to be a new theme in research. Yet, in the contemporary world, the crossing of borders and the transgressive element that comes with it (the gesture of discontent, criticism of what is within the borders) needs to be redefined. Utopian plans for a common Europe, a global world, the idea of citizenship of the world (with its alleged ease of travel and communication, the possibility of living anywhere)[1] have brought an

[1] Julia Kristeva, for example, expressed her concern about the utopian element of cosmopolitanism as follows: "In today's unprecedented intermixing of foreigners on earth, two extreme

illusion of freedom from the burden of borders, and hence of freedom from the experience of emigration—and connected with this: from the potentially painful exposure to other cultures, and hence the experience of becoming a foreigner, subject to other people's hospitality. This, as we know from Jacques Derrida and Anne Dufourmantelle (2000), is not an equal relationship, because it assumes a total tolerance of and agreement to Otherness and strangeness, which cannot be achieved.

For some time, we—or many of us—have wanted to believe that it is possible to do away with borders (first the geographical, then the political, linguistic, social and cultural). There was a sense that the borders of the state could be eliminated, but the collapsing dream of a common Europe seems to confirm their rigidity and persistence, especially in a time of economic crisis, when the rhetoric of opposing sides or allies has a tendency to return. Wisława Szymborska in her well-known poem "Psalm"—from the collection *A Large Number* (*Wielka liczba,* 1976)—sees borders as a human invention, while she describes the whole of nature as disrespecting them. She concludes the poem as follows: "Only what is human can be truly foreign. / The rest is mixed vegetation, subversive moles, and wind." (Szymborska 1995, 100) Maybe this interpretation might provide the concept of the border with a new, or additional function: something that divides into "ours and theirs" (into what is known and what is strange)—the dichotomy may thus become a *sine qua non* of what it means to be human, since to be human is to create that which is strange or foreign ("obce"). In this way the foreigner becomes the guarantor of the human.

Among the examples of contemporary Polish women's writing that I discuss, I shall concentrate in particular on one case of emigration writing, that of Wioletta Grzegorzewska (b. 1974), her experience of dislocation and its inevitable melancholy, but where this melancholy (experienced especially in the poet's roles as a woman, and chiefly as a mother) acquires transgressive value as a criticism of traditional roles, repressive cultural and social structures, and narrow worldviews on both sides of the border.

If melancholy involves a suspension of identity, the painful experience of being in-between, then it also provides a chance for re-evaluation: for a critique of normative culture. Melancholy as a painful path to realization of one's position and its transgressive re-evaluation is perhaps one of the most valuable critical voices to emerge in Polish contemporary literature. Such melancholy in contemporary (e-)migrating women's writing addresses the theme of displacement

solutions are taking shape: either we are heading towards a global united states [. . .] Or else the humanistic cosmopolitanism shows itself to be utopic, and particularistic aspirations force one to believe that small political sets are the optimal structures to insure the survival of humanity" (1991, 98).

juxtaposed with notions of the body, women's social roles, the family, motherhood, romantic love, education or work. Femininity understood in traditional ways is at stake: the role of the heterosexual, submissive woman ("kobieta ofiarnicza") is retold.

Sadness is the lining of the world: three features of writing by Polish women [2]

Literature is born out of pain. It is a desperate attempt to tame the omnipresent disappointment with the world, to restore some kind of sense or meaning to it, some plot or narrative. Writer on melancholy Antoni Kępiński concluded that "sadness is human destiny" (1996, 13). In a similar melancholic spirit, the 19th-century author Eliza Orzeszkowa wrote that "life is lavishly seasoned with sadness" (1896, 1:1)—maybe because, as contemporary writer Manuela Gretkowska puts it, "the world is defective, incomplete" (1999, 8).

Melancholy is inscribed into the structure of reality, into the fabric of the world, just as it is into our individual development (at least that's how we are accustomed to think of it since Freud[3]). The mother is held responsible for this lack—for the sadness, longing and pain of existence. The mother, who gives life and offers momentarily a symbiotic bond, in fact condemns us to painful separation, to isolation, which is always interwoven with the spectre of death. Referring to Freud, but at the same time reinterpreting him, as well as to Luce Irigaray and Kristeva, Judith Butler describes the state of melancholy as follows: "The melancholic refuses the loss of the object, and internalization becomes a strategy of magically resuscitating the lost object, not only because the loss is painful, but because the ambivalence felt toward the object requires that the object be retained until differences are settled." (1990, 62-63) Hence the crucial thing is the loss, which constantly reminds us of the presence and possibility of death. "[. . .] I am obsessed with death. Generic and individual," says the female narrator of Justyna Bargielska's 2010 debut collection of mini prose pieces about loss, written for

---

2 The image "the lining of the world" is taken from Czesław Miłosz's poem "Meaning" ("Sens," from the collection *Provinces,* 1991): "—When I die, I will see the lining of the world. / The other side, beyond bird, mountain, sunset. / The true meaning, ready to be decoded. / What never added up will add up, / What was incomprehensible will be comprehended." (Miłosz 2001, 569) My paraphrase of Miłosz's term "lining of the world" implies a melancholic interpretation of his text. The other side of the world, the one which we long for, and which links us to the destructive instinct for death, is in essence a longing for Kristeva's primordial unity, the Sick or maternal Thing, the bond with the mother that precedes consciousness of self.

3 See, for example, Freud's 1917 paper *Mourning and Melancholia*. In the current chapter, I read Freud through Julia Kristeva's *Black Sun: Depression and Melancholia* (1989) as well as Judith Butler's *Gender Trouble* (1990).

"those who do not like to forget" (see the author's comment on the back cover). "Bronka says she is obsessed too, and quotes me some eighty-year-old woman writer: 'Already as a child, I felt that forcing someone into existence was an absurd abuse. Everyone should be asked whether they wouldn't prefer simply not to be.'" (Bargielska 2010, 18)

The first of the three features of writing by women that I wish to highlight is what I term "melancholic vindication." It is basically a melancholic question about the meaning of existence, a conviction of its senselessness or absurdity. The unending narrative about the existential entity, reason or condition concealed behind the performative "I am" is—or so it would seem—a particular feature of the most recent literature, and especially of prose. This is the perspective from which, for the purposes of the current chapter, I shall regard literary texts published since the beginning of the 1990s, i.e. by writers born in the 1960s or later who have made their debuts since 1990. Prose that appeared since 1989 has its own peculiar character as in any other period, but this does not mean we should not focus on its peculiarity and try to describe it. The twenty-year period 1989-2010 (Chowaniec 2012)—still ongoing, however, and soon to become thirty years—has been a time in Polish culture, as in European culture more generally, particularly disposed towards redefining identity. Hence the unprecedented career of the concept of *identity* (Polish: tożsamość) in the 1990s, and of additional concepts which this category has brought with it: identification, one's own, the foreign, the other (or Other), tolerance, difference, diversity, national identity or belonging, local belonging, globality, and so on. Post-communist transformation on the political and economic level has inspired a genuine revolution in social and cultural relations. The new "freedom" has had to be somehow named, defined and understood (Czapliński 2001 and 2002) while literature itself—even though literary criticism appears to have said good-bye to any kind of engagement of literature in anything—was to record the changes (or rather, the change in values, the various directions taken by discussion and theory, as well as the inspirations), was somehow to capture and narrate it.

It comes as no surprise that this narrative in the version published by the best-known, most widely read and critically acclaimed Polish women writers of the last two decades is not a happy one. And the pessimism of their story is not unconnected with the political dimension to the women's movement. The stories related in contemporary women's prose are a bitter diagnosis of disappointment with the new reality, which promised much but did not deliver—just as bitter as that of Maria Janion in her now famous speech to the First Women's Congress (held in Warsaw 20-21 June 2009), when she concluded that the years 1989-2009 had shown that "Democracy in Poland had a masculine gender."[4]

This disenchantment with reality and the expression of melancholic sadness is, then, one of the most visible features of Polish women's writing of the two decades following the political and economic transformation. Women's sadness also contains an element of reviewing a particular social, cultural and existential position, and the associated vindication of one's rights.

The second feature I wish to stress is the feminist and gender perspective, stressed in Maria Janion's speech. The emphasis on the gender dimension in literary texts by women published during the past twenty years, courageous and self-vindicating (only not in relation to male or masculine perspectives, but also to the oppressively heteronormative culture), has been of crucial importance in redefining culture, although we should note that this has not always been a feature positively received by literary criticism. The feminist commentator and literary historian Kazimiera Szczuka, for example, has tried to counteract some of Przemysław Czapliński's criticisms of literature by women as being boring, passive and formulaic.[5]

Olga Tokarczuk, in her hybrid novel or treatise on travelling entitled *Runners* (*Bieguni,* 2007), combines the gender perspective with the question of existence and its uncertain, unfixed status. At the beginning of the book, in the opening passage entitled "I am" ("Jestem"), we read:

That evening was the far edge of the world, I felt it by chance, while playing, involuntarily. I discovered it because they left me on my own for a moment, weren't keeping an eye on me. [...]. Doors shut, hatches down, blinds drawn. I wanted to go out but there was

4 "For years I was well aware of the clear division between serious and non-serious matters: in times of oppression the struggle for independence is considered a serious matter, and the fight for women's rights is not. [...] I believed that freedom for the whole society should be achieved first, and then, together and peacefully, we would improve women's conditions. To my surprise, it transpired that a woman was to be a 'family creature' in liberated Poland, a creature who—instead of engaging in politics—should take care of the home. It took some time before I realized that democracy in Poland has a masculine gender" (quoted in Chowaniec 2012, 5).

5 "In defiance of Maria Janion and her book *Women and the Spirit of Otherness* (*Kobiety i duch inności*, 1996) [...] and her inclusion of women's writing in Romantic, political and transgressive contexts, Czapliński proposes the formula: 'Women and the Spirit of Identity' ('Kobiety i duch tożsamości'). In his book bearing the significant title *The Effect of Passivity: Literature in Normal Times* (*Efekt bierności. Literatura w czasie normalnym*, 2004) he criticizes novels written by women for women as boring, petty bourgeois [...]. Not only all 'spirit of otherness' but even reality itself has supposedly evaporated from women's literature, making way for escapism and consumption" (Szczuka 2008). Also, in an earlier interview: "Janion's diagnoses about the transgressivity or subversiveness of women's voices in culture are a lot deeper, and reach back to the 19th century, portraying examples of symbolic imagination both Polish and European. Czapliński's diagnoses relate to the social here and now, the current state of mentality. [...] Yet many women, whom we may regard as popular, somehow slip through the net, such as Marta Dzido, author of *Clam* (*Małż*, 2003), a novel written in contemporary language about a young educated woman's experience of the job market"(Szczuka 2006).

nowhere to go. Only my presence took on distinct contours, which trembled, undulated, and that hurt. At a particular moment I discovered the truth: there's nothing to be done: I am. (Tokarczuk 2007, 6)

Tokarczuk goes on to describe the woman traveller and her ways of perceiving a world constantly on the move or in a state of flux. Since she implies that the astonishment or fear of being (fear of that absolute, almost Kafkaesque definition "I am") may somehow be tamed or domesticated through movement, travelling, an existence like that of the eponymous Runners. And this movement, travelling, migration, is the third feature of contemporary women's literature to which I would like to draw particular attention, and on which I shall concentrate in this chapter. My specific emphasis will be on *nomadic existence as a metaphor for loss.*

Since the beginning of the 1990s movement, travel, journeys abroad and returns home have been the much repeated threads of a general leitmotif in prose texts by women. Inscribed into this leitmotif is a multiplicity of associated problems, such as the redefinition of "émigré" or "emigration" literature in the new "liberated" reality (Chowaniec 2011a), the establishment of new identities for the modern contemporary woman, or the contemporary woman traveller (Chowaniec 2010),[6] as well as a critique of the political, economic and social changes that have taken place over the last twenty to thirty years, including changes to borders, to legal regulations affecting the crossing of borders, and to international and interstate relations. In this context two dates have a special significance for the periodization of Polish literature: 1989, as the year marking the end of communism—two important texts by women which deal with this particular theme, each in its own way, are Manuela Gretkowska's novel *We're Emigrants Here* (*My zdies' emigranty,* 1995) and Izabela Filipiak's collection of stories *The Blue Menagerie* (*Niebieska menażeria,* 1997); and 2004, as the year when the European Union expanded to incorporate ten countries of Central and Eastern Europe, including Poland—in this context a number of novels appeared by women, which were weaker from the literary point of view but recorded a new model of emigrant experience, such as Iwona Słabuszewska-Krauze's *Hotel Ireland* (*Hotel Irlandia,* 2006) and Dana Parys-White's *Emigrant by Choice* (*Emigrantka z wyboru,* 2008), or the autobiographical texts by Justyna Tomańska *A Polish Woman in London* (*Polka w Londynie,* 2004) and *A Polish Woman in Madrid* (*Polka w Madrycie,* 2005).

Yet another contingent theme to the subject of movement in literature is its de-

---

[6] On travelling and the changes to identity, essential to the Polish debate on modernity, is Wieczorkiewicz 2008. Here the problem of travel becomes one of consumption, where the question of identity in contemporary society is written into the development of modern capitalism (analysed here through such categories as authenticity and its disappearance, the phenomenon of taking photographs, enjoying new tastes when travelling abroad, or advertising).

nial or negation: the putting down of roots, making oneself feel at home, settling down. In Polish literature, this associated theme established itself as a critique of the historical and political upheavals of the 20th century: movement, leaving or departure, migration, is inscribed into every text of the so-called "small homelands" trend, which became so important in Polish prose of the 1990s (Czapliński 2001). The whole atmosphere of Olga Tokarczuk's novel *Primeval and Other Times* (*Prawiek i inne czasy,* 1996) is pervaded by a sense of threat posed by some catastrophe to an idyllic homeliness (though not one devoid of evil or violence), to the familiarity of one's own world. The possibility of transgressing the mythical boundaries of the home or familiar territory, demarcated for instance by rivers or forests, is already apparent at the beginning of the novel in the threat brought by war and the departure of the man, Michał. However, it is the woman who is the carrier of the values that comprise "rootedness," or "homeliness" or "domestication." Her gesture of indefinite waiting devalues men's transgression of the borders. At the end of the novel, the "small homeland" is ultimately deconstructed by a woman's departure. Her crossing of the boundaries is decisive. Thus when Adelka returns for a moment, her arrival from over there, from far away, becomes a metaphor for the final end of the mythic Home—of what is Permanent. Bidding farewell to Primeval, she turns the coffee-grinder which, like the water mill, is a symbol of transience, the sifting of one state into another, of fluidity itself. *Primeval and Other Times* can be seen as a prelude to the later treatise on travelling, the above-mentioned *Runners,* in which Tokarczuk defines modernity ultimately in categories of movement, change, and the negation of what is Permanent.

Modern, contemporary emigration becomes migration; often it appears to be travelling out of choice, of one's own free will. Contemporary travel or tourism is no longer a temporary distancing from home, but has become a way of life, since Home itself is now always only short-term. Home has been destroyed, as it was for many Poles during World War II—in Ewa Kujawska's novel *Małgorzata's House* (*Dom Małgorzaty,* 2007), for instance—by bombs; or, after the war, by the abortive building programmes of the People's Republic, such as the blocks and housing estates central to Joanna Bator's novel *Sandy Hill* (*Piaskowa góra,* 2009). While I concentrate in the present chapter on post-1989 migration, it is significant that several prominent contemporary Polish women writers connect this present-day experience existentially with the traumatic forced displacement and migration of populations caused by the post-war settlements and shifting westwards of the borders of the Polish state, as in Tokarczuk's *House of Day, House of Night* (*Dom dzienny, dom nocny,* 1998) or Inga Iwasiów's *Bambino* (2008). Home has lost its roots, the ghosts of former generations and the stability of fixed neighbourhood—the things that defined what was Permanent, and has become only a temporary place to stay, an echo of airports, where you put away in a drawer for a while the one stable element and proof of your identity: your passport. Home has therefore become an object of longing of the new emigrant, male or female, of the traveller, of the melancholic.

Migration, homelessness and women's melancholy

Travelling as a metaphor for the loss of Home is clearly a melancholic theme. The Home in *Primeval and Other Times* will never be recovered; it has become instead an impossibility, since it already belongs to a mythical reality (primeval time). Here, however, I should draw attention to the specific nature of the melancholy found in narratives by women, because it does not appear as the particular, individual sadness or nostalgia of the narratorial voice, but as a selection of themes related to the overthrowing or ruination of various orders: the order of integrated traditional stories or narratives, the order of an integrated body, the order of an integrated language (Chowaniec 2011b).

Polish women writers exploit prose in order to bring out the melancholic threads in their critique of traditional narratives, where relationships between the sexes had been established according to exclusively heteronormative categories, often burdened with a priori value judgements (crucial in this context are the themes of madness in Izabela Filipiak and sexuality in Manuela Gretkowska). Lesbian or homoerotic elements are especially crucial here as a means of exploding traditional ways of thinking about loss (for example, the love of Hildegard and Małgorzata in Ewa Kujawska's novel). And this is also a crucial factor in contestations of traditional motherhood—as in the prose of Anna Nasiłowska (2002) or Justyna Bargielska (2010), though the latter do not focus on migration as such.

The gesture of rebellion against heteronormativity is not as frequent, however, as the gesture of revealing the body's physicality: dismemberment of the body, illness, physical pain, while attention is drawn to the body's ugliness and its transparency in literary discourses is questioned, and hence its gendered nature is also emphasized as a melancholic way of criticizing traditional discourses of home-making and/or uprooting. Here of particular note are *Final Stories* (*Ostatnie historie,* 2004) by Olga Tokarczuk, *Polish Cleaner* (*Pani na domkach,* 2006) by Joanna Pawluśkiewicz and *Miscarriage Girls* (*Obsoletki,* 2010) by Justyna Bargielska.

The final feature typical of this melancholy in women's prose is the disintegration of language: the renunciation of a cohesive narrative, the emergence of short and/or hybrid forms rather than single continuous narratives. Here an interesting example is the fascinating quasi-autobiography by poet Wioletta Grzegorzewska entitled *Notes from the Island* (*Notatnik z Wyspy,* 2012).

Note-taking as a way of framing the world: description of a displacement

This section will consist of a close reading of Grzegorzewska's *Notes from the Island.* Grzegorzewska was born in 1974 in southern Poland and has published several collections of poetry, including *Controlled Imagination* (*Wyobraźnia kontrolowana*, 1998), *Relatives* (*Parantele,* 2003), *Orinoko* (2008), *Other Turnovers* (*Inne obroty*, 2010) and *Smena's Memory* (*Pamięć Smieny*, 2011). In 2006, she left Poland and moved to the UK, where she currently resides in the town of Ryde on the Isle of Wight.

Let's begin with a description of the emigrant's displacement:

> 10.04.2007: Life between worlds. Life of the living and the dead. Between rural fullness and urban emptiness. In melodious dialect and Silesian mumbling. In the depths of the Polish language and in the gestation of a foreign tongue. New life in my arms and against my breast. On an autonomous island and in a unified Europe, right out on the edge. (Grzegorzewska 2012)[7]

From the outset, Grzegorzewska's experience of emigration is connected with her position as a mother: her bodily connection to the newborn baby interacts with her struggle to be on various psychological edges or borders: between the past and the present, between her familiar home town and the new place, between the mother tongue and the foreign language. Melancholy slips into the narration as a result of the writer's being in-between, since melancholy is not only a loss of speech, a slow withdrawal from the narrative (hence the "notebook" form) but also the loss of oneself, as Freud famously put it: "In mourning it is the world which has become poor and empty; in melancholia it is the ego itself" (Freud 1989, 585), the statement that was to form one of the starting points in Judith Butler's theory of melancholic gender. In literature, through the aesthetic gesture of writing, the helplessness of melancholy can be overcome by a certain power. "The creative melancholics," writes Noelle McAfee on Kristeva, "are the ones who take part in 'that adventure of the body and signs that bears witness to the affect—to sadness as the imprint of separation and beginning of the symbol's sway'; these are the novelists, poets, and artists, who have been moved to create by the black sun of melancholia." (McAfee 2004, 66)

In Grzegorzewska we see both: the sadness of displacement and the acquisition of a new power connected with the symbolic domain. Thus we have a metaphorical description of the melancholic condition, with its sadness at having left things behind (loss), sense of distraction, helplessness, desperation, reluctance to speak, or perhaps merely disillusion with language as such:

---

7 I wish to thank Marek Kazmierski for his excellent translations of Grzegorzewska's subtle poetic language.

14.09.2007: I have become attached to certain objects, a sure sign that I am ageing. Having moved home many times, I have learnt to evade everything, leave no traces behind. Prior to my departure for England, I burnt my personal letters and private notes. They didn't fit inside my luggage, in my rucksack or my head. And yet, when thinking about my last loft apartment, I find myself missing certain objects, various other imagined fragments which follow me on my travels.

10.09.2006: I meander round this island slowly, between dreams. Feeling halved. When I fall ill, it is for weeks on end.

The melancholy of displacement, this dangerous and painful experience of loss, is slowly overcome in Grzegorzewska through subtle dialogue with the three most important elements that make up the narrator's and central character's—the textual Grzegorzewska's—world: her past, her language and her bodily experience of motherhood.

Beginning with motherhood, it is interesting that the experience of emigration in Grzegorzewska is also a motherly experience. For the narrator, her two children are a way of re-defining and re-evaluating the world:

12.09.2007: At dawn, the Solent is invisible. The needle of the Spinnaker tower pierces the mist. A dark yacht bobs upon the water like a fly drowned in milk. On Surbiton Grove, I notice one red and two grey blotches, which sunlight then turns into cars. My five-month-old daughter is looking out of the window alongside me. How many such sights must she ingest before the world becomes visible to her?

The mother and her little daughter are in a similar situation of acquiring the world: the position of the learner is described here through the melancholic themes of dawn, water, darkness, mist and milk. Both need to learn about the new world ("ingest its sights") in order to domesticate it and make it familiar and understandable. Moreover, the emigrant mother is confronted by her son's language. Her children's tongue is not their mother's tongue, and this causes an interesting tension between them:

30.09.2007: I sneak glances at him through the window as he comes home from school. My Polish boy in his navy blue uniform, stooped, crossing Alexandra Road all alone. He enters the hallway like a cat. Discarding his tie with the Bishop Lovett School crest. Silent. He leaves this time for later. Approaches the kitchen table. Shifting gears in the translation machine.

The son's world is different from the mother's; hence they require the negotiated space of common language, the language of the emigrants' home. Yet, the shared language of intimate space between a mother and her son can become a source of embarrassment, an uncomfortable experience in the public space where foreigners unwillingly meet:

> 15.09.2007: "Watch where you're going, you English bitch," a stranger barks at me in Polish at some car boot sale, unaware that we are both cut from the same language.

It is clear that language can become a foreigner's battlefield:

> 3.02.2008: Talking to a friend recently, I could not recall the Polish for "salmon" (łosoś). Almost twenty years ago, I had to be taught how to speak my native tongue properly, because in my family home we communicated using the local dialect. Then I spent a few years trying to cram Russian and the same for German, then studying for my literature degree I had to listen to the pompously artificial pronunciations of fellow students, and now I am struggling in another new tongue, my reluctance to go over all that again so great I would rather stay silent.

We see both the narrator's awareness of losing her language (which is, of course, a metaphorical home or homeland) while, at the same time, the language itself starts to become a fascinating subject of reflection, but a subject that becomes foreign:

> 17.01.2011: I am becoming intrigued and surprised by the Polish language: its etymology, tame transmutations, ellipses, phraseology and the reflexive pronouns which we overuse. The mechanisms which since birth I have accepted as "mine" and natural are starting to erode and cause me to struggle more and more in my native tongue. And English? To my mind, it is still in its infancy, perhaps never to progress beyond nappy stage. It neither delights nor depresses me. Mr de Saussure, I have got myself into this, so where should I go next? In which language should I seek more of me?

The colloquial locution "ani parzy, ani ziębi" ("it neither delights nor depresses me") is important here: the emigrant may seem detached or unfriendly, but we know "indifference is the foreigner's shield. Insensitive, aloof, he seems, deep down, beyond the reach of attacks and rejections that he nevertheless experiences with the vulnerability of a medusa" (Kristeva 1991, 7). And medusa-like Grzegorzewska—aware of losing her own language—sees the foreign land in a critical light as being a superficial and lonely land:

> 22.09.2007: The Isle of Wight is too cramped for me. I am choked by the stench of rotting roots, seaweed and moss. Local theatres staging farcical murder mysteries. On the High Street, a homeless violinist pumping concerts out of a portable amp. Locals putting on festivals in the name of garlic or tomatoes. Chinese-made junk spilling from shop fronts onto pavements. Yesterday, I enquired about work for a Polish friend in the Long John eatery. Standing by the counter, waiting to speak to the chef, I saw an elderly English woman smiling back at her own reflection in a soup bowl.

The trangressive experience of emigration is a dangerous move: what is at stake is the self, one's properly labelled identity. Grzegorzewska is aware of the ideological dimension to constructed identity and its seizing power (in the sense that it forces one to behave according to regulated, expected patterns). Such labels made her want to escape, yet those same labels are now missing, while the new space has become an amalgam of the disliked, yet idealized past and the disliked but more and more domesticated "present":

> 01.03.2011: I am thinking about Poland. My country is made up of people I met up until 2006, and who in my memories are my fatherland. The places themselves are beginning to fade. Only the odd object continues to hold its shine: colours, smells, details, for example a painted steel mug from a children's ward in a district hospital, dark brown volumes of "The Quiet Don" stamped at the library in Myszków. [...] Why do these and not other things come to mind and play tricks with memory? People have remained intensely alive, even if they have passed away: their private tongues, gestures, phobias, emotions.

The condition of being in-between is eventually resolved. The woman-emigrant, the mother, the melancholic who needs to find another language in order to speak again, finally overcomes the seizing power of melancholy, overpowering those metaphorical waters or mists she was looking at with her daughter, and declares:

> 5.04.2012: I have chosen to stay in Europe, on a small piece of land the guide-books call "Dinosaur Isle," which on maps looks just like a rough-cut diamond. You will find more retirement homes here than you will schools, with many moving, from all over the British Isles, just to die in peace. I have no idea what keeps me rooted to this place, yet, when returning from London to Ryde, crossing the Solent on board a ferry or a hovercraft, I now have the strange sensation I am sailing home.

This is the story of Grzegorzewska's displacement, on various levels: from home, from her body and—probably the most drastic one—from her language. Displacement is a transgression in the dictionary meaning of the word: exceeding a limit or boundary, it suggests behaviour that violates socially acceptable norms. Transgression is an act of aggression. It is a cruel, slow act of de-identification. It is a form of solitude, even the solitude of a mother taking care of a "new life." Of course, the condition of de-identification requires a prior set of identifying labels. And this is guaranteed by home, by a place, by this "somewhere" from where one comes. "Identities are malleable and multidimensional, and I am reluctant to fix my own through reifying labels," writes one author who learned to deal with problems of identity, displacement and homelessness through writing. "And yet," she continues, "we do not only define ourselves; we are also defined by our circumstances, culture, the perceptions of others and—perhaps most of all—the force of an internalized past." (Hoffman 2005, 27)

Identification comes from outside and perhaps increasingly so in the globalized 21st century: from language, from neighbours, from the past, in this sense—from our home. Therefore wherever we are, we search for home while this search is accompanied—especially in the case of emigration—with the difficult struggle with language, so clearly demonstrated by Grzegorzewska.

Notions of citizenship and emigration: women as eternal strangers

The case of Wioletta Grzegorzewska and her emigration brings up the notion of belonging, which is especially important when the category of women's writing is discussed in the Polish context. The use of the feminine forms "Polka" or "obywatelka" (a Polish woman, a female citizen)—even though the Polish language allows them—runs counter to women's attempts at participation in serious (political, philosophical, legal) discourses because of the normative perception of them as inferior and even frivolous. As was demonstrated by Simone de Beauvoir, nouns referring to a political subject, such as politician, senator, minister and citizen, are male. A man is a Subject, a woman is the Other. In Poland, men are the citizens, women are "cudzoziemki" (foreigners). At least this is how Polish women writers have often been described by literary critics (Czapliński 2009, 297-303). Usage of the word "cudzoziemki"[8] itself demonstrates literary criticism's need to locate women's writing within identity politics, rather than to search for the creative and transgressive character of their work (emphasized by Maria Janion, as noted above). Yet, even though second wave feminism, and certainly feminism in Poland since 1990, has not been keen to address the category of citizenship, it is important to discuss it, especially in relation to the category of "foreigner" used as a synonym for Polish woman in critical assessments of women's writing. The questions that arise are: Why have women writers been seen as foreigners in their own country? And why, as a consequence, have they been conceptualized as foreigners who have no chance of ever being at home?

In this context, Izabela Filipiak's short story "Weronika: Portrait with a Cat" ("Weronika. Portret z kotem") from *The Blue Menagerie* (1997) is especially interesting. It is a narrative by and about a female student from the city of Gdańsk, the cradle of the Solidarity movement. The narrator describes in retrospect her stay in the house of Weronika and Weronika's son, Seweryn, in Gdańsk at the time of the movement's birth. The narrator, a "new Polish woman" of the 1990s, does not mythologize the fatherland and its political past. The protagonist depicts the time she spent with Weronika as magical, full of music and art, and ripe with expressions of radical, unconventional attitudes towards the world (they listen to hippy music, smoke, discuss international affairs, literature and art). All this ends the day Weronika and her son become involved in the underground anti-communist movement. The narrator portrays the gradual change in Weronika from an open-minded, liberated, free-thinking woman and liberal mother, into a patriotic freedom fighter, a stereotypical Polish Mother (on the notion of the Polish Mother

8 The word "cudzoziemka" is associated in Polish literary history with the 1935 novel by Maria Kuncewiczowa, of this title. Later this same word was used in the plural ("Cudzoziemki") by Grażyna Borkowska as the title of her 1996 study on Polish women's writing 1845-1918.

in literature see Mrozik 2010 and 2012). This transformation affects not only the relationship between the protagonist and Weronika, but also the formerly close bond between mother and son. The new political circumstances, which require a re-thinking of their duties as citizens, create an unbearable hierarchy between mother and son, as the new order embraces traditional roles and obligations:

> While earlier on she wanted to be everything for him, now she became a law, the defender of national values, family rights and sacred, maternal rights. He hated her, I think, for this transformation. (Filipiak 1997, 151)

The new obligations require not only active participation in the material sense, but the re-evaluation of religion and gender. Weronika's engagement in clandestine (patriotic) work must remain limited to support of her son. Underground activity is generally depicted as a male thing:

> At the back of the church, in the library that was left there and was still being extended, and thanks to the willingness of the academic teachers, a temporary, clandestine university was created. It was a winter evening, when one of my friends, who I knew very well from the meeting in Seweryn's apartment [. . .] stopped me in the front of the church gate and explained, as gently as he could, that I could not come in. My friends discover in these hard times, just like the Renaissance scholars in their day, that the unpredictable female element could interfere with the seriousness of their meeting. (Filipiak 1997, 153)

Filipiak places her narrator in opposition to the mythical aura of Solidarity. The masculine nature of Solidarity as an organization is thereby exposed. Filipiak, as one of the first women writers to emerge in the 1990s, shows the importance of exposing the deceitfulness of the exclusive "manly faces" behind every struggle in so-called "hard times" and the misogynist fear, so well known from history, of "female elements" in politics.[9] Her narrator describes the role of a woman and mother in such hard times, and her inevitable fate. Both are rejected—whether they oppose the traditional female role (as the protagonist does) or conform to it (as Weronika does when playing the role of good mother and carer). Men turn against them as soon as women fulfil their role. Once she has prepared her son for the struggle, even at the cost of sacrificing her relationship with him, Weronika, and indeed the narrator, must be rejected as the alien element which is at odds with, and perhaps even spoils, the serious spirit of the men's clandestine meetings. The choice that women face following this rejection is either to accept their position or to rebel against patriotic exploitation. However, Weronika makes neither of these choices, and consequently goes insane. Weronika's madness, her bodily suffering and death are a literary metaphor for the marginalization of women and their bodies. Weronika's insanity symbolizes her lack of ultimate acceptance of

[9] See also Shana Penn's book, *Women's Underground* (*Podziemie kobiet,* 2003) with the illuminating, though brief introduction by Maria Janion.

her redundancy in patriarchal society. As a punishment she has to be marginalized by the patriarchal order and put beyond social configuration and language.[10]

Through her creation of the narrator and of Weronika, Filipiak represents women who tried to engage in the political and social struggles of the day. The turmoil of the 1980s, even when shown through the deconstruction of its mythical foundations, was nevertheless an important, inherent part of the lives of Filipiak and her peers. Filipiak's retrospective look at the 1980s is critical, as she accuses the past of destroying individual lives (women's lives) through engagement in often illusory roles. Female citizenship, understood as the possibility of gaining agency in decision-making processes, fails in Filipiak's story.

A man can be a citizen and an activist, a woman is only a co-inhabitant and helper... Thirty years after the founding of Solidarity and sixteen after the publication of *The Blue Menagerie* the situation of women in Polish politics does not appear to be any different. "I love women, I understand what they want with this party, but Poland is too poor for your demands," wrote a fan on the internet forum of The Women's Party in 2007, and the statement was later incorporated into book-diary form by Manuela Gretkowska, founder of the party (2008, 114-115). The right of women to be equal players in the Polish public sphere, and hence also efforts to bring women back from the symbolic exile established by the notion of citizenship,[11] seems to be of secondary importance in post-transformational Poland. Despite the strong presence of women on the literary and artistic scene in the 1990s (as in Solidarity in the 1980s!), Polish women have failed to secure for themselves the position of citizens, i.e. equal and serious players in the public realm.

Nevertheless I think that women's writing has taken a particularly interesting turn when it comes to reassessing the "common understanding" of the state and female citizenship in Poland since 1989. As Nick Stevenson argues,

> The power to name, construct meaning and exert control over the flow of information within contemporary societies is one of today's central structural divisions. Power is not solely based upon material dimensions, but also involves the capacity to throw into question established codes and to rework frameworks of common understanding. (Stevenson 2003, 4)

[10] The connection between madness and women's writing was explored at length in the now classic work by Gilbert and Gubar (2000), originally published in 1979.

[11] As Ruth Lister argues in her sub-chapter "The exile of the female," "While the cloak of invisibility is set aside, it is usually to treat the history of women's exclusion from citizenship as no more than an historical aberration or mistake, now more or less effectively remedied. [...] It has been one of the major contributions of feminist scholarship to illuminate the way in which the civic-republican conception of the citizen *was* 'aggressively male,' so that the exclusion of the female [...], far from being an aberration, was integral to the theory and practice of citizenship in both the republican and liberal traditions" (Lister 2003, 70).

This is the case in Filipiak's story, where the heroic mainstream narratives about Solidarity—a landmark in Polish citizens' identity in the 1990s—are challenged. Women writers became involved in presenting women's public and political agency, or women's exclusion from so-called "state" matters ("sprawy wagi państwowej"), in direct or indirect ways. These literary efforts may be called, in the words of Joseph May, "performances of citizenship" that present "sphere[s] of metaphoric, literal and performed possibilities available in different arenas of the everyday through which communities and individuals access (successfully or not) the experience called citizenship." (May 1999, 3) The shift from *being a citizen* to the *performance of citizenship* makes the category more open, especially to individuals who would otherwise be considered "inauthentic" citizens, such as migrants, emigrants, outcasts.

Every society nevertheless has a particular image of the idealized citizen's body, mainly to define the proper citizen's behaviour within his (sic!) rights and obligations. In Poland after 1989 the notion of citizenship needed to be redefined because of the political transformation. Through the vehicle of women's writing, questions were raised surrounding the ideal female citizen, but as result, because a woman does not have a constitutive position in the discourse of citizenship, the debate on female citizenship kept slipping away into other discourses (such as those on motherhood, sexual behaviour, mental health, domesticity and so on), which do not tend to be regarded as part of the general literary discussion of the political, of society, of Polish citizenship and emigration.

The most important themes in writing by women (in novels, short stories, mini-prose, hybrid forms) that bring together notions of the female body, women's participation in public life and citizenship as a means of gaining agency, fall into basically three categories.

First, there is the *body of the political or deliberately non-political emigrant*. Here, we encounter problems associated with emigration devoid of any specific ideological aims. Women emigrants are shown as free-floating nomads, happy with their "uprootedness" ("wykorzenienie") and disengagement with a fatherland which they present—directly or indirectly—as oppressive, as in *We're Emigrants Here* (1995) by Manuela Gretkowska, *Death and the Spiral* (*Śmierc i spirala,* 1991) by Izabela Filipiak and later *The Blue Menagerie* (1997), discussed above, and also *Polish Cleaner* (2006) by Joanna Pawluśkiewicz. The woman emigrant is portrayed as a critic of Polish national discourses of citizenship.

Second, we have the body of a particular type of Polish woman emigrant: *the figure of the cleaning lady abroad*, again in *Polish Cleaner* by Joanna Pawluśkiewicz, as well as in *Room Numbers* (*Numery,* 1999) by Olga Tokarczuk and *Przystupa* (2007) by Grażyna Plebanek. Here the perspective of the cleaning lady working abroad is used as a means of class and economic critique of who is a good citizen.

Third, there is the body of *the melancholic woman mourning the loss of belonging to a state, country, family, idea, identity, class or religion*, as in *Total Amnesia* (*Absolutna amnezja*, 1995) by Izabela Filipiak, *World-Viewer* (*Światowidz,* 1999) by Manuela Gretkowska, *Clam* (2003) by Marta Dzido, *Woman* (*Kobieta,* 2002) and *Sandy Hill* (2009) by Joanna Bator, *Bambino* (2008) by Inga Iwasiów and *Małgorzata's House* (2007) by Ewa Kujawska. The melancholy here is not only related to physical exile or emigration (as in the case of cleaning ladies working outside Poland) but to the internal exile of the "cudzoziemka" at home, and thus provides a particularly interesting perspective on reality, as the melancholic citizen is portrayed as one who has been deprived of her rights, like a foreigner, asylum seeker, or even refugee. The processes of exclusion of women from so-called "big politics" and the physical scars of that omission on the women's bodies are especially evident in the sensitive, sophisticated prose of Kujawska, Iwasiów and Bator.

The melancholic bodies of women excluded from their rights may be conceived of as a field of various intersections or interconnections between gender, religion, and nationality. The sexual body is often portrayed through an ideological prism. The ideologies deconstructed in recent women's writing include the ideology of the traditional family as in Filipiak's *Total Amnesia* and Bator's *Sandy Hill,* but also, for example, in Anna Janko's *The Girl with Matches* (*Dziewczyna z zapałkami*, 2007) or Kinga Dunin's *Taboo* (*Tabu,* 1998) and *Comedown* (*Obciach,* 1999); the ideology of heterosexuality, as in *The Blue Menagerie,* or in *Fool* (*Głupiec,* 2005) by Ewa Schilling; of Catholicism, as in *Katoniela* (2007) by Ewa Madeyska; of antisemitism, as in Bator's *Sandy Hill* and in Sylwia Chutnik's *Pocket Atlas for Women* (*Kieszonkowy atlas kobiet,* 2008) and *Diddums* (*Dzidzia,* 2009).

There is a demand in women's prose for the physical body to be scrutinized as politically relevant. The pain that always accompanies physical existence eludes standard modes of signification. Nevertheless each reader, as participant in the literary communication, reads the pain through their own sufferings. In this way, reading of the body and its pain is always intertwined in a "double decoding": decoding through the body of the reader, and decoding through the political implications of their literary representation. Pain and suffering can be seen as the perfect Other, which needs to be reclaimed by the discursive, even though at the same time it eludes the discursive. This is why the reading of the body and its pain requires constant re-reading, just like the notion of the stranger in the post-colonial context. In order to avoid orientalization, the Other needs to be constantly re-examined in its political position (for example in constructing notions of citizenship) as well as in its particularity and specificity.

Conclusion: Conquered melancholy as a critique of modernity in women's prose

In summarizing my reflections on the movement, travelling, migration, homelessness and melancholy, as well as the exclusion from citizenship portrayed in texts by Polish women after 1989, I would like to emphasize several theses that have emerged from my investigations.

The first is that there is a fundamental difference between women's melancholy as portrayed in these texts and traditional melancholic discourse. A different kind of loss and different means of dealing with it are presented: different themes, different linguistic choices, different genres, different strategies for reaching the reader.

Second, when examining melancholic prose texts, it is essential to distinguish between a *melancholic story* (i.e. one about melancholy, where the narrator and/or protagonist is faced for instance by illness, a narrative which is pessimistic, retrogressive, full of anxiety or fear, portraying a struggle with sorrow, or a process of becoming mute), and a *story about melancholy after the battle has been won* (e.g. against illness)—or from any conquering position, which includes consciousness of having been unfairly used or harmed by patriarchal culture, consciousness that as a result becomes revolutionary and seeks vindication. Sadness thus becomes an active critique of reality.

Third, which is a consequence of the second point, this subversive gesture expresses itself as an accusing one, and makes a plea for fundamental change—for example, a change in attitudes towards women who have lost preterm children through miscarriage (Justyna Bargielska's *Miscarriage Girls*), or a change in the social pressures to get married (Anna Janko's *The Girl with Matches* and Ewa Madeyska's *Katoniela*), or it expresses the truth about the loneliness of the women emigrant and the struggles involved in coping with the distance between her lost home and the alien place (Grzegorzewska).

Claiming normality—i.e. a space where the established norms of society (of any society, though here the emphasis is on Polish) accept the validity of women's experience—is often linked in women's literature to nomadism or vagrancy. A person who has observed something different (the traveller, the vagrant, the outcast, the emigrant) then sees the world—and her own society—in an altered light. Hence the frequent use by contemporary women writers of female protagonists who are tourists, travellers, nomads, vagabonds—they examine the world with fresh eyes, and like less and less what they see.

Meanwhile the instability of the contemporary world, the temporary nature of every state or theory, the impossibility of being right or wrong (in the long term), is likewise reflected in the melancholic themes of contemporary women's writing, both that inspired by actual emigration and that inspired by being an internal "exile" or "foreigner" ("cudzoziemka"). All stable categories—including the patriarchal—therefore require revisiting. In fulfilling this function, women's melancholy becomes an active and subversive gesture that looks forward to changing the world.

Bibliography

Primary sources

Bargielska, Justyna. 2010. *Obsoletki.* Wołowiec: Czarne.
Bator, Joanna. 2002. *Kobieta.* Warsaw: Twój Styl.
—. 2008. *Piaskowa góra.* Warsaw: WAB.
Dzido, Marta. 2003. *Małż.* Kraków Ha!Art.
Filipiak, Izabela. 1992. *Śmierć i spirala.* Wrocław: Wydawnictwo A.
—. 1995. *Absolutna amnezja.* Poznań: Observator.
—. 1997. *Niebieska menażeria.* Warsaw: Sic!
Gretkowska, Manuela. 1991. *My zdies' emigranty.* Kraków: Wydawnictwo X.
—. 1998. *Światowidz.* Warsaw: W.A.B.
—. 2008. *Obywatelka.* Warsaw: Świat Książki.
Grzegorzewska, Wioletta. 2012. *Notatnik z Wyspy.* Częstochowa: E-media.
Iwasiów Inga. 2008. *Bambino.* Warsaw: Świat Książki.
Kujawska Ewa. 2007. *Dom Małgorzaty.* Wołowiec: Czarne.
Madeyska, Ewa. 2007. *Katoniela.* Kraków: Wydawnictwo Literackie.
Miłosz, Czesław. 2001. *New and Collected Poems, 1931-2001.* London: Allen Lane.
Nasiłowska, Anna. 2002. *Księga początku.* Warsaw: W.A.B.
Orzeszkowa, Eliza. 1896. *Melancholicy. Nowele.* 2 vols. Warsaw: Gebethner i Wolff.
Pawluśkiewicz, Joanna. 2006. *Pani na domkach.* Kraków: Ha!art.
Plebanek, Grażyna. 2007. *Przystupa.* Warsaw: W.A.B.
Szymborska, Wisława. 1995. *View with a Grain of Sand: Selected Poems,* translated by Stanisław Barańczak and Clare Cavanagh. London: Faber.
Tokarczuk, Olga. 1996. *Prawiek i inne czasy.* Warsaw: W.A.B.
—. 1999. *Numery.* Wrocław: Ruta.
—. 2004. *Ostatnie historie.* Kraków: Wydawnictow Literackie.
—. 2007. *Bieguni.* Kraków: Wydawnictwo Literackie.

Secondary sources

Barbalet J.M. 1988. *Citizenship: Rights, Struggle, and Class Inequality.* Milton Keynes: Open University Press.

Bauman, Zygmunt. 2000. *Ponowoczesność jako źródło cierpień.* Warsaw: Sic!

Butler, Judith. 1990. *Gender Trouble: Feminism and the Subversion of Identity.* New York and London: Routledge.

—. 2007. *Who Sings the Nation-state? Language, Politics, Belonging*. London: Seagull.

Chowaniec, Urszula. 2010. "O widzialnych i niewidzialnych podróżniczkach w literaturze polskiej dekady 1997-2007." In *Od polityki do poetyki. Prace ofiarowane Stanisławowi Jaworskiemu,* edited by Cezary Zalewski, 269-295. Kraków: Universitas.

—. 2011a. "Displacement, Emigration, and Travel: Contemporary Polish Literature and the Notion of Émigré Literature." In *Contemporary Polish Migrant Culture and Literature in Germany, Ireland and the UK,* edited by Joanna Rostek and Dirk Uffelmann, 133-151. Frankfurt am Main: Peter Lang.

—. 2011b. "'Femme mélancolique,' czyli o pesymizmie najnowszej literatury kobiecej." In *Ćwiczenia z rozpaczy. Pesymizm w prozie polskiej po 1985 roku*, edited by Jerzy Jarzębski and Jakub Momro, 371-408. Kraków: Universitas.

—. 2012. "Feminism Today: Reflections on Politics and Literature." In *Women's Voices and Feminism in Polish Cultural Memory*, edited by Urszula Chowaniec and Ursula Phillips, 1-23. Newcastle: Cambridge Scholars Publishing.

Collins Hill, Patricia. 2000. "Gender, Black Feminism and Black Political Economy." *Annals of the American Academy of Political and Social Sciences* 568: 41-53.

Czapliński, Przemysław. 2001. *Wzniosłe tęsknoty. Nostalgie w prozie lat dziewięćdziesiątych.* Kraków: Wydawnictwo Literackie.

—. 2002. *Ruchome marginesy. Szkice o literaturze lat 90.* Kraków: Znak.

—. 2009. *Polska do wymiany. Późna nowoczesności i nasze wielkie narracje*. Warsaw: W.A.B.

Czerwińska Anna and Joanna Piotrowska, eds. 2009. *20 lat – 20 zmian. Kobiety w Polsce w okresie transformacji 1989-2009.* Warsaw: Fundacja Feminoteki.

Danilewicz-Zielińska, Maria. 1999. *Szkice o literaturze emigracyjnej półwiecza 1939-1999.* Wrocław: Ossolineum

Derrida, Jacques and Anne Dufourmantelle. 2000. *Of Hospitality*. Stanford, CA: Stanford University Press.

Drotkiewicz, Agnieszka and Anna Dziewitt. 2006. *Głośniej! Rozmowy z pisarkami*. Warsaw: Twój Styl.

Freud, Sigmund. 1985. "Civilization and Its Discontents." In his *Civilization, Society and Religion*, edited by Albert Dickson, 243-342. London: Penguin Books.

—. 1989. "Mourning and Melancholia". In *The Freud Reader*, edited by Peter Gay, 584-589. New York: W. W. Norton.

Gilbert, Sandra M. and Susan Gubar. 2000. *The Madwoman in the Attic: The Woman Writer and the Nineteenth-Century Literary Imagination*. 2nd ed. New Haven and London: Yale University Press.

Hoffman, Eva. 2005. *After Such Knowledge: A Meditation on the Aftermath of the Holocaust*. London: Vintage.

Iwasiów, Inga. 2002. *Rewindykacje. Kobieta czytająca dzisiaj*. Kraków: Universitas.

Jarzębski, Jerzy.1998. *Pożegnanie z emigracją. O powojennej prozie polskiej*. Kraków: Wydawnictwo Literackie.

Kępiński, Antoni. 1996. *Melancholia.* Warsaw: Muza.

Kristeva, Julia. 1989. *Black Sun: Depression and Melancholia,* translated by Leon S. Roudiez. New York: Columbia University Press

—. 1991. *Strangers to Ourselves*, translated by Leon S. Roudiez. New York: Columbia University Press

Lister, Ruth. 2003. *Citizenship: Feminist Perspectives*. Basingstoke: Palgrave Macmillan.

McAfee, Noëlle. 2004. *Kristeva*. London: Routledge.

Matynia, Elżbieta. 2009. *Performative Democracy*. Boulder, CO: Paradigm Publishers.

May, Joseph. 1999. *Nomadic Identities: The Performance of Citizenship*. Minneapolis, MN: University of Minnesota Press.

Mrozik, Agnieszka. 2010. "Motherhood as a Source of Suffering: On the Contemporary Polish Discourse of Maternity." In *Mapping Experience in Polish and Russian Women's Writing,* edited by Marja Rytkönen et al., 214-239. Newcastle upon Tyne: Cambridge Scholars Publishing.

—. 2012. *Akuszerki transformacji. Kobiety, literatura i władza w Polsce po 1989 roku.* Warsaw: Instytut Badań Literackich PAN.

Oleksy, Elżbieta. 2008. *Tożsamośc i obywatelstwo w społeczeństwie wielokulturowym.* Warsaw: PWN.

Penn, Shana. 2003. *Podziemie kobiet*. Warsaw: Rosner i Wspólnicy.

Stevenson, Nick. 2003. *Cultural Citizenship: Cosmopolitan Questions.* Maidenhead: Open University Press.

Szczuka, Kazimiera. 2006. *Pióro kobiece*. [Accessed 14 May, 2013] http://kobiety-kobietom.com/feminizm/art.php?art=3702

Szczuka, Kazimiera. 2008. *Rewolucja jest kobietą. Polityka*, 8 December. [Accessed 14 May, 2013] http://www.polityka.pl/kultura/276030,1,rewolucja-jest-kobieta.read

Szkot, Andrzej. 2004. *Leksykon pisarzy polskich przełomu XX i XXI wieku*. Toruń: Literat.

Szpakowska, Małgorzata. 2003. *Chcieć i mieć. Samowiedza obyczajowa w Polsce czasu przemian*. Warsaw: W.A.B.

Voet, Rian. 1998. *Feminism and Citizenship*. London: Sage Publications.

Wieczorkiewicz, Anna. 2008. *Apetyt Turysty. Doświadczenie świata w podróży.* Kraków: Universitas.

Marianna in Bluebeard's Castle: Tropes of Female Authorship in Izabela Filipiak's *Total Amnesia*

Monika ŚWIERKOSZ

> *Let's have a fairytale then. In Bluebeard, Bluebeard's wife has access to all the chambers in his castle except for one—even though she has the key, she is not allowed to enter. This fairy tale is different, though. The female writer in Bluebeard's castle avoids the forbidden chamber because she knows what is inside. She either intuits it or has no illusions about it. (Filipiak 1999)*

One of the most distinctive landmarks in the debate over the place of women's literature within the Polish literary canon, Izabela Filipiak's (b. 1961) essay *Monstrous Literature* (*Literatura monstrualna,* 1999), refers to the tale of Bluebeard. This story, well known from Charles Perrault's version in *Histoires ou Contes du temps passé* (1697), has been frequently invoked by feminist writers in order to lay bare the violence concealed in the patriarchal scenario of the relationship between the sexes, thereby undermining the ethical foundation of male power, and in order to restore women's power to create their own narrative and their own feeling of agency (Gajewska 2008, 138-150). However, with the metaphor of Bluebeard as the guardian of the canon, the author of *Total Amnesia* (*Absolutna amnezja,* 1995) leaves us disillusioned—no feminist revolt can take place within Bluebeard's castle, for two reasons. First, because female writers entering the canon prefer (or rather choose) not to know anything about the women that preceded them. They do not ask—just like Bluebeard's young wife—who his former, now absent wives were. This protects them from finding out the terrible truth about their own fate but also, as Filipiak believes, isolates them from tradition, turning them into "hungry spirits roaming the restrictive and bitterly heterosexual imaginarium" of literature (Filipiak 1999). Second, women's rebellion within the canon also becomes impossible since the female canonical writers (i.e. those few who have been accepted into the established canon), as opposed to the careless prying wife of Bluebeard, will never allow themselves insubordination, mutiny or misdemeanour, because they sense the consequences all too well. For the female canonical writers, the doorstep of the forbidden chamber remains a metaphorical boundary for what a woman should or should not do in "her husband's house," or rather—"in her father's house," since Izabela Filipiak re-writes the family metaphors on which her narration of Bluebeard is based.[1] By replacing the husband figure with the Father figure, she highlights the paternalism (and patriarchy) inherent in the West European definition of authorship or the literary tradition. If—as Harold Bloom claimed—the canon is formed solely as a result of battles between metaphorical "sons" and "fathers,"' then what role may a "daughter's" rebellion play in the process of literary succession? What fate awaits Bluebeard's daughter?

> She [Marianna] didn't like to question the prohibitions she faced, finding in that deceptive action a trap not unlike the one brought by the prohibition itself. She didn't wish to feel even more alienated among her own kind. On the contrary, she decided that if she accepted the house—the way it was—without protesting, without counterbalancing arguments, without judging, its constructions would gradually become transparent to her, it would cease to mean anything. (Filipiak 1995a, 49)

Marianna, the heroine of *Total Amnesia*, is twelve years old at the beginning of the novel, which takes on features of the *Bildungsroman* or story of maturation. She lives in a panoptical prison-house, ruled by her sinister, authoritarian father whom she refers to as the Secretary. Although the name has an ironic meaning here, since the man is in fact the insignificant chairman of a local political party cell—having obvious overtones of the former Communist Party—and financially dependent on his wife, his power nevertheless proves to have real consequences. This is true not just because Marianna's mother—a doctor and anti-communist activist—allows the family to be terrorized by her husband in order to gain for herself relative independence and inviolability in the public sphere; the illusion of paternal authority is also upheld by other traditional means—by the language of symbols that arouses both fear and jealousy in Marianna.

In this novel, the most significant attributes of male power are the perpetually locked, inaccessible room of the Secretary, and the massive wooden clock with a golden face standing inside it. The latter symbolizes the father's power not only over time, but also over the word itself—as he introduces his daughter to the realm of *Logos*:

> Something was almost over when he taught her to recognize letters; inviting her into the yet unknown territories of words, which by degrees became her own land, he deprived her at the same time of trust in this kind of cognition. (Filipiak 1995a, 21)

1 Filipiak refers in her essay to Maria Komornicka's tale *On Father and Daughter* (*O ojcu i córce*, 1900) in order to emphasize the destructive influence of the "Father's authority"—both on the limited number of women writers already accepted and operating within the canon, and those wishing to enter it. Father therefore controls the behaviour of both groups. Literary rebellion would be fatal to both.

The knowledge the father brings divides the daughter's world into some kind of "now" and "before"—thereby making him the patron both of her entry into the territory of her personal history to date (her past), and of her personal narration of that story from then on (her memory of her past). Thus, the Secretary gains power over Marianna's memory, and hence of her biography. The sight of the clock makes the girl feel uneasy and distrustful, even though it has stood idle ever since its mechanism was irreversibly damaged during an argument between Marianna's half-brother Antoni (they have the same mother but different fathers) and his stepfather.

The cobweb-ridden room belonging to the Secretary, locked and forbidden to Marianna, also fills her with ambivalent feelings of jealousy and fear. Even though she lives with her mother in a room not big enough to hold even a desk, she does not initially feel any need to break her father's ban. On the one hand, this is because she perceives anarchy, rebellion and transgression not as strategies leading to freedom but only as ways of deepening her—already painful—alienation. On the other hand, because she suffers from arachnophobia, she is simply afraid to enter the alien territory. Only after her house is visited by Turek—a school-friend and the leader of a boy's gang—does the girl become curious and brave enough to enter the forbidden room. In so doing, however, she feels anxious and struggles to overcome her fear and guilt. Meanwhile Turek, who after all is only a guest, interprets perfectly the map of power relations encoded in the layout of the Secretary's room. "Here resides the authority," he mutters, striding across the room towards the next set of glass doors, behind which he knows all the secrets are lodged. In the drawers of this inner sanctum he finds the Secretary's gold medals, which he examines with great care and undisguised fascination and then tries on. Even though—as he tries to convince Marianna—they are "worthless" to him, he steals one. Marianna sees it, but is initially unable to comprehend the meaning of this act.

Why and for what purpose does Turek—described as a young "barbarian"—take away a state order, a sign of submission to the power of authority? More importantly, how does a boy know about the most important and most carefully protected of all secrets, both the Secretary's and the teachers' at school: the secret phenomenon of child amnesia, which enables adults to shape their pupils' memories according to their own adult needs and objectives? Turek is the first to reveal to Marianna the truth about the institution of school: its main goal is not to teach or educate, but to train the pupils to gradually forget their own—often very traumatic—pasts. Later on the girl herself discovers a black box containing pornographic pictures of naked women and a newspaper article on the phenomenon of child amnesia in her father's bookcase (Filipiak 1995a, 85). Will the knowledge Marianna gains from her secret visits to the Secretary's "bloody chamber" finally show her the path to emancipation and free her from the constraint of paternal authority?

On the one hand, Marianna "grows up" as she comes to understand the controlling mechanisms behind the institutions of school and family, and joins Turek's band, which is preparing for an anarchist revolution (of their generation) against "the old" order, specifically the educational system. The local terrain consisting of a network of ex-German bunkers, reminiscent of the landscape around Gdynia where Filipiak herself grew up, and where the fictional gang hang out, is for a time Marianna's territory of alternative life, contestation, and relative freedom—even though the internal structure of the gang's power relations is based on a caste system and the primitive principle of the survival of the fittest. On the other hand, however, when the time of revolution finally comes, Marianna finds herself excluded—as the only girl—from the brotherly community of rebels. The turning point of the story comes when Marianna enters the headmaster's office. There, she recognizes the signs of the same kind of power from which she had been struggling to free herself. The sight of a massive wooden clock with its golden face in the corner of the room, and also of Turek, now sitting behind the headmaster's desk with the gold order stolen from the Secretary round his neck, recall the power of paternal authority.

The girl is amused by the recent "barbarian's" admiration for these symbolic and institutional signs of power, and this attitude excludes her from the rebellious community, and ultimately banishes her from the "story of youthful revolt." From this point on, Marianna feels as if she is in a bizarre dream "which was dreamt by someone else" (Filipiak 1995a, 98), as if she no longer participates in what is happening, but only observes it from a distance. The change is also visible in the attitude of her friends towards her—she is deprived of her role in the rebellion's scenario which they had planned together. This exclusion manifests itself in the denial of access to language:

> "Why didn't anyone call me?" She asked again.
>
> "That wasn't the most important thing," Turek explained with professional indifference.
>
> Somebody, nobody—she noticed they were talking code. Turek, changed now, had distanced himself into territories unknown. (Filipiak 1995a, 98)

Language creates and consolidates the "brotherly" community, thus revealing its strongly male and paradoxically inter-generational character, based on the tradition of handed-down paternal authority.

Significantly, and amazingly, the story of Turek's gang's rebellion anticipated a literary critical dispute about women's literature—or the so-called "menstrual" literature—that took place in Poland later in 1995, when the appearance of women writers on the literary stage (described by some critics as a "women's invasion") provoked highly ambivalent and sometimes openly negative reactions, even within the previously strong generational community of writers, both men and women, born in the early 1960s, who had been associated with the unofficial (or second-circulation) literary journal *bruLion* in the mid-to-late 1980s. This controversy over women's writing revealed the masculine, conventional and ideological character of literary categories, such as generation, literary conflict and canon itself, as well as the deep conservatism of many former "barbarians." Using family—or paternal—metaphors, Izabela Filipiak later tried to explain the phenomenon of "menstrual literature," which had emerged as a term of denigration in direct reaction to her novel and to the works of other female authors:

> This patronizing insult, spotted in a regional review and then retained unconsciously by Jan Błoński in his research, was passed down to younger men, who embraced it with a certain zeal, as if it were "fatherhood's" gift to "sonhood"; a small gesture, like the touch of a caring hand, a sign that there was a continuum. (Filipiak 1999)[2]

According to the author of *Total Amnesia*, this rhetorical gesture of insult—like institutional rape—was to help young men (young writers) construct and confirm their masculinity, and to sanction the authority of the stronger sex over the weaker sex passed on from generation to generation of men. What can Bluebeard's wife do if—in contrast to the promises in Perrault's version—the brothers do not come to rescue her, but collude with the old, rich and cruel husband (or father)?

After the failed *coup d'état* in her school, Marianna realizes that returning to the underground world of the bunkers will not be possible, because—for her—it can no longer be the place of resistance. The margins now appear to be not so much a negation of the centre, as its mirror image, while the breaking of taboos turns into a trap that makes one even more dependent on the system. This mechanism becomes apparent at the climax of Turek's story when, after a spectacular fall from the top of an industrial chimney (where he has fled to escape the police), he becomes the crippled hero of collective songs, perfectly fitting the Romantic religious myth of the Victim, the converted revolutionary (Filipiak 1995a, 116).

The knowledge which Marianna—the Daughter—gains after entering both her father's room and then the headmaster's office, is tragic: on the one hand, the violation of the prohibition seems a necessary stage on her road to emancipation; on the other, it does not guarantee freedom. Is her radical, yet unsuccessful rebellion also proof of the fact that a woman is inevitably trapped in patriarchal narration, and culturally unable to speak with her own voice? Can the fairy-tale plot used to describe the metaphorical situation of a female writer within the canon be subjected at all to feminist re-interpretation? Is it possible to leave Bluebeard's castle

2 For an overview of this dispute and the role of Błoński and other critics, see Chowaniec 2010, 156-157, and 2012, 31-32.

by another route than by opening the door to the "bloody chamber"? And where should Marianna—the Writer—go after she has discovered what lies inside it?

The traces of the author's (Filipiak's) *self* that may often be found in *Total Amnesia* give us a clue. In one of many paraphrases of parts of Marianna's diary, we find—re-written in the language of intertextual references—a memory of what she saw in her father's room.

In a fragment entitled *Laments* (*Treny*), by reproducing an imagined conversation between the Renaissance poet Jan Kochanowski (1530-1584) and his daughter Orszulka, to whom the poet dedicated a collection of now famous laments with this same title following her sudden death as a small child, the narrator lays bare the "pornographic" and "necrophiliac" aspect of art that makes the body of a dead woman-daughter the object of literary consumption. Suggesting the perverted, incestuous character of fatherly love, Marianna—the Writer—desecrates the literary monument which the *Laments* have become within the Polish literary canon. Yet it would seem that the narrator's aim is, above all, to reveal the relationship of power concealed in the traditional vision of authorship based on the paternal metaphor. It is precisely this relationship that conceals the trap condemning femininity to being no more than a beautiful "masculine vision," the ever tacit object of male worship or aggression. The feeling of confinement within the cage of masculine text that accompanies feminine writing in its initial stages, has been called the *anxiety of authorship* by certain feminist scholars (Gilbert and Gubar 2000, 45-92).

In the excerpt from Marianna's diary which opens *Total Amnesia*, she asks: "I watch, and at the same time I am observed. By whom? Who is my God?" (Filipiak 1995a, 8) In subsequent parts of the novel, the question of the authorship of the text, which we initially perceive as being a biographical record made up of the girl's memories, becomes much more problematic. Graphic breakdown of the narrative into first-person and third-person forms demonstrates that as a protagonist and as one of the narrators, Marianna is not the only trustee of her story, which is thus deprived of explicit authorization. What is more, *Total Amnesia* is not only the title of Izabela Filipiak's novel and of Marianna's diary, but also that of a "corrupt tale" written by Marianna's (female) teacher, Lisiak, in which she finds her "telepathically stolen" words. This woman, who may also be read as one of the future "adult" incarnations of Marianna, admits not only to a lack of power over her own text—"I don't know who puts them in relative order and completes the empty spaces with other clues, thus gracefully leading us astray" (Filipiak 1995a, 143)—but also to an accompanying sense of "fear of violation of a barely achieved harmony" (1995a, 142). Hence the question of literary authorship in *Total Amnesia* is intentionally rendered blurred and is inseparably connected to the fear experienced by the female writer of her own creative potential.

Furthermore, Marianna herself also turns out to be someone else's "incarnation," and her diary the record of another woman's experiences. It is the young Eliza Orzeszkowa (1841-1910), the well-known Polish novelist, creating under a table, away from her mother's reproachful gaze. In the notebook which she finds hidden in a table leg, Marianna recognizes traces of her own past, or maybe it's the other way round: she turns the apocryphal biography of the 19th-century writer into her own story. Thus the trope of authorship, which initially causes Marianna—the Writer—to perceive her own weakness and thus negate her own power over the text, ultimately leads to her regaining the rights over her own story. Through a writing strategy in which someone else's (here: another woman writer's) fragmented and disjointed biography serves as material for her own textual auto-creation, the girl begins to see in her own past or biography not only fear-inspiring echoes of her oppression, but also a space for subversive and life-saving plurality.

The recognition of her own power of authorship comes with her acceptance of womanhood. Menstrual blood, appearing symbolically in the place of sacrificial blood, is a sign here of the cultural emancipation of women's writing from the constraints of patriarchal norms. This positive experience of regained freedom coincides in time with the gruesome vision of the massacre of dolls organized by her father.

> On her way home from school, Marianna noticed smoke curling over the stream and ran to the back of the garden, straight to the kingdom of spiders. She was not afraid of them any more, at least since she discovered that a spider spins two threads, one sticky like a dream, in which it catches its prey, and another, on which it travels safely. She wanted to be like them in their creative artfulness [. . .]. (Filipiak 1995a, 225)

Overcoming her previous fear of spiders is testimony to Marianna's overcoming her "fear of authorship"—as indicated by the arachnological trope (Miller 1988; Szczuka 2001). The emancipation of Marianna the Writer is rooted in establishing distance between herself and the monstrous, yet ultimately absurd and only apparent authority of the Secretary. For the Secretary turns out to be living in the tragic prison of his own past: everything he does is shown to be merely a repetition of the humiliation he endured in a concentration camp during the German Occupation. What Marianna observes now is not so much a horrifying doll's "holocaust," as the Secretary casts them into the fire, but a spectacle of his weakness, arousing in her no longer fear, but pity. The girl's ironic comment addressed to her father when she sees the macabre scene—"What crime have they perpetrated?"—is a sign of this transformation.

This is why Marianna's childhood biography, discovered years later under the table, may be a positive point of reference for her. Her past, contrary to the

Secretary's wishes, has not been forgotten, but deposited in a safe place. Marianna reads it again, and despite the painful experiences, learns it by heart. She does not take it with her when she eventually decides to leave, but puts it back in the table-leg. Thus she reclaims power over that earlier time, which was previously at the exclusive disposal of the Secretary. With her eyes fixed on her own sundial, Marianna sets out on a journey "along the longest ray." Although she promises to return, she does not look back—the retrospective gesture could stop her on her way. On leaving Bluebeard's castle, Marianna regains symbolic control over her biography—both the past one and the future one.

Even though the text of *Total Amnesia* ends at this point, one is prompted to ask: What happened to Marianna after she left her father's house? Where did she go? Did she find a space of freedom as a writer, and if so, where? An answer may be found in the aforementioned essay "Monstrous Literature" in which Filipiak describes a seemingly perverse strategy of female authorship:

> When the canon's food becomes poisoned, she [the women writer] may become an autotrophic organism in order to survive. [. . .] She may find alternative sources of energy and light. She may become the parasite of the canon, use sources not intended for her use, and for her own pleasure interfere with the digestive processes. (Filipiak 1999)

Filipiak's speaking out against the authoritarian power of the (male) canon stems from her fundamental lack of belief in the possibility of it changing its internal, normative structure, even by incorporating new (female) texts into its framework. On the other hand, her position also undermines the relevance of establishing an alternative canon (let's call it: feminist) at its margins. Rather, it encourages individual attempts at anarchist contestation of any hierarchy. Filipiak does not ultimately reject the idea of canon—she appears to regard it as a "necessary hypothesis"—but she does liberate the mind from the limitations of dualistic thinking (in or out, canonical or non-canonical). In determining the place of a female writer within the literary canon, Filipiak goes beyond the opposition of interior and exterior. Instead of declaring a woman writer as belonging to one or other of the clearly defined canonical spaces (inside or outside), she prefers to place herself in the ambivalent, but also unconstrained, sphere of anarchy, where self-sufficiency mingles with parasitic dependency. Although Filipiak does not seek to support the canon unreservedly, she still wishes to remain within its reach—because this is the source of her subversive, "negative" (in the Kristevan sense) otherness, an idea she often refers to in her study of Maria Komornicka (Filipiak 2006). The fictional Marianna likewise uses the ambivalent space of her own past to construct and deconstruct her own genealogy as an author.

Bibliography

Chowaniec, Urszula. 2010. "'Intimately Social': The Experience of Menstruation in Polish Women's Writing." In *Mapping Experience in Polish and Russian Women's Writing,* edited by Marja Rytkönen et al., 150-170. Newcastle upon Tyne: Cambridge Scholars Publishing.

—. 2012. "Listening to Women's Voices: Historical Overview of Women's Right to Write in Poland." In *Women's Voices and Feminism in Polish Cultural Memory,* edited by Urszula Chowaniec and Ursula Phillips, 26-46. Newcastle upon Tyne: Cambridge Scholars Publishing.

Cyranowicz, Maria. 1999. "Z kim Izabela Filipiak dzieli własny pokój." In *Kobiety w literaturze,* edited by Lidia Wiśniewska, 59-65. Bydgoszcz: Wyższa Szkoła Pedagogiczna w Bydgoszczy.

Filipiak, Izabela. 1995a. *Absolutna amnezja.* 2nd ed. Warsaw: Państwowy Instytut Wydawniczy.

—. 1995b. "Niech się stanie sztuczność." [Interview with] Agnieszka Kosińska. *Dekada literacka* 4. Accessed 4 January, 2013. http://www.dekadaliteracka.pl/index.php?id=2342

—. 1996. "O pisarstwie kobiet." [Interview with] Bożena Keff. *Literatura na Świecie* 4: 202-219.

—. 1998. "Literatura jest rodzaju męskiego." [Interview with] Ewa Nawój and Paweł Głogowski. *Magazyn literacki* 1: 39-46.

—. 1999. "Literatura monstrualna." *Biuletyn OŚKi* 1: 1-3.

—. 2006. *Obszary odmienności. Rzecz o Marii Komornickiej.* Gdańsk: słowo/obraz terytoria.

Gajewska, Agnieszka. 2008. *Hasło: Feminizm.* Poznań: Wydawnictwo Poznańskie.

Gilbert, Sandra and Susan Gubar. 2000. *The Mad Woman in the Attic: The Woman Writer and the Nineteenth-Century Literary Imagination.* 2nd ed. New Haven, CT and London: Yale University Press.

Górnicka-Boratyńska, Aneta. 1997. "Odwrotna strona rzeczy, czyli dlaczego Izabela Filipiak jest pisarką feministyczną." In *Od kobiety do mężczyzny i z powrotem. Rozważania o płci w kulturze,* edited by Joanna Brach-Czaina, 330-352. Białystok: Trans Humana.

Helbig-Mischewski, Brygida. 1998. "Histeria historii i historia histerii. Jeszcze raz o *Absolutnej amnezji* Izabeli Filipiak i *E.E.*Olgi Tokarczuk." *Dykcja* 10: 49-59.

Janion, Maria. 1996. "Ifigenia w Polsce." In her *Kobiety i duch inności,* 319-344. Warsaw: Sic!

Miller, Nancy K. 1988. "Arachnologies: The Woman, the Text, and the Critic." In her *Subject to Change: Reading Feminist Writing,* 77-101. New York: Columbia University Press.

Szczuka, Kazimiera. 2001. "Prządki, tkaczki i pająki. Uwagi o twórczości kobiet." In her *Kopciuszek, Frankenstein i inne. Feminizm wobec mitu,* 27-44. Kraków: eFKa.

Szybowicz, Eliza. 2010. "Inne historie kobiet. Apokryfy feministyczne w prozie Izabeli Filipiak." In *Beatrycze i inne. Mity kobiety w literaturze i kulturze,* edited by Grażyna Borkowska and Lidia Wiśniewska, 34-44. Gdańsk: słowo/obraz terytoria.

Warkocki, Błażej. 2002. "Poszukiwanie języka. O twórczości Izabeli Filipiak." *Teksty drugie* 6: 92-112.

—. 2003. "Dziewczyna subwersywna. Wokół *Absolutnej amnezji* Izabeli Filipiak." In *W poszukiwaniu małej dziwieczynki,* edited by Izabela Kowalczyk et al., 97-104. Poznań: Konsola.

Homobiographies and Gay Emancipation

Błażej WARKOCKI

Epistemological breakthrough

In 2009, Polish sociologist, feminist, political activist and literary critic linked to the New Left magazine *Krytyka Polityczna*, Kinga Dunin (b. 1954), observed that:

> We live in a world where a proportion of people happen to have different sexual orientations, but just think of mainstream literature before the year 2000—it's overly populated by straights. I can now say, in all conscience, having been a keen reader of Polish literature for two years thanks to the Nike Literary Awards [established 1997; from 2007 Dunin was a judge—B.W.] that a gay or lesbian character appears in nearly each and every book. If a writer wants to create a so-called social environment and focus on different characters surrounding the protagonist, they inevitably include a gay or a lesbian, usually in the background. (Dunin and Stokfiszewski 2009, 84-85)

What is evident in this short fragment? First, that a rapid quantitative and qualitative change took place at the turn of the 20th and 21st centuries. New characters, virtually absent before, have entered the worlds presented in Polish prose. This change may not necessarily influence the other characters or values of these worlds, since it hinges simply on a kind of "de-naturalization" of *hetero*sexual identity, i.e. on questioning the assumption that heterosexual identity is the only legitimate or even possible one. In other words: the new protagonists of Polish prose are no longer deprived of their sexual identity.

Secondly, the homosexual taboo is fading. The absence in public discourse of the subject of homosexuality before 2000 (let's leave this approximate date, since it is not possible to establish a precise one) did not only affect Polish prose, but also other texts, including literary criticism or theoretical and cultural studies—hence texts which interpret Polish culture in general terms and contribute to its understanding. In all these contexts, the word "homosexuality" appeared extremely rarely and in an alienated manner, where no connection was made with other cultural phenomena. The word "homophobia" did not actually appear in mainstream cultural criticism. Feminist discourse, which entered the Polish cultural scene after 1989, constitutes an undoubted and valuable exception to a rule that tended to marginalize alterative discourses. Put in simple terms, most people were blind to homosexuality itself, to any potential problem associated with it and to any connection between it and Polish culture.

Swiss scholar, philologist and critic of Polish literature, German Ritz (b. 1951), who has contributed enormously to legitimizing reflection on male homosexuality in the discourse of Polish Studies as well as in Polish literary texts themselves, pointed to the research taboo as recently as in 2002, when he commented: "And what do Slavic people say about it? They remain silent" (Ritz 2002, 53). He used an obvious topos originating in the sphere of tabooism (silence). At the same time, he claimed that the lack of reflection on this topic resulted "not only from delay, which is the most frequently suggested cause on such occasions, but also from cultural differences." (Ritz, 53) These differences, however, may be best understood with reference to the dichotomy between "purity and danger," as described by Mary Douglas (2007). Thus the taboo to which Polish literature itself was subjected also affected relevant research into it, as well as the very development and reception of Polish culture as such. This fact is confirmed by Stefan Chwin's 1995 article "Protected Areas: Literature and Taboo in the Post-Yalta Era" ("Strefy chronione. Literatura i tabu w epoce pojałtańskiej"). The point is not that Chwin signals the taboo of homosexuality, but that he does *not mention it at all* (thus expressing even more powerfully the essence of the taboo in Mary Douglas's sense). Homosexuality was inexpressible and hence not subject to discoursivization.

A revolutionary change took place during the first decade of the 21st century, and affected all areas of culture. What was formerly not expressed became a productive literary and media topic. Therefore, it may be reasonable to assume that a unique *epistemological breakthrough* has been taking place in Polish culture during the past two decades.[1] This changing vision, however, is limited neither to a few "gay" novels which appeared in the period, nor to the media-made fetish of homosexuality or even politicization of homophobia, which happened concurrently. What is in question is a specific tectonic shift in culture and in cultural perception, which uncovered what had previously been invisible and now allowed discussion of what had previously been divulged only through silence. Adopting such a holistic anthropological vision allows one to better understand some of the changes that have taken place in the represented worlds of contemporary Polish literature.

---

1 The main thesis of this present chapter crystallized following a discussion at the Warsaw Lambda Association on 24 April 2009 between Tomasz Basiuk, Kinga Dunin, Krzysztof Tomasik, literary author Bożena Umińska and myself. (On Keff-Umińska, see the chapters by Katarzyna Zechenter, Jerzy Jarzębski and Grzegorz Niziołek in the current volume—Ed.).

(Homo-)Biography as a symptom of the times

As a result of the epistemological breakthrough, Polish writers (mainly of the 20th century) have gained a sexual identity which was hitherto transparent. This has become most apparent since the publication in 2008 and subsequent reception of Krzysztof Tomasik's (b. 1978) *Homobiographies: Polish Writers of the 19th and 20th Centuries* (*Homobiografie. Pisarki i pisarze polscy XIX i XX wieku*). The work comprises a series of essays about well-known figures from within the literary canon. Tomasik was most interested—not to ignore the elephant in the room, so to speak—in highlighting affirmed or suspected homosexuality. Apart from Michał Witkowski's novel *Lovetown* (*Lubiewo,* 2005), Tomasik's book had the greatest impact of works referring to such matters published in Poland after 1989.[2] However, his book is not a collection of fascinating gossip about the sexual lives of the Polish intelligentsia—quite the opposite. *Homobiographies* makes the reader aware that homosexuality is not a "fad" but a socio-cultural fact, a part of Polish culture and one of its salient narratives.

There exists nevertheless a subtle and significance difference between the private and the intimate. In his book, Tomasik—like any writer of biography, a fact that stems from the genre's very definition—deals with the private lives of his subjects. What is more, he expresses considerable respect and understanding regarding their life choices. Readers who have encountered *Homobiographies* solely by way of press reviews might receive the (incorrect) impression that the author is interested in intimate—i.e. sexual—matters. This issue is prominent in the reviews by Dariusz Nowacki (2008) and Jerzy Sosnowski (2008). From the perspective of psychoanalytical suspicion, such behaviour is symptomatic: the critics consciously select the scandalous detail (and then proceed to rail against it), ignoring the wider perspective of the whole. With regard to homosexuality, they see only and exclusively "sex," thus eliding "recognition" ("Annerkenung"), which is the actual crux of the matter at hand (Fraser 2005; Bobako 2010). These same critics responded in a similar way to the classic feminist text of the 1990s, Izabela Filipiak's 1995 novel *Total Amnesia* (Warkocki 2007, 154-157).

Homobiographies depicts a paradox. As Tomasik did not have access to certain confidential sources, he used what was already available (mainly published diaries or correspondence), thus voicing what was already generally known, albeit mostly among literary specialists. Still, this "what" had been extensively camouflaged and had not undergone cultural processing or interpretation. It was a secret, but an "open" one—and all "open secrets" have the projective quality of searching for a scapegoat (Sedgwick 1990, 65). A list of synonyms could now also be

2 He has recently published a book on sexual minorities in the pre-1989 communist period (Tomasik 2012).

compiled of strategies euphemizing homosexuality: how to say without telling, or how not to tell everything. In this sense, Tomasik's book names the "open secret" of homosexual identity and demonstrates how it functions within the very centre of Polish culture, how it comprises in fact an essential part of it.

The book also describes a certain unprocessed mourning fostered by the open secret. A characteristic example is the poet Jan Lechoń (1899-1956). An acclaimed "wonder child" of Polish literature, a conservative homosexual, an opponent of communist power, a suicide victim repeatedly "ushered into the closet," and recently an example within right-wing discourse of a "good homosexual."[3] Judging by Tomasik's book, much was done to suppress any attempts to interview Aubrey Johnston (residing in the USA), Lechoń's long-term partner. Biographers were turned away with a slip of paper by Johnston's family and friends; in the best-case scenarios, he was ignored as a "nobody." Not only does this impoverish Polish culture, it also represents symbolic violence against a particular person. The right to a legal union or partnership—frequently invoked in Poland today—is not what is at stake here, however; what is at stake is the right to legal mourning. To be able to publicly express the same pain, to which every heterosexual (following the death of a husband or wife) has a right.

Tomasik's book begs the question as to whether Aubrey Johnston was at Lechoń's funeral? Perhaps he should have been the one to organize it? In truth, his story was dramatic: at the moment of his partner's suicide, he was in Europe and unknowingly sent a few months' worth of letters to an already dead Lechoń. He quickly became illegal, deprived of the right to express any sentiments—and what is most important: the right to legal mourning (Butler 2010). There are many similar stories scattered throughout Tomasik's work.

Today, following *Homobiographies*, it should be quite clear that proponents of the homosexual "closet" are working to the detriment of Polish culture. An extensive interview with Johnston would have been an enormous contribution; it would undoubtedly have enhanced, for instance, the "Więź" edition of Lechoń's collected works that appeared in the mid-2000s. It would have been fascinating and immensely important. Unfortunately, the pro-closet agenda prevailed: Aubrey Johnston died in 2003 and so will divulge no more.

Homobiographies was widely reviewed, and variously received. One is even tempted to entertain the conclusion that Tomasik's book fulfilled the role of *naming* the homosexual secret within Polish culture. In a competent and unpretentious manner, Tomasik provides an account of a self-evident yet complicated issue: the homosexual lives of many actors in the Polish literary canon. The reactions of

---

[3] In right-wing (conservative) discourse, a "good" homosexual is one who never talks about homosexuality and remains in the closet.

both liberals and conservatives have been interesting. Tomasz Terlikowski, a well-known Polish Catholic publicist, declared that we were dealing with the "apotheosis of sin" (2008, 23) even though Jarosław Iwaszkiewicz (1894-1980), another writer with a homosexual past, praised his own marital state until his death—so perhaps was not so entirely deserving of hell? Meanwhile "liberals" (or so-called "liberals"), such as the already mentioned Dariusz Nowacki and Jerzy Sosnowski, also joined the guardians of the "homosexual closet."

The general picture of the book's reception therefore emerges as follows: According to the conservative stance, *Homobiographies* is an aggressive attack on "our" culture (by apotheosizing homosexual sin); liberal opinion, meanwhile, writes it off as blather or gossip, yet in its reinterpretation of homosexual sublimation as simply emancipation, it may prove in the end to be dangerous.

The most symptomatic voice here is that of Dariusz Nowacki. Before turning to a closer analysis of Nowacki, however, one remark must be made. Tomasik's book was much more positively received by certain conservatives: the author of a clandestine review in the Catholic newspaper *Nasz Dziennik*, Stanislaw Krajewski (who does not mention *Homobiographies* explicitly, although the bulk of the review deals with this very work), identifies the book's central issue more perceptibly than Nowacki: namely that the issue is one of redefining culture towards a state where homosexuality is no longer condemned to formal silence. However, Krajewski puts the matter somewhat differently: "The perversion of human gender alongside the destruction of morality must bring negative repercussions to bear on many orders, and in the case of writers, also on the literary order." (Krajewski 2008, 10) Interestingly, this anti-homosexual author paradoxically becomes an "essentialist" like certain pro-homosexual commentators: homosexuality in his view "actively inscribes itself within the very texture of the text," to borrow German Ritz's formulation (Ritz 1990, 54).

Tomasik wrote a book that is popular and journalistic in nature, not academic—not to mention the sales factor, of which the author is completely entitled to take advantage. The book has nevertheless provided encouragement to academics in treating the structural meaning of homosexuality in Polish culture in the second half of the 19th and 20th centuries, in a scholarly fashion. No one has attempted this until now. Tomasik gave us a great work of pop-biography. However, the door is now open to scholars to "queer" Polish culture, meticulously considering every nuance of "historical and cultural contexts, aesthetic paradigms, and societal norms," as Nowacki rightly suggests (2008, 4). It should also be noted that some progress has indeed been made, particularly in the work of German Ritz, in his book on Iwaszkiewicz, and in the ground-breaking *Regions of Otherness: On Maria Komornicka* (*Obszary odmiennosci. Rzecz o Marii Komornickiej,* 2007) by lesbian writer and literary historian Izabela Filipiak (b. 1961). Still, embarrassingly little is known about homosexuality in Polish culture, especially when compared to the number of English-language texts now available on West European culture and literature.

Nowacki perpetuates the typical assertion of the threat posed by emancipation to "real" literature as well as—presumably—to the world order. In former times, according to Nowacki, writers' "hiding" was beautiful and their literature sublime and eloquent. Today, everything has been "banalized," and homosexuality may be mocked on television. In reality, homosexuality is in fact banal, but it is difficult to maintain that such former restrictions were a necessary condition for creating "real" literature. What is more, this conveys a cynical vision of human nature. The fact that homosexuality can now be discussed with ease does not mean that people no longer feel its burden. Dariusz Nowacki unwittingly points to the essential meaning of "the epistemology of the closet" (as coined by Eve Sedgwick) in the construction of Polish high modernism, referring here specifically to Iwaszkiewicz, a modernist poet and prose writer who, at the same time, is now perceived as a kind of emblem of (homosexual) modernism in Poland. Identifying the conditions for this "closeting" (using Nowacki's review as an interesting and symptomatic starting point) might be one important task for future research.

Dariusz Nowacki also remarks, "This pertains also to the media reception, to events that 'might change the way homosexuality is perceived in the public sphere' [he quotes from Tomasik's introduction—B.W.]. Here the jokes stop. Tomasik has no regard for high literary culture." (Nowacki 2008, 6) Let us consider for a moment what the critic is really saying: why do the jokes stop when matters come to an alleged "change in perception"? Why would such a change in the way homosexuality is perceived be wrong, particularly in light of the communist police's anti-gay "Hiacynth" Initiative (1985-1987) or the ideological homophobic paranoia typical of the so-called Fourth Republic (2005-2007), or when homosexuals are faced with the possibility of being outlawed from teaching in schools (in which there are, of course, homosexual teachers anyhow, but on that occasion they were more effectively intimidated than ever[4])? The notion suggested by Nowacki implies a sacralization of violence in the name of some vision of "real" Literature. Such a vision of Polish high modernism—flawed, yet symptomatic of a particular way of thinking—stands guard armed with violence, as embodied in the figure of the "closet."

4 In March 2007 the Polish Ministry of National Education (then headed by Roman Giertych) announced the preparation of draft legislation "banning the promotion of homosexuality and other deviations." Disciplinary dismissals for those who "promote homosexuality" were also announced. It is worth noting that there were no reactions at the time from other institutions (for example universities), but this draft never became law.

The coming-out story

One of the most important narrative structures generated by emancipation is the coming-out story.[5] Its form today tends to follow a clear, fixed and rigid pattern. Let us examine how it was created and how it has evolved.

One of the first stories about gays that appeared on the Polish literary scene after 1989 was the novel by Marcin Krzeszowiec (b. 1958), *The Pain of Existence* (*Ból istnienia,* 1992), now more or less forgotten. In contrast to a number of other authors, Krzeszowiec made no effort to secure his position by using meta-texts to inform the reader he was merely investigating an interesting phenomenon with which he had nothing in common. Quite the reverse—he even suggests an autobiographical pact. *The Pain of Existence* is a complex novel about the life of a gay man at the end of the 1980s which clearly uses an assimilation strategy. It portrays the loneliness and alienation of the hero, and the destructive force of social homophobia, which (in case of the main hero) even results in masochistic self-depreciation. The reader is supposed to understand and sympathize with the message: homophobia is killing us softly.

A similar kind of story can be found in the reportages of Mariusz Szczygieł (b. 1966), where the author refers to a thread in his writings from the 1980s: After publishing an article about homosexuality, a youth magazine receives a plethora of letters from homosexuals (men and women) writing about their loneliness, alienation, unhappiness, invisible stigma and suicidal attempts. What is particularly interesting in this story is the fact that no negative responses come from readers. Not a single letter is received by the editorial office of *Across Country* (*Na przełaj*, for which Szczygieł used to work) protesting against raising the topic of homosexuality in a youth magazine. This prompted the editorial staff to contrive reactions. The reception of *The Pain of Existence* reveals something similar—nobody noticed the novel and it was engulfed by complete silence. A clear difference is evident when such reaction—or rather lack of reaction—is juxtaposed with the situation after 2004, especially following the "Let Them See Us" ("Niech nas zobaczą") action launched in 2003 by the Campaign against Homophobia (which made gayness visible in Polish public discourse).[6] This difference can be inter-

---

5 I mean here: gay coming outs. I will not discuss the lesbian version, which is slightly different and deserves separate treatment.

6 The "Let Them See Us" Campaign was the first socio-artistic campaign to counter homophobia in Poland, and was organized by the Campaign against Homophobia (Kampania przeciw homofobii) in 2003. It presented thirty gay and lesbian couples in photographs that were prominently displayed on billboards in Poland's major cities and in public art galleries. The photos were taken by Karolina Breguła. The campaign initiated a breakthrough in public discourse. It was the beginning of visible LGBT activism in Poland. A year later, in 2004, mayor Lech Kaczyński banned the Gay Pride (Equality) Parade in Warsaw.

preted as follows: silent popular homophobia started to become political. According to the mechanisms observed by postcolonial theory, it could be argued that the ever greater emphasis placed in public discourse (by government, mainstream media) on so-called "real" national identity now encountered an additional Stranger (not merely "the Other"); constructing the homosexual as nationally-alienated derives from the fantasy of a real, unchangeable core of national identity (Czapliński 2009).

As can be seen, the coming-out story from the beginning of the 1990s is denied existence because the other party, the heteronormative Other, is not willing to listen. What happens when it makes the effort? Using this perspective, let us examine the story *Greek God* (*Grecki bożek,* 1993) by Marek Nowakowski (b. 1935), from the volume of the same title. It is a story about a writer who establishes, by chance, contact with a homosexual man. The "true masculinity" of Jureczek, who—in this respect—is portrayed positively in comparison with other clients of the "Alhambra" café, becomes the platform of communication. Jureczek relates to the writer—who is at the same time the first-person narrator—his life story. The life of a homosexual. The writer listens patiently and sympathetically, and—somewhat surprisingly—does not present any counter-discourse, which might serve as a heterosexual safety-valve or "heterosexual buffering" (Sedgwick 1990, 82). In this way, the reader can compare two existential propositions: that of the writer-artist and that of the homosexual. It is clear from the very beginning that the first option is the only realistic choice (*nota bene* the option already chosen by the writer). Thus the coming-out story by Marek Nowakowski ends with a downfall: the downfall of noble (ethically and aesthetically) masculinity. In this story, coming-out and the choice of a homosexual lifestyle are bound to lead to downfall and bodily degradation. There is no room for a happy end. It is better to be an artist than a homosexual.

As a number of critics have noted, *Lovetown* (*Lubiewo,* 2005) by Michał Witkowski (b. 1975) became the turning point, a kind of caesura. The work does not become involved in considerations about gay identity, which it defines for its own purposes. However, coming-out and its possible consequences constitute a boundary also in this story. Coming out is actually the final element in the plot of *Lovetown*. We are introduced to the story of Michalina in a conversation between two friends, one of whom—significantly, it transpires—is planning to go to the opera:

> "Everything, everything, all fatuous twaddle – published! People know about everything now! About the blowjobs, everything, all of it! And just look what happened to Michalina! First they threw her out of every place they could, out of the university, and they took all her money, but what's worse, she's contracted some kind of leprosy! She's lost an eye, half her face is covered in boils, she must be having a relapse. Michalina escaped back to

Switzerland last night, to Zurich [...]. [...] suffice it to say Michalina never made it to Zurich, she ended up going on foot to Roulettenburg, and now she's there playing pontoon on the slot machines, and roulette... She's saving money for plastic surgery! She's never coming back, they say, and she's done with writing, too!" (Witkowski 2005, 290-291; 2010, 336-337).

Michał Witkowski theatricalizes the effect of coming out and, for this reason, refers to *Dangerous Liaisons* (the film version). It is there, at the opera, where the double life of the Marchioness de Merteuil and her hidden secrets are made public. The intended impact of Witkowski's gesture is clear: the potential effect of coming out can be enormous. Coming out is not limited to merely uncovering oneself—it also exposes others living in the closet. The transformative power of "coming out" can be huge and not necessarily positive as it shatters the sensitive, symbolic network of social relations. The final, theatricalized fantasy about "coming out" of both narrator and author (since both instances are deliberately intertwined thereby paying tribute to the sound assumption that whoever writes about "this" topic must surely be involved in it) demonstrates just how strong the metaphor of "inside"/"outside" the closet of privacy remains, confirming also that it does not easily surrender its hold on important mainstream forms of social signification (Sedgwick 1990, 67).

However, does it always have to be like this? Is it possible to find stories about gays which do not follow—more or less directly—narrative schemes focusing on coming out? We shall use this different perspective to examine two novels: *Sand Mine* (*Kopalnia piasku,* 2009) by Paweł Góral (b. 1977) and *Gestures* (*Gesty,* 2008) by Ignacy Karpowicz (b. 1976).

Sand Mine is a debut novel drawing on a number of formats taken from popular literature (the adventure novel, thriller, romance). What is interesting is that the main hero has a homosexual affair, yet it happens only in the second half of the novel. The first part does not even anticipate it. There is not the slightest indication anticipating (and explaining to the reader) what will happen later. The hero is not particularly sensitive to art, does not enjoy listening to opera; nor does he listen to the newest hits of Madonna. On the contrary, while at secondary school, Paweł had an affair with his female teacher, hence nothing foreshadows any deviation from the normative rules of heterosexual romance. Only when he is abroad—an experience which functions rather like a *deus ex machina*—does he enter into a same-sex romance. And although he expresses his views on a variety of topics (films as well as the attacks on the World Trade Centre in September 2001), he has a distinct problem in explaining what happens to himself.

His lover, a PhD history student awarded a scholarship to Berlin, uses a specific style of narration. He presents a kind of simplified version of the modernist sublimation of homosexuality, but at the same time compensatory version of his own identity:

> "Without homosexuals, humanity would never have taken a step forward. The best painters, writers, architects, philosophers and spies felt affection for people of the same sex. The names which make one feel most proud are Michelangelo and Leonardo da Vinci." After mentioning these, there followed a meaningful silence in order to intensify the dramatic effect. Then other names: "Tchaikovsky, Proust, Tolstoy, Wilde and Szymanowski." (Góral 2009, 239)

This legitimizing narration, which is supposed to explain the turning point in Paweł's identity, is received by him with considerable distance (depicted in the irony echoed in the above quotation). For the hero does not want to see his same-sex relationship through the prism of his own identity. The novel clearly shows that it is impossible to act in a non-normative way. If one is part of a same-sex relationship, one has to be homosexual and recognize oneself in one of the already available formative narratives (such as those of the distinguished real artists mentioned in the lover's list). Paweł's lover is eventually murdered after his return to Poland, while Paweł himself dreams about having a wife. *Sand Mine* clearly shows that—to use a metaphorical shortcut—Poland kills off sexually different people, and the only reasonable form of existence is to return to the normative heterosexual story.

Gestures by Ignacy Karpowicz is an excellent psychological novel about a complex relationship between a mother and a son (who is clearly a beneficiary of transformative change in Poland). However, referring to a different order, it is a story about heterosexual melancholy, about the longing for what is impossible—even to imagine it, i.e. the intimacy between one man and another man. A kiss exchanged with a friend from the protagonist's youth, theoretically having no meaning, becomes a sign of this longing. The ambiguous ending of the novel (the friend reappears after the protagonist's death) points to the particular meaning of the kiss as "a sign of the impossible." *Gestures* appears to avoid the coming-out convention and also, as a consequence, obvious identity labels (the implication is that "this" can happen to anyone). Such avoidance may be the reason why this very subtle thread was not noticed by critics (although the novel was highly praised and nominated for the Nike award). If there is no coming-out, the story of same-sex love becomes invisible, transparent. It does not exist.

However, we can appreciate the significance and success of the coming-out story and its form of narrative structure if we juxtapose two autobiographical stories about homosexuality, published in 2010 but written in two different periods: the second volume of Jarosław Iwaszkiewicz's *Diary* (1956-1963) and Michał Głowiński's (b. 1934) *Circles of Alienation* (*Kręgi obcości*).

The main subtext of the second volume of the *Diary* is an introspective narration of Jarosław Iwaszkiewicz's love for the much younger Jerzy Błeszyński. Iwaszkiewicz is an excellent diarist. This second volume could be recognized moreover as one of the most blatantly homosexual Polish texts of the 20th century—as the novel Iwaszkiewicz never actually wrote as part of his official works. The impression that he might have done this on purpose is striking. It is not without reason that his first meeting with Jerzy Błeszyński is recorded in a note which then becomes an attempt at a short story. And it is likewise not without reason that he is fascinated by the biography of André Gide and the sincerity which he himself, in his literary texts, cannot afford. In his private notes, Iwaszkiewicz chose the formula "poetics of love expressed" rather than "the poetics of inexpressible desire," which is German Ritz's formula (2005, 254-276).

The poet's affair with the young man is also set within a complex emotional network. Iwaszkiewicz has a wife whom he loves and who provides him with stability. Błeszyński had a wife whom he divorced. He also has a female lover. Both of them have children and Iwaszkiewicz a grandson in addition. At no point in the story does even a nebulous vision of coming out occur. Such a possibility—let alone an obligation—simply does not exist. The utopia of a non-heteronormative reality is not located in the future but, for Iwaszkiewicz, in the past, in Ancient Greece for instance.

Michał Głowiński's autobiographical novel, in contrast, implements precisely coming-out narrative structures. Hence we, the readers, are confronted by the pain of discovering one's own dissimilarity, by searching for the terrifying term "homosexuality" in the pre-war dictionary, by alienation, loneliness, love triggering a desire to embrace the world (in Paris, not in Poland, which is also symptomatic); in the end, however, we do have a form of therapy which allows confession, precisely a book. The public coming-out must have been a difficult experience, yet the story itself uses the familiar patterns of coming-out narration.

This gay story, this structure of narration, has not been in existence since time immemorial. It has gradually come into being. Thanks to parades, texts, disputes, coming-outs, small and large-scale ones, media ones and modest ones—it has been made possible, in other words, thanks to the whole discursive machinery. If it had been not for these, Michał Głowiński's story would not exist in the form we know it. Nor would its calm reception.[7]

---

[7] Głowiński's biography enjoyed a very positive reception. See for example *Kwartalnik Artystyczny* 2010 (2), which discusses his book and includes reviews by Julia Hartwig, Wojciech Gutowski, Wojciech Ligęza, Jacek Łukasiewicz, Arkadiusz Morawiec, Krzysztof Myszkowski, Andrzej Skrendo, Leszek Szaruga, Piotr Szewc and Wojciech Tomasik.

Conclusion

Perhaps Głowiński's book is the one that best summarizes twenty years of gay emancipation in Poland, but it does so, as it were, unintentionally. Today one thing is certain: virtually all stories about homosexuality published in Poland since the mid-2000s follow one of the narrative variants of the coming-out formula.

I have tried to present the most important parameters of an epistemological breakthrough in Polish literary culture that has taken place during the past two decades. Analysis of Krzysztof Tomasik's book *Homobiographies* demonstrated a symptomatic response to the disclosure of the "open secret" of homosexuality in Polish culture. In the second part of my analysis, I have tried to pinpoint the most characteristic reaction to this situation—the evolution of the coming-out narrative. However, I remain convinced that the relationship between Polish culture and (especially male) homosexuality is still not going well and that we will have to wait for new instalments of this particular novel in future.

Bibliography

Primary sources

Głowiński, Michał. 2010. *Kręgi obcości. Opowieść autobiograficzna*. Kraków: Wydawnictwo Literackie.

Góral, Paweł. 2009. *Kopalnia piasku*. Poznań: Zysk i S-ka.

Iwaszkiewicz, Jarosław. 2010. *Dziennik. Tom II: 1956–1963*, edited by Agnieszka Papieska, Robert Papieski and Radosław Romaniuk. Warsaw: Czytelnik.

Karpowicz, Ignacy. 2008. *Gesty*. Kraków: Wydawnictwo Literackie.

Krzeszowiec, Marcin. 1992. *Ból istnienia*. Poznań: Softpress.

Nowakowski, Marek. 1993. *Grecki bożek*. Warsaw: Wydawnictwo Alfa.

Witkowski, Michał. 2005. *Lubiewo*. Kraków: Korporacja Ha!art.

—. 2010. *Lovetown*, translated by William Martin. London: Portobello.

Secondary sources

Bobako, Monika. 2010. *Demokracja wobec różnicy. Multikuturalizm i feminizm w perspektywie polityki uznania*. Poznań: Wydawnictwo Poznańskie.

Butler, Judith. 2010. *Żądanie Antygony. Rodzina między życiem a śmiercią*, translated by Mateusz Borowski and Małgorzata Sugiera. Kraków: Księgarnia Akademicka.

Chwin, Stefan. 1995. "Strefy chronione. Literatura i tabu w epoce pojałtańskiej." *Res Publica Nowa* 10: 21-29.

Czapliński, Przemysław. 2009. *Polska do wymiany. Późna nowoczesność i nasze wielkie narracje*. Warsaw: W.A.B.

Douglas, Mary. 2007. *Czystość i zmaza*, translated by Marta Bucholc and introduced by Joanna Tokarska-Bakir. Warsaw: Państwowy Instytut Wydawniczy.

Dunin, Kinga and Igor Stokfiszewski. 2009. "Biseksualizm czy kapitalizm? Rozmawiają: Kinga Dunin i Igor Stokfiszewski." *Krytyka Polityczna* 19: 80-94.

Filipiak, Izabela. 2007. *Obszary odmienności. Rzecz o Marii Komornickiej.* Gdańsk: słowo/obraz terytoria.

Fraser, Nancy and Axel Honneth. 2005. *Redystrybucja czy uznanie. Debata polityczno-filozoficzna*, translated by Monika Bobako i Tomasz Dominiak. Wrocław: Wydawnictwo Naukowe Dolnośląskiej Szkoły Wyższej Edukacji TWP.

Krajewski, Stanisław. 2008. "Homoseksualiści i kultura." *Nasz Dziennik*, 29 May: 6.

Mizielińska, Joanna. 2006. *Płeć, ciało, seksualność. Od feminizmu do teorii queer.* Kraków: Universitas.

Nowacki, Dariusz. 2008. "Niedźwiedzia przysługa." *Gazeta Wyborcza*, 27 May: 17.

Ritz, German. 1996. *Jarosław Iwaszkiewicz: Ein Grenzgänger der Moderne.* Slavica Helvetica 47. Bern: Peter Lang.

—. 2002. *Nić w labiryncie pożądania. Gender i płeć w literaturze polskiej od romantyzmu do postmodernizmu*, translated by Bronisław Drąg, Andrzej Kopacki and Małgorzata Łukasiewicz. Warsaw: Wiedza Powszechna.

—. 2005. "Inexpressible Desire and Narrative Poetics: Homosexuality in Iwaszkiewicz, Breza, Mach and Gombrowicz." In *Gender and Sexuality in Ethical Context: Ten Essays on Polish Prose,* edited by Knut Andreas Grimstad and Ursula Phillips, 254-276. Slavica Bergensia 5. Bergen: Department of Russian Studies.

Sedgwick, Eve Kosofsky. 1990. *Epistemology of the Closet*. Los Angeles, CA: University of California Press.

Sosnowski, Jerzy. 2008. "Gej przed Noblem." *Przekrój*, 12 August.

Szczygieł, Mariusz. 2009. "Rozgrzeszanie w PRL." *Replika* 19: 7-8.

Terlikowski, Tomasz. 2008. "Apoteoza grzechu." *Gazeta Polska,* 7 May: 23.

Tomasik, Krzysztof. 2008. *Homobiografie. Pisarki i pisarze polscy XIX i XX wieku.* Warsaw: Wydawnictwo Krytyki Politycznej.

—. 2012. *Gejerel. Mniejszości seksualne w PRL.* Warsaw: Wydawnictwo Krytyki Politycznej.

Warkocki, Błażej. 2007. *Homo niewiadomo. Polska proza wobec odmienności.* Warsaw: Sic!

Women's Archives as Literary Storerooms: Identity Politics in Women's (Auto-)Biographies

Agnieszka MROZIK

> *[...] the historical sense involves a perception, not only of the pastness of the past, but of its presence [...].*
> *(Eliot 1950, 4)*

> *Nostalgia, by sanctioning and soothing utopian images of the past, lets people adapt both to rapid social change and to changes in individual life histories—changes in the latter case, that may lead into social roles and positions in which individual agency, sense of identity and participation in community are severely restricted.*
> *(Tannock 1995, 461)*

Identity, memory and power

The beginning of the 21st century saw an abundance of biographical and autobiographical publications appearing on the Polish publishing market. Currently readers can choose from a wide range of memoirs, journals, diaries, family saga novels, family albums, (auto-)biographies, of which the vast majority were written and published after 1989 but are focused on the period of World War II or the earlier interwar period. Some authors reach back as far as the second half of the 19th century or the turn of the century. Gradually, publications relating to more recent times, namely to the People's Republic of Poland (1945-1989), also began to appear (Tazbir 2006). Amongst the authors of these memoirs, there are many women: writers, artists, journalists, researchers in the field of literature and culture, who often intertwine into an inseparable whole their own biographies and histories of their families with the Big History going on in the background (Czerska 2008).

The fundamental question which I shall attempt to answer in this chapter is the following: why have so many family stories or (auto-)biographical stories with strong family contexts or backgrounds appeared on the bookshelves just now, more than ten years after the overthrow of communism?[1] What is the reason for this popularity, which makes these texts interesting not only as a literary phenomenon, but also, and perhaps more importantly, as a cultural and social one? What role do they play in the process of social, economic and cultural transformation in which we are not only witnesses but also participants?

As has been pointed out by researchers investigating the social phenomena connected with the writing and publishing of memoirs, the imperative to return to one's roots originates in the urge to make coherent and reliable statements about the identity of individuals and communities. The changes that have taken place in Poland and in Eastern and Central Europe generally after 1989 have initiated a process of reconstructing a national identity. Built on the ruins of empire and in opposition to it, in a therapeutic effort to work through the collective trauma, this identity turns to those moments from history that might constitute a solid and immutable point of reference (Said 1994). The politics of re-evaluating and revising history, evident in the actions of every Polish government since 1989, favours recollecting the history of independent Poland (1918-1939) and points to "freedom" as the determining factor in the integrity and coherence of collective identity. This is why in public discourse after 1989 (and I consider autobiographical literature to be a part of this discourse) there are so many nostalgic returns to the history of interwar Poland. This was the period when the sovereign independent state was reborn and the national biography consolidated, while the more recent history of World War II, and especially of People's Poland, is associated with decline, rupture and discontinuity, and has only recently become an object of systematic "biographical work."

The past-centred orientation of modern historical, social and political thought validates the past as a foundation on which both individual and collective identity are built. French historian Pierre Nora notes that we are living in "times of memory," in which only the recollection of the past constitutes a fixed point of reference for individuals and communities in a situation where the shape of the future is uncertain, and where this uncertainty "transposes to the present" (Nora 2001, 37, 40). In a postmodern society, the quest for personal identity comes full circle as the desire to deconstruct identity transmutes into a need to recreate it. This is why writing memoirs can be considered a symptom and indeed an expression of longing for a continuous, rooted identity as well as participation in a larger community.

[1] The research project from which the current chapter has emerged was funded by the National Centre for Science (Narodowe Centrum Nauki), decision reference number: DEC-2011/01/N/HS2/03256. An expanded version of the current chapter appeared in my recent book in Polish (Mrozik 2012, 279-352).

In autobiographies by women, the aforementioned longings, fears and needs are combined with attempts to reconstruct identity both in a personal and collective sense. The culture of individualism, which appeared in Poland after 1989, favours creating stories about the experiences of individual women and stressing the psychological dimension to identity. On the other hand, the history of female experience that emerges from the texts I have analysed is so strongly rooted in family—or more broadly—national history, that any discussion of the identity of women seems inseparable from discussion of national identity. In this chapter I shall examine the following texts: *In the Garden of Memory* (*W ogrodzie pamięci*, 2006) by Joanna Olczak-Ronikier (b. 1934), *A Young Lady in People's Poland* (*Panienka w PRL-u*, 2007) by Jolanta Wachowicz-Makowska (b. 1943), *Frascati Street: An Apotheosis of Topography* (*Frascati. Apoteoza topografii*, 2009) by Ewa Kuryluk (b. 1946), *Here You Go* (*Proszę bardzo*, 2009) by Anda Rottenberg (b. 1944) and *There Was a House… Memories* (*Był dom… Wspomnienia*, 2009) by Anna Szatkowska (1928).

Gender- and nation-oriented research indicates that in the case of national discourse, women play the part of reproducers of familial or national community, responsible for cultivating and transmitting language, tradition and values (Yuval-Davis 1997). It is the family and the history of the nation that constitute the main points of reference for the female authors I have examined, rather than the history of women as a social group, whose rights became a subject of serious debate only after 1989, as a result of the "democratization of history" (Nora 2001: 40). In autobiographies written by Polish female authors the history of individuals becomes relevant only in the context of the history of larger communities. This works both ways: the history of a community finds its reflection in the lives of the individuals who compose it. From these narratives we can deduce a female identity based on (self-)consciousness of national and ethnic background, while other dimensions of identity such as gender, sex and class remain invisible, silenced; and if they are reflected upon at all—stereotypes are often involved. The narrators/heroines of the texts in question often lose sight of the female experience of history: being a woman remains transparent. This is my first thesis.

My second thesis is essentially derived from the first. In my opinion, (auto-)biographies of women not only constitute a response to the politics of memory/identity present in post-communist Poland, but are also an important component in the process of *producing* a past which is subordinated to present interests.

The majority of histories of women and their families that I have analysed have their starting point in the interwar period—in an idealized past, a Golden Age or Eden, which is then lost as a consequence of wars and an externally imposed regime. This loss leads to a feeling of degradation both in the personal and collective senses. The rhetoric of nostalgia, omnipresent in (auto-)biographical texts, operates with such topoi as: the Golden Age, decline and return home, and serves the purpose of reviving the atmosphere of a lost time, or, in other words, of returning to the land of childhood. In the case of authors/heroines of (auto-)biographies born after World War II it is often a return to the childhood of their parents or grandparents, the memory of which is indirect, preserved in family chronicles, letters, diaries, or perpetuated in photographs. The nostalgic ritual return to childhood, to one's roots, one's home, is a return in this case to a past connected with a particular social order, at the centre of which lay the family and private property. (Auto-)biographies are thus a means of restoring that order, for which a "fictitious tradition" subsequently provides legitimacy (Hobsbawm and Ranger 1983).

Identity models of prestige

The starting point of most of these (auto-)biographies is the pre-war world, known to the narrators/heroines either from personal experience (as in the case of Szatkowska or Olczak Ronikier), or, if they were too young to remember it themselves, from the stories of parents, grandparents, relatives and friends (as in the case of Wachowicz-Makowska). The memory of pre-war reality with its established social and economic order, its rich cultural life and atmosphere of joy and enthusiasm resulting from Poland's having regained independence in 1918—all this merges in their consciousness with the memory of childhood, of the family home, and images of loved ones. This leads to an idealization not only of childhood itself but also of the historical, social and economic circumstances that constitute its background (Eliade 1961, 1978). A sense of the stability, peace and safety of the home is transposed into a sense of the stability, peace and safety of the whole era. Echoes of nostalgia, of longing for a "Golden Age," "paradise," "Arcadia," resound in these (auto-)biographies, especially in the context of its later "loss":

> I was born on the ruins of the pre-war world. This is not in the least a poetic metaphor. My childhood took place during the second half of the forties and at the beginning of the fifties. (Wachowicz-Makowska 2007, 5)

> Only now do I realize, how much I envied my mother's and my grandmother's past in my early years. Pre-war Poland seemed to me Arcadia, a lost paradise, the sweetness of which I have never known. (Olczak-Ronikier, 2006, 187)

The past, of which only a faint (if any) memory is preserved, is present mainly in the stories told by parents and grandparents, often recalled in situations of crisis, tension, danger. For Joanna Olczak-Ronkier, a memory of this world is brought back by one of the last photographs taken before the war, in which she herself appears as a four-year-old child lying in the grass at the feet of her grandmother and sister. The memory appears suddenly, bringing with it a feeling of bliss but at the same time disbelief that such a stable and safe world once existed, and then vanished:

> There is something idyllic in this picture. A fragment of life frozen forever, as if in a drop of resin. Soon the era of peaceful holidays in summer resorts and lazy afternoons in wicker chairs will be over. Soon destiny will throw me out of this sunny resort into a fearsome world. (2006, 186)

Susan Sontag remarks that "photographs are not so much an instrument of memory as an invention of it or a replacement." Their meaning consists in the fact that "they give the texture and essence of things" (Sontag 2005, 128) and hence enable the emergence of the past in a more tangible form than reaching for associations, which is the strategy of Proustian realism: "It is not the reality that photographs make immediately accessible, but images. [...] their force comes from their being material realities in their own right, richly informative deposits left in the wake of whatever emitted them, potent means for turning the tables on reality—for turning it into shadow" (Sontag 2005, 128-129, 141). Along with the tatters of memories, bits and pieces of stories, family souvenirs and even common household appliances, the photos build up the framework of the lost world while leaving free spaces which can easily be filled with any content—one may complete, and at the same time *create* them: "Through photographs, each family constructs a portrait-chronicle of itself—a portable kit of images that bears witness to its connectedness" (Sontag 2005, 5).

The world known from memories or rather flashes of memories, from the stories of relatives and friends, from photographs and family souvenirs, is to a large extent a world that has been imagined, dreamed about, longed for, and on the basis of these very longings, dreams and visions—reconstructed. This means that narrators/heroines of (auto-)biographies can furnish it as they please, drawing on the above-mentioned sources as well as their own imaginations, which, however, were not shaped in a social, economic and cultural vacuum. The pictures of family homes and the reality that surrounds them suggest a certain habitus (Bourdieu 1984) of the authors/heroines: they mirror their social background, financial status and education.

In most cases these are idyllic pictures that exemplify family happiness, wealth, patriotism, engagement in promoting Polish culture (even if the family was of Jewish origin) and the good taste typical of aristocratic or bourgeois intellectuals—in short: everything that determines class and cultural distinction. Against the backdrop of the gloomy reality of People's Poland, and then the gaudy, flashy and tasteless images of early capitalist Poland, the pre-war period seams elegant, subtle but at the same time fragile. It was swept away so easily by the wind of History:

> I was raised in a home in which every object, every trinket had its own history. This is how I remember the world of my childhood—as a sort of work of art created day by day with much physical and intellectual effort, but also with much heart. (Wachowicz-Makowska 2007, 25)

It is a world of beautiful, lavishly furnished, spacious apartments in tenement houses, of old mansions with histories, of stylish and costly furniture, artefacts, books; a world of trips to spas, holidays in the countryside, outings to the opera, theatres and cafés, Sunday walks and dinners in the company of other family members. It is a world of entrepreneurs (Olczak-Ronikier, Wachowicz-Makowska, Kuryluk, Rottenberg), landowners (Szatkowska) but also of artists, writers, animators of culture and science (Kuryluk, Szatkowska, Olczak-Ronikier), of the wealthy bourgeoisie, aristocracy and self-employed professionals. These are the groups that represented the social, economic and intellectual elite of the Second Polish Republic, and in some cases also of the People's Republic of Poland (e.g. the father of Ewa Kuryluk was one of the few pre-war leftist intellectuals who worked his way up after the war). It is also a world where it was not seen as extraordinary for wealthy people to employ servants and dictate the rules of proper behaviour in both the public and private spheres.

Mary Margaret Steedly notes that "the transfer and transcription of historical experience—in names, monuments, genealogies; in collective fantasy and in the regulated social intercourse of everyday life; in law, property, and desire; in stories inhaled with the common air of a shared place or time—is the movement through which subjectivity is produced" (Steedly 1993, 22). The impression of middle-class women one gets from reading the (auto-)biographies in question, is that of intellectuals and patriots, but also of traditionalists in their approach to gender roles and relations between the sexes. The world which they miss and which constitutes their only point of reference is the pre-war world of high society: elegant, tasteful, neat and subtle. Compared to the reality of People's Poland—grey, morose and vulgar—it is a true "Golden Age," Arcadia, a paradise lost in the whirlwind of history, and now regained by means of a nostalgic vision of a return to home.

The power of nostalgia

Stuart Tannock notes that the ideological function of nostalgia that puts to use such rhetorical figures as the "Golden Age," "the decline," "fall," "return home" consists in presenting a vision of the past that is "universally good," "ideal," cleansed of everything that might constitute a flaw on its spotless surface, such as dissonances connected with class, race, ethnicity, gender, religion, as well as the social, political and cultural injustices that arise from them (Tannock 1995, 453-464).[2] Simultaneously, thanks to the figure of "return to the beginning," nostalgia carries a promise of fulfilling the dream of recreating the structure of paradise, which was taken from us as a consequence of sin. However the ultimate end does not consist in a literal "return to the past" but in its recreation in a form that legitimizes the modern social and economic order. Hence anything that might disturb the remembered (or imagined) view of the blissful past, any element that does not fit into the definition of the desired norm of identity which, when interiorized, would guarantee the "restoration of Arcadia," is silenced, erased, and forced into the sphere of collective oblivion.

In Poland class divisions, as well as socialism as an ideology promoting social justice, restrictions on private property, rejection of the capitalist idea of the free market and—in its communist variant—the creation of a classless society, are affected by a kind of "collective amnesia." For this reason, in the (auto-)biographies in question, the category of class and class conflicts, of economic inequality, rarely appears, much like the issue of engagement in the pre-war socialist movement. As for the People's Republic, it is either entirely omitted in the narration or almost exclusively demonized.

Of all the authors I have analysed, only Ewa Kuryluk notices the problem of social stratification in pre- and post-war Poland. The class issue appears here as an element in the family conflicts between the egalitarian father, a leftist journalist and later civil servant, and the elitist mother who comes from a wealthy Jewish family.

The narrator of *Frascati Street* focuses on the tragedy of Jews, but does not pass over forms of social exclusion based on factors other than ethnic ones (such as class). She confesses that as a child she perceived servants as a depersonalized "mass" that appeared and disappeared, yet was in a way always present, just like objects of everyday use. Her mother was concerned that "people of a certain social status" had servants and that these should know their place. Her father in turn strove to eliminate feudal relations in his home:

While Mummy was away at the sanatorium, the "nice ladies" slept on the couch in her room and ate with us in the dining room. As soon as Mummy, who used to call the "nice

---

[2] In this context Tannock mentions of the ideas of Raymond Williams, which analyse the nostalgic "structure of feeling" (Williams 1977, 128-135) and point to a correlation between the private/social experience of longing for a given place or time and the rhetorical practices/strategies of narration used to express this experience, always within a certain social, cultural and political order: "Nostalgia, it can be said, is universal and persistent; only other men's nostalgias offend. A memory of childhood can be said, persuasively, to have some permanent significance. But again [...] a perpetual recession into history turns out, on reflection, to be a more complicated movement: Old England, settlement, the rural virtues—all these, in fact, mean different things at different times" (Williams 1973, 12).

ladies", "home helps", "housekeepers" or "house maids", came home, they moved back to their rooms, served at the table and ate in the kitchen. We also had rows about the "servants" who were being treated by Łapka [the narrator's father—A. M.] as if they were "gentry". (Kuryluk 2009, 132)

Kuryluk is the only one among my authors who does not univocally condemn People's Poland. There is certain disillusionment with the hypocrisy of the government and the faults of a system that promised social equality yet gave birth to a new elite, that promoted concepts of peace and empathy yet engendered indifference and callousness, and so on. On the other hand, the writer demonstrates that for some people, such as her father and his friends, socialism, or even communism, was a grand purpose, an ideal goal that was not fully realized, but still remained worthy of respect for its tradition of sensibility to human suffering and struggle against social exclusion.[3]

Kuryluk is isolated in her views on both pre- and post-war socialism. In the majority of the texts socialism, communism and People's Poland, often used as synonyms, are valued negatively as a "time of repression" (Szatkowska 2009, 347), "red plague" (Wachowicz-Makowska 2007, 127) and "diabolical power" (Olczak-Ronikier 2006, 343). In the rhetorical structure of nostalgia, People's Poland is a figure of decline: it is the evil that came from outside and led to the end of the ideal pre-war world, in which multi-generational intellectual families had cherished Polish culture and promoted traditional values. People's Poland is held responsible for the atomization of society, the crisis in the institution of the family, the collapse of moral values, in short—for everything that is supposed, in reconstructed form, to be the new, post-1989 basis of individual and collective identity. "The unremembering" (Ricœur 2007, 107) of People's Poland seems to be a condition for returning to the ideal state before the fall and promises to satisfy individual and collective needs: the consolidation of biographies, the continuation of tradition, and an anchor for identity:

Two demonic forces that have made an alliance to destroy us. [. . .] People without roots, deprived of memory, connections, values transmitted by the former generations do not see a purpose to their lives and have nothing to offer to their own children. Luckily, we have survived all these dangers, we have found each other and our common past, which will

[3] The memories of Kuryluk also form part of the aforementioned nostalgic current although in a different way from the stories of other authors. At the centre of her story we find her father—an idealist and communist; the entire era of "real socialism" is seen through the prism of his personality. In the writer's autobiography, her childhood, which coincided with the early days of the People's Republic of Poland, is subject to mythologizing, which extends also to the sociopolitical reality. People's Poland seen through the eyes of a child seems to be an Arcadia, overshadowed only by the illness of her mother and early loss of her father. His death initiates the collapse of the project of People's Poland—in *Frascati* we begin to notice an echo of disappointment with its very idea.

help us understand better who we are and where we are heading. (Olczak-Ronikier 2006, 343)

The texts I have analysed contain the promise of a return to paradise. It is however a return to a certain place in paradise—one woven out of fantasy, dreams and longings, which mirror the author's habitus on the one hand, and present-day power relations on the other. When they focus on family, they promote a particular form of it (traditional, patriotic, intellectual) but they cast a veil of silence over the feudal relations of power that lay at its very basis. Social inequalities, violence and exploitation, i.e. internal factors which also led to the destruction of Arcadia are absent from these stories: the ideological function of nostalgia consists in creating an image of serene past times, shattered by an evil that came from the outside world. A return to paradise would be possible, if only this external evil were overcome. Leading us into the "garden of memory," nostalgia draws our attention away from existing inequalities and neutralizes any rebellion against the traditional social order with its intrinsic relations of power. This is how it participates in the reproduction of a status quo.[4]

Histories of women—women in history

The starting point for the stories told by the authors is a state of abundance: family happiness, harmony and wealth. All of them come from traditional multi-generational families, spearheaded for ages by men. It was men who earned money to support their wives, daughters and sisters by doing business, working intellectually or operating in the field of politics. Women from these families took care of the households and supported the men in their work, passions and aims. The image that emerges out of the memories of daughters and granddaughters, backed up by family stories and photographs, is one of a traditional, patriarchal family, in which women and men had fixed duties and privileges (Flandrin 1979). This type of family had perished as a consequence of the war and the transformation of the social structure that accompanied the establishment of People's Poland: many men died, others went missing, hence the duty to survive and support other survivors was assigned to women (Fidelis 2006). Herein lies the source

[4] Referring to Nietzsche, Fredric Jameson comments that nostalgia confirms our belief that "there is only the present and it is always 'ours'." The power of nostalgia has its source in the fact that it dissipates fears brought about by the past, but also—and perhaps above all—by the future: "the fear of proletarianization, of slipping down the ladder, of losing a comfort and a set of privileges which we tend increasingly to think of in spatial terms: privacy, empty rooms, silence, walling other people out, protection against crowds and other bodies" (Jameson 1991, 286). Paradoxically, the rhetoric of nostalgia serves the end of strengthening our conviction that we are in fact living in the "best of all possible worlds."

of my protagonists' clearly evident nostalgia for a traditional family, which had in fact passed away together with the entire pre-war world.

A deeper reading of the aforementioned (auto-)biographies convinces us, however, that the tale of such an ideal patriarchal family is full of flaws and fractures, which expose strong emotions and passions on the part of women, such as anger and desire, where the traditional family often constitutes a golden cage with bars made from conventions and rituals. If we scratch the surface of the monument, we will bring to light a female revolt, a dream of freedom, a longing aroused again and again, and then finally extinguished, only to return in the convulsions of the body and the ravings of a haunted mind.

Reading the histories of the protagonists, we see that many came from families built upon misalliance—an inverted version of the story of Cinderella and her prince. Their mothers came from the privileged classes of society, while their fathers were merely trying to climb the steps of the social ladder. For example, the mother of Anna Szatkowska—Zofia Szczucka (1890-1968)—came from the famous Kossak family, and was already a well-known writer when she met her second husband, the father of Anna. The mother of Ewa Kuryluk, who was born into a wealthy Jewish family, married a Pole who was of a lower social status. The mother of Anda Rottenberg was Russian—which, in the years immediately following the war, could guarantee certain privileges in Poland—while her father was a Polish Jew from a rather orthodox, lower-class family.

The privileged position of the family had an impact on the condition of its women. They were highly educated, spoke foreign languages and were well travelled. Some of them, such as the grandmother of Joanna Olczak-Ronikier, had worked before the war. It must be stressed, however, that both in the Polish and Jewish communities, the "idleness of women" was an indicator of the family's economic status (Veblen 1994). Beautiful and educated ladies were treated as showcases of wealth—a classic example of "merchandise on the market," which Luce Irigaray described as serving the sole purpose of multiplying men's goods (Irigaray 1985). In the case of most of these women—the mothers and grandmothers of my protagonists—marriage put an end to any dreams about realizing their own desires, and forced them to transfer all their ambitions onto family life.

In many Jewish families women were not only wives and mothers but also "managers" of the family business, understood as the household itself (directing the kitchen, giving instructions to servants, taking care of the education of children) but also the family company, run by women in the absence of men (Umińska 2001; Czerwonogóra 2009). This is the case of the family of Joanna Olczak-Ronikier, where women made all decisions concerning investments and finances, while men were busy with scientific research or political activity. When writing about women in her family, Olczak-Ronikier uses the following terms: resourceful, having initiative, clever, determined (2006, 23). Men on the other hand are described as impractical "sensitive intellectuals," chasing after great ideas. Traditionally, women are responsible for everyday matters connected with the body and the material world, while men are cut out for higher ends: matters of the spirit and mind. Women are "guardians of the family hearth," "pillars of the home." Men are guests in the house, wayfarers who come and disappear, which is a source of evident frustration to the narrators: it transpires that a woman's capacity to create a home for a man is not enough to keep him there. Although proud of the fact she is surrounded by wonderful, strong women, who ably manage "their little state," Olczak-Ronikier exhibits an internalized social expectancy for the family to be run by men: grandfather, father and brothers. Without a "man's hand" at the helm, the family is perceived as defective, incomplete, inferior: "[. . .] my family home was a damaged one, one deprived of the masculine element, ruled by women [. . .]" (2006, 210).

Masculine power legitimizes women's sacrifice, its sense and meaning. The absence of men, as in the home of Olczak-Ronikier (whose great-grandfather died prematurely, grandfather committed suicide and father divorced her mother soon after their wedding), or the presence of weak men, as in the family of Anda Rottenberg (whose father was sickly, and from a certain point entirely dependent on his wife and daughter), alongside strong confident women, seems to be a warning not to reverse traditional gender roles, as this leads to a family crisis. The vision of a "sane" or patriarchal model of the family enforced by culture and then internalized, arouses a feeling of guilt in those women who have been raised in a different kind of family, far removed from this model, and have been accustomed to types of human relationship different from those pertaining in a traditional household. Caught in the pitfall of social expectations, which are very different from what they have seen in their own homes, they struggle with a feeling of guilt, blaming themselves and others: the state, parents, partners and children. Unhappy in their relations with men and women, parents and children, they long for the ideal: a fantasy of a family that they have never known, but the memory of which they carry within themselves.

This was the case with Anda Rottenberg, in whose family women lived longer than men, the victims of wars, deportations and imprisonment. They were also psychologically stronger, more resistant and resourceful. Her mother, who was Russian, survived the siege of Leningrad, proving her fortitude and will to live. Together with her husband, a Polish Jew, she decided to leave for Poland, abandoning her fatherland and her loved ones, demonstrating her need for change and adventure. When describing her brave and independent mother, the narrator is torn between admiration for her vitality and firmness, and a certain fear when confronted by her power, capable of crushing anything in its way. She wants to be like her mother, but at the same time is afraid of this similarity, runs away from it: “Our mothers. Good and wise, courageous and strong, hardened by the side of weak men. Shaped by war, exile, hunger and unfulfilled dreams, and forming us in their likeness.” (Rottenberg 2009, 298)

In the case of Rottenberg’s narrator, the admiration and anxiety provoked by her mother are closely intertwined with an ambivalent attitude towards her father—a Polish Jew who had lost his closest family during the war, and also his formerly strong personality as a result of his marriage to an energetic Russian woman. In contrast to the exuberant and lively mother, the narrator’s father seams dull and featureless. He will be remembered by his daughter for his love-affairs, trips to the sanatorium and inclination to gamble—real and symbolic escapes from a rather unhappy life. She will also recall the sharp contrast between the generous curves of her mother’s body and the shrinking, sickly body of her father, which provoked in the author—at that time a child—feelings of compassion and pity. The weak, ill father was no role model or mentor for his daughter. On the contrary—he was the exact opposite of the traditional model of masculinity, since he was unreliable and unable to support her.

There is often a strong tension in the women’s (auto-)biographies—usually not expressed directly, but nevertheless present between the lines—that springs from the need to define oneself, to state one’s identity, between the spheres of gender, sex, nationality and ethnicity. A firm identity brings a sense of being settled and belonging, but at the same time carries the danger of determinism: the risk of being confined within a narrow definition. Especially the category of “femininity” creates many problems, which however remain unexpressed, as there is a silent assumption that “one is a woman” and does *not* ”become a woman” as in Simone de Beauvoir’s sense (Beauvoir 1989). This silence surrounding “gender trouble” in the (auto-)biographies under discussion is significant, bloated, like a swollen body rejecting toxins that have been accumulating for years. Doubts concerning what it means to be a woman, a Polish woman, a Polish Jew, a woman of Jewish, Russian, German or other origin, but also concerning the duties and rights connected with being a woman—vibrate beneath the surface of the women’s texts, and only seldom shine through the cracks that occasionally appear.

This hesitation is only part of a deeper dilemma that may be summarized by the following question: how to reconcile the image of a traditional family—i.e. a certain fantasy, strongly rooted in patriarchy—with a social reality that forces the transformation of such a family model, opening up the possibility for different forms of human relationships (Tyszka 2003).

In Poland, the longing for a traditional, patriarchal, multi-generational family is an element of the nostalgic tale about the past: the pre-war or even pre-Partition reality of freedom and independence, based on indigenous (not imposed) values, customs and culture. In this tale, the traditional family with its fixed roles for men and women is perceived as the solid foundation on which a clear and certain Polish identity may be built. It is a Catholic and heterosexual one, and even if an element of foreign ethnicity enters, the conceptions of gender, sex and body remain traditional, while everything that is considered evil—lack of balance between the sexes, awakened sexual desire in women, the crisis of the family—is perceived to be the effect of external forces, of external rule, which have disrupted the existing order and created a space of doubt regarding models of femininity, masculinity and the family. The yearning for what was, for the patriarchal family, for "true" femininity or masculinity, would seem to be a yearning transmitted by the national legend: a mythologized monument frozen solid, Paradise before the Fall, a past in whose image the traditional family is tightly bound to the free nation. Often, this is a yearning that one feels against oneself, against one's parents (especially the mother) and even against one's own experience of family life and observation of surrounding reality. This yearning, when materialized, often loses its charm, leaving only bitter disappointment, as in the case of Anda Rottenberg. She was trained by her father to become a "lady of the house" and entered the traditional role of a Polish mother, but had to pay a very high price for this accomplishment: many years of depression.

The national, patriarchal but also capitalist discourse dominant in Poland since 1989, in which the traditional family, with the woman in the role of wife and mother, figures not only as a symbol of the nation's vitality but also as a showcase of its wealth, has required however some careful retouching of its ideal model, i.e. a covering up of the flaws and fractures that might reveal its oppressive nature, or the possible existence of different models that might potentially damage the monument from the inside. This is why in all the examined (auto-)biographies, there occurs a nervous process of adjusting personal and family history to fit the existing model. But all this patching, stitching and mending ultimately appears to be futile in most cases, as the signs of a different model, a different tale remain visible underneath, demanding to be brought to light, named and uttered.

In one of the analysed (auto-)biographies, there is the story of a woman that deserves special attention. It occupies a separate place in the narrator's tale, as if it, or maybe its heroine, kept haunting the author. As though she could not pass over it, look away from it. It is the story of Kamila Horwitz—the sister of the grandmother of Joanna Olczak-Ronikier, an "emancipated woman" of the pre-war world: well educated, one of the first female doctors in Poland, an activist of the socialist movement, a single mother in times when this condition entailed social ostracism. It is a story of female power, will, determination, the stubborn endeavour to attain a once chosen goal, against all conventions or social expectations about "fulfilling a woman's duty." It is an emancipatory tale, the testimonial of the struggle of women oppressed by patriarchy, a tale buried in the collective female oblivion, and reclaimed today; one of many threads out of which the history of women is woven. It is an adventure story, the kind girls believe only happen to boys. No wonder the narrator of *In the Garden of Memory* relates it almost breathlessly. It is however very different from the everyday life of her grandmother and other women of her times; therefore she puts much effort into covering up her admiration with conventional sermonizing about women's duties:

> To walk straight ahead without elbowing one's way and trampling on others. To be proud of one's own achievements without confusing pride with conceit. To fight against the feeling of inferiority without falling into arrogance. To prevent disappointment from turning into bitterness. To take other people's feelings into account, but without servility and hypocrisy. Generally speaking, to build internal acceptance of one's fate but never give in, never lose one's dignity. All this sounds extremely high-flown but people treated life very seriously back then. (Olczak-Ronikier 2006, 52)

We will not find many similar stories, and when we do, they are scattered and often ambiguous. It is well worth the effort, however, of bringing them into the daylight, gathering them together, as they complement the official tale about the past—in which the traditional family and "natural" gender differences are inseparable elements—by means of this other dimension to women's experience, strung somewhere between desire and suppression, oppression and revolt, conventionalism and the challenge to society. A layer of plaster scraped off the surface of the monument allows us to reach valuable material underneath: it is a different memory, a different story which is alive and vibrant beneath the surface (Bobako 2009). If we are to grasp it, we must hurry before the plaster sets.

Bibliography

Primary sources

Kuryluk, Ewa. 2009. *Frascati. Apoteoza topografii*. Kraków: Wydawnictwo Literackie.
Olczak-Ronikier, Joanna. 2006. *W ogrodzie pamięci*. Kraków: Znak.
Rottenberg, Anda. 2009. *Proszę bardzo*. Warsaw: W.A.B.
Szatkowska, Anna. 2009. *Był dom... Wspomnienia*. Kraków: Wydawnictwo Literackie.
Wachowicz-Makowska, Jolanta. 2007. *Panienka w PRL-u*. Warsaw: Czytelnik.

Secondary sources

Beauvoir, Simone de. 1989. *The Second Sex*, translated by Howard M. Parshley. New York: Vintage.

Bobako, Monika. 2009. *Powrót kobiet do historii – niedokończony projekt?* Biblioteka Online Think Tanku Feministycznego. Accessed 1 May, 2012. http://www.ekologiasztuka.pl/pdf/f0083bobako.pdf

Bourdieu Pierre. 1984. *Distinction: A Social Critique of the Judgment of Taste*, translated by Richard Nice. Cambridge, MA: Harvard University Press.

Czerska, Tatiana. 2008. "Historia rodziny – rodzina w historii." In *Prywatne/ publiczne. Gatunki pisarstwa kobiecego*, edited by Inga Iwasiów, 193-232. Szczecin: Wydawnictwo Uniwersytetu Szczecińskiego.

Czerwonogóra, Katarzyna. 2009. "O doświadczeniach polskich Żydówek." In *Gender: kobieta w kulturze i społeczeństwie*, edited by Beata Kowalska, Katarzyna Zielińska and Ben Koschalka, 35-54. Kraków: Rabid.

Eliade, Mircea. 1961. *The Sacred and the Profane: The Nature of Religion*, translated by Willard R. Trask. New York: Harper Torchbooks.

—. 1978. "The World, the City, the House." In his *Occultism, Witchcraft, and Cultural Fashions: Essays in Comparative Religions*, 18-31. Chicago, IL: University of Chicago Press.

Eliot, Thomas Stearns. 1950. "Tradition and the Individual Talent." In his *Selected Essays 1917–1932*, 3-11. New York: Harcourt, Brace.

Fidelis, Małgorzata. 2006. "Czy 'nowy matriarchat'? Kobiety bez mężczyzn w Polsce po II wojnie światowej." In *Kobieta i rewolucja obyczajowa. Społeczno-kulturowe aspekty seksualności. Wiek XIX i XX*, edited by Anna Żarnowska and Andrzej Szwarc, 421-436. Warsaw: Wydawnictwo "DiG"; Instytut Historii Uniwersytetu Warszawskiego.

Flandrin, Jean-Louis. 1979. *Families in Former Times: Kinship, Household and Sexuality*, translated by Richard Southern. Cambridge and New York: Cambridge University Press.

Hobsbawm, Eric and Terence Ranger, eds. 1983. *The Invention of Tradition.* Cambridge and New York: Cambridge University Press.

Irigaray, Luce. 1985. "Women on the Market." In her *This Sex Which Is Not One*, translated by Catherine Porter with Carolyn Burke, 170-191. Ithaca, NY: Cornell University Press.

Jameson, Frederic. 1991. "Nostalgia for the Present." In his *Postmodernism, or, The Cultural Logic of Late Capitalism,* 279-296. Durham, NC: Duke University Press.

Mrozik, Agnieszka. 2012. *Akuszerki transformacji. Kobiety, literatura i władza w Polsce po 1989 roku.* Warsaw: Instytut Bada? Literackich PAN.

Nora, Pierre. 2001. "Czas pamięci," translated by Wiktor Dłuski. *Res Publica Nowa* 7 (154): 37–43.

Ricœur, Paul. 2007. *Pamięć, historia, zapomnienie*, translated by Janusz Margański. Kraków: Universitas.

Said, Edward W. 1994. *Culture and Imperialism*. New York: Vintage.

Sontag, Susan. 2005. *On Photography*. New York: RosettaBooks.

Steedly, Mary Margaret. 1993. *Hanging without a Rope: Narrative Experience in Colonial and Postcolonial Karoland*. Princeton, NJ: Princeton University Press.

Tannock, Stuart. 1995. "Nostalgia Critique." *Cultural Studies* 9(3): 453–464.

Tazbir, Janusz. 2006. "Splątane korzenie." *Polityka* 5: 66–68.

Tyszka, Zbigniew. 2003. *Rodzina we współczesnym świecie*. Poznań: Wydawnictwo Naukowe Uniwersytetu Adama Mickiewicza.

Umińska, Bożena. 2001. *Postać z cieniem. Portrety Żydówek w polskiej literaturze*. Warsaw: Sic!

Veblen, Thorstein. 1994. *The Theory of the Leisure Class: An Economic Study of Institutions*. New York: Penguin Books.

Williams, Raymond. 1973. *The Country and the City*. London and New York: Oxford University Press.

—. 1977. *Marxism and Literature*. Oxford and New York: Oxford University Press.

Yuval-Davis, Nira. 1997. *Gender and Nation*. London: Sage Publications.

Motherhood and the Transmission of Memory in Texts by Polish-Jewish Writers

Katarzyna ZECHENTER

"The greatest tragedy that can occur between mother and daughter is when they cease being able to speak and to listen to one another" wrote Marianne Hirsch emphasizing the bond between mother and her child. (Hirsch 1989, 199) This relationship is enshrined in all cultures but, at the same time, is mocked through various jokes about the "manipulative Jewish mother" (Ravits 2000, 4) or the overprotective "Italian mamma" overfeeding her already fat children, which suggests degrees of complexity in interpretations of mothering. In the so-called second generation—the children of Holocaust survivors who live "at a further temporal and spatial remove from the decimated world of their parents" (Hirsch 1996, 659), the relationship between mother and the children serves also as one of the most important, if not the most important, channel of transmission for knowledge of the Holocaust, although culture and cultural memory also play an important role. It affects not only how these children perceive the world in general, but also how they see modern Poland and Poles sixty years after the Holocaust and what knowledge they transmit to the next generation, personally and through their works as writers, publicists and painters. Margaret Feinstein argues that "mothering and motherhood figure prominently in the personal narratives of women survivors of the Holocaust," while the fathers are often absent (Feinstein 2007, 155); an observation supported by medical science (Yehuda 2008, 1004). I argue that the same is true in texts written by the daughters of survivors even in cases when the mother is not Jewish yet went through the trauma of World War II, and that the transmission is aided by referring to a specific cultural construct—the ideal of the Polish Mother strengthened by existing antisemitism.

In this chapter I ask what strategies are used to transmit the memory of the mothers and what strategies are used by the daughters to deal with "such knowledge," including the construct of the Polish Mother (Matka Polka). I also ask how daughters construct their own identities in the face of parental trauma and what the past means to them when they are faced with antisemitism. Finally, I investigate how memory passes down through the generations, how the mothers' private stories translate into the public sphere, how the adult children deal with the gaps in their mothers' stories and how they construct their postmemory, often in their own works.

My investigation is based on three autobiographical works: Bożena Keff's *Song on Mother and the Fatherland* (*Utwór o Matce i Ojczyźnie*), *Frascati Street: An Apotheosis of Topography* (*Frascati. Apoteoza topografii*) by Ewa Kuryluk, and *Here You Go (Proszę bardzo)* by Anda Rottenberg—all published in Warsaw in 2008 and 2009.[1] What unites these texts (apart from the randomness of the date of publication) is the fact that they were written by mature women who learned how to cope not only with their mothers' legacy of survival, their subsequent traumas and eventual deaths, but also, and more importantly, used their mother's trauma as material for their own artistic works.

In many ways these texts form part of the narrative of Holocaust survival that has become exceedingly popular in Poland since the 1980s,[2] although here I address a slightly later period when the country had grown more diverse (although not without its problems[3]) and accepting of differences, partly as a consequence of Poland's membership of the European Union (since 2004) that facilitated easier movement between Poland and other European countries (Łodziński 1999). More importantly, there has also been a progressive normalization of Polish-Jewish relations associated with growing understanding of the role of the Holocaust, as noted by many influential critics and historians including Antony Polonsky (2009) and Maria Janion, who stated in her *Jewish Lectures*: "Although we do not always realize it, the Holocaust informs the entire system of contemporary culture, all the questions and dilemmas of postmodernity." (Janion 2009, 63)

It is also important to note that these women writers are united by their education in the People's Republic of Poland and their acceptance of communism (albeit to varying degrees) or, in the case of Ewa Kuryluk, by belonging to a group that significantly benefited (financially and otherwise) from their parents' support for the system (the so-called "red bourgeoisie"[4]). They all went to Polish schools with their strict hierarchical curriculum, which means that they read the same texts about mothering as all other Polish children and became familiar with the same

---

1 The works by Kuryluk and Rottenberg are discussed also by Agnieszka Mrozik in her contribution to this volume, but from a different angle—Ed.

2 Szacka and Castle argue that while the collective memory of the Holocaust arose at the end of the 1950s, the broad discussion of Polish-Jewish relations from the time of World War II appeared only during the Jedwabne debate (Szacka and Castle 2006, 18).

3 Bożena Umińska-Keff focuses in another work *Barricades: Chronicles of Obsession 2000-2006* (*Barykady. Kroniki obsesyjne lat 2000-2006,* 2006) on the struggle between narrowly understood Polishness and the Other (that is gays, lesbian, feminists and Jews) in modern Poland.

4 This derogatory term is used to describe the children of communists who benefited financially from their support for the system while the rest of the society struggled (e.g. they had free apartments, cars, private medical clinics, trips abroad, separate or shops with goods not available elsewhere). Janusz Głowacki described them as early as 1968 in his collection of short stories entitled *The Nonsense Spinner* (*Wirówka nonsensu,* Warsaw: Państwowy Instytut Wydawniczy, 1968).

cultural concepts such as the Polish Mother (Matka Polka) and the Marian cult, even though they were not Catholics. It also means that they were exposed to the popular imagery of mothers with its "emphasis on suffering and pain, with portraits of grieving mothers" (Porter 2005, 160), to mention just one poem essential in this context, namely Adam Mickiewicz's "Do Matki Polki" (1830)—obligatory reading in all Polish secondary schools. This particular poem unites Catholicism with suffering for the sake of the country's future independence, while the Polish mother herself is presented as preparing for the suffering of her children and their subsequent death in the name of Poland's freedom.

My three chosen works represent different forms of autobiographical texts, to employ Małgorzata Czermińska's classification, with the emphasis on "witnessing," and although none represents "the pure" autobiographical form as defined by Philippe Lejeune (Ryan 1980, 5), the authors focus on expressing what happened to their mothers and to themselves (Czermińska 2000, 5-22). Within the wider context, these texts narrow the gap between the mothers and the readers despite the probability that the audience might not be able to understand them fully (Langer 1991, xviii-xv). However, the reader should remember that "given the distortions of memory and the mediation of language, narrative is always a story about the past and not the past itself" (Ellis and Bochner 2000, 745), and as such these three works tell stories about how memory works for the daughters, rather than providing an accurate picture of each one's mother's life.

In the cases of Kuryluk and Rottenberg the greater emphasis is on discovery of certain facts about their parents and families exterminated during the war, while in Keff's text the emphasis is on the difficulty of mother-daughter relations, the child's right to free herself from patriarchal and matriarchal dominance as well as on modern antisemitism or rather the absurdity of modern antisemitism. However, all three texts are written in the name of women from the traumatized generation by their daughters, whose mixed backgrounds added to their confusion: Kuryluk's mother was Jewish but her father was a Pole and a communist; Rottenberg is the daughter of a Russian woman from Leningrad, a "Soviet," and a Polish Jew who survived a camp in the Soviet Union. Both Bożena Keff's parents were Jewish: her father, a devoted communist, committed suicide in 1954 (Bielas 2008) yet his daughter was named Umińska which concealed her ethnicity.[5]

This mix of identities, including Jewish and Russian, adds to the complexities of the daughters' lives as they choose their own identities or even their first language, as was the case with Rottenberg who spoke mostly Russian at home. They perceive their origin as strongly contributing to their identity, but also as responsible for their Otherness, as Rottenberg emphasizes (2009, 14); or they might

5 In *Song on Mother and the Fatherland,* the narrator states only that her father committed suicide.

change their last name so that their Otherness would be more clearly marked. Keff's father, who served in the army in communist Poland, for instance, was ordered to change his name to a Polish-sounding one, and so his daughter was born as Umińska but started using her father's real surname—Keff—after 1989 to mark her Jewishness and thus clearly define her identity (Bielas 2008).

Transferring the trauma through talking

The most visible strategy for the transfer of the mothers' trauma is through communicative memory "based exclusively on everyday communications" which constitute the field of oral history where texts are characterized by, among other things, a certain degree of disorganization, to use Jan Assmann's term (Assmann and Czaplicka 1995, 126) and the fact that "each individual composes a memory which is socially mediated and related to a group" (1995, 127). Since communicative memory has a limited temporal horizon linked to an average human lifespan, it can exist between grandparents and their grandchildren but no further, which has implications for the texts since the authors did not have grandparents, and hence communication is restricted to two, not three, generations.[6] Consequently these three texts are rooted in conversations between traumatized mothers and their daughters and very limited contacts with their grandchildren (Rottenberg).

The daughters—not the mothers themselves—convey the mothers' memories to the reader, mostly through conversations. As such, the daughters—who are the narrators—had to prepare the texts to fit their own artistic objectives and emotional needs: Rottenberg, for instance, wrote *Here You Go* in order to cope after the disappearance of her only son and survive her anger against the police who for ten years were unable to find his body (Kim 2009), while Kuryluk's story creates an idealized portrait of her parents. In short, the stories told by the mothers are narrated by the daughters for different reasons: not only to tell what happened to their mothers during World War II but also to understand the trauma of their own postmemory (Kuryluk, Rottenberg), to relate how the mothers lived their postwar lives with the trauma (Kuryluk, Rottenberg, Keff), how they benefitted from their husbands' participation in the system (Kuryluk), or not (Rottenberg), and how the daughters managed their own lives, burdened but also enriched by that memory (Rottenberg, Keff), or fighting against overidentification with mother's trauma (Keff, Kuryluk). More importantly, however, the daughters also examine themselves and their own emotions, trying either to find out the "truth" about

6 Although Rottenberg's Russian grandparents were still alive, she was able to see them only twice because they lived in the Soviet Union and travel was restricted. Her Jewish grandparents were dead.

themselves as mothers (Rottenberg) or to free themselves from it (Keff), yet always remaining firmly within their mothers' pasts and traumas (Kuryluk) and as targets of antisemitism.

Frascati Street is constructed as a long conversation with Kuryluk's mother, Miriam Kohany, who was saved from the L'viv (Lwów) ghetto by her future husband Karol Kuryluk[7] and to a large degree repeats elements of Ewa Kuryluk's earlier work, *Goldi*.[8] The story of her survival is central to an understanding of Kohany's constant fear, although the connection between her trauma and subsequent mental illness, schizophrenia, remains unclear in the text (Shanan 1988-9, 42-71). Karol Kuryluk was a pre-war communist strongly supportive of communism in post-war Poland, later rewarded with the prestigious position of Minister of Culture (April 1956-April 1958) in Józef Cyrankiewicz's government and then ambassadorship to Austria (1959-1964); he died suddenly of a heart attack in 1967. Among many benefits, he received an apartment in devastated post-war Warsaw located on a prestigious street called Frascati, hence the title of Ewa Kuryluk's book.[9] The flat played an important role in the life of the family: both Kuryluk's mother and Ewa herself present this apartment as their haven, the only safe place in an uncertain world: "I don't need anything more in order to be happy. [...] I have found in Frascati my Italy, *meine zweite Heimat*" (2009, 61).[10]

Miriam Kohany's entire post-war life as Maria Kuryluk was affected by what she went through during the Holocaust. After World War II she sees the world around her exclusively from a position of survivor-guilt and constant fear of a new Holocaust. Thus even some of her misfortunes, such as the protein allergies of her son, constitute in her mind a form of "revenge" for her very survival: "if this was not my fault, then it is *their* fault. [...] They could not forget that the

---

7 Karol Kuryluk (1910-1967) was founder and editor-in-chief of *Signals* (*Sygnały*), a pre-World War II cultural weekly. During the war he saved his future wife, Miriam Kohany, as well as another woman, Peppa Frauenglas and her two sons, for which he was honoured by Yad Vashem as one of the Righteous Among the Nations.

8 Kuryluk's *Goldi* (2004) is devoted mostly to Kuryluk's mother and the pre-war photographs of her family. Although *Frascati Street* does not bring new information or approaches, it reaffirms the depth of the trauma both of the mother and daughter.

9 Frascati Street was an exclusive location in devastated post-war Warsaw, not destroyed, with large villas with gardens. First Secretary of the Central Committee of the Polish United Workers' Party, Władysław Gomułka, had a villa there.

10 Kohany's identity is also complex: her daughter writes that she was a "German-Polish Jew" (Kuryluk 2009, 236) and although she spoke Polish, preferred to use German in her writings and whenever emotions got the better of her: she calls her children *meine Kleine* or *meine arme Kleine* and uses German words when she cannot remember the Polish ones; she is attached to German culture, especially literature. Kohany also remained a friend of her German teacher Mathilde despite the fact that Mathilde had joined the NSDAP [Nationalsozialistische Deutsche Arbeiterpartei] "long before the war" (2009, 197).

cattle truck left without me, they took revenge on my baby." (Kuryluk 2009, 70, emphasis as in original) Such guilt as experienced by Kohany may be recognized as typical of those who survived while their families did not (Leys 2007, 43-44), yet in her case it was also augmented by her later mental illness. Thus Kohany easily recognizes herself in one of the characters in her daughter's book *Trio for the Hidden* (*Trio dla ukrytych*, 2005) as a person who transforms herself from a Jewess who wants to hide from the Germans into a Jewess who wants to denounce herself because she believes that she is blameworthy for having survived (Kuryluk 2009, 136).

Similarly, Keff's mother, called Meter in the text, talks relentlessly to her daughter but underneath she feels guilty because she survived by abandoning her mother, who did not.[11] Her guilt manifests itself in her conviction that her daughter is unable to understand her simply because she has never been faced with such dramatic choices, and she treats her daughter accordingly as a perpetual child who has no right to her own voice or opinions.

According to Rottenberg, however, being a victim is not something that the daughters can avoid, although victimhood does not have to be the result exclusively of the Holocaust. Her difficult relations with her parents (their failure to show emotion towards her was a conscious educational strategy on the part of her mother, the emotional absence of the father) eventually result in her becoming a victim, although she tried "so hard not to be one. This mechanism worked in me outside my consciousness, instinctively—just as in Pavlov's dogs." (Rottenberg 2009, 267) Thus it seems that although victimhood is ingrained in the second generation and transmitted through communicative memory, it is not restricted to those whose parents who survived the Holocaust, especially in Poland, where it is additionally connected with the suffering of women as socially and historically respected, even admired, in the style of the traditional stereotype of the Polish Mother.

In each text, the monologues are designed to serve various purposes. Most obvious is the need to learn about the familial past (Kuryluk, Rottenberg) and mother-daughter relations. In Kuryluk's text, the daughter prompts the conversations with multiple questions which result in long, not always coherent stories about the past, the illness of her brother (Piotruś also had schizophrenia and attempted suicide several times), Poles of their own times, Ewa Kuryluk's artworks and exhibitions, or the various pets the family had over the years. The constant presence of the trauma is visible in the fact that Miriam Kohany is sometimes

11 "And so today in this place of Oral Writ we are/ there where she abandoned her mother, to save herself./ Take heed, voluntary passer-by, of this /significant moment—" ("A więc dziś w tym miejscu Pisma Oralnego jesteśmy / tam gdzie ona opusciła matkę, żeby się ratować./ Zważ dobrowolny przechodniu ten moment /znaczący—") (Keff 2008, 15).

unable to distinguish between the time of World War II and present-day Poland, because her traumatic experiences express themselves in her behaviour (cf. Hoffman 2004, 54). Thus the terrible experiences seem to her to be being replicated in modern Poland; she believes, for example, that patients in mental institutions are swollen with hunger, that tooth extraction is carried out in hospitals without anaesthetic or that nurses might kill patients at night. Such perceptions are rooted in her trauma and mental state and although her individual memories might be inaccurate from the historical point of view, they may be read according to Langer's argument that they might well convey a deeper layer of previous suffering (1991, xv).

However, when her daughter presents modern Poland in uniformly negative terms (unlike her mother), this kind of perception suggests not only overidentification with her mother's trauma, the trauma of postmemory, but also the importance to her of stressing antisemitism, despite evidence to the contrary. In *Frascati Street,* Ewa Kuryluk presents today's Poland as a kind of caricature, as a terrifying antisemitic place where young rustics relish torturing and killing animals, hospital patients are left to starve or beg the nurses on their knees for water, where doctors and nurses are indifferent, crude and scandalously incompetent or even sadistic, where Solidarity is an organization of virulent antisemites who use Nazi terminology (lice) to describe Jews, abuse people whom they suspect of being Jewish, and regret that not all of them were gassed, and where patriotism is equivalent to antisemitism and nationalism. Poland as presented by Kuryluk is a country populated by poorly educated or uneducated people from backward villages who speak poor Polish or even believe that electricity can evaporate through electric sockets, where it is safer not to criticize the Polish Pope and where a Jewish child saved by a family of peasants becomes as crude and cruel as his adoptive peasant parents. Even nursery teachers in the 1950s are presented as no better than Nazis—in the way they hiss at children whom they suspect are Jewish, telling them they will be sent to the gas chambers if they are naughty (Kuryluk 2009, 29, 58, 61, 114, 133, 141).

Such uniform negativity strongly suggests that the daughter is fixated on the negative aspects of life in Poland, overlooking all positive experiences, because of the fear instilled in her by her mother's trauma and later illness. The daughter attempts to present modern Poland only as an antisemitic space, despite the mother seeing her life within a larger context: "'After Teddy's death [Miriam Kohany's first husband—K.Z.], I convinced myself that we were all victims of evil.' 'That's true to a degree,' I said. 'Not in my case,' she retorted. 'I had to live through murderous times, but I was saved by goodness.'" (Kuryluk 2009, 158) Also, unlike her mother, who feels guilty for the ease with which she accepted the benefits of the totalitarian system, Kuryluk prefers not to discuss it focusing either on antisemitism or the perceived superiority of her family.

Although Kuryluk's narrative appears to end positively, it does not: her life is not defined by her being an artist and writer but by living with her mother's trauma and her failure to save her mother and brother from insanity, and her brother from suicide. At the end of her narrative, Kuryluk goes to L'viv to see her father's old house and the ghetto from which her mother had escaped. She has a sensation of being led through the streets by her mother who is now dead. Kuryluk dreams about saving her mother who, with her husband, would perform in front of Emperor Franz Joseph: "and, dear reader, we need to end here. Our ending is a happy ending because dream has vanquished reality." (2009, 312) Such an ending, however, with the emphasis on dreams conquering reality and final glamorizing of her parents, suggests that the reality as presented by Kuryluk could not have been equally positive.

In Keff's text, the conversations with her mother are constructed differently. Although the mother survived the war and thus belongs to the first generation of Holocaust survivors, it is as if the reader is dealing with a moment already crystallized in "forms of objectivised culture" (Assmann and Czaplicka 1995, 128) because s/he learns not about the specificity of the mother's situation but rather about abstract figures of memory under the general heading of suffering, such as "hunger in Volgograd" or "ghetto in L'viv" (Keff 2008, 39). This could, however, also be read in the light of what Saul Friedlander calls "deep memory" of the Holocaust (Friedlander 1993, 55, 61), where a deep memory, as a trauma, remains inexpressible although it does actually exist, as, for instance, in the case of the trauma of abandoning one's mother to save one's own life, the very case of Keff's mother, to which the narrator draws the reader's attention.

Rottenberg's story is not structured around conversations as they do not comprise the core of the book designed as a diary of events in 2007 and 2008. On the contrary, the focus is on Rottenberg's search for her missing son, that is, on her being a failed mother, her constant doubts, struggle with depression, as well as search for her unknown Russian and Jewish relatives who had been wiped out by either the Nazi or Soviet totalitarian systems. Rottenberg also provides multiple photographs of her family and friends strengthening the autobiographical context of her text.

The Matka Polka figure

Ever since the Romantic period, sacrifice was seen in Poland as a necessary part of motherhood and many women have felt ennobled by their true or imagined victimhood. Although the attitude towards sacrifice has changed, the sacrifice of mothers is still well represented among the younger generation born years after World War II: "But as I listened to the litany of sorrow I knew that these women were passing on to me one more important message. They wanted me to know that all their loss was a sacrifice I have to remember and respect. For I was another woman of the family and this legacy of sacrifice was now mine." (Stachniak 1995, 75)

The Polish Mother figure was and is still visible in various cultural registers: it has been discussed both in the press[12] and in specialist works, notably those by Maria Janion, the leading scholar on Polish Romanticism (Janion 1996) or Agnieszka Graff (2001). Like all Polish children, Keff would have become familiar with the concept through school, if not in the home. During the partitions, when Poland did not exist on the political map (1795-1918), this suffering figure was represented in many ways, as Poland lying in her grave, epitomized in Mickiewicz's Epilogue to *Pan Tadeusz* (1834, also obligatory reading in school), in Artur Grottger's panel of pictures entitled *Polonia* (1863), or Jacek Malczewski's painting *Melancholia* (1894). The Polish Mother was a heroine capable of raising her children as patriots and thus preserving the nation's identity and religion. Above all, her glorified motherhood allows, even requires, her to sacrifice herself and her children for an ideal. It was her ability and willingness to suffer alongside the men in their struggle for independence which gave her, in Mickiewicz's eyes, the right to be equal to them in suffering: a Polish woman struggles not to be free, but to sacrifice herself (Kowalczyk 2010, 51). Although the Polish Mother myth is supposed to be dead, Izabela Kowalczyk argues that even during the communist period and for some years afterwards, the ideal of the Polish Mother manifested itself through a woman's constant sacrifices made for her family and her double burden, i.e. her work at work and her work at home, by her standing in long queues to provide for the family, and later through supporting anti-communist activities, even watching her child die, as in the popular opposition song about a young boy killed by the state police during the 1970 strikes in Gdynia, entitled *Ballad of Janek Wiśniewski* (*Ballada o Janku Wiśniewskim*): "Don't cry Mother, it is not in vain" (Kowalczyk 2010, 57).

Although the Matka Polka figure is not common in fiction of the communist period, it can be found in Polish cinema. Suffice it to mention *A Pearl in the Crown* (*Perła w koronie,* 1972) directed by Kazimierz Kutz, and especially Janusz Zaorski's *Mother of the Kings* (*Matka Królów,* 1982, released 1987) or Andrzej Wajda's *Man of Iron* (*Człowiek z żelaza,* 1981). A more recent revival of the myth can be found in Jerzy Wójcik's *Complaint* (*Skarga,* 1991), based on a

---

12 See the stormy press discussion on motherhood provoked by Zbigniew Mikołejko's article "My War Against the Pushchair Pushers" ("Moja wojna z wózkowymi"), 5 September 2012 and later, in *Gazeta Wyborcza. Wysokie Obcasy.*

true story, although this was already read as anachronistic. Even in 1995, in Jerzy Kawalerowicz's film *For What?* (*Za co?*), the myth of the Polish Mother is central to an understanding of the story, as it is in Jan Jakub Kolski's *Keep Away from the Window* (*Daleko od okna*, 2000). This film presents the story of a Jewish mother who is forced to give away her daughter during the war and who later, after the war, does not want her back because she reminds her of the horror she had to go through (Haltof 2012, 168-169).

Thus I would argue that Keff and Kuryluk employed the Matka Polka concept, ever present in both Polish literary texts and film and prominent in public discourse on women and their role since the transition to democracy, as something that could still be readily understood by modern Polish readers, and probably in other Eastern European countries as well (Watson 1997, 146-147). Its appeal is reinforced not only by the continuing popularity of the Marian cult with its emphasis on motherhood, devotion and sacrifice but also because of the continuing discussion of the role of women in Polish society, even by feminist writers from the youngest generation, such as Sylwia Chutnik in her *Pocket Atlas for Women* (*Kieszonkowy atlas kobiet*, 2008) because "nationalist discourses tend to be heavily gendered in ways that limit women's agency." (Graff 2007, paragraph 8 of 20)

In *Frascati Street* Kuryluk presents her mother not only in the context of her past suffering, but also through icons of Polish cultural memory. In her mind, Miriam Kohany sacrificed herself for her children to the point where she literally risked her life, when she stopped taking her medication during the antisemitic campaign of 1968; this resulted in serious bouts of schizophrenia since she believed that her children would not be expelled from their flat on Frascati Street if she became gravely ill:

> "You pretended you were insane to save Frascati? Did you?" I couldn't speak. "There was no other way," she murmured. "I figured they wouldn't throw a crazy old woman out onto the streets." "Is that why you screamed?" "I screamed as loud as I could so everybody in the building would know." (Kuryluk 2009, 115)

In this particular dialogue the mother presents herself as a tragic widow in the tradition of probably the most famous Polish Mother—Mrs Rollison from Mickiewicz's *Forefathers' Eve. Part III* (1834), because "they [i.e. the system—K.Z.] knew how to catch a widow with her orphans." (2009, 114) By using this device, Kuryluk relies on cultural icons which any Polish reader can recognize from the readily available "library" of suffering Polish mothers and thus sympathize with the victim, even if the metaphor does not fit reality at all: at the time Kohany's children were not children, but adults—Ewa Kuryluk was twenty-four (and living independently abroad) while her brother was eighteen.

In Keff's *Song,* the elevation of the complexities of mother-daughter relations in patriarchal society over and above those of learning about the traumatic past (the case of Kuryluk and to some degree of Rottenberg) indicates yet another approach. Maria Janion and Izabela Filipiak, in their Afterword read the character of the Mother (Meter) as a Polish Mother figure where "the Jewish mother does not differ from the Polish mother in her acceptance of messianic elevation through suffering." (Keff 2008, 84) The mother presents herself as one whose duty it was to sacrifice everything for her child according to traditional patriarchal, Polish and Jewish stereotypes (Antler 2007)[13]: she finds validation in her sacrifice, while remaining a double victim: a victim of history and a victim of the patriarchy that demands that mothers sacrifice all for their children, something that indeed the very title of Keff's work suggests: "'You!!!' she barks. 'It was because of you I married that bastard (łajdak).'" (Keff 2009, 23)

At the same time, Rottenberg's book is also about struggling against victimhood and suffering as a woman, as a mother and as a Jew, "because I was not raised to be a victim, because the concept of victimhood remains as alien as ever, even when I understood its Christian context." (Rottenberg 2009, 486) Her attempt to shake off victimhood is the result of her mother's upbringing, which had had its faults but also allowed her to free herself from stereotypical Polish patriarchy. And yet, the very last sentence of the book suggests that despite this it is almost impossible for a woman in Poland not to become a victim: Rottenberg concludes that she has known this "for a while and although I don't want to know it, I know that nothing will be spared me in life. I have done some good deeds, but nothing will be spared me, nothing will pass me by. [...] And that maybe someone will shoot me in the back." (Rottenberg 2009, 489) In short, she could well become the perfect victim, despite everything, simply for being a woman and a mother.

Each of the three texts under discussion offers a different analysis of mother-daughter relations, although it seems logical that children raised by parents who survived the Holocaust would bear some scars of the trauma, since it has long been assumed that the extreme traumatization experienced by Holocaust survivors has had a detrimental effect on their capacity for parenting.

> Typically, Holocaust survivor parents have been regarded as too anxious, depressed and pre-occupied with mourning their multiple losses to be able to provide an adequate maturational environment for their children. As a result, such mothers and fathers have been thought to pass on their emotional burden to their sons and daughters thus creating child-rearing problems around both attachment and detachment. (Kellermann 2001, 58)

---

[13] Joyce Antler's *You Never Call! You Never Write! A History of the Jewish Mother* (2007) focuses on the stereotype of the anxious, neurotic, overprotective and despotic Jewish mother in American cinema and fiction, and the persistence of such a stereotype.

However, each text repudiates this assumption, albeit to varying degrees, just as actual studies carried out on Holocaust families have also repudiated it, since it is largely based on generalizations drawn from merely anecdotal evidence. In these three texts, for instance, none of the daughters had what one might call a "normal childhood," but for other reasons, such as the mental illness of Kuryluk's mother, the emotional absence of Rottenberg's father and the widowhood of Keff's mother, whose husband committed suicide—an additional trauma both for the wife and the child. All these other traumas added to the disturbed childhood of the daughters, which thus included extra experiences not connected with the Holocaust; Rottenberg's mother, for example, "spent her life remembering the hunger in Leningrad." (2009, 346)

In Kohany's case the post-war trauma was intensified by her mental illness, later augmented by her decision not to take her medication. The relationship between the old, very ill, tired and intelligent woman, and her daughter, at the time of writing a recognized artist in her sixties living in America, is described by the latter as ideal, with the daughter being fully understanding, fully compassionate and fully supportive. All family members, including the narrator's mother, grandmother, husband and son, are presented as exceptionally intelligent and talented, devoted and strong, coming from a household of equally exceptional people where even the dogs are musical and play the piano (Kuryluk 2009, 81). This extraordinarily positive familial picture, clearly idealizing the family, is nevertheless troubled by the underlying trauma transmitted not only through the mother's illness, but also through the general Polish, nation-specific cultural memory as manifested in, for example, newspaper articles on ghettos during World War II and above all in the antisemitism which, according to Ewa Kuryluk, is omnipresent in Poland. For instance, although the mother does not want her children to know the history of the Jews during the war (and does not tell them that she is Jewish), knowledge of it is easily accessible from other sources: the daughter chances to see some photographs of people wearing the Star of David in a newspaper, or she hears antisemitic abuse directed at another girl in the nursery. The result remains the same: although the daughter did not experience the war she "was wounded as if during the war" (Kuryluk 2009, 29), which hints at "the paradoxes of indirect knowledge" haunting "many of us who came after" (Hoffman 2004, 25).[14]

The main vehicle of transmission remains the atmosphere at home created by the erratic and incomprehensible behaviour of the mother, who, during bouts

---

14 Ewa Kuryluk's identification with Jews, whose pictures she saw in newspapers, or when preparing herself and her brother to commit suicide (Kuryluk 2009, 172) in case of war, strongly suggests that since early childhood she knew that she was Jewish but preferred to omit that information in *Frascati Street* most probably in order to emphasize her conviction of the omnipresence of antisemitism in Poland.

of her illness, relives the wartime trauma again and again, and is feared by the children, especially by Kuryluk's small brother, who is unable to understand his mother's illness yet able to absorb the general fear that accompanies it. It is also strengthened by the existence of antisemitism. The specific knowledge about events is transmitted only to the daughter and only when she is in her fifties, but even after the death of her mother Kuryluk is still unable to find out such basic facts as the circumstances of her mother's first husband's death or even how she was saved by Karol Kuryluk. Despite that, however, the transmission of trauma is obvious.

Antisemitism as a factor in the transmission of trauma

An important factor in the process of transmission of trauma, according to the daughters, is thus the presence of antisemitism. In Kuryluk's story, the children repeat the abuse they hear outside, such as when the young Kuryluk yells at her brother that he will be turned into a lampshade, to which he responds with a panic attack. This suggests not only some form of knowledge about what happened during the Holocaust, but also the atmosphere of fear at home, augmented by the mother's illness and her conviction that she and her children are constantly in some kind of danger. The children's behaviour (for example, the way they hide under the table or collect mercury so as to be able to commit suicide in the event of a future war) strongly suggests that fear is being ingrained in them and augmented by the world outside, even when the parents are trying to protect them from such knowledge.

According to other widely held views about parents who survived the Holocaust, fear visible in the mother's overprotective attitude also adds to the process of transmission. Sometimes a simple command such as "eat up" has been described as containing a more desperate and anxious undertone: "'Don't leave any food on your plate, because… *then and there*, we we had nothing!'" Regarding trust: "'These people are all anti-Semitic, they would kill us immediately if they could.'" (Kellermann 2001, 59) This attitude is easy to find in all three books discussed here, since the mothers and the children remain trapped in the past: "'Trauma is like a taboo,' she complained, 'it is passed on from mother to child, from generation to generation.'" (Kuryluk 2009, 136) In Kuryluk's case, the trauma becomes not only the mother's main story but also one of the themes of the daughter's artistic works, emphasized in *Frascati Street* by the inclusion of photographs of Kuryluk's installations and quotations from her earlier books (Kuryluk 1981, 265).

In *Song on Mother and the Fatherland* the mother—called Meter—provides a continuous narrative of her trauma and demands the unlimited and undivided attention of her daughter. Unlike Kuryluk, Keff is not interested in the specificity of the events in her mother's "pre-history" but rather in their general significance and the dangers of modern antisemitism. This means that the daughter neither needs nor has any specific knowledge of the events, while the knowledge that she does possess comes across as a figure of memory, such as "the ghetto in L'viv" (Keff 2008, 39) that she can easily share with the reader. Thus Keff writes from a perspective of postmemory which is not mediated by any archival material such as photographs, as is the case of Rottenberg or Kuryluk, where such material emphasizes the autobiographical character of the texts. Also, it is not the trauma *per se* that informs the text but rather the relationship between the mother and the daughter as a result of the trauma. The mother simply demands to be the only important thing in her daughter's life because of what she went through and because she is alone after her husband's suicide, expecting her daughter to function as a surrogate for the mother's destroyed world: "So you will be my husband, my mother-father," she demands (2008, 23). In order to achieve this, she does not shy away even from emotional blackmail—"she takes out a knife to stab herself"' (2008, 23) and attempts to instil in her daughter a feeling of constant guilt for not being a dutiful daughter, which in the present case means having an unlimited capacity to listen to her mother's complaints. Again, it is not the stories that the daughter has to listen to, but rather the running commentary on what is happening currently to the now older mother, especially her health problems and mental state as a lonely woman whose capabilities are restricted to what little her trauma permits. Unlike Kohany, however, Keff's mother is presented as being angry at, but not afraid of modern antisemitism: in 2006, while watching a monument to Roman Dmowski being erected in Warsaw on the television news, the mother says: "Look, this dastardly fascism is everywhere, always the same rascals" (2008, 61), consequently transmitting her general experience of persecution but without the fear that pervades Kuryluk's mother's stories.

The hostility Rottenberg experiences as an adult is the result of her Jewish name and not her Russian origins (which remain obscure because of her Jewish name), suggesting an homogenization of the way Jews may be perceived (Sienkiewicz 2012). It was not much of an issue in the post-war years when as a child in Legnica she "was not the only one with a strange surname and not the only one to use more than one language at home," since differences were common (Rottenberg 2009, 222). Her teacher's decision that Polish should be her first language duly simplified her life and provided "a safe haven for her uncertain identity" (2009, 223). But as an adult Rottenberg realizes that although as a child she wanted to be like everybody else, later on she was in fact "richer than they because of this second region that was included neither in the school curriculum nor in the typical home curriculum of a Polish child. These riches, however, also deepened my Otherness while the choice I made during my first class [to speak Polish at school—K.Z.] did not end my problems." (2009, 224)

Surprisingly, knowledge of the Holocaust and the trauma associated with it comes mainly from her Russian mother who did not experience it, not from the father, whose family did fall victim to the Holocaust. He keeps mostly silent about the events and Rottenberg, unlike Kuryluk or Keff, does not provide any explanation for his behaviour. Again, Friedlander's concept of "deep memory" might help explain his inability to express his trauma (1993, 61). Rottenberg's mother, however, is presented as more emotional about her own past and about the Holocaust when she learns about its extent through public forms of remembrance. After she comes back from seeing Auschwitz, she spends a few days lying on the sofa because "she could not stop crying" as she spoke to her acquaintances about the place and the piles of suitcases, glasses and shoes. She does not tell her daughter about it so as to protect her from "such knowledge," yet the daughter hears her mother talking to the neighbours. As a result Rottenberg "developed a phobia about the word Auschwitz and never went there" (2009, 140), which suggests another indirect way of transmission through places of public remembrance and early crystallization into cultural memory, but also the process by which the word "Auschwitz" became *the* cultural icon of the Holocaust. Consequently, Eva Hoffman's observation that "insofar as we identify ourselves as children of survivors, our narratives have been structured mostly by our relationship to the past" proves correct in the context of these three narratives (Hoffman 2004, 241).

Being Jewish and belonging to the second post-Holocaust generation in Poland also involves having to address the issue of communism, in part because of the stereotype of the so-called "żydokomuna" (Michlic 2007, 135-176). Both Rottenberg and Kuryluk address this issue, although each does so in a different way, according to their parents' past and degree of involvement in the system. Rottenberg openly addresses the question of "the presence of Communists of Jewish origin in significant positions in the security apparatus" (Polonsky 2012, 17). Her father was offered a job as Director of Prisons in the Ministry of Justice, but turned it down on the grounds that, as a tailor, he was not qualified for the position. Setting aside the important question as to why a tailor was offered a top position in the prison hierarchy in the first place, Rottenberg talks about her "deep gratitude" to him because, thanks to his refusal, she did not have to feel "burning shame at his actions" or at any involvement he might have had in prosecuting members of the political opposition, which that at that time included the torture, murder and general abuse of innocent prisoners. If Rottenberg's father had become an important figure within the totalitarian system, Rottenberg would have belonged to a privileged social class and enjoyed a lifestyle denied to the majority, and might even have had articles about her family published in the national press as was the case of Ewa Kuryluk (Kuryluk 2009, 117). Rottenberg's father's rejection of the job offer was made more difficult by the fact that he, like Karol Kuryluk, was offered a large apartment in Warsaw where his wife wanted to live, while his refusal left them in provincial Legnica, which neither of them liked.

Keff, whose own story about her father negates—like Rottenberg's—the assumption of unconditional Jewish support for communism,[15] mentions her father's suicide but omits any contextually relevant explanation: before the war, her father had been a Jewish communist and later an officer in the Polish army.[16] Yet he refused to be a witness in a staged trial of officers, some of whom were Jewish, committing suicide instead (Bielas 2008).

Keff is at pains to stress that the focus of her text is not her father, partly because she wishes to concentrate on the patriarchal system in general, where the mother alone is responsible for raising children, because "patriarchy is the most general definition of slavery." (Keff 2008, 67) Keff ends her *Song* with an Epilogue entitled "Song from a Doctor's Waiting Room" and a subtitle inviting the reader to "recognize this homespun song-book" (2008, 73). The Epilogue is a conversation between a group of elderly and poorly educated people within a stereotypical antisemitic discourse, where Jews are presented as responsible for all evil: they are accused of supporting both Hitler and Stalin, of promoting contraceptives to destroy Poland while having children themselves, being ungrateful and scheming: they "rule" modern Poland where even Polish-language newspapers are "Jewish." It ends with attacks on Czesław Miłosz and Wisława Szymborska (because both poets "supported" the Jews), on homosexuals, feminists, capitalism, unemployment and the state of Israel. Eventually the choir demands a disability pension from "the Jews" because "our country was like a Mother to them, like their own Mother, and a Mother deserves a pension," and ends by chanting that football clubs are Jewish, even the football club called "Polonia" (Keff 2008, 77-79). In short, "the Jewish conspiracy" is responsible for all the ills of Poland and the wider world. In *Song*, outrage against antisemitism unites mother and daughter, while the focus on it in the Epilogue suggests that hatred of Jews is entrenched in the older generation of Poles.

Frascati Street focuses to a high degree on antisemitism which for the mother constitutes such a danger she does not let her daughter know she is Jewish, and demands she does not go researching the past. On the one hand, Kuryluk's mother sees in communism an alternative to fascism, nationalism and antisemitism, an

---

15 "This view is offensive both to the majority of the Jews who did not want to live under Communism and left Poland, and because it implies that different moral standards can be applied to judge Jewish and Gentile moral behaviours."' (Bartoszewski 1990, 29) See also Kersten (2000).

16 At that time the Polish army included a significant number of Soviet officers serving as "*ersatz* Poles" (Chodakiewicz 2003, 17).

attitude which seems to have been widespread among Jews in post-war Poland (Kersten 2000, 138) On the other hand, Kohany is aware of the complexities of the post-war political situation in Poland and the fact that some of her writings conceived as documents about the past of Polish Jews constitute in fact a form of propaganda that supported the totalitarian system, despite her partial knowledge of its crimes (Kuryluk 2009, 176-177). Ewa Kuryluk downplays the communist connections of her family, the degree of her own indoctrination such as praying to Stalin (Kuryluk 2009, 160) and the benefits she received as a result of her father's support for communism. Unlike her mother, who feels guilty because of the ease with which she accepted the favours and benefits of the system such as trips abroad, contacts with famous western actors such as Vivien Leigh and politicians such as John Kennedy or Nikita Khrushchev, Kuryluk focuses on her mother's trauma and on antisemitism, thus avoiding a deeper discussion about the rather contentious issue of her parents' support for communism.

Conclusion

In the three texts discussed in this chapter, mothers are without doubt the most important channel of transmission of knowledge about the Holocaust, even if they themselves are not Jewish. However, growing up in Poland at such a short remove from the horrific past constitutes a second, equally important way of transmission for the daughters, whose lives are strongly affected by the knowledge and trauma of their mothers and the existence of antisemitism. In general, the daughters position themselves as supporters of their mothers while employing well-known cultural figures (Polish Mothers) to help convey a more culture-specific meaning to their mothers' suffering as women. The daughters remains trapped by their memories and knowledge of the Holocaust, understood as a "cataclysmic episode in Jewish history within the context of persecution as a recurrent theme throughout Jewish history" (Stein 1984, 5), augmented by the persistence of antisemitism.

At the same time the daughters use their knowledge about the past as material for their artistic works, both directly and indirectly as writers or painters. However, they are also affected by their lack of knowledge of what it means to be Jewish in a "normal" place such as post-war or post-1989 Poland, which is still strongly marked by the memory, and the meaning of the memory, of the Holocaust, and by the presence of antisemitism, which corrupts the possibility of these women seeing themselves and being seen as "normal," and not as the Other. More importantly however, they remain imprisoned by their postmemory and "concerned less with the past than with a sense of that past in the present" (Langer 1991, 40) while continually awaiting and fearing another disaster.

Bibiography

Primary sources

Keff, Bożena. 2008. *Utwór o Matce i Ojczyźnie.* Afterword ("Zmagania z Matką i Ojczyzną") by Maria Janion and Izabela Filipiak. Kraków: Ha!art

Kuryluk, Ewa. 2009. *Frascati. Apoteoza topografii.* Kraków: Wydawnictwo Literackie.

Rottenberg, Anda. 2009. *Proszę bardzo.* Warsaw: Wydawnictwo W.A.B.

Secondary sources

Antler, Joyce. 2007. *You Never Call! You Never Write! A History of the Jewish Mother.* Oxford and New York: Oxford University Press.

Assmann, Jan and John Czaplicka. 1995. "Collective Memory and Cultural Identity." *New German Critique* 65: 125-133.

Bartoszewski, Władysław T. 1990. *The Convent at Auschwitz.* London: Bowerdean.

Bielas, Katarzyna. 2008. "Nielegalny plik." *Gazeta Wyborcza*, 27 May. Accessed 25 August, 2012. http://wyborcza.pl/duzyformat/1,127291,5250183,Nielegalny_plik.html?as=3

Brom, Danny, Revital Kfir and Haim Dasberg. 2001. "A Controlled Double – Blind Study on Children of Holocaust Survivors." *Israel Journal of Psychiatry and Related Sciences* 38(1): 47-57

Chodakiewicz, Marek Jan. 2003. *After the Holocaust: Polish-Jewish Conflict in the Wake of World War II.* East European Monographs 613. New York: Columbia University Press.

Chutnik Sylwia. 2008. *Kieszonkowy atlas kobiet.* Kraków: Ha!art.

—. 2009. "Polskie symbole: Matka Polka, Matka Boska, mama aktywna." [Interview with Agata Grabau]. *Przegląd* 28. Accessed 4 April, 2013. http://www.przeglad-tygodnik.pl/pl/artykul/polskie-symbole-matka-polka-matka-boska-mama-aktywna

Czermińska, Małgorzata. 2000. *Autobiograficzny trójkąt. Świadectwo, wyznanie i wyzwanie.* Kraków: Universitas.

Ellis, Carolyn and Arthur P. Bochner. "Autoethnography, Personal Narrative, Reflexivity: Researcher as Subject." In *Handbook of Qualitative Research,* edited by Norman K. Denzin and Yvonna S. Lincoln, 733-768. 2nd ed. Thousand Oaks, CA: Sage.

Engelking, Barbara. 1994. *Zagłada i pamięć.* Warsaw: Instytut Filozofii i Socjologii PAN.

—. 1993. *Na łace popiołów. Ocaleni z Holocaustu.* Warsaw: Cyklady.

Feinstein, Margaret Myers. 2007. "Absent Fathers, Present Mothers: Images of Parenthood in Holocaust Survivor Narratives." *Nashim: A Journal of Jewish Women's Studies & Gender Issues* 13: 155-182.

Friedlander, Saul. 1993. *Memory, History and the Extermination of the Jews of Europe.* Bloomington, IN: Indiana University Press.

Głowiński, Michał et al., eds. 2005. *Stosowność i forma. Jak opowiadać o Holokauście?* Kraków: Universitas.

Goldhagen, Daniel. 1996. *Hitler's Willing Executioners: Ordinary Germans and the Holocaust.* London: Little, Brown.

Goodman, Nancy R. and Marilyn B. Meyers, eds. 2012. *The Power of Witnessing: Reflections, Reverberations, and Traces of the Holocaust: Trauma, Psychoanalysis, and the Living Mind*. New York and London: Routledge.
Graff, Agnieszka. 2001. *Świat bez kobiet: płeć w życiu publicznym*. Warsaw: W.A. B.
—. 2007. "The Land of Real Men and Women: Gender and E.U. Accession in Three Polish Weeklies." *The Journal of the International Institute* 15(1). Accessed 20 February, 2013. http://quod.lib.umich.edu/j/jii/4750978.0015.107?rgn=main;view=fulltext
—. 2008. *Rykoszetem. Rzecz o płci, seksualności i narodzie*. Warsaw: W.A.B.
Haltof, Marek. 2012. *Polish Film and the Holocaust: Politics and Memory*. New York and Oxford: Berghahn Books.
Hirsch, Marianne. 1996. "Past Lives: Postmemories in Exile." *Poetics Today* 17(4): 659-686.
—. 1997. *Family Frames, Photography, Narrative and Postmemory*. Cambridge, MA: Harvard University Press.
—. 1989. *The Mother/Daughter Plot: Narrative, Psychoanalysis, Feminism*. Bloomington and Indianapolis, IN: Indiana University Press.
Hoffman, Eva. 2004. *After Such Knowledge: Memory, History, and the Legacy of the Holocaust*. New York: Public Affairs.
Janion, Maria. 1996. *Kobieta i duch inności*. Warsaw: Wydawnictwo Sic!
—. 2009a. *Bohater, spisek, śmierć. Wykłady żydowskie*. Warsaw: W.A.B.
Janion, Maria and Monika Rudaś-Grodzka, eds. 2009. *Honor, Bóg, Ojczyzna*. Warsaw: Dom Spotkań z Historią.
Kellermann, Natan P.F. 2001. "Perceived Parental Rearing of Behavior in Children of Holocaust Survivors." *Israel Journal of Psychiatry and Related Sciences* 38(1): 58-68.
Kersten, Krystyna. 2000. "Żydzi – władza komunistów." *Jidełe. Żydowskie Pismo Otwarte* (Wydanie specjalne): 131-140.
Kertzer, Adrienne. 2002. *My Mother's Voice: Children, Literature, and the Holocaust*. Peterborough, ON: Broadview Press.
Kim, Renata. 2009. "Dziennik: Anda Rottenberg o swojej książce i powikłanym życiu." *Dziennik*, 24 March. Accessed 29 June, 2012 http://gazeta.teatr.legnica.pl/index.php/akt-artykuly/1766-dziennik-anda-rottenberg-o-swojej-ksiazce-i-powiklanym-zyciu
Kowalczyk, Izabela. 2003. "Matka-Polka kontra supermatka?" *Czas Kultury* 5: 11-21.
—. 2010. *Matki-Polki, Chłopcy i Cyborgi... Sztuka i feminizm w Polsce*. Poznań: Galeria Miejska "Arsenał."
Krajewski, Stanisław. 2005. *Poland and the Jews: Reflections of a Polish Polish Jew*. Kraków: Austeria.
Kuryluk, Ewa. 1981. "On My Artistic Development Leading to Drawing on Fabrics." *Leonardo* 14(4): 265-270.
—. 2004. *Goldi. Apoteoza zwierzaczkowatości*. Warsaw: Twój Styl.
Langer, Laurence. 1991. *Holocaust Testimonies: The Ruins of Memory*. New Haven, CT: Yale University Press.
Leys, Ruth. 2007. *From Guilt to Shame: Auschwitz and After*. Princeton, NJ and Oxford: Princeton University Press.
Lichtman, Helen. 1984. "Parental Communication of Holocaust Experiences and Personality Characteristics among Second Generation Survivors." *Journal of Clinical Psychology* 40: 914-924.

Łodziński, Sławomir. 1999. "Foreigners in Poland: Selected Issues in Poland's Migrational Policy 1989-1998." *Polish Sociological Review* 126: 301-321.

McGlothlin Erin H. 2006. *Second-Generation Holocaust Literature Legacies of Survival and Perpetration*. Rochester, NY and Woodbridge: Camden House.

Michlic, Joanna. 2007. "Soviet Occupation of Poland, 1939-41, and the Stereotype of the Anti-Polish and Pro-Soviet Jew." *Jewish Social Studies* 13(3): 135-176.

Polonsky, Antony. 1990. *"My Brother's Keeper?" Recent Polish Debates on the Holocaust*. London: Routledge.

—. 2012. "Jews and Communism in the Soviet Union and Poland." American Association for Polish-Jewish Studies. Accessed 28 August, 2012. http://www.aapjstudies.org/manager/external/ckfinder/userfiles/files/Polonsky%20Jews%20and%20Communism.pdf

—. 2009. *Polish-Jewish Relations Since 1984: Reflections of a Participant / Stosunki polsko-żydowskie od 1984 roku: refleksje uczestnika,* Polish translation by Malgorzata Ornat [bilingual edition]. Budapest and Kraków: Austeria.

Porter, Brian. 2005. "Hetmanka and Mother: Representing the Virgin Mary in Modern Poland." *Contemporary European History* 14(2): 151-170.

Ravits, Martha A. 2000. "The Jewish Mother: Comedy and Controversy in American Popular Culture." *MELUS* 25(1): 3-31.

Rowland-Klein, Dani and Rosemary Dunlop. 1998. "The Transmission of Trauma across Generations: Identification with Parental Trauma in Children of Holocaust Survivors." *Australian and New Zealand Journal of Psychiatry* 32(3): 358-369.

Ryan, Michael. 1980. "Self-Evidence: *Le Pacte Autobiographique* by Philip Lejeune." *Diacritics* 10(2): 2-16.

Shanan, Joel. 1988-9. "Surviving the Survivors: Late Personality Development of Jewish Holocaust Survivors." *International Journal of Mental Health* 17(4): 42-71.

Sienkiewicz, Karol. 2011. "Zachęta – decydujące starcie." *Dwutygodnik*, 26 June. Accessed 28 June, 2012. http://www.dwutygodnik.com/artykul/2977-zacheta-decydujace-starcie.html

Stachniak, Eva. 1995. "Why Did We Not Become Feminists? Women in Poland." *NWSA Journal* 7(3): 69-80.

Stein, Howard F. 1984. "The Holocaust, the Uncanny, and the Jewish sense of History." *Political Psychology* 5(1): 5-35.

Szacka, Barbara and Marjorie Castle. 2006. "Polish Remembrance of World War II." *International Journal of Sociology* 36(4): 8-26.

Szczuka, Kazimiera. 2009. "Matka Polka/Matka Żydówka." In *Honor. Bóg. Ojczyzna*, edited by Maria Janion and Monika Rudaś-Grodzka, 181-198. Warsaw: Dom Spotkań z Historią.

Umińska-Keff, Bożena. 2006. *Barykady. Kroniki obsesyjne lat 2000-2006*. Kraków: eFKa.

Watson, Peggy. 1997. "(Anti)feminism after Communism." In *Who's Afraid of Feminism: Seeing through the Backlash*, edited by Ann Oakley and Juliet Mitchell, 144-161. New York: The New Press. Yehuda Rachel et al. 2008. "Maternal, not paternal, PTSD is related to increased risk for PTSD in offspring of Holocaust survivors." *Journal of Psychiatric Research*, 42 (13): 1104-1111.

Into the Well of Memory: Michał Głowiński's Jewish Childhood during the Holocaust

Joanna MICHLIC

Introduction

Pre-1939 Poland was an impressive, vibrant centre of Jewish literary life expressed in three main languages: Yiddish, Hebrew and Polish. Even though the post-1945 remnant Polish Jewish community has been numerically insignificant compared to its pre-war predecessor, and its cultural output cannot match the artistic and literary achievements of the pre-Holocaust period, it has nevertheless produced a salient body of belles-lettres. The distinguished critic and historian of Polish literature Jan Błoński called it the "Jewish school of Polish literature" (Błoński 1986). Child Holocaust survivors, born in 1929 and after, constitute one important subgroup of this school, and are today the last living witnesses to the Holocaust. Some of them, such as Henryk Grynberg (b. 1936) have dedicated their entire literary oeuvre to bearing witness, and have created almost without ceasing an imaginative Holocaust literature of various genres: stories, novels and poetry. In contrast, the literary critic and historian Michał Głowiński (b. 1934), author of the personal Holocaust memoir/autobiography, *The Black Seasons* (*Czarne sezony*), first published in Poland in May 1998, is a latecomer. However, this is not to suggest that Głowiński is so atypical as the author of a late personal Holocaust memoir, or that his case is unique to Poland because of the legacy of the country's communist past and the existence of various social, cultural and political taboos on Jewish matters which had prevented child survivors from speaking out and writing about their experiences until the 1990s and 2000s. On the contrary, we can speak of an almost universal boom in late Holocaust testimonial memoirs in the 1990s and 2000s of both non-literary and varied literary value by child survivors of different national origins. For example, Susan Rubin Suleiman, an accomplished American literary scholar of French literature and a Hungarian child survivor turned to writing her autobiographical memoir in the same period. In *Budapest Diary: In Search of the Motherbook,* published in 1996, Suleiman explores—among other topics—her Jewish childhood in pre-war and wartime Hungary, and the memories of it as she revisits the place where she was born and survived the war. The Israeli writer Irit Amiel, a child survivor from Częstochowa, Poland, has embarked only today at the age of eighty on writing her autobiography.[1] Though Amiel became a successful Israeli author in middle age, writing in Hebrew and Polish moving poetry and arresting short stories about Holocaust survivors of her generation—about those who survived but were "scorched" for life because of what they went through and because of their losses, she wrote almost nothing about herself. In all her published prose, she has alluded to her personal and family wartime history in only two stories, "Leaf from a Diary," the opening story of the *Scorched* volume originally written in Hebrew (2006), and "Ancestors" ("Przodkowie"), a story included in her latest collection *A Double Landscape* (*Podwójny krajobraz*, 2008), written in Polish.

How might Głowiński's testimonial memoir be interpreted? Does Głowiński's memoir represent a new genre of Holocaust writing in Poland? Does it belong to a specifically Polish school of writing about the Holocaust or does it rather exhibit features of Holocaust testimonial literature written by child survivors in different languages? What is the relationship between imaginative autobiographical Holocaust literature and Holocaust testimony produced by child survivors? At what point does the traumatic memory surface among child survivors, and how does the memory unfold? These are the core questions I shall explore in the present chapter.

Głowiński represents a sophisticated, complex and highly self-reflexive voice among child survivors. He is an eminent literary theoretician, and his expertise as a scholar would appear to inform the linguistic-narratological strategies in his autobiographical writings. Representatives of this generation, called by Susan Rubin Suleiman the "1.5 generation" (Suleiman 2002; 2006), could not have had an adult understanding of what happened to them during the war and in the immediate aftermath of the Holocaust. The inability of children to possess and articulate an adult understanding of the world was the main reason why until the "era of witness" in the 1990s (Wieviorka 1998; 2006), their voices have remained almost totally unheard and unnoticed by historians. In addition, for those child survivors from Poland like Głowiński who remained, for various reasons, in the country after the war, the specific political and social situation in Poland between 1945 and the fall of communism in 1989 also contributed to the creation of a thick veil of silence covering their wartime past.

Głowiński's *The Black Seasons* and his other autobiographical wartime writings present the voice of a child survivor from Poland with a distinct set of wartime and post-war experiences. His testimonial works are of literary value, and *The Black Seasons* was even nominated for the prestigious Polish Nike literary award.

1 Author's interview with Irit Amiel, Tel Aviv, 29 August 2011. In this interview, Amiel emphasized that she had to "hurry up" with her autobiography and that her desire to write about her child survivors' generation had been "inside her" throughout her entire adult life. She became an author at the age of fifty thanks to taking a Polish-Hebrew translation course.

However, his writings can only be fully understood in the context of the massive body of late Holocaust testimonies by child survivors of various national origins, both literary imaginative works and straightforward referential accounts devoid of any literary value. Głowiński's preoccupations, concerns and obsessions, and his choice of the short story as the main medium for his autobiographical writing, demonstrate that his work is informed by an awareness of the complexities associated with memory, narrating trauma and representation. Despite its artistry and structure as a story, Głowiński's testimonial writing is primarily pressed into the service of facts. He anchors his writing in a commitment to recall solely his actual autobiographical experiences. In this he places himself within the massive body of Holocaust writings articulated in various genres, including autobiography, fictional autobiography, imaginative literature and poetry, and other artistic works by Holocaust survivors (including even those by the second generation)[2] which are wedded to the same commitment.[3] His way of telling his remembrance makes his writing a work of memoir and history rather than literature in the stricter sense of belles-lettres. Like many other testimonial works by Holocaust survivors, it thus reveals the inadequacy of conventional generic boundaries with regard to Holocaust literature. Głowiński and other child survivors such as Irit Amiel, Henryk Grynberg and Hanna Krall (b. 1935), have created and are continuing to create, in the Polish language, some of the most nuanced examples of Holocaust literature, and in doing so, are bringing something new to Polish writing. There is no tradition in Polish literature of this genre.

Michał Głowiński's confession of memory

How did Głowiński's writing of his wartime recollections begin? In his 2008 personal essay "In the Shadow of the Holocaust?" ("Czy w cieniu Zagłady?"), Głowiński matter-of-factly reveals that for him and his surviving family, the Holocaust was a highly sensitive subject they never mentioned in daily conversations, reminiscences or reflections. At the same time, he describes the Holocaust as "the fundamental subtext of life" (2008, 22). Though never discussed and suppressed from memory, the events of the war have accompanied him throughout his postwar youth and adulthood. In every stage of his life, Głowiński could not escape

2 For example Art Spiegelman, a son of two Holocaust survivors from Poland, has consistently insisted since its publication in 1986 on interpreting his graphic novel *Maus* as a work of history and memory, rather than as literature. For a thoughtful discussion of Spiegelman's work see Horowitz 1997, 2-8. On Spiegelman's commitment to truth, see also the article by Dwight Garner on his recent work *MetaMaus* (Garner 2011).

3 On the commitment to truth in Holocaust imaginative writing, see Horowitz's introduction (1997, 1-33).

the basic realization that his wartime past inevitably marked him as different from his peers of ethnic Polish background. In the climate of Communist Poland with its lurking antisemitic political and social undertones, his peers could not comprehend, much less empathize with, the fate of a Jewish boy who went through the experience of two ghettos, first in Pruszków and next in Warsaw, and then lived as a Jewish fugitive on the Aryan side. They could not understand and accept that in the social environment on the Aryan side some of his compatriots subjugated him to daily acts of dangerous curiosity, insults and blackmail. Neither could they comprehend the feelings of a Jewish boy who had been forced to adopt a brand new social identity as a Christian Polish orphan under fear of death.

After escaping with his parents from the Warsaw Ghetto and hiding with his mother on the Aryan side, first in Warsaw and then in the countryside in central Poland, Głowiński spent the rest of his wartime childhood moving from one orphanage to another. First he was placed in a Catholic home for very young children in Otwock, where he remained only for a couple of days because of his visibility as an older child. Next he was relocated to Czersk near Góra Kalwaria from where he was taken to the Boduen Catholic children's home in Warsaw. During the war this place served as one of the main transit centres for Jewish children in hiding and from there in the winter of 1944 Głowiński was finally and fortuitously moved to the Catholic orphanage run by the Sister Maidservants of the Holiest Virgin Mary in Turkowice, in the southeastern part of the country. Turkowice became his haven where he spent a year and a half before one of his surviving aunts brought him back to his parents.

Yet, despite suppressing the Holocaust almost to oblivion, so it would not interfere with his post-war professional and social life, Głowiński, like many other child survivors, felt compelled to revisit it. The conditions in post-communist Poland in the 1990s, with the sudden boom in the theatre of memory about Jews and the Holocaust, encouraged him to face up to and recollect his youth. Reading Głowiński's account of his personal eruption of memory in the 1990s, it is clear that his writing was never envisaged as a purely literary venture. Far from it, this writing is itself a document of the profound existential and psychological experience of "coming out of the closet" as a child Holocaust survivor, by revealing his own suppressed ethnic identity and overcoming the fears associated with his wartime past.[4] For Głowiński, writing short stories that evoke his core wartime

---

4 Ten years later in *Circles of Otherness: An Autobiographical Tale* (*Kręgi obcości. Opowieść autobiograficzna*) he offers an elaborate account of his long-lasting and well-kept secret about his Jewish roots and Jewish family life before, during and after the Holocaust, but in the same work he also comes out publicly as a middle-aged gay man. The latter personal confession can be viewed as his contribution to the new and intense public debate about gay rights in Poland (see also the chapter in this volume by Błażej Warkocki).

autobiography is part of a complex process of coming to terms with his traumatic past[5]:

> As the years went by, I was contemplating more and more intensely an idea I had carried within me since my youth: of trying to write about my own fate during the Holocaust, about the way events in my life had unfolded, about how I had escaped alive and how I perceived what I had gone through. For a long time I kept postponing this project for later years, for various reasons—not just because I was busy writing other books. I wasn't at all certain I was up to this challenge; I was afraid I would be helpless when it came to coming to grips with it; but, first of all, I had to overcome my various inhibitions. [...] One of the reasons why these narratives have been so important to me was that, by writing them, I learned to speak in public about the Holocaust and I overcame the fear associated with it. (Głowiński 2008, 31-32)

Głowiński's "awakening of memory" has triggered in him the challenging process of "returning to his suppressed childhood," and thus of "returning to himself." *The Black Seasons* is the tangible record of this process. This "return to himself" is dynamic and ongoing, judging by his most recent writings, some of the wartime stories included in his volume *Magdalene Sister from Brown Bread* (*Magdalenka z razowego chleba,* 2001), the volume *History of One Poplar and Other Tales* (*Historia jednej topoli i inne opowieści,* 2003) and the first part of his major autobiography *Circles of Otherness: An Autobiographical Tale* (*Kręgi obcości. Opowieść autobiograficzna,* 2010). All these writings demonstrate that Głowiński as author, narrator and protagonist is compelled to retell, again and again, the same core traumatic events of his wartime autobiography. This is like a ritual of repeatedly putting down on the page crucial parts of one's life that were previously confined only to intimate "silent recollections" in the author's mind. Głowiński admits he longed to share his wartime past for a long time, and yet even after he began to put on paper the traumatic accounts of his childhood, the fears and anxiety associated with reliving them through the act of writing did not entirely dissolve and leave him alone:

> I've told this story to various people, and I've long wanted to commit it to paper as a testimony of those times. Yet something always restrained me. In essence I was protecting myself from it, as if the act of transcription would summon those events back to life in all their horror. I confess that even now I take up the task with difficulty, I struggle against my resistance, yet I don't want this story to remain forever in my memory alone. (Głowiński 2005a, 59)

The published interviews conducted with Głowiński in the late 1990s and 2000s also show that for the author coming to terms with his traumatic childhood, mak-

5 A similar interpretation underlies Knut Andreas Grimstad's discussion of *The Black Seasons* (2010, 209-210).

ing it public is crucial.[6] In a sense, for Głowiński, sharing that experience with a sympathetic listener, the reader, constitutes an integral part of "returning to himself": to that primal past cut out of his autobiography. The author regards the presence of the listener as having some intrinsic healing qualities for himself. Many hidden child Holocaust survivors, not only from Poland but also from other former Nazi-occupied countries, have undergone a similar late "awakening of traumatic memories within themselves" in different circumstances and for different reasons. For some, this process takes place during long, exhausting hours of audio and video-taped oral testimonies, whereas, for others, it occurs on the pages of their written memoirs and autobiographies of varying literary quality. The challenging but cathartic "return to themselves" follows on after the "awakening of memory."

We can trace the beginning of Głowiński's public "awakening of memory" to an interview with the journalist Cezary Gawryś of the Catholic liberal monthly *Więź*.[7] The interview was conducted in 1987, the year when the Holocaust and the painfully protracted discussions about Poland's dark past had just begun, slowly, to enter the public sphere. At that time hidden child survivors living in Poland did not yet come out of the closet and speak up in a full and free voice about their wartime childhoods. The subject was still very much taboo. Therefore Gawryś decided that Głowiński and other child survivors who were saved in Turkowice should be interviewed under different names from their own. In the interview Gawryś addresses Głowiński by the personal name Łukasz. Interestingly, although Głowiński lived under several false family names on the Aryan side, he retained his own personal name Michał throughout that period.[8] Keeping one's own personal name and thus retaining an intrinsic part of one's true personal identity was rare among Jewish child fugitives. As a rule they were forced to adapt and internalize new, full Aryan names more than once during the war. Those who were in Głowiński's situation, consider themselves today to have been lucky. In the interview with Gawryś, Głowiński paid tribute to the late Irena Sendlerowa, one of the central figures in the rescue of Jewish children from the Warsaw ghetto during the Occupation. Sendlerowa was responsible for placing nine-year-old Głowiński and thirty other Jewish children in the Catholic orphanage in Turkowice run by the Sister Maidservants of the Holiest Virgin Mary, and thus for saving his life. Głowiński also recollected certain traumatic moments faced by his family

---

6 See, for example, two interviews conducted with Michał Głowiński by Teresa Torańska (Głowiński 2005b and 2010c), interview with Dariusz Zaborek (Głowiński 2010a) and the earlier Głowiński 2001b.

7 Cezary Gawryś republished the interview in 1997 (Głowiński 1997, 38-40).

8 Author's interview with Głowiński conducted on 29 October 2011. In the interview Głowiński disclosed that he was working on a new wartime story dedicated to his retaining his own personal name during the war.

in the Warsaw ghetto and how lucky his parents, one set of grandparents and his two aunts with their children had been in escaping death and surviving the war. He also briefly recalled the atmosphere in the orphanage in Turkowice, and his quotidian activities there. Towards the end, Głowiński briefly and matter-of-factly mentioned his baptism that took place after the end of the war on his request and with the agreement of his mother who had visited him in Turkowice during the cold February of 1945.

The short story *Emil* was the first piece of testimonial writing that Głowiński published under his own name. Before *Emil* became an integral part of *The Black Seasons*, Głowiński prime autobiographical wartime memoir, it was published in the literary journal *Arkusz* in July 1994, and then in the collection *Black Year... Black Years...* (*Czarny rok....Czarne lata...*), one of the first consisting of straightforward, non-literary, referential short testimonies of Polish child Holocaust survivors (Śliwowska 1996, 273-276). This publication, by the Association of Child Holocaust Survivors in Poland, appeared two years before the first edition of Głowiński's *The Black Seasons*. The collection *Black Year... Black Years...* signifies the rise of a collective memory boom among child Holocaust survivors in Poland in the 1990s, and their need to articulate their wartime past in public. By publishing *Emil* in *Black Year... Black Years...*, Głowiński explicitly asserted his belonging to and identification with the minute yet diverse community of child survivors in Poland. The group includes other child survivors who, like Głowiński himself, possess a complicated multi-layered social identity: Jewish, Catholic and Polish. The similarity in the titles of the collective testimonial volume and Głowiński's first wartime autobiographical memoir is striking, and suggests a common visual reflection about Holocaust childhood in which black is the most dominant colour. In fact, Głowiński originally planned to title his first testimonial work *Black Hours* (*Czarne godziny*), but because of the publication of *Black year... Black Years...*, he renamed it *The Black Seasons*.[9]

The publication of *Emil* among the short, straightforward, referential testimonies in *Black year... Black Years...* also reveals Głowiński's commitment to truth, underscored by most of the survivors, including authors of various imaginative Holocaust writings and artistic visual representations. In *Emil*, and all his other testimonial Holocaust writings, Głowiński emerges as a author guided by what the French literary scholar and theorist Philip Lejeune calls the "autobiographical pact": an "implicit or explicit contract" between author and reader in which the autobiographer commits himself to a sincere effort to come to terms with and represent his own life (Lejeune 1988). In *A Thousand Darknesses*, the American literary critic Ruth Franklin notes that, "such an autobiographical pact

[9] The author would like to thank Głowiński for sharing this information.

is a familiar feature of the holocaust memoir, which is often prefaced by an assertion of the truth value of its content," articulated in a different form such as a foreword (Franklin 2011, 9). Głowiński's autobiographical writings fit well into this category.

Emil is not only an integral part of, but also a prologue to *The Black Seasons* in which the reader observes the breaking down of the cognitive and emotional barriers that kept the wartime experience safely in the past. In *Emil*, Głowiński not only mourns the death in the Warsaw ghetto of his two female tutors Panna Julia and Pani Bronisława, but also his perished classmates, those whom he knew and those like the boy named Emil whom he did not meet, because they were murdered prior to the possibility of their actual encounter. It pains Głowiński that the perished children do not have a voice, that their life stories will remain unvoiced and lost forever. Thus, *Emil* is a sorrowful elegy written in prose for the entire generation of Jewish children who were murdered in the Holocaust. It is an epitaph for his generation. Głowiński struggles to comprehend their death and to absorb the Holocaust. He wrestles with the fundamental existential and moral question survivors constantly pose: why of my generation did I survive, while others, smarter and more talented perished? Why am I alone left alive?

> It is difficult to think of oneself as the only witness and still more difficult to live with that awareness. After all, I can't help but question why I am the one among the living and not the marvellous and exceptional "Emil," Suzi with her odd Polish, or the unruly Tadzio. Why? There is no answer to this kind of question. One can only reflect upon whether Emil, for example, would have better, more wisely, more creatively made use of the unusual gift of life—the life of a person who was condemned to extermination while still in his childhood. (Głowiński 2005a, 15-16)

In *Emil* as in the rest of *The Black Seasons*, the reader becomes not so much a listener to the story as a witness to the ongoing acts of remembering, to the coming and fading of memories, and, above all, to the coming out of memories from oblivion. In this respect, Głowiński's confession of memory closely resembles that of Aharon Appelfeld, a child survivor born two years earlier than Głowiński (in 1932) in the small town of Zhadova (Sadhora) close to the multi-cultural city of Czernowitz (Yiddish name) in Bukovina in pre-1939 Romania, from 1944 part of the Ukrainian Soviet Socialist Republic and since 1991, of the independent Ukrainian state (Ukrainian Chernivsti, Romanian Cernăuţi). Before 1939 Czernowitz was a vibrant political and cultural centre in the lives of East European Jews. Today, Appelfeld is an acclaimed Israeli writer of more than thirty books, known for his poignant stories of the loss of childhood and devastating loneliness of young Jewish fugitives during the war. Not unlike Głowiński in postwar Poland, Appelfeld, as a youngster who arrived alone in Palestine/Israel at the age of fourteen, consciously confined his wartime past to oblivion. Although this past would attempt from time to time to rise to the surface, Appelfeld admits in his personal memoir *The Story of a Life* that the power of suppression was stronger and succeeded in shutting it up "under lock and key" (Appelfeld 2004, viii). Appelfeld's opening note to the reader in *The Story of a Life* is strikingly similar to Głowiński's in *The Black Seasons*. Both authors introduce their works as testimonial memoirs portraying their struggle to dig up and uncover the layers of memories of their deeply buried childhoods, the struggle to articulate the traumatic past into something resembling a coherent narrative. Appelfeld writes:

> This book is not a summary, but an attempt (and perhaps a desperate attempt) to integrate the different parts of my life and to reconnect them to the wellsprings of their being. The reader should not expect a sequential and precise account in this story of a life. These are the regions of my life that have been packed together in memory, and they are alive and pulsating. Much has been lost and much corroded by oblivion. At first it seemed that very little remained, and yet, when I laid one piece alongside another, I saw that not only have they been made whole by the years, but they have even achieved some level of meaning. (2004, ix)

Similarly Głowiński admits:

> When I first began to set down these stories in writing, I did not anticipate their comprising a book. Each of them is a relation of an experience, emerging from flashes of memory, neither embracing the entirety of the event nor encompassing all of my life and the history of how I survived during those years. These stories are rather of a different character, and I was unconcerned with their unity. I was unable to sketch a continuous record—the gaps in my memory revealed themselves to be too great. (Author's Note 2005a, 3)

In contrast to Appelfeld, who immerses himself in the well of his ruined memory in order to uncover and bring to life the lost and painful past, Głowiński frequently pauses to share with the reader his experiences of the process of the recovery of his memories: what emerges from the ruins of his memory and how it does so, and which events do not come to the surface. He exhibits a great deal of self-reflection regarding the general state of his memories of the past, and more specifically the memories belonging to a child survivor who is still chronologically a child. He is curious about how the memory of a child was shaped by fragile, limited and non-adult knowledge of the world. Thus Głowiński not only transmutes fragments of his memory into the testimonial story of his wartime childhood, but also writes about the ways his wartime remembrances became imprinted in his memory and then unfold. His reflections on his ways of remembering shape and frame all the recollected moments of his essential wartime autobiography: the portrayal of members of his family, grim and scary events in the Warsaw ghetto and on the Aryan side, the colours and smells of the ghetto, and his own wartime self-portrayal. He admits that some aspects of his wartime autobiography remain outside of the recollections articulated in writing, that they are not "awakened," or are too traumatic to be "awakened" and to be shared.

Głowiński is concerned with exactitude, truthfulness, forgetting, and the many gaps or black holes in his memory of his wartime childhood and family. He differentiates between "what I remembered" and "what I know now" and between "what I remembered as a child" and "what I remember about my childhood right now with the knowledge acquired from relatives and books." He consciously attempts to eliminate the latter memories from his wartime stories. One encounters a similar type of reflection about personal memory in video-taped testimonies of the 1990s and 2000s of child survivors, and in some written autobiographical memoirs. However, in contrast to written testimony, the video-taped testimonies also offer us a direct gaze into the ways the child survivors as adults instantly react to their recollections of their wartime past—through their silent pauses and strong emotional outbursts prompted by reliving the past during interviews.

In *The Black Seasons*, Głowiński uncovers the primal account of his wartime childhood. The author builds blocks of personal narratives of various wartime experiences. Such experiences constitute the essence of his wartime biography and define who he became during the war. The core group of these experiences includes those of an especially shocking and traumatic nature, such as his learning of his grandfather Lajzar Głowiński's suicide, and his spending long dreadful hours on his own in an apartment in the Warsaw ghetto. He recalls how he was surprised and disturbed on the streets of the ghetto after a starving beggar boy stole—in a second—a piece of pastry from his hand. He recounts playing a long game of chess with a blackmailer in an attic on Srebrna Street in January 1943, while his aunt Teodora desperately sought funds to pay off the blackmailer and save their lives. He remembers being watched and suspected of being Jewish by onlookers in a coffee shop on the Aryan side, while his aunt Maria left him to make a phone call. These experiences are, to cite the pioneering American psychologist William James, "events so emotional as to leave a scar upon the cerebral tissue."[10]

The theoretical literature on Holocaust writing often underscores the problem of drifts in memory in survivors' testimonies and their lack of reliability and competence. It also warns us that we live in an age when false memoirs proliferate. In contrast, the historian Yehuda Bauer argues that memory does not necessarily fade with age, but becomes "sharper." Bauer suggests that the passage of time does not make a testimony less truthful, but on the contrary, makes it more so by creating

---

[10] William James stated this in "The Principle of Psychology" in 1890. His main argument was that although memory is not always perfect, a memory can sometimes accurately preserve a moment in time; cited in Kensinger (2009, 99).

"detachment" from the traumatic events and their emotional impact (Bauer 2001, 24).[11]

Głowiński, as a literary historian who teaches the literature of the Holocaust, is concerned with the problem of authenticity and veracity in this genre. He believes kitsch or embellishments are necessarily limited in works where the author is committed to telling his own personal story and describe his own observations, even if the recollections are dull and mundane. For Głowiński, a story is the ideal form for writing Holocaust testimonial memoirs because, he argues, it operates according to the rules of a non-fiction medium (Głowiński et al. 2005, 7-20). He sees the story as a medium able to represent events in a concrete way, and thus close to representations found in a strictly referential report, court proceeding or journalist essay. He correctly assesses that the story is one of the dominant forms of Holocaust narration. Głowiński's observations about the importance of the "I" voice or first-person narrator and the "story" as the medium of Holocaust narration, serving the purpose of bearing witness, are useful for understanding his own striving as an author for the least mediated representations of his childhood. They also assist us in perceiving how he self-categorizes his own writings. *The Black Seasons* and his other testimonial writings demonstrate that child survivors' works provide a serious forum for reflections about the Holocaust. Through these writings, child survivors grapple with how the genocide affected them as young individuals and as adults, as well as affected their families, friends and entire generation. Głowiński's *The Black Seasons* is testimony to an ongoing trauma, although the author attempts to dissociate his past from the present, insisting somehow that it does not have much impact on his present life. It is a record of returning to oneself through the challenging process of awakening the memory of the traumatic, primal events of one's childhood. This is a common experience among hidden child survivors, those capable of writing about their pasts in a sophisticated way that has literary worth like Głowiński, and those only able to verbalize it in oral interviews or straightforward referential written testimonies. Głowiński's process of awakening memory and thus returning to himself illustrates the validity and depth of the statement made by French writer and theorist Maurice Blanchot, that: "Whoever wishes to remember must trust to oblivion, to the risk entailed in forgetting absolutely, and to this wonderful accident that memory then becomes."

[11] Bauer's observations are confirmed by scientific research by psychologists investigating the nuances of memories of emotional events, particularly of negative valence, in older adults; see Kensinger 2008 and 2009.

Bibliography

Amiel, Irit. 2006. "Leaf from a Diary." In her *Scorched: A Collection of Short Stories on Survivors,* translated from the Hebrew by Riva Rubin, 1-2. London: Vallentine Mitchell.

Appelfeld, Aharon. 2004. *The Story of a Life,* translated by Aloma Halter. New York: Schocken Books.

Bauer, Yehuda. 2001. *Rethinking the Holocaust.* New Haven, CT: Yale University Press.

—. 2008. "Przodkowie." In her *Podwójny krajobraz,* 47-50. Warsaw: Proszyński i S-ka.

Błoński, Jan. 1986. "Is There a Jewish School of Polish Literature?" *Polin* 1: 196-211.

Franklin, Ruth. 2011. *A Thousand Darknesses.* Oxford and New York: Oxford University Press.

Garner, Dwight. 2011. "After a Quarter-Century, an Author Looks Back at His Holocaust Comic." *New York Times,* 12 October. Accessed 23 October, 2011. http://www.nytimes.com/2011/10/13/books/metamaus-by-art-spiegelman

Głowiński, Michał. 1997. "Turkowice, śmierć i ocalenie." In *Ścieżka ocalenia* [Interviews conducted 1987-1996], edited by Cezary Gawryś, 38-40. Warsaw: Biblioteka Więzi.

—. 1999. *Czarne sezony.* Warsaw: OPEN.

—. 2001a. *Magdalenka z razowego chleba.* Kraków: Wydawnictwo Literackie.

—. 2001b. "Zapisy Zagłady." *Tygodnik Powszechny. Kontrapunkt* 1-2, 25 March: 14-15.

—. 2003. *Historia jednej topoli i inne opowieści.* Kraków: Wydawnictwo Literackie.

—. 2005a. *The Black Seasons,* translated by Marci Shore. Evanston, IL: Northwestern University Press.

—. 2005b. "Polskie gadanie." [Interview conducted by Teresa Torańska]. *Gazeta Wyborcza,* 23 May. Accessed 30 May, 2005. http://serwisy.gazeta.pl/df/2029020,34471,272112.html

—. 2008. "Czy w cieniu Zagłady?" In *Myślenie po Zagładzie. Głosy z Polski,* edited by Sebastian Rejak, 19-34. Warsaw and Kraków: MUZA SA.

—. 2010a. "Amator kwaśnych jabłek." [Interview with Dariusz Zaborek]. *Gazeta Wyborcza,* 2 November. Accessed 4 November, 2010. http://wyborcza.pl/2029020,75480,8590576.htlm?sms_code

—. 2010b. *Kręgi obcości. Opowieść autobiograficzna.* Kraków: Wydawnictwo Literackie.

—. 2010c. "Michał Głowiński." In *Trzy rozmowy Teresy Torańskiej. Śmierć spóźnia się o minutę,* edited by Teresa Torańska, 103-154. Warsaw: Biblioteka Gazety Wyborczej.

Głowiński, Michał, et al., eds. 2005. *Stosowność i forma. Jak opowiadać o Holokauście?* Kraków: Universitas.

Grimstad, Knut Andreas. 2010. "The Rhetoric of Present Absence: Representing Jewishness in Post-Totalitarian Poland." In *Contesting Europe's Eastern Rim: Cultural Identities in Public Discourse,* edited by Ljiljana Saric et al., 203-217. Bristol: Multilingual Matters.

Horowitz, Sara R. 1997. *Voicing the Void: Muteness and Memory in Holocaust Fiction.* Albany, NY: State University of New York Press.

Kensinger, Elizabeth A. 2008. "How emotion affects older adults' memories for event details." *Memory* 17: 1-12.

—. 2009. "Remembering the Details: Effects of Emotions." *Emotion Review* 1(2): 99-113.

Lejeune, Philippe. 1988. *On Autobiography,* translated by Katherine M. Leary. Minneapolis, MN: University of Minnesota Press.

Semprun, Jorge. 1997. *Literature or Life.* New York: Viking.

Śliwowska, Wiktoria, ed. 1996. *Czarny rok... Czarne lata...* Warsaw: Nakładem Stowarzyszenia Dzieci Holocaustu w Polsce.

Suleiman, Susan Rubin. 1996. *Budapest Diary: In Search of the Motherbook.* Lincoln, NE: University of Nebraska Press.

—. 2002. "The 1.5 Generation: Thinking About Child Survivors and the Holocaust." *American Imago* 59(3): 277-295.

—. 2006. *Crises of memory and the Second World War.* Cambridge, MA: Harvard University Press.

Wieviorka, Annette. 1998. *L'Ère du témoin.* Paris: Plon.

—. 2006. *The Era of the Witness,* translated from the French by Jared Stark. Ithaca, NY and London: Cornell University Press.

Polish Holocaust Writing after Testimony, or the Relevance of Piotr Paziński's *The Boarding House*

Knut Andreas GRIMSTAD

At the core of this chapter's interest is the construction of memory and identity in a seemingly new period of Polish postmemorial Holocaust writing. We are nearing an age "after testimony" when all works will have to come to terms in some way with the historical reality that accounts of survivors have tried to communicate, and when the actual witnesses will have died out. My concern here is with trends and tendencies among younger Polish-Jewish writers whose approach may well be a projection of their own generation, their own human affairs and doings. Referring to the "passed down" memory inherited by writers who have no personal recollection of the events, Ewa Kuryluk draws attention to those, of her age and younger, who are moving away from the Holocaust as such to writing about growing up in the post-war world. Characteristically, they "try to describe the universal and local sources of Holocaust as well as its 'afterlife'—in mentality, society and the individual self."[1] In this respect, *the grandchildren* of Polish-Jewish Holocaust survivors represent a complex phenomenon grappling with postmemorial trauma as well as the persistent shadow of history. Since we are dealing with the subject matter of Holocaust, we are also necessarily dealing with the relation between aesthetics and ethics, and with the relation between aesthetics and transmission. Hence I propose to explore this budding third-generation writing and ask *how* it has been created, and how it has been created most effectively. While the question of what constitutes a literary generation has never lent itself to sacrosanct answers and has often generated a profusion of conflicting positions, the fact remains that the majority of writers whose texts constitute the hitherto modest corpus of third-generation Polish Holocaust texts, were born well into the 1970s and made their publishing debuts after 2004, the epochal date of post-totalitarian Poland's accession into the European Union. An intriguing case in point is Piotr Paziński (b. 1973).

[1] Personal communication to me 19 March 2012.

A poetics for the retrival of memory

In 2009, Paziński was launched as the first literary voice of Poland's third post-Holocaust generation (Sobolewska 2009).[2] Since then, his slender little book of some 130 pages has received the "Paszport Polityki" (awarded by the weekly newspaper *Polityka*), has been shortlisted for the Nike Award, has sold more than 8000 copies and been translated into several languages.[3] *The Boarding House* (*Pensjonat*) is a quasi-autobiographical novel about a man who journeys by train back to a Jewish guesthouse where he used to spend summers as a child with his grandmother, a Holocaust survivor. The first-person narrator focuses on the "events" of a single day, during which he evokes the ghosts of the dead residents—Jewish traditionalists, assimilationists, ex-communists—while realizing that the past cannot easily be summoned without a feeling of inadequacy and incongruity.

To the extent that Paziński is staging himself as a Polish-Jewish writer of Holocaust literature, it may be useful to cite some of his many published comments on the novel's inception, its main features and ambitions. As Paziński explains to online journalist Katarzyna Kazimierowska, he concentrated first and foremost on "reconstructing a world from my recollections, not from stories heard in childhood" (Kazimierowska 2009a).[4] It should be emphasized here, as elsewhere, that he presents himself as a writer of fiction whose work is a fantasy based on childhood memories or, as he puts it himself, "perhaps it is a testimony of a generation, perhaps just an author's record of his own reflections—I do not know" (Paziński 2010).[5] More unambiguous is the structure of the narrative: first, there are the episodes from the narrator's childhood spent at the guesthouse in the late 1970s—told from a child's perspective, these involve his grandmother and the other Jewish boarders; and second, there are the vicissitudes of the adult narrator's return: these are told in the here and now, depicting the boarders from his childhood who have survived, as it were, into the postdependence era, where they continue their squabbles. Significantly, as in the prose of Bruno Schulz (1892-

---

2 This epithet might also be ascribed to Mikołaj Łoziński (b. 1980), another award-winning Polish writer of Jewish origin. But although his latest novel *Książka* (*A Book*, 2011), fraught with absurd humour as it is, deals with questions related to the Holocaust and the war, this forms only a sub-theme. In this "family saga," more strongly present are the so-called *żydokomuna* (Jewish communism) and victims of the 1968 antisemitic witchhunt.

3 These figures were communicated to me by Paziński's publisher Nisza (15 March 2012).

4 See also Paziński's own comments on the novel's fictionality in an interview with Paweł Dunin-Wąsowicz (2009).

5 Given that the author's experiences have been transmitted to him in such a profound and affective way as *to seem* to form memories in their own right, his "postmemorial connection" to the past is, to paraphrase Marianne Hirsch (2001, 2008), not so much mediated by recall as by imaginative projection and creation.

1942), the Polish-Jewish short-story writer and artist, less emphasis is placed on dramatic action than on dream-like atmosphere.[6]

From the prologue onwards, there is a subdued and soberly reflective tone, a "serene melancholy" (Huelle 2010; Sobolewska 2009), which has not been lost on readers. According to many reviewers, it is "a story about melancholy as the driving force of literature," in which "dwelling on loss is a way of maintaining the past" (Kurkiewicz 2010); to others, it offers a "melancholic 'archeology of memory'" (*Gazeta Wyborcza* [no author] 2010). Some literary scholars have conceived of the boarding house as a privileged heterotopia, or space displacement, within which Jewish survivors meet in a "melancholic landscape" (Szczepan 2011, 254); others, in a similar vein, have likened the narrator's experience of an identity gap to "rituals of melancholy" (Dąbrowski 2011, 268).[7] I should like to add that melancholy, as *a feeling of pensive sadness*, is useful because it tends to be easily recognized as a condition in which the Holocaust victim displays inner torment.[8] More precisely, for Paziński's readers it is a trusted identity, or at least allows them to believe that they better understand the feelings of the afflicted, regardless of the generation to which a person belongs. As to the transmission of postmemorial trauma, we may thus surmise that Paziński is a retriever of memory but without the historian's imperative of seeking causal explanations for the events.[9] Instead of understanding, the rememberer seeks emotion—especially the emotion of melancholy. But is melancholy the only emotion associated with memory? I think not. Because it chronicles the experience of a rememberer who recreates a vanished childhood world, *The Boarding House* reads more like a contemplative tale about the passing of all things. It is significant here that Paziński describes his novel as "an attempt to answer the question: what kind of crazy notions [zajoby] do you have?" (Dunin-Wąsowicz 2009) Inasmuch as his narrator is driven by a traumatic past that he has not experienced personally, but which has somehow been transmitted to him—albeit unconsciously—by his grandmother and the guesthouse residents, it seems fair to conjecture that the author's "crazy notions" point to a poetics encompassing a revival of memory, wherein his Jewish identity could be shaped by echoes, shadows and, to paraphrase James E. Young's expression, memories of memories (Young 1998). Moreover, Paziński's obsessions with memory, because

6 In addition to Bruno Schulz, Paziński's book has invited comparison with an impressive line of memory-oriented writers, ranging from the deceased Thomas Mann, Marcel Proust, Georges Perec and Julian Stryjkowski to contemporaries such as Jonathan Safran Foer, Irit Amiel and Michał Głowiński. See, among others, Sobolewska 2009, Dunin-Wąsowicz 2009, Huelle 2010, Jankowicz 2010, Rutkiewicz 2011 and Dąbrowski 2012.

7 "Heterotopia" is used here in the Foucauldian sense (Foucault 1984).

8 For this definition, see Oxford Dictionaries: http://oxforddictionaries.com/definition/melancholy?q=melancholy (Accessed 6 July, 2012).

9 I have borrowed the phrase "retriever of memory" from Charles S. Maier (1995).

of the very fact that they are obsessions, are not something that can be made to go away. And so his novel becomes more than tinged with an aura of nostalgia.

In relation to Paziński's memory poetics, nostalgia—understood as an emotional state and used in purely psychological terms—refers as much to a temporal as to a geographical site, meaning the narrator may primarily be longing for a *time* called "home". With this shift from place-loss to time-loss, the narrator's nostalgia is transformed into something irrevocable, since the flow of time cannot be reversed. Let us consider another of Paziński's comments: "A bit of nostalgia, yes, but perhaps more important than nostalgia is the melancholic statement that the world which we remember already belongs exclusively to our memory, it is founded upon it and if we do not keep a record of it—it will perish along with us" (Kurkiewicz 2010). In an interview with Kazimierowska, he stresses that we have to live with our parents' and grandparents' stories but must also stake out the course for our own life (Kazimierowska 2009b). In my opinion, these and other declarations point to the *disingenuousness of nostalgia* as well as to the author's attempt to fully absorb the traumatic Holocaust events. For as yearner he does not really wish to go back, instead he wishes to continue to yearn to return, meaning it is the yearning itself that is desired, and not the actual return (Horowitz 2010, 49ff).

A strategy of nostalgia

In the remainder of this chapter, I will examine Paziński's novel with the aim of establishing the strategy of nostalgia that he seems to have adopted in an attempt to be relevant to segments of the Polish public. I have in mind mainly third-generation post-Holocaust Poles, Jewish or not, who continue to express their sorrow over the absence of Jews in present-day Poland, and who read the author's fictionalized personal account against the turbulent history of Polish-Jewish relations.[10] In tracing descriptions of belonging and communality that are particularly poignant, my hypothesis is twofold. First, I argue that Paziński performs a

[10] Judging by numerous articles on blogs and other websites, *The Boarding House* was particularly well received by younger readers. See, for example, Kazimierowska 2009b, Rahoza 2009, Wieliczko 2009 and Jankowicz 2010. As to the grandchild-generation of all Poles and their thematization of the country's missing Jews, consider the popularity of Kraków's annual festival of Jewish culture. According to Paweł Pijanowski (2012), it has increasingly "undertaken to reflect on the Annihilation in a profound manner, touching upon such questions as: (post)memory and the experience of trauma among successive victims of the Holocaust, the limits of artistic decorum and the problem of education (cf. the interesting panel "How to teach successive generations about the Holocaust")." Consider also the virtual Movement for Polish-Jewish Renaissance (Ruch Odrodzenia Żydowskiego w Polsce, 2010) and the Polish-Israeli film *Nightmares* (*Mary Koszmary,* 2007) directed by Yael Bartana, in which left-wing intellectual and activist Sławomir Sierakowski plays a leading role. As he said to the Danish weekly *Weekendavisen* (10

"working through" of memory material using melancholy balanced with low-key humour, in order to cut right to the hearts of his readers. This ambiguous process involves what might be called Paziński's *quiet voice* and takes place across the dimensions of location, characters, objects and time. Second, I will contend that the author's ultimate aim is to negotiate and reconfirm a dual (Polish-Jewish) identity—and to suggest that his self-presentation expresses truths to which contemporary society at large should attend.

Location

Referring to the guesthouse as it appeared immediately after the Second World War, Paziński uses the word "pensjonat" (literally "pension"), which implies both a sanatorium (as in a medical facility for long-term illnesses) and an asylum (as in a sanctuary or refuge). In so far as the boarders are people sick with melancholy following the cataclysm of the Holocaust, the association with pathology is justifiable. Briefly stated, the location is populated with traumatized people who depend on storytelling: whether they are portrayed as dead or living, the guests at this "health resort" have a bent for the healing exchanges of stories.[11] The narrator sets their stories in motion and, what is more, he is capable of recording and editing them. Just as the guesthouse had been a sanatorium in both the pre-war and post-war past, so too in the novelistic present it has become an isolation ward. For in addition to separating its "inmates" from the outside world, it also—owing to their weakening or deliberately weakened memory—isolates them from the past. Away from the city, they live inside of their community, squabbling over difficult matters that outsiders cannot easily understand.

To some extent Paziński draws on first-generation writer Bogdan Wojdowski (1930-1994), whose posthumous novel *The Other Side* (*Tamta strona*, 1997) is also set in a dilapidated guesthouse owned by the post-war remnants of the Polish-Jewish community. Moreover, the main hero arrives for a two week "holiday," whilst the boarders are unable to free themselves from the memories of the Holocaust; they talk, think and dream of it continuously. Pathologically speaking, the survivors' lives have been destroyed by trauma. However, Wojdowski's title refers to the majority world that exists beyond the ghetto walls, an "outside" to which neither the first-generation Jewish author nor his characters have access. In *The*

March 2012), "The loss is almost tangible [. . .] it is a strange feeling to live in Warsaw knowing that in your city there lived until relatively recently about 350,000 people with an altogether different culture, language, customs, history [. . .] the absence of Jews also means something for the Poles' perception of their own national identity."

11 I am indebted to Inga Iwasiów (2010) for drawing attention to the medical aspect of Paziński's novel.

Boarding House, however, the narrator is a third-generation Jew who comes from this outside, but who wishes to enter the "side" of his retrieved childhood,[12] as is the case in one of his initial encounters, a dialogue featuring a certain Pani Mala:

"Me? To my room," I mumbled.
"To your room?" She was obviously feeling indignant. "This is a holiday resort [. . .]."
"I know and I would like to go inside."
"Why do you want to go inside?" She was suspicious.
"I'm from here." I did not know how else to explain myself. "I lived here once."
"You lived here. What do you mean 'lived'? And who are you? I haven't seen you here before."
"Long ago, I was here a long time ago." It didn't sound very clever. (Paziński 2009, 11)[13]

In reply to the old Jewess, the narrator insists that he is "from here" and "lived here once" but soon after feels the strangeness and inadequacy of these phrases. Dwelling upon one recollection after another, he seems to have arrived from the world of the living in order to visit the half-dead, who (unlike Wojdowski's boarders) attempt at all costs to forget their past. In spite of (or because of) their resistance, he brings to the surface a conversation with a certain Pan Jakub and the guesthouse caretaker, both of whom are curious as to the whys and hows of his visit.

"Are you staying for long?"
"For a few days."
"For a few days. So you're passing through. A short visit. Young people are always on the move [. . .]."
"And what brings you here?" The caretaker decided to join in the conversation.
"That old Jewish dilemma, as they say. Once a man is a Jew, he wants to sit awhile among his own folk."
"There are very few people now, less and less," the other one sighed. "Everywhere in the world people arrive, only with us it's the other way around."
"In the Jewish way, it's all different," Pan Jakub remarked in a tone of light sarcasm. "Go outside the tent. Look at all the stars! Do you remember our forefather, Abraham?" (Paziński 2009, 31)

In the rendering of this dialogue, the narrator emphasizes the temporary quality of his sojourn to the close-knit community ("for a few days," "passing through"). At the same time, though, with the light-hearted reference to his own Jewishness, he indicates a yearning to belong (he "wants to sit awhile among his own

[12] This point is also made by Grzegorz Jankowicz (2010). In so far as *The Boarding House* is "an attempt to show the same world from a different perspective, since he writes from the perspective of an old man, and I from that of a child" (Kurkiewicz 2010), we might perhaps say that Paziński enters into a dialogue with his predecessor.

[13] Translations from the novel are my own. At the time of writing, there is no complete published English translation.

folk"). There are many such wistfully humorous scenes in which identity issues are treated ambiguously, while it becomes clear that the guesthouse is a crisis heterotopia, a separate space where coping with post-traumatic stress may take place out of sight.

Characters

The boarders exist solely within the narrator's memory; or rather, they are emanations which he evokes from his childhood world. Moreover, they are portrayed in connection with ordinary guesthouse situations—walks in the forest, rest-cures in the open air, dining-room meals, card-playing and so on. As part of his strategy, the narrator makes a point of describing how he felt at home and happy in their company:

> On such misty days, I used to meet Pan Abram and Pan Leon in the garden [. . .] They would sit me down between them and begin to spin yarns to which I could listen endlessly [. . .]. Then everything would cease to be important, the world around us vanish [. . .]. (Paziński 2009, 91)

As to why the boarders engaged in brawls and similar displays of conflict, a significant role is afforded to the abovementioned Abram. Like his namesake, the patriarch of the Bible, he has an uncritical attitude to God's commandments:

> "Quarrels are our speciality," Pan Abram remarked. "Didn't we quarrel in the desert? All the time, without a break! This is bad, that is bad, the food is tasteless, the neighbours no good, family members not like they should be."
>
> Back then we had something to quarrel about. We had just begun the wandering. What now, when we have almost finished it? How will we quarrel after this? Will it still make sense? And perhaps Pan Abram and Pan Leon have brought our march to a close? The last of the quarrellers from there? (Paziński 2009, 108)

Now here the narrator renders himself as an insider, a pensive co-member of an ancient community ("What now, when we have almost finished it?"). Having crossed over from the other side, from the outside world, he identifies with both biblical and present-day Jews. It is characteristic, therefore, that he lets Abram, a latter-day representative of the old faith, address the problem of "damned assimilation" ("przeklęta asymilacja," 115):

> "Tell me, how is it that a Jew, a wise Jew, well even a stupid one, though few Jews are born stupid, how is it that he can believe in the foolish idea that a Jew can change his skin, be somcone he isn't?"
>
> "But Pan Abram, there are those who have succeeded," someone remarked.

> "Succeeded? In becoming goim? Changing their clothes, walking and dancing, when they start playing for them? Do you think it's so difficult to change your name?"
>
> "Rubinstein, the one who played the piano," recalled Pani Mala.
>
> "But Rubinstein, he isn't a converted Jew!" protested Pani Tecia. "He only left the temple. After all, he's a cultured person."
>
> "Cut off the nose," Pan Leon laughed out loud. "Where I come from, this is what they told a fellow who was drinking in a bar with the locals. Shiker vi a poyer, drunk like a peasant. It's just the nose!" (Paziński 2009, 115-116)

Note how the narrator gives the dual theme of belonging/non-belonging a tongue-in-cheek treatment. But although he is drawn to the world of the guesthouse, he never feels quite at home among its Jewish residents. Judging from this and other dialogues where the prevailing melancholy is lightened with humour, the only alternative to "wandering" appears to be to settling for an integrated identity, to become if not a secular then "a cultured person."

Objects

The narrator recalls and describes his discovery of things that are marked with peoples' fates, thus linking the past and the present. The objects "speak" and become mnemonic devices with which to focus on his relationship with the individual boarder. As indicated, the two determining factors of sanatorium narration are stories and medicine. Hence the narrator's detailed description of various black-and-white photographs, or the look and smell of tables full of flasks and phials containing medicinal substances—and, in this connection, of the many Jewish doctors. One in particular has left an indelible impression on the narrator's memory:

> Doctor Kahn had a little bird's head instead of a nose, like Uncle Motia, and on it sat a pair of gold-rimmed spectacles, which I later saw worn only by doctors. I loved staying with Doctor Kahn and skimming through his very thick books [...] I also thought highly of Doctor Kahn for another, perhaps more prosaic reason; there was always a small bowl of big pink fruit-flavoured candy with white filling, stuck together in one lump, waiting for me in his room [...]. I also liked Doctor Kahn a lot because once, when I was ill, he came to me in a white apron, looked me over carefully and administered medicine [...]. (Paziński 2009, 36-37)

Here we can say that the mention of glasses, books, sweets, aprons and medicine is an important facet of the memory poetics, in the sense that each object underscores the narrator's feeling of closeness and inclusion. A more painful and pessimistic example is the description of Pan Abram who has turned to hoarding as a sort of compensation for loss and privation. After years of writing biographical notes on used tram tickets, he intends to publish an encyclopedia of the fates of Polish Jews. It is doubtful whether the frail old Jew succeeded in his endeavours. Characteristically, however, the story about the failed biographical project is balanced by a series of more optimistic images, notably featuring the amiable Doctor Kahn who

> also had at his place a shelf of crime fiction. The books stood in the neighbouring room, right next to a small cupboard full of mysterious objects, which now and then, when I kept asking, Doctor Kahn would take out [...] Treasures from his travels, from the wanderings of doctor Kahn. What could you not find there! [...]. "Ma tovu ohalecha...," he began to sing. Jacob's tents. Why did we have to live in tents? To roam such a very long way through the desert only to find ourselves here, where we are?" (Paziński 2009, 60-61)

As evidenced by the narrator's rendering of this and similar scenes, crippled objects and unfinished stories fill the empty space of the guesthouse—now with consoling, now with burdensome memory. Kahn's reference to the Jews' desert wandering and their blessing "How fair are your tents, O Jacob" (Numbers 24:5) are significant, because what is blessed is a type of world unity in which people have different opinions, outlooks on life and acceptance of one another. On the whole, however, the narrator is left with a more jarring feeling of incompetence and alienation, of "life on an island" (Paziński 2009, 134), which in turn highlights the ambivalence of his identity.

Time

The narrator embarks on a journey through time, setting out by train for the guesthouse in the morning, leaving it in the evening. But his expedition is not made in any particular year or at a particular moment in his now adult life. Rather, it is the sum total of many remembered visits to this place, in both winter and summer. Thus he is free to shift between different levels of memory. The primary time reference for his rendering of the guesthouse are the pre-war years, but the pre-war and the post-war pasts blend together. And here the rendition of his experiences indicates that although he lives in an eternal present, he cannot escape either collective destiny or his own recollections.

> Their life and my life, among shadows, amid spirits and together with spirits—instead of rays of fresh sun. The taste of transience was too bitter. And there was too much old age. Too much medicine, occasional coughing, as well as memories of those who were no longer. Who were killed during the war. Who later died, emigrated or somehow vanished across the world. A melancholic landscape [...]. (Paziński 2009, 74)

In so far as the main focus is on time-loss, and the flow of time cannot be reversed, we could say that underlying the narrator's yearning is a nostalgia, whose model is Adam and Eve's expulsion from the Garden of Eden. For like them, he cannot return to his original "home" but must go on to live in the real world, being human, being one of us. In one of the concluding scenes, Pan Jakub addresses the narrator's ambivalent feeling of attachment, then expands on a story about his biblical namesake.

"Sad to be with old people, isn't it?"

He did not wait for my reply. "But then you had only a few days here anyway… Passing through…" Passing through, young people are always on the move. I am sure he wanted to add […].

"It is said that on the night when Jacob fell asleep in Beit El, the Lord God allowed him to see the entire history of the world […], when he awoke, he had the strength only to cry: 'What a terrible place this is! Surely, God has been here and I did not see anything, Veani lo yadati!'" (Paziński 2009, 128-129)

According to one Jewish traditional interpretation (Philo of Alexandria), Jacob's dream of the ladder points to the communal life of the Jews, who are subject to constant ups and downs as they strive for moral and spiritual improvement; or, it symbolizes the entanglement of human destinies.[14] Towards the end of our narrator's account, this entanglement seems to be solved (echoing the unity motif of Jacob's tents) by an evocative image of all the boarders marching as deceased spirits. While being witness to the procession, however, the narrator is uncertain as to whether it actually takes place before his eyes or whether it is played out in the eyes of Pan Jakub:

I wanted to run away, but felt held back by some power […].
"I am coming to you!" I cried.
"No, no, why do you say that, where did you get that idea from? He's gone mad, simply gone mad! What nonsense he's talking!"
"It's our forest and we don't need anyone here!"
"It's Bronka's grandson. Where will he go now?" (Paziński 2009, 134)

In the end, the narrator separates himself from the spectacle of phantasmagorical characters and reaches the railway station. Here the grandson is left on his own, "the last of the generational links, attached to the very end" (Paziński 2009, 134). And so he has enacted a return to the place that formed his identity—that is, he has gone "home" again. But it turns out not to be the home of memory, the Jewish home for which he has yearned, because the guesthouse has changed over time, and is no longer its former self. It has become a space of otherness, which is neither here nor there, simultaneously physical and mental. In addition, the adult returner has changed from the person he used to be as a child. In this res-

[14] A similar point is made by Huelle 2010.

pect, *The Boarding House* becomes an accessible and all-inclusive book, or, to cite Kazimierowska: "Called 'the first Polish literary voice of the third Holocaust generation,' it also, if the truth be told, brings us—the third generation of non-Jews—to heel. What will we do and what are we doing with the memory of our grandparents?" (Kazimierowska 2009a)[15]

Concluding remarks

Paziński's third-generation fiction debut is an example of how the Holocaust continues to drive the motivations and actions of Polish-Jewish writers and their readers living in Poland today. As seen can be from our discussion of mnemonic devices—images, scenes and themes that are particularly poignant—the novel is composed according to a poetics of retrieved memory. In view of the seriousness of its subject, we have shown that Paziński does not opt for pathos and idealization, or for sensationalism. Instead, he recreates a personal world by balancing melancholy with low-key wit and humour. This is tantamount to the author's using his *quiet voice*, a manner of writing about postmemory which seems to represent a new, less dramatic trend in Polish Holocaust writing. Considering his ambiguous working through of memory material, we could say that his first-person narrator does not feel at home either on "this" or "the other" side of the guesthouse world. But this is the crux of the matter: because as fictionalizer, the narrator always retains a safe measure of distance from the past; his contemplation of it allows him to mark how far beyond it he has progressed. In this way, nostalgia for his grandmother's Jewish community allows him to reflect on his own progress from despondency, insecurity and alienation in a Polish society where he may always be perceived as both an intrinsic part of it and the Other. Finally, in our contemporary understanding of the world, the notions of home and identity are multi-layered, diasporic and fragmented—a result of the development of migration and globalization. And here, Paziński may be said to have captured the generational momentum: in so far as his life story expresses mnemonic solidarity with a new community of readers, and contributes to defining the parameters of various tensions and conflicts both in Poland and the wider world, *The Boarding House* can be said to possess a universal dimension.

15 I concur here with Renata Plaice that Paziński actualizes Poland's Jewish heritage and "opens space for contemporary literature's engagement with the Holocaust" (Plaice 2012, 45).

Bibliography

Dąbrowski, Bartosz. 2011. "Postpamięć, zależność, trauma." In *Kultura po przejściach, osoby z przeszłością. Polski dyskurs postzależnościowy. Tom 1: Konteksty i perspektywy badawcze,* edited by Ryszard Nycz, 257-270. Kraków: Universitas.

Dunin-Wąsowicz, Paweł. 2009. "Otwock – Niedoszły syjonista, wywiad. Piotr Paziński rozmawia z PDW." *Lampa* 9. Accessed 6 July, 2012. http://www.sztetl.org.pl/pl/art\-icle/otwock/16,relacje-spomnienia/11402,niedoszly-syjonista-piotr-pazinski-rozmawia-z-pawlem-duninem-wasowiczem-redaktorem/

Foucault, Michel. 1984. "Of Other Spaces (1967). Heterotopias," translated by Jay Miskowiec. Accessed 6 July, 2012. http://foucault.info/documents/heteroTopia/foucault.heteroTopia.en.html

Gazeta Wyborcza [no author]. 2010. "Piotr Paziński: Pensjonat." 25 May. Accessed 6 July, 2012. http://wyborcza.pl/1,106966,7937179,Piotr_Pazinski__Pensjonat.html

Grimstad, Knut Andreas. 2010. "The Rhetoric of Present Absence: Representing Jewishness in Post-Totalitarian Poland." In *Contesting Europe's Rim: Cultural Identities in Public Discourse,* edited by Ljiljana Śarić et al., 203-217. *Journal of Multilingual and Multicultural Development* 29. London: Multilingual Matters.

Hirsch, Marianne. 2001. "Surviving Images: Holocaust Photographs and the Work of Postmemory." *Visual Culture and the Holocaust*, edited by Barbie Zelizer, 146-214. London: The Athlone Press.

—. 2008. "The Generation of Postmemory." *Poetics Today* 29 (1): 103-28.

Horowitz, Sara R. 2010. "Nostalgia and the Holocaust." In *After Representation? The Holocaust, Literature, and Culture*, edited by R. Clifton Spargo and Robert M. Ehrenreich, 41-58. New Brunswick, NJ: Rutgers University Press.

Huelle, Paweł. 2010. "Piotr Paziński, 'Pensjonat.'" *Zeszyty Literackie*, 13 January. Accessed 6 July, 2012. http://www.zeszytyliterackie.pl/index.php?option=com_content&task=view&id=972&Itemid=88

Iwasiów, Inga. 2010. "Literatura sanatoryjna." *Tygodnik powszechny*, March 9. Accessed 6 July, 2012. http://tygodnik.onet.pl/0,42579,literatura_sanatoryjna,komentarz.html

Jankowicz, Grzegorz. 2010. "Ta strona." *Tygodnik Powszechny*, 19 January. Accessed 6 July, 2012. http://tygodnik.onet.pl/1,39974,druk.html

Kazimierowska, Katarzyna. 2009a. "Gdy nie ma już kogo zapytać, czyli Żydzi tacy jak my." *Kultura Liberalna*. Accessed 6 July, 2012. http://kulturaliberalna.pl/2009/08/03/kazimierowska-gdy-nie-ma-juz-kogo-zapytac-czyli-zydzi-tacy-jak-my/

—. 2009b. "Przedmioty mówią za ludzi...—K. Kazimierowska rozmawia z P. Pazińskim." *Kultura liberalna*. Accessed 6 July, 2012. http://kulturaliberalna.pl/2009/08/31/przedmioty-mowia-za-ludzi-k-kazimierowska-rozmawia-z-p-pazinskim/

Kurkiewicz, Julian. 2010. "Piotr Paziński: Istniejemy jeszcze-jeszcze." *Gazeta Wyborcza*, 16 June.

Maier, Charles S. 1995. "A Surfeit of Memory? Reflections on History, Melancholy and Denial." *History and Memory* 5: 136-152.

Molisak, Alina. 2007. "Figures of Memory: Polish Holocaust Literature of the 'Second Generation'." *Imaginary Neighbors: Mediating Polish-Jewish Relations after the*

Holocaust, edited by Dorota Glowacka and Joanna Zylinska, 205-222. Lincoln, NE: University of Nebraska Press.

Paziński, Piotr. 2009. *Pensjonat*. Warsaw: Wydawnictwo Nisza.

—. 2010. "Łączę z Piotrem Pazińskim – relacja z e-spotkania." *Niedoczytania. Pismo innego uczestnictwa w kulturze* (22 December). Accessed 6 July, 2012. http://niedoczytania.pl/lacze-z-piotrem-pazinskim-relacja-z-e-spotkania/

Pijanowski, Paweł. 2012. "I koniecznie coś w jidysz." *Popmoderna*. Accessed 6 July, 2012. http://popmoderna.pl/i-koniecznie-cos-w-jidysz-kultura-zydowska-we-wspolczesnej-polsce/

Plaice, Renata. 2012. "Holocaust Memory in Recent Polish Literature: Andrzej Bart's *Fabryka muchołapek* and Piotr Paziński's *Pensjonat*." *Journal of European Studies* 42 (1): 34-49.

Rahoza, Agnieszka. 2010. "O debiucie Piotra Pazińskiego." *Dwutygodnik* 24. Accessed 6 July, 2012. http://www.dwutygodnik.com/artykul/854-o-debiucie-piotra-pazinskiego.html

Rutkiewicz, Pawel. 2011. "O pewnym hotelu bez gwiazdek—czyli debiut debiutowi oraz 'Paszport Polityki' a działalność charytatywna." *WAKATonline*. Accessed 24 January, 2012. http://www.sdk.pl/wakat/nr11/PawelRutkiewicz.html

Sobolewska, Justyna. 2009. "Recenzja książki: Piotr Paziński, Pensjonat. Taniec z cieniami." *Polityka*, 30 July.

Szczepan, Aleksandra. 2012. "Polski dyskurs posttraumatyczny. Literatura polska ostatnich lat wobec Holocaustu i tożsamości żydowskiej." In *Kultura po przejściach, osoby z przeszłością. Polski dyskurs postzależnościowy. Tom 1: Konteksy i perspektywy badawcze, edited by Ryszard Nycz, 239-256. Krakow: Universitas.*

Sierakowski, Sławomir. 2012. "Polen i post-politikkens tid." *Weekendavisen*, 9 March.

Wieliczko, Karolina E. 2009. "Niewypowiedziany kadysz. Paweł [sic] Paziński 'Pensjonat'." *Teksty Niekulturalne*. Accessed 6 July, 2012. http://teksty-niekulturalne.umcs.lublin.pl/index.php/krytycznie-literacko/172-niewypowiedziany-kadysz-pawe-paziski-qpensjonatq.html

Wojdowski. Bogdan, 1997. *Tamta strona*. Wrocław: Wydawnictwo Dolnośląskie.

Young, James E. 1998. "The Holocaust as Vicarious Past: Art Spiegelman's *Maus* and the Afterimages of History." *Critical Inquiry* 24: 666-699.

Constructing a Memory of Polish/Jewish Community in Tadeusz Słobodzianek's *Our Class*

Paul VICKERS

Introduction

This chapter explores Tadeusz Słobodzianek's drama *Our Class* (*Nasza klasa*), comparing two versions—one shortlisted for the 2008 Gdynia Dramaturgy Prize (Gdyńska Nagroda Dramaturgiczna) and another, published in 2009, which won the 2010 Nike Prize (Słobodzianek 2009 and 2009a).[1] The play's world premiere performance at London's National Theatre in September 2009 was based on Catherine Grosvenor's English translation of the published drama. The October 2010 Polish premiere took place at Warsaw's Teatr na Woli, where Słobodzianek had recently become artistic director.[2]

I argue that *Our Class* contributes to ongoing Polish efforts to confront the memory of ethnic Poles' crimes against their Polish Jewish neighbours and classmates during World War II, something which entered public consciousness following publication and discussion of Jan Tomasz Gross's *Neighbors* (Gross 2000; 2001). Słobodzianek's drama also highlights the complexities of pre-war relations between ethnic Poles and Jewish Poles, a fact hidden by collective memory's vision of idylls shattered by war, as well as efforts towards constructing a Polish/Jewish community of memory, where—with reference to Maria Janion—"our dead" are imagined as a group which is no longer homogeneous, but instead incorporates also Jewish Poles, their memory and suffering, including that caused by ethnic Poles (Janion 2000, 5-7, 243-258).[3] Słobodzianek's drama also reflects the consequences for the paradigm of Polish national identity and memory, as

[1] The earlier, twenty-lesson version, nominated for the Gdynia Dramaturgy Prize is available at: www.gnd.art.pl/baza/nasza_klasa.doc, Accessed 13 November, 2010.

[2] I saw this version twice while living in Warsaw during my AHRC-funded doctoral research. Meanwhile, I would like to thank participants of the Polish Literature Since 1989 conference held at UCL SSEES in November 2011 for their comments on an earlier version of this chapter. I am supremely grateful to my supervisor Elwira Grossman at the University of Glasgow for our inspiring discussions on the subject of *Our Class* and related issues.

[3] In her 2001 essay, "Taboo Topics in Polish and Polish/Jewish Cultural Studies," Halina Filipowicz argues that the slash is the most apt symbol in attempting to approach in discourse relations between Poles and Jews in the Polish lands: "A space between the two terms allows proximity, while separating and thus denying any possibility for productive interaction. In contrast, a hyphen can be seen as a site of intercultural connection, but the intrusiveness of the hyphen drives a wedge between the two terms and keeps the second term at arm's length. The slash

traditionally unquestioned pillars of Polishness—God, Honour and Fatherland—are disrupted following reflection on relations between Jewish Poles and ethnic Poles.

Our Class: overview and context

Our Class presents the lives, deaths and afterlives of ten classmates—five ethnic Poles and five Polish Jews (one of whom converts to Christianity during the war)—in an unnamed town in north-eastern Poland. The protagonists, born between 1918 and 1920, die between 1941 and 2003, some in the same town, others in New York, Israel, or outside Warsaw. The pivotal event in the classmates' lives is the massacre of almost the entire Jewish population of the town in summer 1941 as Soviet occupiers are replaced by Nazi-German troops. This mass murder was executed by predominantly Christian ethnic Poles against classmates, neighbours and their families. Two Jewish classmates—Jakub Katz and Dora—perished in the pogrom; two survived, while Abram had already left for America in 1938 to train as a rabbi. One ethnic Pole was killed by a Polish classmate later in the war: Władek kills Rysiek, who was active in both the Nazi-sponsored police and a Polish underground organization. Rysiek had attempted to deport Władek's now Christian wife Marianna, formerly Rachela, alongside Jews cleared from a nearby ghetto. Menachem, another Jewish survivor, became an agent of post-war Poland's communist-sponsored security services, torturing some of his former classmates before being coerced into leaving post-Stalinist Poland for Israel where he worked on a kibbutz before committing suicide in 1975. Zygmunt, a local Party official,

in *Polish/Jewish* functions both as part of the name and a confession of failure to name, the sign of a perception of the area as resistant to naming, transitional, suspended, perhaps permanently indeterminate. Moreover, the slash functions as a paradoxical metaphor of both wound and suture. It tropes the trauma of the troubled history of the relations between Jews and Poles on the one hand and the cultural interaction between them on the other. Thus the slash, even more eloquently than the hyphen, resists the danger of repairing historical injuries by amalgamative thinking. Stitching some kind of seam into the encounters between Jews and Poles, the slash is also a scar." (Filipowicz, 2001) Słobodzianek's approach in *Our Class* appears to embody the symbolism of the slash as the play works towards constructing a community of memory based on acknowledgement of scars and injuries actually suffered and inflicted or subsequently felt by both communities. Słobodzianek seeks to avoid employing either images of a pre-war idyll or notions of irreconcilable differences and distance between the two groups, since both of these frameworks serve as means to overlook troubling aspects of the past which can disrupt established notions of identity based in memory and culture. Słobodzianek thus depicts the seams which symbolized sites where Polish and Jewish communities bonded and interacted productively, while also symbolizing sites where they could be torn apart. *Our Class* studies the scars that have emerged at such points both as a result of the events of recent history and also as a consequence of the later return to public consciousness of the memory of these events.

also died in 1975 following his own mental breakdown. Another Pole, Heniek, became a priest, before dying in 2001 simultaneously with Władek, whose wife followed a year later. Zocha, who became Menachem's lover whilst hiding him, during the Nazi occupation, was abandoned by him once he secured her passage to the USA. She died there in 1985 having maintained contact with New York-based Abram, the last to die, in 2003.

A recent article by Bryce Lease has explored two stagings of *Our Class* and critical responses to them (Lease 2012).[4] Here I concentrate instead on *Our Class* as a dramatic text. Briefly, however, the London performance, directed by British Iranian Bijan Sheibani, appeared to be a more literal interpretation highlighting attempts to later falsify and manipulate memory of the massacre. The play's exploration of efforts to preserve local and national dignity reflects the broader context of post-Gross debates on relations between ethnic Poles and Jewish Poles. Ondrej Spišák's Warsaw version, meanwhile, revealed more explicitly *Our Class's* potential as a theatre of death and memory, something perhaps easier to achieve when staging the play in Poland and in Polish. In this Polish dramatic convention, the dead appear, inciting present-day reflection on the past and its significance. Although Spišák's staging is most obviously reminiscent of Tadeusz Kantor's *Dead Class* visually, the play's treatment of memory and the dead also invokes the dramas of Adam Mickiewicz and Stanisław Wyspiański.

Słobodzianek's drama is inspired by massacres carried out in late June and July 1941 in north-eastern Poland, also drawing on the murders' place in individual, local and national memory. The killing of Jews by Poles, particularly in the town of Jedwabne, became the focus of investigations by historians, politicians, prosecutors and journalists. Until March 2001, before revelations about the 10 July 1941 pogrom entered public consciousness following the publication of Gross's *Neighbors*, a memorial in the town, erected under communism, stated 1600 Jews were killed by "the Gestapo and Nazi gendarmerie." Once claims of German responsibility were undermined, the number was revised downwards, with the Polish Institute of National Remembrance (IPN) concluding that at least 340 Jews were killed by Poles (Ignatiew 2003, 199-200). In writing *Our Class* Słobodzianek took inspiration from works by Gross and Anna Bikont, as well as from historical investigations and documentary films exploring the pogroms (Słobodzianek 2009, 98).[5] Certain parallels therefore exist between actual individuals involved—as victims, bystanders, rescuers and killers—and the play's protagonists. Indeed, Słobodzianek's contact with Bikont enabled him to meet some

4 Initial drafts of this chapter were completed before the publication of Lease's article.

5 In a brief postscript, he lists the Polish versions of Irena Grudzińska-Gross and Jan Tomasz Gross (1981) and Gross (2001); Machcewicz and Persak (2002); Bikont (2004); and films by Marian Marzyński and Agnieszka Arnold.

of the area's inhabitants, with Bikont noting how the encounter with Stanisław Ramotowski and his wife Marianna, formerly Rachela Finkelsztejn—saved from the Radziłów pogrom on 7 July 1941—proved particularly inspirational (Bikont 2004, 223).[6] Władek and Marianna (in the play) in their experiences, though not attitudes towards each other, mirror Stanisław and Marysia-Rachela. The play's Abram Piekarz (Baker), meanwhile, evidently resembles an eponymous New York rabbi. Zygmunt features aspects of the unrepentant Laudański brothers, particularly his namesake. Menachem is modelled partly on Szmul Wasersztejn, who was saved by Antonia Wyrzykowska (Zocha in the play) and provided initial witness testimony triggering investigations in 1949 and 1953. However, Menachem also becomes a security service (UB) agent, as historian Tomasz Strzembosz (2004) suggested Wasersztejn also was. Strzembosz quickly retracted this claim, although not before this witness had entered the popular imagination as a Stalinist collaborator.

The drama is not a documentary reconstruction of the Jedwabne or Radziłów pogroms, or any of the estimated twenty-nine others in the region. The play's class was created from various sources, although the massacre itself, with Jews herded into the town's marketplace and then burned alive in a barn, resembles the pogroms in Jedwabne and nearby Radziłów. Słobodzianek felt the revelations instigated by Gross's book were a transformative moment for his identity as an artist, Pole and Catholic. The playwright was born in 1955 in Siberia to parents deported in 1944 by the Soviet authorities from their homelands in the Lwów/L'viv and Wilno/Vilnius borderland regions. Słobodzianek was under one year old when his mother decided the family should return to a geographically reconfigured Poland. They settled in Białystok, where Słobodzianek was again resident when public controversy over Jedwabne erupted in mid-2000 (Bikont and Słobodzianek 2010). He was involved at that time with the Wierszalin theatre group, inspired by ideas of investigating peripheral regions. But revelations instigated by Gross's *Neighbors* shattered any illusions of idyllic borderlands in this once multicultural, multi-faith region.

> My vision of the borderlands was a dream that I believed in for many years. I was awoken from the myth of Wierszalin by Jedwabne. I understood that the borderlands weren't some idyll [*sielanka*], but were instead lined with hate and crimes; I understood it was necessary to account for spilled blood. (Bikont and Słobodzianek 2010)

6 Bikont's diary entry for 21 October 2001 reads: "I go with Tadeusz Słobodzianek to the Ramotowskis. Tadeusz is considering a further version of his planned work on Jedwabne. Perhaps the central axis would be the wedding of 1941 with the Ramotowskis as bride and groom? I can see that following his talk with Staś [Ramotowski] his appetite grows further for the project."

Beyond its significance for his personal and professional life, Słobodzianek considered the Jedwabne debate transformative for Polish theatre and indeed the nation. Speaking to Anna Bikont in August 2003, Słobodzianek argued for a necessarily new approach towards a "post-Jedwabne theatre":

> We must write differently. Dramaturgy must be different because our consciousness is now different. Poland—whose mission was to suffer on the cross; the Church—which had been united with the nation in suffering: it's all unravelled now. We have become in this sense a normal nation. The Church must account for its baleful role and this is today a subject of which the young dramatists I am working with are aware. (Bikont 2004, 337)

The extended writing process lasting from 2001 to 2009, typical of Słobodzianek's dramaturgy, was particularly significant for *Our Class*, allowing the author to reflect upon and incorporate other discourses—historical, academic, legal, media, religious, popular, political—regarding Jedwabne, while tracing their transformative effect on the pillars of Polishness. Lengthy observation and reflection meant that over time *Our Class* increasingly resembled a meditation on more universal questions of fate and humanity. Słobodzianek notes:

> The writer must ask: Why did this happen? How did it transpire? Who is responsible? But my role is not finding answers to these questions. My role is posing them. *Our Class* also asks questions about freedom and fate, questions to which each spectator, in identifying to some extent with each protagonist, must respond while also sensing what they would do in the same situation.
>
> If we Poles fail to confront the subject then someone else will do it for us. We must face this task which is a fundamental duty stemming from our consciousness, both individually and in terms of general humanity, regardless of where we live; it is a duty, too, of civic consciousness. There are certain psychological theories which state that until perpetrators seek reconciliation with victims, then society cannot be fully normal and healthy. (Słobodzianek 2010)

To become a "normal" country as regards the relationship with its past and its dead, Słobodzianek advocates confronting the past which demands a shift in mentality from Poland's traditional victim identity. For him this is a patriotic task, since only by working through troubling aspects of the past can Poles construct a community of memory that includes Jewish Poles and thus find a suitable identity which Poland, particularly since joining the European Union in 2004, can present to the twenty-first-century world. Such a process became known in German as *Vergangenheitsbewältigung*—a term conceived in West Germany as broader public discussion developed regarding the role of ordinary Germans in both World War II and the Holocaust, and also the implications of this for subsequent generations. Confino and Fritzsche argue that the problem of explaining and historicizing the historical extremes of world war and mass death has more or less defined the topic of memory in Germany. The basic imperative of German memory is widely regarded to be the collective responsibility of coming to terms with the past, or *Vergangenheitsbewältigung*. (Confino and Fritzsche 2002, 2)

Against such positive generalization, however, Wulf Kansteiner notes: "Even with hindsight it is difficult to determine to what extent Germany's remarkably self-critical historical culture reflected the historical consciousness of its population." He warns of the "impressive degree of miscommunication between champions of [*Vergangenheitsbewältigung*] in positions of power and significant segments of the population." (Kansteiner 2006, 137)

Whether *Our Class* as performance or text can speak to "significant segments of the population," remains to be seen. Nevertheless, it contributes to a growing discourse, increasingly popular in its reach, promoting collective coming to terms with the troubling past, regardless of its potential to disrupt certainties of imagined national identity. As Lease also argues, "[w]hat is at stake in this debate over Polish culpability is the notion of a collective identity of a people." (Lease 2012, 88) According to Marta Kurkowska-Budzan, an academic and social scientist born in Jedwabne, radical revelations about Jedwabne could become, as she stated in 2001, a moment of national trauma. Drawing on Frank Ankersmit's ideas, she notes:

the one and only moment in which the past exposes itself to us is in the moment of trauma, which causes surprise and pain. Trauma causes our convictions, categories and expectations to shatter. History is created as a result of traumatic collective experiences. History, according to Frederic [sic] Jameson, is what hurts. Trauma does not register events from the past but records the power of experiences that cannot be assimilated, cannot be accepted. This is the paradox of trauma: it cannot be forgotten and cannot be remembered. "Normal" history can be acquired, adopted, domesticated; traumatic history cannot. In this way the traumatic past, whether private or national, exists in ourselves like a foreign body that we cannot get rid of. (Kurkowska-Budzan 2004, 202)

Vergangenheitsbewältigung does not permit the past to be confronted and then mastered, allowing those bearing witness today simply to move on and ultimately forget. Yet Ewa M. Thompson's problematic recent article suggests that one Polish "way of remembering" is based on "closure," achieved once guilt, responsibility and victimhood have been allocated (Thompson 2011, 231).[7] Thompson claims that it is primarily Polish-Russian memories that remain irreconcilable—because of essential Russian intransigence. Remarkably, she also states that "the depar-

[7] Thompson states that "certain traumas have already reached the point of closure in Poland, including that of Polish-German relations. The Germans have acknowledged their guilt concerning the Jews. There is a consensus in Poland as to what happened to Christian Poles under Nazi occupation" (Thompson 2011, 231).

ture of the Russian army in 1993 brought significant changes to the remembrance of the Shoah in Poland, and the trauma of Auschwitz is beginning to achieve its proper closure." (2011, 231) However, Thompson's failure to confront the transformative impact of discourses around Jedwabne enables the continued reinforcement of the paradigmatic foundations of Polishness. In her text, Poles actually emerge as victims of communist "mendacity" over the Holocaust which she believes prevented open confrontation with the past (2011, 230). Although psychoanalytically inspired terminology proves problematic for studying collective remembering, as Kansteiner and Weilnböck (2010) have argued in theory and Thompson demonstrates in practice, the Jedwabne revelations have nevertheless traumatized, or wounded, Polish national pride as it strives to uphold traditional identity concepts. Instead of denying their impact by imagining closure, the *Vergangenheitsbewältigung* model appears particularly apt in suggesting the past should be constantly worked through, leaving individuals today conscious of lessons learned while paying respect to the dead, whoever they are. For both Kurkowska-Budzan and Słobodzianek in *Our Class*, the revelations about Jedwabne and Poles' role in massacring their Jewish neighbours initiated a certain transformative trauma that demanded re-examining past relations between Poles and Jews, the Holocaust and indeed Polishness critically, uncoupled from the prerogatives of the Church and national megalomania.

My reading of *Our Class* is informed by Maria Janion's call of 1999 (2000, 257): "Into Europe—yes, but together with our dead" ("Do Europy tak, ale razem z naszymi umarłymi").[8] Presaging the following year's revelations about Jedwabne,[9] Janion envisions a transformation of national memory into a site of contestation where Polish dead are joined by the dead of others. For Janion, this meant revising the "romantic cultural paradigm in Polish culture" (Janion 2000, 246) including its central conviction that "through death one enters history and achieves greatness." (2000, 248) For Janion, "our dead" does not mean simply the Polish dead, but all dead of lands once and now Polish, which for a long time, she notes, had been a shared, if far from idyllic, Polish/Jewish space (2000, 254; 257). The challenge now is to work towards a Polish/Jewish community of memory, with a concomitant revision of national self-images: "How are we to recover the memory of that which happened here beside us?" For Janion, "only by means of critiquing *our own* myths" (2000, 164) does it become possible to be guardians of a Polish/Jewish memory instead of reinforcing the Romantic cultural paradigm's

---

8 See "Rozmowa o końca wieku. O duszy" [Janion in conversation with Katarzyna Janowska and Piotr Mucharski for the Polish television channel TVP, 1999] (Janion 2000, 243-258).

9 See her reactions to Gross's *Neighbors* in an essay in the same collection "Spór o antysemityzm—Sprzeczności, wątpliwości i pytania" (2000, 127-66).

pillars of God, Honour, Fatherland—which uphold traditional Polish memory and identity concepts:

> Those who today still write and say "God, honour, fatherland" while imagining Prince Józef Poniatowski and believing they behave according to this maxim, act in fact romantically. But this does not mean at all that they have read Romantic poetry. They just know, often intuitively, that behaving according to such rules is part of Polish tradition. (Janion 2000, 247)

Our Class, then, is more than a reminder of horrors perpetrated by Poles against their Jewish neighbours and classmates. It also depicts ongoing contestations over Polish national memory, including failed attempts to suppress memories of Polish Jews and resist their entry into a re-imagined community of "our dead."

My investigation here considers the evolution of *Our Class* as a text. Indeed, it is not unusual for Słobodzianek to rewrite his texts, with *The Prophet Ilja* existing in "seven or eight" different versions, each adapted for different performances (Bikont and Słobodzianek 2010).[10] *Our Class* evolved from the version shortlisted for the 2008 Gdynia Dramaturgy Prize following initial rehearsals with Spišák in 2007 and also altered in the context of developments in discourses on relations between Jewish Poles and ethnic Poles. A shift in form is evident between the two versions, with the Nike-winning play more evidently a mnemonic séance of a Polish/Jewish dead class, as the classmates' fates appear inextricably and fatefully bound together. This second version also generates a sense that having attacked the pillars of an exclusivist identity and memory, alongside presenting forceful reminders of Poles' role in destroying communities of Jewish neighbours, Słobodzianek offers readers a certain order expressed in the form of a cosmic source of justice, absent from the earlier version, where the protagonists' post-war fates proceed in relative isolation from their classmates as they head toward death.

Despite Słobodzianek's winning the Nike Prize for the written text, discussion in Poland has been generated primarily by the Warsaw performance, which received expected criticism from the Catholic right-wing press where Gross's claims continue to be disputed. *Our Class* has been considered "anti-Polish" or even an incitement to violence against Poles (Stankiewicz-Podhorecka, 2010). The respected daily newspaper *Rzeczpospolita*, meanwhile, published dismissive opinion pieces presenting Słobodzianek's work as less nuanced even than Soviet propaganda: "Even the most anti-Polish books, plays and films clearly differentiated between pre-war bloodsuckers—'Polish lords'—and Polish working people of towns and villages. Propaganda at least did not attack all Poles as such." (Masłoń

[10] The first version of *The Prophet Ilja* was for Polish Television's (TVP) "Teatr Telewizji" programme in 1994, with the latest premiere coming on 31 March 2012 at Teatr na Woli, also directed by Ondrej Spišak.

2010, 16-17) Some left-wing opinion, centred on the journal *Krytyka Polityczna*, also considered the play too simplistic for its depiction of Polish antisemitism as a feature of lower-class, poorly educated Poles while also perpetuating gender stereotypes (Mrozek 2010; Michalski 2010).[11] Praise for *Our Class*, meanwhile, stressed Słobodzianek's success in avoiding historical recreation in favour of exploring the complexity of relations between the groups, while suggesting themes of more universal nature regarding questions of crime, punishment, guilt, responsibility, fate and memory. Słobodzianek was applauded for avoiding simplistic characterization with the protagonists displaying diverse motivations for their actions and attitudes (Derkaczew 2010).[12]

My reading finds that Słobodzianek toned down his shortlisted drama before publication in 2009, realizing that constructing a broader, inclusive community of the dead, and thus national memory, is something that in itself contributes to delegitimization of the Romantic cultural paradigm highlighted by Janion. Blunter attacks on imagined Polishness—together with responses to such—could overshadow the traumatic experiences of the dead, hence the published version's focus on the classmates' symbolism as a Polish/Jewish memory community, built on different foundations than the traditional trinity of pillars of Polishness: honour, fatherland and God.

Honour

The published play's clearest comment on "honour" concludes Lesson XII as the class recites: "Sienkiewicz taught us/ Son of this nation/ That yesterday's glories/ Are bricks we can build on." (Słobodzianek 2009, 73; 2009a, 79)[13] Almost every scene features a verse or song commenting on the lesson's events. Here the verse offers a bitterly ironic perspective on Abram learning from Zocha what really happened in the town during the war. He previously believed Zygmunt's letters' claims that the massacre, in which most of Abram's family was murdered, had

[11] I appreciate Izabela Filipiak's comments given at the London conference on the earlier version of my chapter as well as Mrozek's *Krytyka Polityczna* article. However, it is evident that Mrozek missed the historical context of the play and its particular geographical location, as well as the implicit presence of the antisemitism of state officials whose pre-war decrees regarding Christian prayer in the classroom created the first division of the class.

[12] For a fuller set of links to Polish reviews of *Our Class* see: http://www.e-teatr.pl/pl/repertuar/38529,szczegoly.html (Accessed 14 November, 2010).

[13] Quotations will be given in English. It should be noted, however, that the published translation is not always a literal approximation of the original Polish, thus offering alternative imagery, and also adapted for stage performance. Where a significant discrepancy occurs that has a bearing on my commentary and interpretation, the Polish original will also be given in a footnote. The first page reference will be to the Polish original and the second to the translation.

been perpetrated by Germans. This lesson thus acquires significance as a critique of broader Polish denial or silencing of events in Jedwabne and elsewhere.

Słobodzianek's efforts to revise paradigmatic attitudes towards honour and heroism subject Henryk Sienkiewicz's (1846-1916) patriotic literary legacy to a particular critique. Even Władek, who saved Marianna by hiding and marrying her, emerges as an ambivalent character. Indeed, no protagonist in *Our Class* appears unequivocally evil or good. When Rysiek tries to take Marianna for deportation, Władek emerges on horseback. Marianna compares him to Skrzetuski, the hero of Sienkiewicz's novel *With Fire and Sword* (*Ogniem i mieczem,* 1884) coming to assist Oleńka (Słobodzianek 2009, 64).[14] Yet in the same lesson we learn that Władek most probably suffocated their only child, born soon after this *With Fire and Sword*-style scene. Thus while saving one life, Władek stifled the continuation of the Jewish race. The Skrzetuski reference suggests, on the one hand, that Władek rescued a woman out of loving desire or at least a chivalrous sense of honour. On the other hand, Jan Skrzetuski—by chance—saved Poland's enemy, the Ukrainian rebel leader Bohdan Khmelnytsky. Władek's later off-hand, antisemitic remarks make his apparently honourable deed appear more ambiguous than might be expected of the Righteous Among the Nations. Furthermore, their child was most likely conceived as a result of rape, with their marriage consummated without Marianna's consent. In this context, the verse concluding Lesson VIII: "In a Paris salon/ Luxurious and smart/ Peasant violinists/ Played on in Chopin's heart" (Słobodzianek 2009, 41; 2009a, 44)—acquires additional irony, suggesting even Chopin's music and the associated mythology acquires different resonance, given peasants' involvement in Jedwabne. Likewise, Lesson VI concludes with an alienating and ironic verse referring to the Kościuszko peasant uprising (1794), consequently questioning paradigmatic concepts of "fatherland": "He marched at the forefront/ His rebels at hand/ For God will help those/ Who will fight for their land [the Polish has literally "fatherland"—P.V.]." (2009, 31; 2009a, 34) Copernicus, too, is implicated in Słobodzianek's critique of national pride. Concluding Lesson XI, the class recites: "We look at the stars/ Our hearts fill with pride/ At our country and people/ The Copernicus kind." (2009, 69; 2009a, 73) Gross also argued that Jedwabne disrupts the unquestioned sanctity of Poland's canon of "Great Men," the founding fathers of imagined national identity.

> Usually the canon of collective identity is assembled from deeds that are somehow special, striking, or remarkable. It is made up, in other words, of actions that depart from routine, that are unusual. And even though it is only a Fryderyk, a Jan, or a Mikołaj who has

[14] "Skrzetuski na pomoc pannie Oleńce!" (Słobodzianek 2009, 64) The translation here alters the cultural context: "He was hurtling towards us on that thing like Errol Flynn charging to save Mary Pickford" (2009a, 68).

> actually performed such deeds, as constitutive components of the canon they also belong to the collective "us". Hence Polish music, most deservedly proud of "our" Chopin; Polish science of "our" Copernicus; and Poland thinks of itself as a "bastion of Christianity" in no small part because King Jan Sobieski defeated the Turks in an important battle near Vienna. For this reason we are entitled to ask whether deeds committed by the likes of Laudański and Karolak [mayor of Jedwabne during the pogrom—P.V.] since they were so striking and unusual—engage Polish collective identity as well. (Gross 2001, 136)

Słobodzianek's critique of national pride, together with the identity and memory paradigm it reinforces, resounds with Gross's argument. Both believe pride expressed as the deeds of "Great Men" should be balanced by recognition of criminal deeds of other members of the nation. Słobodzianek's use of children's nursery rhymes generates a subtle but significant alienation effect, generating space for reflection along such lines. However, the critical verses questioning the canon of Polish Great Men were all absent in the Gdynia version. Equally, blunter attacks on another canonical source of Polish honour, namely the Polish partisan underground, were omitted from the published version. Lesson XIII of the Gdynia text features pointed criticism of antisemitism among elements of the underground. Only part of this scene remained in the published twelfth lesson: Zygmunt comes to Zocha's house accompanied by a group of partisans declaring he knows she had hidden Menachem. Notably, he remains in hiding, fearing his former classmates' vengeance even with the war over. Zygmunt and his group impose their vision of justice on Zocha, whom they assault and rob. In the published version they also rape her, meaning all three women in *Our Class* suffer rape. Zygmunt, who collaborated with the Soviet NKVD and the Nazis before becoming a local Party official, declares: "We're not just some gang of hooligans we're the Polish fucking Army, right? If we don't find that Bolshevik scum, we'll be back. And you and me'll have a different sort of conversation. You'll be shot. In the name of the Republic." (2009, 70; 2009a, 74) In the published play, Zocha and Menachem subsequently head to Łódź to work at a cinema. Zocha has an abortion there because she is unsure whether Menachem or Zygmunt is the father (2009, 76). She subsequently leaves for America, while Menachem becomes a security service agent.

In the earlier version, they join a touring song and dance troupe in Łódź. Returning from one trip, their train is raided by a forest-based gang (*banda*). A boy of twelve or thirteen "in a pre-war scout cap" scanned the train. Reaching Zocha and Menachem's compartment he shouted, "There's a Jew here." Men with red-and-white armbands, indicating membership of patriotic underground organizations, removed an elderly man before shooting him and another dead (Słobodzianek [2008], 33). Zocha adds that Poles then seemed obsessed with Jews. Researchers have indicated a number of incidents in post-war Poland where Jews were hunted down in trains. Joanna Tokarska-Bakir suggests that at least 200 Jews suffered such a fate at the hands of partisan units belonging to the underground National Armed Forces (Narodowe Siły Zbrojne or NSZ) (Tokarska-Bakir 2004, 77). In the Gdynia version, it is not concern over the identity of father but the fact that she doesn't "want to have children in this country of bandits!" that motivates Zocha to have an abortion (Słobodzianek [2008], 44). The implication is the same as in the published version, but there finds more subtle expression. Perhaps this episode was revised for publication and performance to avoid present-day controversies rooted in memory regarding the actions of NSZ groups in the late wartime and post-war periods, since even brief mention of such partisan organizations as murderers could potentially overshadow the play's depiction of the classmates' inextricable bonds, even as they were dead or dispersed around Poland and the world. The issue of the Polish underground's attitude towards Jews is removed in favour of focusing on the class's symbolism as a Polish/Jewish mnemonic community of the dead which could potentially restore memories of a heterogeneous fatherland.

Fatherland

The earlier version of *Our Class* divides the surviving protagonists roughly into pairs with each duo effectively sharing one lesson. The survivors narrate their post-war experiences relatively isolated from the community of classmates. Menachem and Zocha, after their stint as Duo Marinelli, die alone on opposite sides of the globe. Heniek the priest and Zygmunt the Party official form a close friendship and professional relationship, with both buried in the town. Marianna and Władek are married, of course, but rarely interact with their classmates. Abram, meanwhile, has some contact with Zocha in New York and briefly visits Heniek when attending a post-millennium ceremony marking the massacre. This initial version lacks, however, one of the more Nike Prize-winning text's more powerful aspects—namely the protagonists' memory-based disputes and interactions occurring beyond the grave, which suggest frameworks for confronting the past. In the published version, Słobodzianek's dead class become a channel for projecting back onto audiences more grotesque aspects of contemporary discussions on Jedwabne and other massacres. It is only in this version that while Dora narrates how she and her child suffocated to death in the burning barn, Abram, Zygmunt and Heniek interject, presenting competing claims over numbers killed (Słobodzianek 2009, 46). Słobodzianek also added, in the published version, further correctives to popular memories serving in Polish public discourse as mitigating narratives, such as when Heniek claims at the opening of Lesson V: "The Jews erected an arch to welcome the Red Army" and Władek counters: "Jews *and* Poles hung red flags outside their houses." (Słobodzianek 2009, 10; 2009a, 21)

The published play, however, lacks certain cultural references included in the first version which indicate how the generation of Słobodzianek's dead class had since childhood together enjoyed cultural works created by Jewish Poles. The Gdynia text's second lesson opens with the class reciting Julian Tuwim's poem *ABC* (*Abecadło*), a prescient indicator of the traumatic events and disruption to the established order that would come. In the Nike-winning version, Tuwim is replaced by a prophetic verse highlighting the innocence of childhood crushes which knew no religious or ethnic boundaries. The classmates gently rib Rysiek for liking Dora, whom he would later rape and lead to her death, while Dora's name is his final word before she appears as a ghost, bringing him into the community of the dead (Słobodzianek 2009, 65). While Rysiek's death scene featured in both versions, the childhood song included in the published Lesson II indicates the text's transformation, with notions of fate and inextricable bonds becoming central (Neuger 2009, 101-108). Zocha's heartbreak in Lesson IV, with Menachem cajoled into inviting her to the cinema, likewise presages their fate (Słobodzianek 2009, 19-20).

Słobodzianek also cuts Jakub Katz's appearance as Charlie Chaplin, singing *That Famous Moustache* (*Ach, ten wąsik*) by Marian Hemar—a Jewish Pole, cousin of Stanisław Lem—who collaborated with Tuwim in various artistic cabarets and projects. However, one song featuring at a crucial moment in both versions is *Tango milonga*. The lyrics to *Tango milonga* were written in 1929 by a Jewish Pole Andrzej Włast (real name Gustaw Baumritter) while the music was composed by another Jewish Pole, Jerzy Petersburski, a member of a famous Klezmer family. While Petersburski lived to 1979, Włast/Baumritter died in the Warsaw Ghetto in 1942. The song became a global hit in the 1930s as *Oh Donna Clara*, maintaining only the music rather than the sense of the Polish lyrics. *Tango milonga* is played at Władek and Marianna-Rachela's wedding in Lesson X after the ghastly gift-giving. The newlyweds receive goods looted from Jewish neighbours' homes. The absent Jews—murdered, in hiding or in America—appear at the wedding and comment horrified at the gifts. At one point—evident only on the page—Rachelka "reappears," remarking on a gift received as Marianna: tablecloths and napkins looted from her house by Zocha's husband. On the page, Rachelka is named as one of the characters commenting on the gifts. On stage, however, Władek, seeks to ease the tensions evoked by the repressed memory of Rachelka by requesting the song for the guests at his and Marianna's wedding to enjoy. Yet its lyrics provide ironic commentary on memory, remembering and community following the massacre.

Tango milonga, jak dawniej, grajcie mi znów./ Tango milonga, play it again for me, just like old times.
Zabijcie tę dręczącą ciszę./ Kill this agonizing silence.
Żegnajcie, dawne wspomnienia./ Farewell, old memories.
Żegnajcie, burze i serce uniesienia./ Farewell, storms and passions of the heart.
Czas wszystko odmienia. / Time changes everything (Słobodzianek [2008], 34)[15]

The old times cannot return, except as a spectral séance, a hallucinatory elucidation of repressed memories and traumas escaping from the unconscious. This song—written by Jewish Poles and sung by the Polish and Jewish classmates—thus evokes a further ghastly spectacle rather than grants closure to old memories. Dora's ghost asks Rysiek to dance. He tries justifying his behaviour during the pogrom—beating Dora rather than saving her from the crowd of Jews led to the barn—before trying to shoot down her ghost as his heart's stormy passions overwhelm him. Zygmunt sends home the apparently drunk Rysiek before himself being grasped by Jakub Katz's ghost, who reminds Zygmunt of his role in betraying fellow ethnic Poles. Heniek then parallels Abram, who calmed the first classroom conflict between ethnic Poles and Jewish Poles by announcing his departure for America; this time, Heniek attempts an exorcism by announcing his departure to a Łomża seminary (Słobodzianek 2009, 58). In the initial version, ghosts haunt survivors on their deathbeds, appearing—as in Władek's case, for example—as silent spectral reminders of repressed memories and a guilty conscience (Słobodzianek [2008], 59). Consequently, the twenty-lesson play fails to symbolize contemporary contestations over memory that work towards a heterogeneous community of memory. The epic fourteenth lesson, which is the final one of the Nike-winning text and forms almost one fifth of its length, becomes a séance in which memories are contested and revised, and reconciliation is intimated.

In the initial version, Zygmunt, for example, dies of a long, painful heart attack during which he endures haunting visions of Jakub, Menachem, Zocha and Dora. In the published version, by contrast, his decline is even more prolonged with a breakdown causing him to spend days in silence, smoking, staring into the distance, before declaring: "We pissed our lives away Heniek. What a Godless waste." (Słobodzianek 2009, 85; 2009a, 94)[16] Heniek's deathbed guardianship over Zygmunt—dictated, Władek suggests, by the desire "to make sure Zygmunt didn't blab before he croaked" (Słobodzianek 2009, 86; 2009a, 94)—plays out

[15] Translation is mine—P.V. The lyrics were not published in the Nike-winning text but were sung on stage in the Warsaw productions.

[16] It is a shame that the power and significance of Zygmunt's rhetorical question ("Where was God?") is lost in the English version: "Przesraliśmy to nasze życie, Heniek. Gdzie był Bóg?" (2009, 85).

as an ironic Catholic confession and absolution. Heniek remarks on Zygmunt's death:

> Zygmunt's death shook me to my core. Memento Mori. I started to realise that in the face of our mortality, we will be judged... not on the irrelevant details of our lives... but on greater matters. In the final reckoning... faith, patriotism, honour... these are the things that will count. (Słobodzianek 2009, 86-87; 2009a, 95)[17]

Here—only in the Nike version—the imagined trinity of Polishness is subjected to stinging ironic criticism. The scene also reflects attempts to continue excluding Jewish Poles from national memory, with the Church portrayed as a significant agent of this. This section of Lesson XIV also indicates the futility of purely Polish-Polish discussions on the past, whereby apparent penitence seems empty without engagement with Jewish ghosts, their experiences and versions of events. Heniek's unconscious consequently reveals upon his deathbed, as he is haunted by hallucinations, the extent of his exorcism's failure: "Jews tangling themselves around me. Of Jakub Katz. Eluś the tailor. Dora with little Igor. Sometimes Zygmunt would come to me. [...] there was no escape! There was no God." (Słobodzianek 2009, 94; 2009a, 103) He thus receives an answer to Zygmunt's question. For Zygmunt—and ultimately Heniek, too—God had abandoned the town by allowing so much evil to befall it.

God

God—or organized religion at least—is allocated a larger role in the published play. Whereas Zocha ended her days in the Gdynia version in the House of Broken Dreams retirement village in Florida (Słobodzianek [2008], 52), the published *Our Class* places her in the "St Thérèse of Lisieux Retirement Home" (Słobodzianek 2009, 89; 2009a, 97). She finds the poker-playing Catholic women she lives with "weren't too keen on Jews" (Słobodzianek 2009, 89: "coś nie lubiły Żydów"; 2009, 98). Dying alone in 1985, she is haunted not by her classmates, but by the fact her late antisemitic Polish-American second husband had hidden his father's Jewish heritage. This formerly repressed ghost of the past returns, causing Zocha to reassess memories of her husband and her life. Zocha visited the town in 1981 where she and Heniek reached a somewhat grotesque agreement that $50 should provide sufficient penitence and compensate Heniek for praying for *all* the dead classmates as well as her family. Zocha leaves feeling "uplifted" by this act (Słobodzianek 2009, 89). Another critique of religious influence added to the final version comes with Menachem having only the Bible to read when hidden

[17] Punctuation transcribed as in the original—P.V.

by Zocha. Its violence and message of justified vengeance—an eye for an eye—apparently serves as his guiding principle when using sadistic methods as a UB officer (Słobodzianek 2009, 62). Marianna also remarks (in the published version only) on the eye-for-an-eye principle: she fears her Christian neighbours might employ it, should she testify against them in the post-war trial (Słobodzianek 2009, 79). In the final version particularly, institutionalized religion appears as the chief source of repression and falsification of the memory of the wartime massacre, with both Heniek and Abram complicit in this. Despite full awareness of the facts, during his return to the town in 2001, Abram speaks to Heniek, who is happy to confirm his classmate's imagined pre-war idyll where the rabbi and priest were ultimate authorities in a happy community. Władek again interjects with a corrective:

Heniek: We chatted away about old times. About how in the good days before the war, Jews and Poles had studied together, worked together, played together. How the Priest and the Rabbi would club together to resolve any contentious issues . . . .

Władek: Yeah, like how much the Jews should pay for a new church roof or to avoid being attacked on Good Friday. (Słobodzianek 2009, 92; 2009a, 101)

Heniek readily confirms Abram's mythologized version of events in summer 1941, with the rabbi said to have led a crowd of Jews to their deaths—at the hands of Germans and a Polish mob (not ordinary Poles, like Heniek)—holding the Torah, apparently blessing victims, killers and witnesses, before preparing for Kiddush Hashem in the barn (Słobodzianek 2009, 93; 2009a, 102). Abram subsequently repeats this version, with additional martyrological embellishments, for an audience of dignitaries and potentially millions of television viewers worldwide. In a further addition to the published version of *Our Class*, Heniek happily bears false witness, along with his bishop, when the "provocation" against the town—and by implication the national monolith of memory—emerges in 2000. Heniek consulted the bishop: "Perhaps I should make a partial confession. The Bishop took my head off. Are you out of your mind father?" (Słobodzianek 2009, 90; 2009a, 98-99) Yet he is prepared to condemn to eternal damnation Władek, who reveals more about the events of summer 1941 to the world.

I am not convinced Słobodzianek's argument is helped by making Heniek, in the published version, a caricature degenerate priest: a gambler and suspected paedophile, as well as an egomaniacal believer in Poland as the Christ of Nations and a bearer of false witness. However, Słobodzianek's criticism of the Catholic Church's role in turning, generally, a blind eye to the fate of Polish Jews then permitting and promoting silence over the role of Poles in killings, together with his critique of Judaism's institutional representatives exploiting victims for theological purposes, nevertheless powerfully underscores his belief that the Judeo-

Christian tradition cannot provide a simple foundation either for reconciliation between ethnic Poles and Jewish Poles or for a Polish/Jewish memory community. Rather, *Our Class* indicates that revising exclusivist Polish national tradition requires moving towards a community of memory built on both everyday and popular traditions of mixed Jewish and Christian towns and cities, and also recognition of some responsibility for the tragedy that befell them. It should avoid idealized memories of supposed pre-war idylls, while confronting difficult and horrific moments of relations between Jewish Poles and ethnic Poles throughout history, even if this means appreciating the disruptive significance of now irrepressible spectres of the past. Yet, having chipped away in both versions at the trinity of pillars upholding an exclusivist Polishness, Słobodzianek seems to find that the earlier text's representation of wartime traumas remained too raw. Hence, the published play features a search for order. If God is absent, and His agents on earth are a (perhaps all too convenient) source of the concealment of traumas, Słobodzianek presents fate as a hoped-for source of justice.

Order

Władek and Heniek's dying within hours of each other appears to be the Gdynia version's only cosmic or fateful parallel. However, the published text's Lesson XIV features a more telling parallel between Zygmunt and Menachem. Both have lost sons in tragic circumstances. On 22 May 1970, Menachem's young son Jakub was shot dead attempting to save a female classmate during a terrorist attack on an Israeli school bus.[18] On 24 June 1970, the anniversary of Jakub Katz's murder, Zygmunt's son was the only fatality in a boating accident. Menachem subsequently committed suicide having been barred from seeking vengeance as an Israeli secret service agent, while a breakdown accompanied Zygmunt's withdrawal from public life. Słobodzianek demonstrates an urge to offer readers some hope, beyond religion, that justice will be done, yet this hope proves ambivalent as justice takes cruel forms causing children to suffer for forefathers' deeds. Indeed, future generations' responsibility to atone for predecessors' misdeeds is crucial in *Our Class*. Zygmunt's letter to Stalin asking not to be considered an enemy of the people despite his father's arrest, provides the framework for Słobodzianek to question future generations' immunity from the consequences of predecessors' deeds (Słobodzianek 2009, 14; 2009a, 27).[19] The playwright suggests parallels

[18] This was the date of an actual terrorist attack on a school bus travelling from Avivim to Dovev in Israel (Fine 2008).

[19] This principle takes an ironic twist with Zocha's second husband's sense of having been sinned against by his father's Jewishness. Her father-in-law's identity suggests something of the desire to suppress the memory of hybridity and heterogeneity among the national community.

with the task facing Poles today following the Jedwabne revelations. They can bring about justice for the community of the dead by revising national mythologies of innocence and heterogeneity promoted by their forebears, working instead towards what Słobodzianek terms "normality" (Słobodzianek 2010).

The poems and songs in *Our Class* offer increasingly ironic reflections on events. Thus, the concluding poem read by all the classmates is a tribute to the Pole star, "constant and still in the sky," which, according to wisdom learned in childhood, will always guide the classmates. Indeed, when Rysiek first thought he was to be killed, this star was his final thought (Słobodzianek 2009, 30-31). Furthermore, the play ends with the stanza: "So fear it no longer/ And puff out your chest/ There's North and there's South/ And there's East and there's West." (Słobodzianek 2009, 97; 2009a, 107-108)[20] Clearly Słobodzianek considered this poem significant, given its position, moving it from the end of the earlier text's Lesson XIV, where Menachem learns that his Polish classmates' 1949 trial had collapsed (Słobodzianek [2008], 49-50). This poem could be an ironic comment on the idyllic, simple logic learned as children which proves increasingly unfeasible, particularly when facing traumatic experiences. Perhaps, like the song "Resurrection" that concludes Krzysztof Warlikowski's *(A)pollonia*, a performance—especially in its final parts—concerned with exploring the Holocaust and attitudes towards Polish Righteous Among the Nations, *Our Class* in concluding with this poem, also seeks to offer audiences succour and a sense of order? Such a conclusion may offer some hope of succeeding in endeavours towards coming to terms with the past, and transforming the Polish cultural paradigm by welcoming Jewish neighbours and classmates into the shared community of "our dead"?

Conclusion

Some critics, such as Witold Mrozek, have suggested *Our Class* merely repeats well-known facts, as if the memory of Jedwabne and its cultural aftershocks had become normalized or commonplace in Poland.[21] Perhaps in Mrozek's milieu such critical perspectives are commonplace, but Ewa M. Thompson's article shows that even academic elites remain prepared to blank experiences disruptive of canonical national memory. Conversely, Mrozek's *Krytyka Polityczna* colleague Cezary Michalski suggests Słobodzianek's "radical centrist" vision deserves praise (Michalski 2010). This perhaps accords with Polonsky and Michlic's

[20] "I już więcej nie zabłądzisz,/ pójdziesz dalej bez strachu./ Tutaj północ, południe,/ a tam wschód jest i zachód."

[21] Mrozek (2010) suggested that *Our Class* is merely a transfer of Gross's *Neighbors* onto the stage in a neat form, reminiscent of amateur school theatre, thus the play "doesn't say anything new."

proposed approach to writing the history of the Holocaust and relations between ethnic Poles and Jewish Poles:

> It should be possible to move beyond strongly held, competing, and incompatible narratives of the past and to reach some consensus that will be acceptable to all people of goodwill and will bring about a degree of normalization both in Poles' attitudes toward the past and in Polish-Jewish relations, while also increasing awareness in the Jewish world of the complexity of the Polish situation between 1939 and 1945. Some have questioned whether normalization is a desirable or realizable goal. The past is too near and painful for that. (Polonsky and Michlic 2004, 43)

Indeed, Słobodzianek's search for a radical centrist position proceeds by highlighting ethnic Poles' crimes against neighbours while also indicating the complexity of relations between ethnic Poles, Christian Poles and Jewish Poles. This is perhaps why Menachem, a Jewish victim, also appears as an agent of the Polish communist secret police inspired by the Old Testament. Meanwhile, supposed Polish patriot Zygmunt also serves the communist regime. Słobodzianek thus questions *żydokomuna* stereotypes (see also Lease 2012, 88), while shifting away from the victim/perpetrator binary which underwrites Polish national pride and mythology (Strzembosz 2004). Rather than suggesting the memory and impact of Jedwabne has become normalized in Poland, the coming to terms with the past requires constant reminders, like *Our Class*, which confront the irrepressible ghosts of the past inhabiting Polish (and formerly Polish) spaces as well as Poles' memories. As Leonard Neuger notes in his afterword to the published version: "Jedwabne has become, whether we like it or not, a metaphor for all Poland. The word, once released, cannot be returned to the sphere of silence." (Neuger 2009, 106)[22] Likewise, Polonsky and Michlic question whether normalization (or closure) is a welcome or indeed possible goal, suggesting instead that for a Polish/Jewish community of memory to develop a "tragic acceptance" of each group's fate is more desirable (Polonsky and Michlic 2004, 43). *Our Class* treats Jedwabne as a tragic event transformative of Polish discourses of national memory and identity. The play's epic form contributes to this process by chipping away at the pillars which increasingly struggle to uphold an exclusionist vision of who may belong to the community of the dead. Following Janion's call, Słobodzianek and his dead class contribute to Poland's mnemonic "Europeanization" by working towards a Polish/Jewish community of memory.

Bibliography

Bikont, Anna. 2004. *My z Jedwabnego*. Warsaw: Prószyński.

[22] My translation. Neuger's afterword does not appear in the published English translation.

Bikont, Anna and Tadeusz Słobodzianek. 2010. "Pójdziesz za mną w ogień." *Gazeta Wyborcza. Duży Format* supplement, 24 October. Accessed 3 November, 2011. http://wyborcza.pl/1,76842,8546696,Slobodzianek__Pojdziesz_za_mna_w_ogien.html?as=2&startsz=x

Confino, Alon and Peter Fritzsche. 2002. *The Work of Memory: New Directions in the Study of German Society and Culture*. Urbana, IL: University of Illinois Press.

Derkaczew, Joanna. 2010. "Nasza osierocona klasa." *Gazeta Wyborcza*, 24 October. Accessed 13 November, 2011. http://www.e-teatr.pl/pl/artykuly/104482.html

Filipowicz, Halina. 2001. "Taboo Topics in Polish and Polish/Jewish Cultural Studies." *The Journal of the International Institute* 9(1): [no pagination]. Accessed 3 January, 2013. http://quod.lib.umich.edu/j/jii/4750978.0009.103?rgn=main;view=fulltext

Fine, Jonathan. 2008. "PLO Policy towards the Christian Community during the Civil War in Israel." Herzliya, Israel: International Institute for Counter-Terrorism paper (July 2008). Accessed 3 November, 2011. http://www.ict.org.il/Articles/tabid/66/Articlsid/291/currentpage/5/Default.aspx

Gross, Jan Tomasz. 2000. *Sąsiedzi. Historia zagłady żydowskiego miasteczka*. Sejny: Pogranicze.

—. 2001. *Neighbors: The Destruction of the Jewish Community in Jedwabne, Poland*. Princeton, NJ and Oxford: Princeton University Press.

Grudzińska-Gross, Irena and Jan Tomasz Gross, eds. 1981. *War Through Children's Eyes: The Soviet Occupation of Poland and the Deportations, 1939-1941*, translated by Ronald Strom and Dan Rivers. Stanford, CA: Hoover Institution Press.

Ignatiew, Radosław J. 2003. "Postanowienie o umorzeniu śledztwa." [IPN report issued 30 June]. Warsaw: Instytut Pamięci Narodowej. Accessed 15 October, 2011. http://www.ipn.gov.pl/ftp/pdf/jedwabne_postanowienie.pdf [no longer active] See also: Accessed 24 January, 2013 [hyperlink to paragraph on Jedwabne inactive]. http://ipn.gov.pl/kszpnp/sledztwa/oddzialowa-komisja-w-bialymstoku-stan-na-sierpien-2012-r./sledztwa-zakonczone-wydaniem-postanowienia-o-umorzeniu

Janion, Maria. 2000. *Do Europy tak, ale razem z naszymi umarłymi*. Warsaw: Sic!.

Kansteiner, Wulf. 2006. "Losing the War, Winning the Memory Battle: The Legacy of Nazism, World War II, and the Holocaust in the Federal Republic of Germany." In *The Politics of Memory in Postwar Europe*, edited by Richard Ned Lebow, Wulf Kansteiner and Claudio Fogu, 102-146. Durham, NC and London: Duke University Press.

Kansteiner, Wulf and Harald Weilnböck. 2010. "Against the Concept of Cultural Trauma (or How I Learned to Love the Suffering of Others without the Help of Psychotherapy)." In *A Companion to Cultural Memory Studies*, edited by Astrid Erll and Ansgar Nünning, 229-240. Berlin and New York: de Gruyter.

Kurkowska-Budzan, Marta. 2004. "'My Jedwabne': Excerpts from a lecture given at UCL 19-21 June 2001." In: *The Neighbors Respond: The Controversy over the Jedwabne Massacre in Poland*, edited by Antony Polonsky and Joanna B. Michlic, 200-206. Princeton, NJ and Oxford: Princeton University Press.

Lease, Bryce. 2012. "Ethnic Identity and Anti-Semitism: Tadeusz Słobodzianek Stages the Polish Taboo." *TDR: The Drama Review* 56(2): 81-100.

Machewicz, Paweł and Krzysztof Persak, eds. 2002. *Wokół Jedwabnego*. 2 vols. Warsaw: Instytut Pamięci Narodowej.

Masłoń, Krzysztof. 2010. "Głós wojującego bezbożnika." *Rzeczpospolita. PlusMinus* supplement, 30 October-1 November 2010: 16-17.

Michalski, Cezary. 2010. "Moralitet bez morału." *Krytyka Polityczna*, 2 November. Accessed 14 November, 2010. http://www.krytykapolityczna.pl/CezaryMichalski/Moralitetbezmoralu/menuid-291.html

Mrozek, Witold. 2010. "Czytanka o Jedwabnem." *Krytyka Polityczna*, 24 October. Accessed 14 November, 2010. http://www.krytykapolityczna.pl/Serwiskulturalny/MrozekCzytankaoJedwabnem/menuid-305.html

Neuger, Leonard, 2009. "Splot: Refleksje nad *Naszą klasą* Tadeusza Słobodzianka." In *Nasza klasa: Historia w XIV lekcjach,* by Tadeusz Słobodzianek, 101-108. Gdańsk: słowo/obraz terytoria.

Polonsky, Antony and Joanna B. Michlic, eds. 2004. *The Neighbors Respond: The Controversy over the Jedwabne Massacre in Poland*. Princeton, NJ and Oxford: Princeton University Press.

Słobodzianek, Tadeusz. [2008]. *Nasza klasa: Historia w XX lekcjach* [version submitted for the Gdynia Dramaturgy Prize]. Accessed 13 November, 2011. www.gnd.art.pl/baza/nasza_klasa.doc.

—. 2009. *Nasza klasa: Historia w XIV lekcjach*. Gdańsk: słowo/obraz terytoria.

—. 2009a. *Our Class*, translated by Catherine Grosvenor, adapted by Ryan Craig. London: Oberon.

—. 2010. "Tadeusz Słobodzianek o *Naszej klasie*." Accessed 3 November, 2011. http://www.teatrdramatyczny.pl/index.php?option=com_content&view=article&id=850

Stankiewicz-Podhorecka, Temida. 2010. "To zagrzewanie do nienawiści wobec Polaków." *Nasz Dziennik* 249 (23-24 October). Accessed 3 January, 2013. http://stary.naszdziennik.pl/bpl_index.php?dat=20101023&typ=my&id=my82.txt

Thompson, Ewa M. 2011. "Ways of Remembering: The Case of Poland." In *New Perspectives on Polish Culture: Personal Encounters, Public Affairs*, edited by Tamara Trojanowska et al., 221-235. New York: PIASA Books.

Strzembosz, Tomasz. 2004. "Collaboration Passed over in Silence." In *The Neighbors Respond: The Controversy over the Jedwabne Massacre in Poland,* edited by Antony Polonsky and Joanna Michlic, 220-236. Princeton, NJ and Oxford: Princeton University Press.

Tokarska-Bakir, Joanna. 2004. "Obsessed with Innocence." In *The Neighbors Respond: The Controversy over the Jedwabne Massacre in Poland,* edited by Antony Polonsky and Joanna Michlic, 75-86. Princeton, NJ and Oxford: Princeton University Press.

Ressentiment as Experiment: Polish Theatre and Drama after 1989

Grzegorz NIZIOŁEK

Polish fear of ressentiment

The systemic turning point of 1989 created the ideal conditions for ressentiment to blossom in Poland. Idealized, ideologically guaranteed equality is, according to Max Scheler, the natural environment for ressentiment.[1] This is for the simple reason that the reality is unable to fulfil it, and thus becomes the object of imagined vengeance. The basic mechanism of ressentiment is one of external passivity, combined with the production of fictional scenarios of moral superiority over one's oppressors. We should note right from the outset that the production of this sort of fiction with its powerful libidinal charge contains a strong element of theatricality and of alternative, imagined historical scenarios. Myths of community including the myth of national solidarity, which were (it should be stressed) effective tools of political transformation, inevitably had to come up against new rules of power distribution, new mechanisms creating social inequality in all spheres of life. *Traum oder Trauma*—this was how Grzegorz Dziamski diagnosed the shock that came with the loss of the utopian dream accompanying the integration of Poland and other Central European countries into the West after 1989 (Dziamski 2004, 172). At the same time, a group of self-declared guardians of betrayed ideals emerged. New ressentiments were supported by old ones: the perpetrators of the new "wounds" were those who had once betrayed Poland and the Poles: the Germans, who had attacked Poland in 1939, and the West, which had orchestrated and acquiesced to the resolutions of the Yalta Conference. Thus there was, on the one hand, an ideological battle to accept the conditions by which "Poland would be accepted into Europe" (with a whole array of corrective norms), while on the other, social frustrations caused the stakes to continually rise in the daily game of politics. Small wonder social ressentiments were perceived as especially hazardous forces impeding political transformations, as well as the integration process with the West. Political correctness demanded that they be suppressed.

Fear of ressentiment had a somewhat older genealogy, going back to the times of the People's Republic. In the mid-1960s—alongside the formation of increasingly powerful communities in Poland independent of the centralized communist

[1] A longer version of this chapter was published in 2012 in Polish as "Resentyment jako eksperyment," *Didaskalia* 112: 45-53.

government, which became a storehouse for future political opposition—a battle began against social ressentiments, in particular those shaped by the experience of World War II. The end of the 1960s brought dramatic and shameful political events (the eruption of antisemitism, the oppression of intellectual and literary communities by the authorities), their dynamic and effective nature the result of ressentiments skilfully manipulated by communist state ideologists. These ressentiments ensured for a time the effective cooperation of a large part of society with the disgraceful actions of the authorities. The task of defusing ressentiments was so difficult, however, that the call to gain knowledge about Poland's past became linked by opponents of the communist regime to efforts to make the central conflict remain the relationship between society and the authorities. Other conflicts were to be mollified, or to be presented as the result of the authorities' manipulations (attempts were made to interpret the Kielce pogrom of 1946 and the events of 1968 in this manner).

The Second World War and particularly relations with the Germans were subjected to special ideological exploitation in the 1960s (the situation was complicated by the existence of two German states—one "good" and one "bad"). Polish antisemitism was useful here too, as from 1945 onward it could exist only in smothered or camouflaged forms. On the one hand, memory of the crimes committed by the Germans against Polish and European Jews was an invaluable tool for provoking anti-German sentiments (owing to the gravity of the facts, the numbers involved, and the "spectacular" nature of the crimes), while on the other, the sufferings of the Jews evoked in Poles the familiar mechanism of competing to be seen as the greater victims. Hence every attempt was made to "universalize" the war crimes, to present Polish society as having had the most harrowing experiences during the war. The overt and clamorous incitement of hostility toward Germany was accompanied in the state propaganda by a discreetly waged and carefully encoded release of antisemitic feeling. Something that appeared historically and logically contradictory (the use of the Holocaust both to incite anti-German sentiments and to support antisemitic attitudes) worked out effectively in collective terms.

This also explains why the famous call of the Polish bishops to the German bishops in 1965 to perform the real service of working through the frightful past ("We forgive, and we ask for forgiveness"), was a masterful, though risky political manoeuvre. The Church was risking an unwanted conflict with the social majority, but it was also stripping the authorities of their most powerful ideological tool for manipulating collective emotions. The stakes and the condition for the success of the whole operation was the Church's authority, which was put to the test—and ultimately prevailed. This is also why stifling ressentiment toward the Germans became the fundamental ideological premise of the growing opposition movement (political, intellectual and artistic). We must bear in mind that the political elite who were to run the country after 1989 came from precisely this community, and that good relations with the united German state became one of its priorities at the time. Therefore, if there still was ressentiment associated with the Polish-German past, it was effectively kept under ideological lock and key (at any rate, it was Poland's communist past that stirred the most emotions when embarking upon the new independence after 1989).

Postcolonial theory has revealed other aspects of the ressentiment tied to Poles' long period of political servitude. According to this theory, it was important to *free oneself* from ressentiment in order to discard the ballast of the colonized (and, in Poland's case, also the colonizing) society's bad experiences: thus, to this way of thinking, the cultural process is akin to the therapy process, ending in a cure. In 2006, Ewa M. Thompson called upon Poles on the pages of the conservative paper *Dziennik* to discard their ressentiments and return to their Sarmatian roots, to the pre-partition-era culture and traditions, and thus to bracket off their entire history composed of various partitions, the loss of the state, the 19th-century national uprisings, the Romantic national ideology, two world wars, the restoration of independence, and its subsequent loss. She demanded not only liberation from Romantic myths of sacrifice (produced by Polish culture over the last two centuries), but also kindled a hope of avoiding confrontation with various facts that were less than compatible with the community's idealized self-image. Instead of the considerable effort required to work through the mirage of quick therapy by means of postcolonial discourse, here was the promise of a radical and joyful (Sarmatian) catharsis:

> The pre-partition literature was neither great nor worthy of moral admiration, but it was a healthy literature. A great gulf divides the normality of Pasek from the neuroses of Mickiewicz, the peace of Kochanowski from the bitterness of Wyspiański. Even if we admit that the richness of the Polish literature of the last two centuries considerably exceeds the literary achievements of the pre-partition period, there is no denying that there is a fundamental psychological difference between them. (Thompson 2006, 11)

Ewa M. Thompson uses the tool of ressentiment in a manner that does not so much counteract the effects of the old colonialism as goes to serve a new colonialism, establishing a hierarchy of "healthy" (Western) and "sick" (Central European) societies, and formulating a mission for society against the "worse" part of the world (one aspect of this mission is the categorical desire to dispose of ressentiment). Thompson does not inquire into the relationship between "healthy" societies and their colonial past (insofar as "health" is conditioned by past inflicted violence), and she uncritically and superficially reads the concept of ressentiment in Nietzsche's work as a slur correctly aimed at weakness of all sorts. She does not recognize that ressentiment is an ideological fiction that ought to be disarmed. While accusing the Polish intellectual elite of retroactively adopting Western intellectual trends, she herself is incapable of proposing anything beyond this (i.e. beyond using tools developed elsewhere to describe the local situation).

My own proposition is an attempt to apply the concept of ressentiment in an analogous fashion to how the epithet "queer" has been used in queer studies. This offensive term was adopted by those whom it was meant to offend, and used as a tool in battling the discriminatory discourse. In the case of ressentiment, we also ought to reveal the violence contained in the concept, its potential to normalize and to exclude, and to unmask the position of the "user of the term as the emblem and vehicle of normalisation" (Butler 1993, 230).

Defenders of ressentiment

Our impulse is to define ressentiment as a negative, poisonous and destructive facet of social life. This automatically negative apprehension of ressentiment as a psychological, moral and social phenomenon ultimately makes us pause for thought, however. So too, the ease with which we tend to side ourselves with those forces free of ressentiment (in Nietzschean terms: with the side of the "masters"). All the more so, given that there is a fascinating tradition in defence of ressentiment. It suffices to recall Max Scheler's *Ressentiment* (1913), Jean Améry's essay "Resentments" in his book *At the Mind's Limits: Contemplations by a Survivor on Auschwitz and its Realities* (1980; originally published as *Jenseits von Schuld und Sühne,* 1964), or the concept of "authentic ressentiment" developed by Fredric Jameson in his study *The Political Unconscious* (1981).

It is Jameson's concept which will particularly interest me here, because it identifies ressentiment with an "experimental" capacity to deal with the contradictory demands of social life. Ressentiment, paradoxically, opens up this prospect. Moreover, Jameson sees in ressentiment the last residue of the utopian in 19th-century political reality, grappling with a realist conception of the world (a deterministic world easily "naturalizing" its rules, conceivable in a single unified, coherent convention). And hence a world which—from this point of view—is always determined and easily "naturalizes" (and imperceptibly normalizes) its rules. An all-too-"objectively" represented reality eliminates space for experimentation, obstructs projects for change. Moreover, this kind of representation frames all desire for change within an image of caricaturized evil resulting from vengeful powerlessness—i.e. within the realm of ressentiment. For Jameson, ressentiment is the fundamental "ideologeme" of the 19th century. The main attribute of all ideologemes is that they can exist in two forms: as "pseudo-ideas," opinions, and superstitions, and as narratives, libidinal fantasies legitimizing class divisions.

This duality allows them to affect both the conscious and the unconscious. According to Jameson's concept, ressentiment is central to ideological practices that give us flawed tools for interpreting reality; by the same token, however, they cannot entirely conceal their self-referentiality, and cannot complete the procedure of self-masking and naturalizing the images of the world they produce (Jameson 2002, 189). According to Nietzsche's definition, ressentiment is a reviled and condemned strategy of imagined revenge on reality, though in essence it is a model for every ideological intervention that masks our own activities and attributes them to others. In other words: it should not be ressentiment we analyse, but the socially invisible ideology that produces the concept of ressentiment (it is "invisible" because of the "visibility" of ressentiment as such). In this sense, ressentiment is a purely theatrical phenomenon. In the sphere of reality a stage is created upon which caricaturized figures appear in garish roles, with primitive story lines. Ressentiment must thus be associated with bad taste in order to fulfil its ideological task.

Jameson's real contribution to the theory of ressentiment is the self-referentiality of this phenomenon: he or she who formulates a theory of ressentiment also produces ressentiment, because other people's ressentiments are often a particularly grating subject of one's own ressentiment.

Améry's defence of ressentiment is based on other principles. He does not consent to the formulation of a post-war ideology of forgetting and forgiveness from a position of political power as a condition for belonging to the civilized world. Améry lays bare his traumatic experiences as a victim of Nazi fascism and presents the demands *not to* remember that were made of him, as extreme oppression: he locates the defeated Germans on the victors' side, and their victims among the defeated. Améry formulates his right to ressentiment as man's right not to submit to "nature" (meaning here: the "natural" process of forgetting, since ressentiment is always perceived as a phenomenon against "nature"—rather as proof of its theatricality). As his right to desire that something never occurred, as a demand for the "suspension of time." And thus Améry—like Jameson—recognizes the experimental, critical, and utopian value of ressentiment. Ressentiment opens up a space—the only one Améry accepts—for victims and perpetrators to meet; it has an ethical, empathic, and intersubjective dimension. The experience of the victim must be acknowledged and directly shared by his/her recent perpetrator (and thus the reverse of what Ewa M. Thompson would want, in her demand that the colonized free him/herself from the experience of being the victim, and match the "health" of the colonizers). Only ressentiment—or the fact of it being acknowledged by others—can disarm the destructive power of the experience of violence, and release us from the isolation of having survived these harrowing experiences.

Once again, according to Nietzsche, ressentiment is tied to an excess of memory and paralyses the processes of forgetting that are required for living and the creative attitude, poisons individual and collective life, turns values on their head, and subordinates reality to the mechanisms of projection. If we remove the negative valuations, however, that Nietzsche and other constructors of this ideologeme impose, this definition reveals the "experimental" spirit of ressentiment, its conditional mode and the utopian dimension which Jameson describes. This can be seen in Nietzsche himself:

> [. . .] the man of *ressentiment* is neither upright nor naive in his dealings with others, nor is he honest and open with himself. His soul *squints*; his mind loves bolt-holes, secret paths, back doors, he regards all hidden things as *his* world, *his* security, *his* refreshment. (Nietzsche 2008, 24)

Such a histrionic definition of ressentiment is simultaneously a definition of subversive theatre, in its complex game of undermining reality.

The category of ressentiment interests me chiefly in three of its aspects: its experimental relationship to time (the past is present, the present recreates the past), its refusal to forget the victim's experience, and its exposure of an "unjust" relationship to the past. Ressentiment is based on the memory of the body: the necessity to halt the immediate, instinctual response to the insult incurred. It might be compared to the rhetorical figure of *catachresis*, with its principle of building metaphors on the basis of the body and its tactic of extreme deformation of meanings. Catachresis can be a powerful intervention into the symbolic order—it is the speech of those attempting to assert power over the language that excludes them, or condemns them to silence as subjects of ressentiment. In a sense, the reading of ressentiment proposed by Jameson and Améry can be seen as a catachresis of the Nietzschean idea of ressentiment.

Polish theatre of oblivion

Thus conceived, ressentiment allows us to grasp the breakdown of the forgetting strategies that Polish theatre and, more generally, Polish culture have tried to produce and mobilize in the years since 1989. If Jameson proposed that ressentiment, as a key 19th-century ideologeme, can always be stated in narrative forms, we might risk the hypothesis that wariness of ressentiment has paralysed the ability to tell stories. This wariness manifested itself initially in a cult of the classics (i.e. in tales *previously* written), in a search for ambiguity and universality in the themes presented on stage, and in the marginalization of contemporaneous drama (to put it succinctly). The critic Tomasz Plata once pointed out the remarkable popularity of Anton Chekhov's dramas in the Polish theatre in the first years of the political transformation, in the early 1990s (Plata 2006, 221-222). Perhaps addressing the theme of silence and passivity was the first move in taking aim at the experience of ressentiment? If Jameson could call Joseph Conrad the poet of ressentiment (2002, 257), turning unresolved political conflicts into moral, psychological, and aesthetic issues, could not the same be said of Chekhov in Polish theatre after 1989?

References to history, if they emerged at all, underwent a complex encoding and metaphorization, or provocatively vanished (prompting critics to repeatedly express their impression of the past received from plays and theatrical productions as being sealed and increasingly remote). As part of this forgetting strategy, I would also cite the centre-stage placement of the monster-protagonist, the polar opposite to representations of all forms of victimization. The famous staging of Witold Gombrowicz's play *The Marriage* (*Ślub,* 1948) directed by Jerzy Jarocki in 1991 (staged at the Stary Theatre in Kraków) could be read as an attempt to force the perpetrator's perspective into Polish culture and history: a Polish soldier fighting on the Western front during World War II was represented as an unscrupulous patricide, debunking all the cults of the past and tradition. Identifying with such a strong and sadistic protagonist was a source of pleasure for the Polish viewers of the time. It should not be difficult to unravel the subterranean motif of Nietzsche's call to triumph over history.

We ought to ask ourselves at once if the forgetting strategies that characterized this type of theatre were merely a delayed accession to a pact of amnesia demanded by the new political order after 1945 in Western Europe, as described by Tony Judt (with the key moral obligation "to forgive the Germans")—an amnesia whose blessings Polish society could not know in the time of the People's Republic, being pummelled by propaganda that built ressentiment towards West Germany. (This went as follows: those who lost the war and performed atrocities are better off than us; the criminals have got off scot free and are living well.) Over time, this ressentiment underwent a powerful and effective suppression, because the propagandistic motives stirring it became increasing evident to society, and were thus eyed with suspicion. On the other hand, memory of the war remained acute, and was passed down through the generations in family stories. Layers of unspoken emotions thus accumulated; Polish theatre was to uncover them a decade after the political and economic transformations of 1989-1990, and allowed them to explode. We might therefore ask: Did these forgetting strategies have a distinct affective logic and their own local justification in Poland?

Did they arise from the conviction that we had reached the limits of history, of which nothing more could be said, and which could not be altered? Again we find a vision of the excessively objectified reality that Jameson describes, and the problem that Améry so passionately struggled against: a concept of political life that is too closed to the traumatic past. The noble attempt to overcome ressentiment involved a high degree of conformity to one's own society: it assumed outright a collective historical omniscience, and by the same token indicated its superfluity. It designed its own utopias for reality. It freed people from taking up the considerable effort of grappling with the past.

Przemysław Czapliński writes about the delusion of transformation periods being characterized by a collective understanding of the past. The turn of the 1980s and 1990s produced a stereotypical and provisional image of the past, and of World War II in particular, made up of a few allegedly irrefutable truths: the equation of German crimes and Russian ones (Kolyma was to appear alongside Auschwitz from then on), the innocence of the Poles (even when speaking of shameful acts, they were recalled alongside evidence of greatness and heroism) and above all the conviction that the threads of the private, familial transfer of tradition and values had not been broken, and could serve to rebuild society's values according to old, and purportedly mass-accepted formulae (Czapliński 2009, 63-80).

This collectively developed and powerful ideological construct had a great deal of political potential; it served to protect society in a transformational period, and thus the illusions tied to it needed to be upheld for as long as possible. In the theatre, no one had the courage to make a full frontal attack; instead, too many political circles with real authority were working to protect Polish society from ressentiment. Tadeusz Kantor's (1915-1990) final plays, staged in Poland in the early 1990s—*I'll Never Return Here* (*Nigdy już tu nie powrócę,* 1989) and *Today is My Birthday* (*Dziś są moje urodziny,* 1990)—demonstrated such a position of historical omniscience and integration of society. In his theatrical performances, Kantor presented an image of the "entire" history of the 20th century in this part of Europe, while his stage metaphors could be encapsulated in various synthetic formulae, such as the "century of barbarism"—against which Jean Améry had protested so passionately, demanding a more concrete and diversifying approach to history, one based on ressentiment. Kantor, for one, began providing the illusion that the painful and brutal past had been worked through, and that the audience was in full agreement as to its meaning.

I consider two performances in particular, of 2001 and 2008, to be the culminating (though paradoxical) experiences of the art of forgetting in Polish theatre. Characteristically, these are the plays that evoked perhaps the liveliest discussions among theatre critics of the past decade, and met with a powerful emotional response from the Polish public. They became cult performances, and were well attended by young audiences. The first was a production of Sarah Kane's *Cleansed* (translated into Polish by Krzysztof Warlikowski and Jacek Poniedziałek), directed by Warlikowski in 2001 at the Rozmaitości Theatre in Warsaw. The second was *Factory 2* directed by Krystian Lupa, being the director and actors' "collective fantasy" on Andy Warhol and his crew, created in 2008 (at the Stary Theatre, Kraków). It is characteristic that both tried to define collectivity within microcosmic environments entirely outside the context of Polish history.

The naked human body was central to both performances or, more accurately, the body clearly extracted from the structure of history. In these productions, anguish does not spring from historical experience. Pain is experienced in an eternal "now" (in Warlikowski), and in narcissistic gratification within the frame of a staged "here" (in Lupa's play). Both contain a strong libidinal element, releasing the circulation of energy. If the body of the man of ressentiment is a map of his wounds (evidence of inflicted violence), in such a stage reality it can speak differently. The game revolves around the image of a humiliated man. Curiously, in Warlikowski's play many stage situations alluded to Jerzy Grotowski's *Akropolis* based on Stanisław Wyspiański's 1904 drama of the same name (let us recall that the protagonists of this legendary production of 1962 were Auschwitz prisoners), while Lupa's *Factory 2* struck up a dialogue with Kantor's "Theatre of Death" and its images of the degraded man captured in freeze-frames of the past.

Yet we might well ask: behind these directors' exposure of the shamelessness of those who had become degraded and excluded from mainstream society, is there no trace at all of any unresolved (and thus libidinally effective in shaping viewers' reactions) historical ressentiment? Does not the motif of the experimenting community, so powerfully present in both plays, draw its energy from this sphere of excluded social experience? It acquires a new scope and dignity. It liberates this sphere from narrow definitions and embarrassment.

There were, however, directors who were not afraid to reveal the ressentiment at the heart of Polish culture. For the opening of the National Theatre's 1997 season, Jerzy Grzegorzewski directed Wyspiański's *November Night* (1904). The director transformed the mystery-play structure of the drama addressing a great national catastrophe—the disastrous November Uprising of 1830—into a monstrous and monumental parody. The Greek gods overseeing the course of history were drawn more from an Offenbach operetta than from the Homeric epics and Eleusinian Mysteries. National heroes were defeated by national traitors (as the more interesting characters, and as people who had been painfully humiliated by the moral majority). The audience was utterly disoriented as to the director's intentions, which could be interpreted as creating radical distance from national myths, national misfortunes, and national victim narratives. Grzegorzewski provoked a situation of incomprehension, which should be read as the result of the forgetting process that was taking place—liberation, once and for all, from the burdensome past and its accursed myths. The message was simple: If we no longer understand Wyspiański's odd, ghostly play, if we (Poles) observe it with a detached sense of tedium, then it means that we have finally freed ourselves from the myths of martyrdom and have become, in the Nietzschean sense, healthy. At one point, however, the realistic sounds of aeroplanes rang out overhead in the theatre. A telling silence descended over the audience. There could be only one association: war, the bombardment of Warsaw in 1939 and 1944. On the one hand, Grzegorzewski was reminding Poles in affective terms of their condition as victims of history, in a way that preceded conscious reactions (and as such, reached down into layers of ressentiment that lingered on, repressed and as yet uncorrected). On the other, he was exposing the relativity of temporal distances. Viewers who were too young to witness the bombing were also affected by the scene. Thus it was not direct experience, but the vitality of ressentiment that was the condition for viewers being moved by the performance, and for their affective participation in it.

Another director attuned to the layers of ressentiment in the Polish experience is Jan Klata. On the occasion of Poland's accession to the European Union (2004), Klata directed a play based on Stanisław Ignacy Witkiewicz's *Janulka, Daughter of Fizdejko* (*Janulka, córka Fizdejki,* 1923). He changed this "medieval" tale of the Teutonic Knights invading Lithuania into a story of the colonization of Poland by German EU politicians. Significantly, Klata's production was created in Wałbrzych, a mining town which had belonged to Germany before World War II, became an important mining town in communist Poland, and increasingly succumbed to economic and social degradation after the political transformations of 1989.[2] Klata superimposed various layers of time: the medieval war with the Teutonic order, the 19th-century resistance to Germanization, the memory of World War II, and events that were entirely contemporaneous. One might say that Klata was simply trying to uncover Polish ressentiments. In reality, however, the play operated more subversively: it fuelled them. As a symbol of colonization, two emaciated men appeared on stage in striped concentration camp suits, eating crisps with terrifying crunching sounds, pulling them greedily from shiny, crinkling packages. Viewers found it difficult to control their feeling of inappropriateness: the hunger of the concentration camp prisoners was satisfied by crisps; signs of the traumatic past overlapped with present-day symbols of consumption. The real famine of the concentration camps was a metaphor for the hunger of a society seeking to find itself among advanced consumer societies. In other words: the economically powerful Germans had "compensated" for their past crimes at a cut price. The brilliant ellipsis of the image not only unearthed a still vital sense of maltreatment; it also unmasked the political taboo in contemporary political

[2] Wałbrzych and its post-1989 decline have featured in various Polish cultural artefacts since 1990—for example in numerous texts by Olga Tokarczuk, the novels of Joanna Bator (published 2009, 2010 and 2012) as well as in Tomek Tryzna's *Miss Nobody* (*Panna Nikt,* 1994) and Andrzej Wajda's 1996 film of the same (Kraskowka 2010).

correctness surrounding the phenomenon of overlapping past and present ressentiments. The audience's lively laughter, which had theretofore greeted the performance, ceased abruptly.

Both Grzegorzewski and Klata thus seem to confirm the view that untangling oneself as a Pole from the status of victim as well as the postulate of forgetting are not only difficult tasks, but perhaps also undesirable and damaging to social self-consciousness. Both directors were able to reveal the existence of ressentiment through the use of powerful effects, by staging plays in which audiences experienced radical shifts in their emotional reactions.

Carnivalesque ressentiment

Nonetheless, the most fascinating experience of ressentiment associated with the memory of World War II has been revealed and developed in several recent dramatic texts—or rather in texts which may not have been called dramas by their authors, but which use dramatic forms, such as in Bożena Keff's *Song on Mother and the Fatherland*. It is in this way that contemporary Polish drama has broken into the theatre once more, disrupting the latter's defence mechanisms, undermining its sophisticated forgetting strategies.

Of the most important texts written during the past few years, none before 2005, I shall discuss five as being the most illustrative: *Night* (*Noc*, 2005) by Andrzej Stasiuk (b. 1960), *Everything's All Right between Us* (*Między nami dobrze jest,* 2008) by Dorota Masłowska (b. 1983), *Child's Play* (*Sztuka dla Dziecka,* premiere 2009, unpublished) and *Long Live War!!!* (*Niech żyje wojna,* 2011) by Paweł Demirski (b. 1979), and *Song on Mother and the Fatherland* (*Utwór o Matce i Ojczyźnie,* 2008) by Bożena Umińska-Keff (writing as Keff, b. 1948). Interestingly, these authors represent different generations; their perceptions are therefore not necessarily "generation specific."

All have provided the basis for important and fascinating performances (which is not always the case in contemporary Polish drama). In all these works memory of the war is presented as returning from a personal, emotionally charged perspective, not one that is objectified and historical. They all put the victim's perspective centre stage. In all of them the "experimental" and "theatrical" nature of ressentiment reveals itself in its full force and gains strong support from the author, who does not succumb to the temptation to be above ressentiment. Finally, they all contain a utopian motif: they change the course of history by putting things in the conditional mode, i.e. by creating alternative versions of history within a fictional framework. They carry out the revenge of the imagination, inspired by ressentiment and so condemned by Nictzschc, reshaping it into a tool of critical and—politically, historically, morally—incorrect action.

They all also use comedy as a strategy—but in order to explore the audience's standpoints, and not with the clear intent to ridicule. It suffices to recall Stasiuk's *Night* and Masłowska's *Everything's All Right between Us*, whose world premieres took place in German theatres. They initially met with guarded audience responses, uncertain of whether it was appropriate for a German viewer to laugh at Polish ressentiments.

Things are sketched out most simply, perhaps, in Stasiuk's work: the "drama" is a "tribal song," a piece about "memory that has sunk deep into the bone" (Stasiuk 2005, 22) through the tales of mothers and grandmothers. It is the story of a Polish thief of German cars who dies and donates his heart to the owner of a stolen car—who is also his killer. The Polish heart saves the life of the German murderer—a motif as loaded with all the complications of ressentiment and good-willed forgiveness as it is with secret revenge for injuries past. The tale is set against a sprawling landscape of collective memory, based on the same, eternal patterns. The war rages on: both in the living memory of the chorus and in the present day. Germany represents a colonial powerhouse, a developed technological civilization and an elevated spiritual tradition; Poland remains a country of barbarians, suppliers of biological materials—donors of hearts, kidneys and livers. The Polish car thief is first killed by the car owner, and later becomes his heart donor. The Pole is always the victim and the German always comes out on top.

Ressentiments survive, which allows them to be assimilated; in a paradoxical way, they allow Poles to forge bonds, closeness, and give mortal enemies the chance to unite. "Ripping off a BMW" is ultimately read by the car owner as an expression of Polish admiration for German culture, and becomes a platform for a tender reconciliation between the German and the Pole (the latter appearing before his killer as a ghost, obviously). In the final scene, they lie together on a hospital bed, clearly supplied by the author for mutual therapy. Stasiuk uses ressentiment in a conciliatory, kind-hearted fashion; soothing rather than stoking it, turning it into music or a song.

In Masłowska's text too, the war rages on. At first only in the grandmother's memory (this "gendered" motif of the female memory, also present in Stasiuk, is characteristic—it assimilates and mollifies). The main issue of the drama is first raised as follows: "Ah, I remember the day the war broke out." And the granddaughter replies: "What broke out?" thereby giving convincing expression to her unfamiliarity with history and her lack of interest in it (Masłowska 2008, 6). The generational conflict of languages and experiences is brilliantly overcome in Masłowska's drama. In the finale, the howl of sirens, the rattle of automobiles and the echoes of dropping bombs ring out. Grandmother and granddaughter dig through the ruins of their home together. Regardless of their differences in language and the experiences of their separate generations, the vitality of their ressentiment transcends generations and provides them with a common plane of understanding, if not a sense of community.

The conclusions we draw might be dismal, but Masłowska seeks less to offer diagnoses than to examine the emotional transferability of cultural subcodes, in a way that is almost akin to Wyspiański's strategy in his play *The Wedding* (*Wesele,* 1901). The political significance of this drama is its attempt to extract disparate realms of subconscious social communication from beneath the hegemony of nationalist ideologies and their summary political applications.

The grandmother dies in the rubble, thus calling into question the real existence of her daughter and granddaughter: Masłowska splendidly differentiates between the realness of history and the fictions of ressentiment. The whole drama thus has a double conditional mode, or even a negative one: we see figures on stage who—following the armed cataclysm—have had no chance to be born, alongside those who exist in the realm of fiction, a film that is just being made, another narrative about Polish misfortune. Masłowska collects clichés and distorts them as she pleases: she doesn't so much defuse them as explores (again, like Stasiuk) their effectiveness in creating a community—the *Everything's All Right between Us* of the title. She mitigates our fear of ressentiment, allowing it to operate with full force.

In Paweł Demirski's dramas and Bożena-Keff's text, the conciliatory intentions are less evident. The ressentiments sound threatening here, and can be truly destructive. The author's personal attitudes are more sharply drawn.

Stasiuk appeals to tribal instincts, allowing viewers to see a gang of car thieves as a collective image, which could form the basis of a general identification. Polish viewers may accept this demeaning image as a representation of the entire nation; well-rehearsed in acts of self-degradation, they instinctively permit it and are even, to some degree, ready to affirm it. The author does not negotiate with his audience here. Viewers accept in all humility a stereotype that should enrage them. An insult becomes the basis for an identity. This acutely recalls the "queer" political strategy: an insult is made the basis of an identity, thus disempowering those who oppress. Masłowska also requires viewers to be ready and willing to identify with Poland as a lesser, miserable, repellent country. She walks in Gombrowicz's footsteps, though she does not deride Polishness sadistically; her belittling leads to utter absurdity—as well as to something like empathy for Polish poverty.

We find nothing of the sort in Demirski and Keff. First, because they both introduce the Jewish theme into their texts, thus complicating the Polish myths of victimization, and second, because the subject of their ressentiment is experience whose trauma has not faded. Demirski ruthlessly evokes these in both dramas mentioned above. We encounter images of bestiality, gang crimes, rape, and death. The author furiously attacks attempts to culturally assimilate them: national myths, popular cinema or television series, the politics of memory, and museums devoted to crimes of all sorts. Small wonder that such an approach inspires a distilled sort of ressentiment: every gesture that does not serve degradation is nevertheless degraded. *Child's Play* is a violent protest against the ideology of trauma, while trauma is viewed at the same time as the ultimate argument against all ideologies. The action of the play takes place in a fictional Europe, in which the Nazis have won the war and have forced upon everyone a ritualized nursing of guilt. According to Améry, however, this Europe is in fact far from fictional. In Demirski's drama the world knows only one crime—the Holocaust—and is mired in its obscene contemplation. He drags Polish ressentiment associated with the massacre of the Jews into the light of day, playing a risky game with it, and mercilessly striking at the very foundations of the Polish culture of victimization. We search in vain for a foothold. The mechanism Jameson described is at work: ressentiment is always self-referential, it rebounds towards itself and always frames another ressentiment.

Bożena Keff also demonstrates the vitality of ressentiment: her imaginary revenge on the Mother and the Fatherland is characterized by boundless invention. This is the tale of a person utterly excluded from history—both from Jewish history, represented by the Mother saved from the Holocaust, and from the experiences of the Polish community, because of its antisemitic attitudes. Polish society appears as an aggressive "tribe," fed on myths of the harm they have suffered and indifferent towards to the suffering of others. This very lack of "participation" releases the narrator's overactive imagination. *Song on Mother and the Fatherland* is the most radical summons to a personal and risk-laden appropriation of history: not through forgetting, but through an uncompromising, dauntless *catachresis* produced by the mechanism of ressentiment. This text is exceptional in that ressentiment does not become the basis of a commonality (as in Stasiuk, Masłowska and even Demirski); on the contrary, it entails extreme alienation, but without the satisfaction gained from a sense of individualism. The situation of the subject of this tale is more complex—she has no prospect of joining a community or of translating her experience into political rebellion. The Polish tribal culture of victimization inspires contempt and horror in Keff, for it is seen from the perspective of a victim of this culture, from the perspective of one excluded from it. The violence of the Jewish mother's traumatic experiences, in turn, changes this authentic victim of history into a terrifying monster, who makes her own daughter (i.e. the subject or narrative "I") the victim of psychological and verbal violence.

Conclusion

Has the political fear of ressentiment been defused by theatre and drama? On the basis of the works discussed above, we may suggest that they have indeed turned ressentiment into a creative power, which in no way means that its defence in the sphere of art should be transferred directly into the field of politics. In Demirski's dramas, especially, the language of hatred sometimes comes rather too close to what is practised on the current political stage. And it is precisely the defence of the principle of theatricality that, to my mind, becomes valuable for ressentiment: it creates the chance to open up a utopian space, a field for critical thought. Each of the authors mentioned above performs a deep analysis of linguistic mechanisms, in order to fully grasp them and subvert the speech of ressentiment. The discovery of new combinations of words, the proposition of different rhythms and intonations and the chance to hear them in living speech on stage, provides not only a valuable impunity, but above all, an effective intervention into the symbolic order. The victims' ressentiment bounces back towards themselves: it is there that the source of violence is recognized and acknowledged (victims themselves appear as oppressive monsters, or phantoms, particularly in Demirski and Keff), as is the memory of harm committed, written in the body's speech, and thus impossible to relativize or forget.

Bibliography

Primary sources

Demirski, Paweł. 2011. *Parafrazy*. Warsaw: Wydawnictwo Krytyki Politycznej.

Keff, Bożena. 2008. *Utwór o Matce i Ojczyźnie*. Krakow: Korporacja Ha!art.

Masłowska, Dorota. 2008. *Między nami dobrze jest*. Warsaw: Lampa i Iskra Boża.

Stasiuk, Andrzej. 2005. *Noc. Słowiańsko-germańska tragifarsa germańska*. Wołowiec: Wydawnictwo Czarne.

Secondary sources

Adorno, Theodor W. 2003. "The Meaning of Working through the Past." In *Can One Live after Auschwitz?* edited by Rolf Tiedemann, 3-18. Stanford, CA: Stanford University Press.

Améry, Jean. 1980. *At the Mind's Limits: Contemplations by a Survivor on Auschwitz and its Realities,* translated by Sidney Rosenfeld and Stella P. Rosenfeld. Bloomington and Indianapolis, IN: Indiana University Press.

Butler, Judith. 1993. *Bodies That Matter: On the Discursive Limits of "Sex."* New York and London: Routledge.

Czapliński, Przemysław. 2009. *Polska do wymiany. Późna nowoczesność i nasze wielkie narracje*. Warsaw: Wydawnictwo W.A.B.

Deleuze, Gilles. 1983. *Nietzsche and Philosophy*, translated by Hugh Tomlinson. New York: Columbia University Press.

Dziamski, Grzegorz. 2004. "Hybrydyczna tożsamość Europy Środkowej po 1989 roku." In *Dylematy wielokulturowości*, edited by Wojciech Kalaga, 163-176. Kraków: Universitas.

Janion, Maria. 2000. *Do Europy tak, ale razem z naszymi umarłymi*. Warsaw: Sic!

Jameson, Fredric. 2002. *The Political Unconscious*. London and New York: Routledge.

Judt, Tony. 2005. *Postwar: A History of Europe since 1945*. London: Heinemann.

Kraskowska, Ewa. 2010. "W Wałbrzychu, czyli nigdzie? O karierze miasta Wałbrzych w literaturze i filmie lat ostatnich." In *Nowe dwudziestolecie (1989-2009). Rozpoznania, hierarchie, perspektywy,* edited by Hanna Gosk, 245-260. Warsaw: Elipsa.

Nietzsche, Friedrich. 2008. *On the Genealogy of Morals*, translated by Douglas Smith. Oxford: Oxford University Press.

Plata Tomasz. 2006. "Osobiste zobowiązania." In *Strategie publiczne, strategie prywatne. Teatr polski 1990-2005*, edited by Tomasz Plata, 217-238. Warsaw: Świat Literacki.

Scheler, Max. 1973. *Ressentiment*, translated by William H. Holdheim. New York: Noonday.

Sobolewski, Tadeusz. 2002. "Dzieło bezstronne." *Gazeta Wyborcza* 123 (28 June): 4.

Thompson, Ewa M. 2006. "Sarmatyzm i postkolonializm. O naturze polskich resentymentów." *Europa. Tygodnik Idei* 46: 11.

Wood, Nancy. 1998. "The Victim's Resentments." In *Modernity, Culture and "the Jew,"* edited by Bryan Cheyette and Laura Marcus, 257-267. Cambridge: Polity Press.

Transnational or Bi-cultural? Challenges in Reading post-1989 Drama "Written outside the Nation"

Elwira M. GROSSMAN

By comparing and contrasting two plays "written outside the nation": *Antigone in New York* (1992) by Janusz Głowacki (b. 1938) and *Cherry Blossom* (2008) by Catherine Grosvenor (b. 1978). I would like to investigate closer the possibility of creating a transnational drama/performance that is supposed to facilitate mutual understanding and intercultural experience. What prompted me to combine these two plays were their Scottish premieres held in the same year: 2008.

Although both pieces share the same broadly defined theme of "migration," one could not find more diverse plays in terms of their main focus, approach, dramatic convention and stage design. While *Antigone in New York* has had an impressive production history all over the world and been translated into more than twenty languages since its original 1992 publication in Polish, *Cherry Blossom* was written "collaboratively" and staged for the Traverse Theatre in Edinburgh. It was designed as an artistic response to the huge wave of post-2004 Polish migration to the British Isles in general, and Scotland in particular.

The common theme of displaced and dispossessed individuals, however, is not the only shared platform of exploration here. I am more concerned with how the two plays respond to the challenge of the "globalized world" that brought down the Berlin Wall and opened all borders to all citizens, including those of former communist Eastern Europe. How do these two dramatic texts "written outside the nation" (Seyhan 2001)—in a time of no political barriers between "home production" and "émigré writing"—deal with the challenge of addressing their respective audiences, or perhaps a shared transcultural and/or transnational spectatorship? Whom they are written for, is a vital question. But equally important are the questions as to who reads them, who watches them and who assesses them. And who has the power to issue verdicts on their artistic merit and aesthetic values (which, after all, are culture-based and historically determined)?

Addressing these challenging questions would seem quite urgent since discussion of "intercultural readers" and writers receives a lot of scholarly attention, yet this attention does not appear to be directed at the Slavonic world. The works written between or among different nations defy easy national classifications or definitions and scholars struggle to coin the proper terminology and methods for researching them. Among the most notable efforts are the following proposals: nonterritorial, transnational/translingual or nomadic writing; "the grey zone writing" (Ugresić 2007); the "third scenario" writers (Hall 1989); the "third space" (described by Homi K. Bhabha "as a spatial movement of cultural representations," 2004); "writing for the planet" (initiated by Gayatri Spivak but developed further by Wai Chee Dimock, 2001); "writing for a new belonging" (Bromley 2000) and the well-established concept of "minor literature" discussed by Deleuze and Guattari which has been challenged by Azade Seyhan in her 2001 study *Writing Outside the Nation*. The term "minor literature" has also been adopted by Halina Filipowicz in her attempt to re-conceptualize émigré writing in Polish (Filipowicz 2001). All these attempts have been made in order to grasp the challenging phenomenon of "transcultural/transnational writing" to which both plays under discussion in the current chapter belong, albeit in different ways.

First, it is necessary to establish some basic facts and background in order to address the major, more pertinent aspects of my analysis. Głowacki originally wrote *Antigone in New York* in Polish, but the play premiered in both Poland and the USA in the same year: 1993. The English text was translated (or, I would say, was rewritten/adapted) by the author himself and Joan Torres. *Cherry Blossom*, on the other hand, was intended to be bilingual from the start and much effort was invested by the writer and her collaborators in order to meet this challenge. This constitutes one of the plays' major differences. While Głowacki put a lot of effort into rendering the language issue transparent and into focusing on the problem of homelessness presented through intertextuality "beyond the language," the producers of *Cherry Blossom* made the conscious choice of situating the language at the very centre of their two parallel plots: one fictional, describing the migration experience of Grażyna Antkiewicz, and the other based on the real story of Robert Dziekański, who died in police custody at Vancouver Airport in October 2007. Approximately forty per cent of the script was spoken in Polish in both locations (Scotland and Poland) while the translation was projected onto the stage using multimedia devices. The point was to reinforce the confusion experienced by migrants (or should I say, displaced people) who do not know the language of the host country. But the confusion conveyed onstage was not limited to its linguistic dimension. It involved in addition all the different aspects of a broadly defined culture. Thus, while *Cherry Blossom* was played by the same cast and used the same script in Poland and Scotland, *Antigone in New York* was significantly amended by the writer to suit the needs of each culture. Yet, surprisingly enough, the two separate versions of *Antigone* have never been compared even by bilingual reviewers and scholars. It has been commonly assumed that one is the clone of the other, which is most certainly not the case. Moreover, some interpretations of the play were based on misleading assumptions. A case in point is

Elżbieta Baniewicz's reading of the play's language (2001), to which I shall return shortly.

Let me now briefly outline the basic differences between the two *Antigones*: the first and most significant one is the dramatis personae. Since the play roughly follows the Sophoclean episode of an unlawful burial, the change of name is more than just a minor adjustment. The Americanness of John/Paulie is established by different references. In the English-language version, his name is Paulie and he is called a WASP; while in the Polish text, he is introduced as John and described as "an aristocrat from Boston" ("arystokrata z Bostonu"). What seems far more important here is the matter of direct family kinship established in English by the play's mythical framework (Paulie versus the prototype of Sophocles's Polyneices). This connection is far less transparent in Polish and one could argue that in the original version, national identity counts more than the mythical family ties. The Polish text depicts the homeless characters by including episodes that never feature in the English "translation." For example, there is the story of a homeless man who manages to get out of the park by selling second-hand books. Then there is the rumour about a boiler room owner who organizes pilgrimages to the Vatican to see the Pope, and also an ironic mention of "lessons in existentialist philosophy" that people living in America might find interesting. By the same token, specific episodes and dialogues—absent in the Polish version—are introduced in the English edition of the play. There is, for instance, talk of Anita's earning money by pissing into a bottle for Jenny, who—being a drug user—would not be able to pass the drug test at work. Interestingly enough, the Polish play never explains where Anita got her money to bribe Sasza and Pchełka into stealing Paulie's body. One could argue that these are minor cultural adjustments, but the fact that they exist indicates that Głowacki had in mind two different types of audience and two different cultural contexts which he considered carefully when preparing each version of the play.

One of the most striking textual differences in this context (apart from the John/Paulie name) is the introduction of a phrase in scene 4, Act I, which hints at seeking a "final solution" to the homeless problem (Głowacki 1997, 35). In the Polish version, a similar exchange between Sasza and Pchełka is moved to scene 9, Act II, a literal translation of the Polish here being: "there is a plan to finally resolve the problem of the homeless" ("jest plan, żeby rozwiązać problem bezdomnych ostatecznie"). By comparison, the Polish phrase "ostateczne rozwiązanie" seems much milder than the English term "final solution," especially given its historical associations and connotations. Although this could be a matter of individual readers' opinions, it is highly unlikely that an English-speaking spectator upon hearing the words "final solution" would not make the Holocaust connection instantly. Interestingly, the hint at a "final solution" is not the only "transfer" that makes its way into Głowacki's depiction of a Western world that praises itself for its unconditional application of democratic values. The figure of the Policeman in both versions illustrates a truly "Eastern European" paradox: while praising truth, he tells lies; while referring to equality and respect, he carries out violent orders. In short, his rhetoric masks the real meaning of his actions, and in the end his monologue becomes so convoluted it obscures the points he makes rather than explains them.

There is one more example in both versions where common associations reveal drastic differences between East and West, and that is the unbearable yelling in the park. It reminds Sasha of the KGB interrogative methods he experienced back in Leningrad. In Russia, he would muffle the sound with radio music, while in the Tompkins Square Park he uses a broken tape recorder playing a Frank Sinatra tune.

All these ostensibly "minor" episodes strike me today as a sign of Głowacki's amazing creative insight, which courageously suggests that the "West" gets "easternized" much faster than we are willing to admit and that the open borders secure the traffic in both directions—not just in one. "East" indeed gets "westernized" (and there is a rich media discourse being developed along these lines) but "West" does not remain immune to the flow of "Eastern" experience either, and it is a pity that this particular phenomenon is so rarely commented on. The point seems more obvious today but it was less so in 1993, and yet surprisingly strongly present in Głowacki's take, in both versions of the play, on the "Promised Land," for example, approximating the symbolic "West."

Let me now return to Baniewicz's 2001 interpretation of the play. The case in point is Głowacki's total erasure of the language issue in his depiction of the homeless characters who are non-native speakers of English. I subscribe to the view that behind each erasure stands a powerful ideology, but I can just as well suspend my disbelief and redirect my attention to the play's intertextual and mythical fabric (Grossman 2008). However, not all critics and scholars—on both sides of the ocean—privilege this approach (Wanat 1993; Trojanowska 2003; Chmielewski 2002). Helena Morawska-White in a conversation with Kevin J. Harty pointed out that "Certainly, with Sasha's charm and education and Flea's verbal skills, both could have achieved more." (Morawska-White and Harty 1997, 119) Baniewicz followed a similar train of thought but constructed a more sophisticated argument. In her interpretation of the play, she assumed that Głowacki wrote it in English and that the characters spoke pigeon English which contributed to the play's humour, deeper meaning and aesthetic qualities. She criticized the "smooth linguistic version of the authorized Polish translation" (sic!) and wondered what the polyphony of "pigeon Polishes" would be like if the play were to be faithfully translated into Polish (Baniewicz 2001, 362-363). The fact that Baniewicz's imagination became energized by the prospect of *Antigone in New York* as a truly transcultural text is actually quite insightful. It reveals the potential offered by "cross-cultural transfers," including the new perspective on the reader's own culture. The new perspective here brings up the concept of "pigeon Polishes," which was triggered by Baniewicz's imagination rather than by the actual state of affairs. This example shows that much can be gained through intercultural reading even when the bi-cultural perspective is largely imagined; although a crucial amendment needs to be made, in that "interculturality" does not always work the way we assume or imagine it does, which is precisely what Baniewicz's misreading illustrates so well. All this evidence proves that Głowacki's erasure of the language issue may return like a boomerang in critics' comments and interpretations, demonstrating that staging migration while paying no attention to language issues, breathes confusion at worse and curiosity at best.

In the light of the above comments, Catherine Grosvenor and Lorne Campbell's audacious objective of placing the language at the centre of their theatrical project *Cherry Blossom* should not be surprising. The following quotations taken from the Traverse Theatre website confirm how conscious their creative approach was. While working on the production, Lorne Campbell remarked,

> There is no global truth about migration but a thousand of small truths that contradict each other. However, the language problem was what all the stories shared. What I mean by "language" is not just a set of new words and rules but also a set of cultural codes and different social customs. You are unable to become yourself until you learn this code. You are nobody until you master a new language to such an extent that it conveys your skills and abilities.

In Neil Cooper's review, Campbell is quoted as saying:

> I don't believe that theatre can change the world or human consciousness but all we could do is to offer a different perspective; to allow the audience to step for a moment into emigrants' shoes and feel what it's like to be excluded, to find yourself outside the natural milieu. Perhaps through this experience the audience can understand the migration phenomenon better.

Meanwhile, the drama critic Łukasz Chotkowski is also quoted on the Traverse Theatre website:

> We didn't want to evoke sympathy for migrants but to convey their universal experience; the experience of transgression and border crossing in all possible meanings of these words. We wanted to centre on what migration does to a human being. The two stories of *Cherry Blossom* illustrate different aspects of this problem.[1]

[1] Material published on the theatre's website (http://www.traverse.co.uk) relates only to current productions and information about older productions is removed after a time. However, interested readers can contact the website and request archival information.

The Scottish critics praised the project and revealed much appreciation of its didactic scope. Joyce McMillan of *The Scotsman* pronounced,

> There's a paradox at the heart of 21st-century theatre, and it goes something like this: language is the lifeblood of the art form and is the fact that distinguishes it from dance, music and visual art; yet language divides a world that increasingly needs to think globally. And it's because it tackles this question of language head-on, using all the available firepower of mid-scale 21st-century theatre, that the new Traverse show, Cherry Blossom—co-produced with the Teatr Polski of Bydgoszcz, Poland—is a landmark theatre event in Scotland. (McMillan 2008)

Writing also for *The Scotsman*, Susan Mansfield even used the Polish phrase in the title of her review: *Polish Theatre—Przelamywanie Barier Jezyka* [i.e. "przełamywanie barier języka," meaning: breaking down the language barrier—E.G.]. It was a touching editorial choice as it gave Polish readers the impression that their language was welcomed and just for once was given equal treatment. It was a symbolic gesture of acknowledging its co-existence with English rather than an aggressive demand to give it up. All such gestures are invaluable for displaced people who are desperate to protect their dignity in a new home country. They are also important lessons for those who host them. *The Herald's* reviewer, Neil Cooper, concluded that despite the simple story line "the actors' performances left him feeling humbled."

Yet the praise of the Scottish press was hardly matched by the Polish critics who openly blamed the focus on language for lowering the artistic merit of the play (Derkaczew 2008; Kiss-Orsk, 2008; Łubecka 2008; Pawłowski 2008). This time it was Polish critics who found the linguistic reality of migration as too obvious a theme for the point to be mentioned in an artistically worthwhile performance. They criticized the play's predictable plot, the reduction of characters' needs to economic aims and found the didactic aspect quite superfluous. In short, everything seemed too obvious and not sufficiently imaginative to them. Derkaczew was the only one who noted the positive element of the play concerning the empowered female character who becomes assertive abroad whereas she did not seem to be so while in Poland.

So what conclusions can be drawn from this brief comparison of the reviews? Let me summarize. One truly intercultural text exposed to two different types of audience/readers produced two drastically different responses. This clearly indicates how mighty the power of a specific cultural context is. It also challenges the idea of "intercultural spectatorship" per se. It is amazing how little attention was paid in the Polish reviews to the pioneering notion of "interculturality" in this spectacle. Here we have one script, one cast, a mixture of two languages (not a translation, but a brave attempt of doing away with the hegemonic role of English) and yet there was not a single commentary in the Polish press regarding this innovative aspect of the performance. Moreover, nobody even commented on the authors' and performers' admirable attempt to give up the binary division between "them" and "us," whereas the switching of languages and characters' roles is very effective in this respect. There were no questions raised regarding the intercultural actor who acknowledges his or her autonomy and agency as an artist but at the same time crosses over to the other side (Nascimento 2009). No points were mentioned regarding the gains in performance through cultural (and linguistic) heterogeneity.

In *The Art of Stillness*, Paul Allain explains that "Interculturalism grew out of the ideological, social, and racial aspirations of multiculturalism in the 1970s which filtered into artistic practices." (Allain 2003, 93) Although his comments refer to a different cultural context, *Cherry Blossom,* as a performance, could be said to pioneer a similar kind of undertaking for Eastern Europe. It opened up a very interesting dimension for the emergence of hybrid theatrical forms (within this particular type of media theatre), for changing socio-political contexts and for negotiating new intercultural spaces of exploration. The performance addresses in its own way many vital issues discussed by Claudia Nascimento in her study *Crossing Cultural Borders through the Actor's Work* (2009) and as such has the potential to mark a new stage in the history of post-1989 intercultural theatre in Eastern Europe (paradoxically, this strikes me as true even if it has gone unnoticed in the press). The performance has contributed to the discussion on linguistic diversity as well. Joanna Rostek and Dirk Uffelmann adopt the concept of "subaltern" in relation to language which only reinforces the hierarchy of languages by privileging English over all other tongues. Following Spivak's hugely influential essay, they ask if the subaltern can be heard and investigate many examples of exilic art, including the *Cherry Blossom* performance. However, their fine discussion prompts another question: if the subaltern is heard, doesn't this mean that it ceases to be "subaltern"? (Rostek and Uffelmann 2010, 311-334) To me, the innovative aspect of *Cherry Blossom* lies precisely in its attempt to dismiss this hierarchical way of thinking when narrating the migrants' experience and, in so doing, it effectively subverts the key question. What seems most urgent in this discussion is that we, as scholars of drama and theatre, need to develop a language for naming and discussing such phenomena, since their power to reinforce mutual understanding and respect cannot be overestimated, and it is my belief that it should occupy more space in current scholarship in both languages.

In conclusion, let me add one final comment as an epilogue regarding *Cherry Blossom*'s intercultural dimension. I dare to claim that this ostensibly simplistic play seems to make a promising (if not futuristic) point regarding the language trap. The authors themselves, as well as critics and commentators, compare the stories of Grażyna Antkowiak and Robert Dziekański, stressing that she lived but he died. Although Grażyna and Robert represent the same generation (both are forty-three years old), their reactions to the challenge of migration differ. There are crucial reasons that account for this difference such as their background and family situation: Dziekański's parents awaited him in Canada and he left Poland following their invitation, while Grażyna had no family network in Scotland but left determined to help them all back home. Dziekański, however, as a single male who experienced both communist and post-communist Poland, makes a worthwhile comparison with another single male in the story: Grażyna's son Jasiek, who being twelve years old represents a new upcoming generation. Unlike Robert Dziekański, Jasiek ignores the reality of the country he lives in and disappears into "computer" land. His computer addiction develops to such an extent that he appears to be autistic. Jasiek refuses to speak, but I would argue that his staged muteness is not devoid of a language. On the contrary, all his attention and energy have been invested in learning Netlish and/or Netspeak, to use a term borrowed from Emily Apter (2006, 226-40). His computer "literacy" points towards a global futuristic world in which "all is translatable" and the hierarchy of languages no longer matters. In short, he appears to be a real transcultural agent who places himself beyond cultures, nations and languages. To what extent his choice facilitates and to what extent it obscures communication is a different question. His character, as constructed in the play, clearly resonates with the core issue posed by Deleuze and Guattari: "How to become a nomad and an immigrant and a gypsy in relation to one's own language?" (1986, 19)[2]

Bibliography

Allain, Paul. 2002. *The Art of Stillness*. London and New York: Routledge.

Apter, Emily. 2006. "Everything is Translatable." In her *The Translation Zone: A New Comparative Literature,* 226-240. Princeton, NJ and Oxford: Princeton University Press.

Baniewicz, Elżbieta. 2001. "Janusz Głowacki, *Antygona w Nowym Jorku*. Antygona w Tompkins Park." In *Dramat polski. Interpretacje. Część 2: po roku 1918*, edited by Jan Ciechowicz and Zbigniew Majchrowski, 355-363. Gdańsk: słowo/obraz terytoria.

Bhabha, Homi K. 2004. *The Location of Culture*. 2nd ed. London and New York: Routledge.

Bromley, Roger. 2000. *Narratives for a New Belonging: Diasporic Cultural Fictions*. Edinburgh: Edinburgh University Press.

Butler, Judith. 2000. *Antigone's Claim: Kinship between Life and Death*. New York: Columbia University Press.

[2] I would like to thank Ursula Phillips for her editorial suggestions in preparing the final draft of my chapter. I am also indebted to the participants of the November 2011 conference for their comments and questions which helped me to improve the chapter for publication.

Chmielewski, Paweł. 2002. "Muchy, karaluchy, pchły. Emigranci i emigracja wewnętrzna. *Kopciuch, Polowanie na karaluchy, Antygona w Nowym Jorku* Janusza Głowackiego." In his *Słowacki w supermarkecie. Szkice o polskim dramacie,* 47-70. Gdańsk: Czarny Kot.

Cooper, Neil. 2008. "Cherry Blossom, Traverse Theatre. Edinburgh." *The Herald* [Glasgow], 29 September.

Deleuze, Gilles and Félix Guattari. 1986. *Kafka: Toward a Minor Literature*, translated by Dana Polan. Minneapolis, MN: University of Minnesota Press.

Derkaczew, Joanna. 2008. "Teraz idą emigrantki." *Gazeta Wyborcza* 254 online, 27 October. Accessed 23 March, 2013. http://wyborcza.pl/1,75475,5859179,Teraz_ida_emigrantki.html

Dimock, Wai Chee. 2001. "Literature for the Planet," *PMLA* 116 (1): 173-188.

Filipowicz, Halina. 2001. "Beginning to Theorize 'Polish Émigré Literature'." In *Between Lvov, New York, and Ulysses' Ithaca: Józef Wittlin—Poet, Essayist, Novelist,* edited by Anna Frajlich, 225-242. Toruń: Nicholas Copernicus University; New York: Columbia University Press.

—. 2004. "Shifting Cultural Paradigm: Between the Mystique and the Marketing of Polish Theatre." In *Over the Wall/After the Fall: Post-Communist Cultures through an East-West Gaze*, edited by Sibelan Forrester, Magdalena J. Zaborowska and Elena Gapova, 164-180. Bloomington and Indianapolis, IN: Indiana University Press.

Głowacki, Janusz. 1992. "Antygona w Nowym Jorku." *Dialog* 10: 5-74

—. 1997. *Antigone in New York*, translated by Janusz Głowacki and Joan Torres. New York and London: Samuel French.

—. 2004. "Antigone in New York." In his *Z głowy,* 211-216. Warsaw: Świat Książki.

Grossman, Elwira. 2008. "Nowojorska Antygona w Glasgow." *Przegląd Polski,* 18 July: 5

Grosvenor, Catherine. 2008. *Cherry Blossom*, in collaboration with Lorne Campbell, Mark Grimmer and Leo Warner. London: Nick Hern Books.

Hall, Stuart. 1989. "Third Scenario Theory & The Politics of Location." *The Journal of Cinema and Media* 36: 4-32.

Kiss-Orska, Dominika. 2008. "Kłujący kwiat wiśni." *Gazeta Pomorska* 246, 21 October.

Krajewska-Wieczorek, Anna. 1994. "Two Contemporary Antigones." *New Theatre Quarterly* 40: 327-30.

Łubecka, Michalina. 2008a. "Emigranci bez polotu." *Gazeta Wyborcza (Bydgoszcz)* 247, 21 October.

—. 2008b. "Dobry festiwal, słabszy Aneks." *Gazeta Wyborcza (Bydgoszcz)* 248, 22 October.

McMillan, Joyce. 2008. "Language lessons." *The Scotsman*, 3 October.

Mansfield, Susan. 2008. "Polish Theatre—Przelamywanie Barier Jezyka." *The Scotsman,* 26 September.

Morawska-White, Helena and Kevin J. Harty. 1997. "Janusz Głowacki's *Antigone in New York*: A Dialogue." *Periphery* 3 (1-2): 117-119.

Nascimento, Claudia Tatinge. 2009. *Crossing Cultural Borders Through the Actor's Work: Foreign Bodies of Knowledge*. London and New York: Routledge.

Pawłowski, Roman. 2008. "Kwiat emigracji." *Gazeta Wyborcza* 228 online, 29

September. Accessed 23 March, 2013. http://wyborcza.pl/1,75475,5743464,Kwiat_emigracji.html

Rostek Joanna and Dirk Uffelmann. 2010. "Can the Polish Migrant Speak? The Representation of 'Subaltern' Polish Migrants in Film, Literature and Music from Britain and Poland." In *Facing the East in the West: Images of Eastern Europe in British Literature, Film and Culture*, edited by Barbara Korte, Eva Ulrike Pirker and Sissy Helff, 311-334. Amsterdam and New York: Rodopi.

Seyhan, Azade. 2001. *Writing Outside the Nation.* Princeton, NJ and Oxford: Princeton University Press.

Trojanowska, Tamara. 2003. "Many Happy Returns: Janusz Głowacki and His Exilic Experience." In *Living in Translation: Polish Writers in America*, edited by Halina Stephan, 259-287. Amsterdam and New York: Rodopi.

Ugresić, Dubravka. 2007. "What is European about European Literature?" In her *Nobody's Home: Essays,* 162-176. London: Telegram.

Wanat, Andrzej. 1993. "Antygona 93." *Teatr* 3: 26-27.

A Transformation in Verse: Reconnaissance of Developments in Polish Poetry since 1989

Wioletta GRZEGORZEWSKA and Marek KAZMIERSKI

An end to Polish poetry as we knew it

The collapse of the Polish communist state in 1989 meant the end of the ominously-named Main Bureau for Control of the Press, Publishing and Public Performance (Główny Urząd Kontroli Prasy, Publikacji i Widowisk). However poetry publishing, although suddenly freed from the censors' potential interference, now had to contend with a new and hitherto unknown problem: free market forces. Poetry volumes begun appearing in ever smaller print runs, stripped of support from state-funded distribution and promotional networks, becoming a niche phenomenon in the process. Yet, within literary circles of the early 1990s, there existed the expectation that this dramatic shift would also have a positive effect on poetry writing and a new generation of poets would emerge to follow not only state-sanctioned poetry, but also the poets established by scholarly criticism and western translators, such as Czesław Miłosz (1911-2004), Zbigniew Herbert (1924-1998), Wisława Szymborska (1923-2012) and Tadeusz Różewicz (b. 1921), to shape and comment on a free Poland in a similar way to their predecessors, who in their various ways had undermined the totalitarian system, using their pens to anticipate the new freedoms. Alternative cultural circles popped up all over the country, countless new fanzines and art magazines were produced on previously inaccessible photocopiers, along with alternative newspapers and freely-organized live readings (Dunin-Wąsowicz 2002). Students set up their own literary journals in Kraków, Warsaw, Poznań, Gdańsk and in Silesia, which also inspired the publication of many new volumes of poetry—both collections and volumes by individual poets (Gałuszka, Maroszczuk and Nęcka 2010). At the same time, however, we should not overlook the fact that the established poets mentioned above, as well as a number of other prolific poets of several generations—Julia Hartwig (b. 1921), Ewa Lipska (b. 1945), poets of the 1968 or "New Wave" generation, such as Stanisław Barańczak (b. 1946) and Adam Zagajewski (b. 1945), for example—continue to write and publish post-1989. This current survey will concentrate on specifically new trends, on the generation(s) of poets born in the 1960s or subsequently.

The watershed began as early as 1986, however, with thc publication of the now-famous "blue issue" of the journal *Literatura na Świecie* (7), its cover depicting a ticket to the Museum of Modern Art in New York. This ground-breaking publication contained the work of such poets such as Frank O'Hara, John Ashbery, Kenneth Koch and others associated with the New York School, translated by Piotr Sommer (b. 1948) and Bohdan Zadura (b. 1945), both well known Polish poets in their own right. This particular issue had a huge impact on a new wave of Polish poets, causing a seismic shift in influence from Russian and French poetry to that being published in the long-forbidden English-language West (although we should not forget certain important exceptions, such as Miłosz's influence by Walt Whitman among others).

Brulion—sketching the new

In 1986 in Kraków, a group of friends, led by Robert Tekieli, set up the literary quarterly *Brulion* (or *bruLion*, as it was usually written); it was published 1988-1999. The name translates as "rough sketchbook" and was, according to the founding editor, to be a departure from conventional high-brow journals, something of a "rough draft of our whole culture" (Klejnocki and Sosnowski 1996; Dunin-Wąsowicz 2000a; 2000b). *Brulion*, not unlike publications from the turbulent and culturally diverse independent Poland of the 1920s and 1930s (*Zwrotnica*, *Kwadryga*, *Żagary*), began its operations with aesthetic provocations. Its editors challenged cultural hierarchies, making fun of such high-minded poems as "The Power of Taste" by Zbigniew Herbert from his volume *Report from the Besieged City* (*Raport z oblężonego miasta*, 1983), publishing interviews with a porn star, a skinhead, a masochist, alongside notorious antisemitic texts by Louis-Ferdinand Céline and deliberately controversial poems such as "Cunt Crumbs" ("Flupy z pizdy") by Zbigniew Sajnóg (*Brulion* 1991, 16, 63). The magazine developed a sizeable readership, being Poland's biggest alternative culture platform at the time, achieving a print run of 16,000 copies by 1993. Among its authors were some of today's best-known Polish writers, such as Andrzej Stasiuk (b. 1960), Marcin Baran (b. 1963), Miłosz Biedrzycki (aka MLB, b. 1967), Marcin Sendecki (b. 1967), Krzysztof Koehler (b. 1963), Grzegorz Wróblewski (b. 1962), Izabela Filipiak (b. 1961) and Manuela Gretkowska (b. 1964).

At this time, in the early 1990s, any poet born in the 1960s was lumped together with the "*Brulion* Generation." And yet this collective was made up of poets representing a range of very different poetics: so-called "classicists" and "barbarians," O'Harists and Ashberyists, "banalists" and "Totartists" (Dunin-Wąsowicz and Varga 1995; on the O'Harists, see also Niżyńska 2007). Apart from *Brulion*, this period saw the appearance of many other publications produced by local cultural centres and universities steering the development of contemporary Polish poetry (but not only poetry: they also covered and continue to cover broader cultural and artistic developments). These included *Nowy Nurt*, *Czas Kultury*, *Kresy*, *FaArt*, *RED*, *Pogranicza*, *Tygiel Kultury*, *Portret*, *Fronda* and *Nowa Okolica Poetów*.

Many interviews published subsequently with contributing authors seem to suggest that the "*Brulion* collective" was a temporary and somewhat accidental phenomenon. Young artists born in the mid-decades of communist rule had no plans to create anything communal. They all simply wanted to write for themselves, for the sake of poetry (or prose fiction) itself. Andrzej Stasiuk, poet, novelist, journalist and founder of the Czarne publishing house, once declared: "Poetry and literature are a form of competition between me and the rest of the world. Writing is nothing but a form of loneliness." (Burkot 1996, 147)

Jacek Podsiadło and Marcin Świetlicki

Two poets from the *Brulion* generation, who had a considerable impact on younger followers and therefore deserve special mention, were Jacek Podsiadło (1964) and Marcin Świetlicki (b. 1961). In 1990, Podsiadło published his first volume of poetry entitled *Sad in Amusement Parks, Silly in Bawdy Houses* (*W lunaparkach smutny, w lupanarach śmieszny*). His life story, which includes stints of working on building sites and in a foundry, along with active engagement in anti-war and ecological movements, helped make both the poet and his poetry the stuff of legend. The work of Podsiadło was a kind of shaman's diary, of a traveller describing his adventures with skill and poetic invention. Love, recollections from his childhood and teenage years, and, of course, tales from the Road (always written with a capital letter), were his favourite themes. Podsiadło regularly invoked Edward Stachura (1937-1979), a poet who preceded him by thirty years, as he attempted to describe everyday existence as a fascinating adventure, presenting his protagonists as lost in the civilized world and himself, at the heart of the poetry, set against both state and society. No friend of the formal educational system, Podsiadło refused to allow his poems to be published in school textbooks, because he rejected the idea of becoming a "living monument" as had happened to other well-known Polish bards of his generation.

Two years later, in 1992, Marcin Świetlicki made his début with the volume *Cold Countries* (*Zimne kraje*), heralding new approaches and linguistic experiments in poetry. The speaker in Świetlicki's poetry is a provocateur, the "eternal youth," who reflects upon reality with cynical glee. Świetlicki brought poetry closer to the prose form, celebrating such simple situations as sweeping the streets or buying leeks for supper. His poetry, like that of Rożewicz before him, showed that the language of verse must be stripped bare of all falsity and pretension, cleansed of cheap adornments and metaphors, rid of bad ways of communicating, in order to attract a wider readership—helped also by the music the poet recorded with his rock band, Świetliki.

The end of the beginning

In the second half of the 1990s, the poetry of Marcin Świetlicki and Jacek Podsiadło become increasingly popular. Another poet popular and influential in the late 1990s was Andrzej Sosnowski (b. 1959), who had also made his debut earlier in the decade with two books of poetry: *Life in Korea* (*Życie na Korei,* 1992) and *A Season in Hel* (*Sezon na Helu,* 1994). Poet, translator, and member of the editorial board of *Literatura na Świecie*, lecturer in English Literature, he became a real inspiration for younger poets born in the 1970s. His unique style, imitated however by others and known as "sosnowszczyzna," opened Polish poetry up to unexpected paths in the innovative use of language, metaphors, and thereby influencing a new generation of poets.

Yet this "experiment with freedom," a term coined by Piotr Śliwiński (2002), did not bring about the expected fundamental transformations within Polish poetry. After the gaining of political independence, the Brulion poets announced great changes would start to happen, yet this did not happen in any collective sense. Poets continued to be influenced rather by new verse being translated from the West and especially the United States. Readers expecting a leap in aesthetics, a fresh approach to the art of the written word, waited for a new bard to appear: a Poet for all Poles. However, the "Brulionites" did not produce this new leap forward—they made a powerful entrance as a group, yet each individual then went his or her own separate way. Though Marcin Świetlicki outgrew this generation and developed a distinct poetic language of his own, many critics considered the Brulion generation to be a direct continuation of the previous generation of "New Privacy" poets—figures such as Bronisław Maj (b. 1953), Jan Polkowski (b. 1953), Krystyna Lars (b. 1950), Grzegorz Musiał (b. 1952), Zbigniew Machej (b. 1958), Urszula Benka (b. 1953), and others. Meanwhile the pantheon of grand masters, recipients of the most prestigious prizes, ever present in the media (Różewicz, Miłosz, Szymborska) published their books in huge print runs with major publishers such as Znak, Czytelnik, Muza, A5, and had new work printed in prestigious literary magazines such as *Odra* and *Zeszyty Literackie*. This "old guard" put huge pressure on the new generation of poets who had rejected the language of earlier masters, unable to help pitting their expectations against them, and thereby expressing a generational clash between parents and offspring.[1]

[1] On the generational clash between parents and offspring as represented in post-1989 prose fiction, see the chapter by Jerzy Jarzębski in the current volume.

A new wave of talent

Polish critics began to make reference to the "Seventies generation," i.e. those born in 1970s, a term coined by the magazine *Pro Arte,* and the lyricism of the so-called "emboldened imagination" (Marecki, Stokfiszewski and Witkowski 2002; Nowaczewski 2003). From the early 2000s, poets still gathered in informal collectives. In Silesia, the group of poets named "In the Wild" ("Na dziko") was formed, its poetry known as the "Silesian school of the poetry of life" (Pawelec 2004). As the name itself implies, the main features of its poetics were a free-flowing verse construction, use of common-place language and a preference for concrete imagery. In the view of the poets associated with this group, a poem should develop in a spoken-word style, taking on the feel at times of reportage, punctuated with local vernacular and even vulgar language. Meanwhile, in Warsaw, the Neolinguistic Movement (Ruch Neolingwistyczny) publicized its manifesto and published the anthology entitled *Chatter! Box It? [P]anthology of Neolingualism* (*Gada!zabić. [P]antologia neolingwizmu*), edited by Maria Cyranowicz and Piotr Kozioł (2005), taking sound and image as the key elements of their verse, as opposed to purely linguistic features.

Students in Kraków set up the avant-garde, multi-disciplinary publication Ha!art, which has since become a well-known publisher of innovative and alternative artistic and poetry initiatives. The journal published articles on new media art, street art, socially conscious literature, hypertexts, political literature, gay and lesbian literature, avant-pop, book art, cyberpunk, internet publishing, minimalism, as well as work by the Warsaw school of Neolingualism, both poetry and prose by authors born in the 1970s. In 2002, Ha!art, under the direction of Piotr Marecki, published *Tekstylia,* a dictionary of modern Polish culture, although the project did not meet with success, as it focused too exclusively on fragments of the most recent poetry being published.

Studium was another influential publication, making its first appearance in 2000, labelling itself "A journal of new literature," edited by Roman Honet, Mariusz Czyżewski, Grzegorz Nurek and Ewa Sonnenberg, and notable for its original approach to literary criticism which focused on interviews with young writers. Within a short space of time, *Studium* became perhaps the most important literary publication in Poland, printing the series of poetry volumes called *New Polish Poetry,* including some by future stars, all born in the 1970s or later, such as Justyna Bargielska, Joanna Wajs, Roman Honet and Jacek Dehnel, as well as the key collective volume *Anthology of New Polish Poetry 1990-1999* (*Antologia nowej poezji polskiej 1990-1999*), edited by Czyżewski and Honet (2000). This latter collection was a sizeable and professionally produced selection of poems by authors born in the 1960s and 1970s, though it failed to include a number of female poets writing on the peripheries of the main scene (out of 106 poets in the book, only twelve are women, a regrettably common feature of Polish poetry criticism and publishing, although, curiously enough, not in shortlists for prizes and awards). For the generation of poets born in the 1970s, the collapse of *Studium* in 2008 was as a symbol of the beginning of the end of paper publications in Poland, especially as other literary magazines were similarly publishing only at irregular intervals because of the cut in government funding.

Females and festivals

The first decade of the 21st century saw the publication of important volumes of poetry written by women, beginning at the turn of the century with Marta Podgórnik's (b. 1979) *Paradiso* (2000), Agnieszka Wolny-Hamkało's (b. 1979) *Powerfully Sought* (*Mocno poszukiwana,* 1999) and *November on the Narva* (*Listopad nad Narwią,* 2000) by Julia Fiedorczuk (b. 1975). The Kraków publishing house Zielona Sowa attracted the most promising female poets, publishing their debut collections in the series entitled *Biblioteka Dwumiesięcznika Literackiego-Artystycznego Studium.* Agnieszka Kuciak (b. 1970) made her debut in 2001 with the volume *Retardation* (*Retardacja*), followed in 2003 by the experimental *Phantom Somnambulapains* (*Somnambóle fantomowe*) by Joanna Mueller (b. 1979), and the sophisticated volume *Dating sessions* by Justyna Bargielska (b. 1977). The year 2002 also saw the publication of Izabela Filipiak's *Madame Intuita,* the first collection of openly lesbian poetry to be published in Poland, challenging the dominance of the male voice with its obvious reference to Herbert's *Mr Cogito.*

In 2004 Joanna Wajs (b. 1979) published her volume *Pocket Mirror Sellers* (*Sprzedawcy kieszonkowych lusterek*), described as "one of the most remarkable debuts of recent decades" (Mikołajewski 2004), as did Justyna Radczyńska (b. 1965) her collection entitled *Jola Grosz's Deception* (*Podmiana Joli Grosz*). The second part of this decade was dominated by female poets, as they developed their craft by publishing verse and exchanging opinions on web portals and forums. Anna A. Tomaszewska (b. 1968) made her debut in 2005 with *Poems for Reading* (*Wiersze do czytania*). In 2007 Elżbieta Lipińska published *Farewell to the Colour Red* (*Pożegnanie z czerwienią*). The following year belonged to Julia Szychowiak (b. 1986), who received the prestigious Wroclaw Silesius Poetry Award for her volume *After Myself* (*Po sobie,* 2008).

In 2009, the collection *Solo Women: Anthology of Women's Poetry 1989-2009* (*Solistki. Antologia poezji kobiet, 1989-2009*) was published in Warsaw and advertised as the "missing link in Polish poetry [. . .] containing forty-one women engaged with language." Even before going to print, the book caused heated debate on literary internet forums and drew the attention of critics. However, the publication was not altogether a success. A number of well-known poets, who might have shown just how varied and highly developed poetry written by women had become since 1989, were not included (such as Jolanta Stefko, Genowefa Jakubowska-Fijałkowska, Joanna Wajs, Anna Janko, Joanna Lech, Anna Tomaszewska)—the editors preferring to choose instead a confrontational stance (in language, themes and form) towards the patriarchal world.[2] The anthology contained several young poets from the Warsaw scene, such as Natalia Malek or Anna Weiser (who had not published any separate volumes of their own), while excluding the above key names, some of whom had in fact influenced the youngest generation of women poets.

Of notable cultural impact in the second half of the 1990s were festivals and competitions organized outside official cultural centres, such as the Golden Centre for Poetry (Złoty Środek Poezji) in Kutno, Tychy Winter of Poetry (Tyska Zima Poetycka), and the All-Poland Bierezin Competition (Ogólnopolski Konkurs im. Jacka Bierezina) in Lódź, which published many post-competition volumes including such future stars as Krzysztof Siwczyk, Marta Podgórnik, Jacek Dehnel, Justyna Bargielska, Edward Pasewicz, Bartosz Konstrat, Przemysław Witkowski, Joanna Lech, Klara Nowakowska, Magdalena Gałkowska and Justyna Krawiec. In 1996, the first European Congress of Young Writers held in Legnica gave rise to the influential publishing outfit Biuro Literackie and the literary festival and magazine Port Wroclaw, which published debut volumes alongside well-established names, among them Krystyna Miłobędzka, Piotr Sommer, Bohdan Zadura, Jerzy Jarniewicz, Eugeniusz Tkaczyszyn-Dycki, Dariusz Suska, Dariusz Sośnicki, Julia Fiedorczuk and Justyna Bargielska. They also published anthologies, theory and criticism (Bartczak 2009; Gutorow 2011; Stala 2011), along with new or previously published translations from American, English, Irish, Scottish, Russian, Hungarian, Ukrainian, French and Czech poetry.

The coming of the Net

2002 saw the launch of the internet poetry portal *nieszuflada* (Maliszewski 2007). In Polish, you can say you write "for your own desk drawer" ("do szuflady") meaning only for yourself, amateurishly—"nieszuflada" thus means "not-the-desk-drawer" and alludes, among other things, to Herbert's poem "Drawer" written under conditions of communist censorship, when the dissident poet had no alternative but to write for his own desk drawer. The new portal became immensely

[2] It is debatable also whether the volume was successful even as a feminist project; see, for example, the review in *Tygodnik Powszechny* "Stracone złudzenia" (Kałuża 2009). For a detailed survey of poetry written by women since 1989 and its reception, see Pawluś 2009.

influential, publishing almost all important young names. The portal marked the beginning of the "online poetry movement" and the rise of many other similar portals: *Poezja Polska, ArtPapier, Współczesna Poezja Polska, Niedoczytania, Cyc Gada, Cegła, Pro Arte, Fundacja Karpowicz, Liternet,* and others. Not only did they provide a new platform for sharing work, they also allowed spontaneous, heated debates about the role and relevance of poetry in the modern world.

Poetry published in printed form, however, did still appear to be noticed in Poland in the new millennium—many of the most important literary prizes were awarded to poets from small, independent presses, functioning outside the mainstream, such as *Instytut Mikołowski, Portret, Zeszyty Poetyckie, Biblioteka Arterii, Staromiejski Dom Kultury and Mamiko.* In 2009 Eugeniusz Tkaczyszyn-Dycki (b. 1962) won the Nike Prize for his volume *Songs of Assignments and Addictions* (*Piosenki o zależnościach i uzależnieniach,* 2008); this was a major event, an upset even, as his body of work is a very provocative and unconventional project: personal, immersed in eschatological themes and traces of discreet homoeroticism. Dycki's favourite themes include death, schizophrenia, illness, decomposition, his friends—the favourite themes of Baroque lyricists (Śliwiński 2007, 246). He is a poet who can, in a single sentence, "combine the language of a hoodie and a Mickiewicz" (Sobolewski 2009).

Conclusions

According to Katarzyna Janowska, "[. . .] in the year 2000, around 800 volumes of poetry were published in Poland." (Janowska 2005, 35-40) By 2010, this figure had exceeded a thousand, which does not include certain independent, self-published titles without ISBN numbers, of which there are many. Some commentators joke that these figures should be recorded in the Guinness Book of Records. Yet while everyone scrambles to have their own book published—something that is becoming ever easier with the advent of cheap digital printing techniques—the journals and periodicals, which in the 1990s provided critical analysis, thereby helping to shape and nurture talent, are disappearing from bookshelves.[3]

[3] 170 literary journals were founded after the year 1989. From the mid-90s, due to lack of funding, the number of published magazines fell considerably. Grants for the development of cultural magazines are awarded each year by the Ministry of Culture and National Heritage. The Book Institute (Instytut Książki) makes decisions about which organizations should receive a grant, and how much. In 2000 minister Andrzej Zakrzewski announced a list of 39 magazines, which were to receive a three-year grant. After two years, however, it transpired that there wasn't enough money, so cuts were made and some magazines deleted from the list (Marecki 2005). In 2011, minister Bogdan Zdrojewski guaranteed the existence of only 34 magazines from a list of 152. Many important literary journals that reviewed books and discussed new authors did not receive the grant, including *Fa-art, Tekstualia, artPapier, Nowa Okolica Poetów, Tygiel Kultury.*

Faced with such a reality, it is hardly surprising that contemporary poetry appearing in Poland is changing in tone as it moves ever closer to internet dependency. Poems are published immediately on various open forums and dedicated portals, yet are mostly read within certain closed circles. This has given rise to the new concept of the "internet poem," constructed as a composition of words with multimedia elements, in which metaphors are replaced with links to musical uploads, while the text itself is embellished with images. The 21st century may turn out to be the age when e-books, web poetry, twitter-literature, self-publishing and the growth of numerous online poetry portals take over from traditional publishing, at least in the field of poetry.

Benjamin Paloff, meanwhile, offers the following assessment:

> Polish poets publish too much. Such a generalization flirts with heresy in a country with so many lionized bards, and where for much of the twentieth century state censors steered extraordinary poets into long careers of writing "for the drawer." There are certainly exceptions to this overexposure, including Adam Zagajewski, Wisława Szymborska and the late Czesław Miłosz. But some of their colleagues haven't been so prudent. In Poland it is not uncommon for a poet to "debut" (their term, thankfully, not ours) by the age of 25 and to crank out a book every eighteen months thereafter. One consequence of this prolificacy is the staggering volume of garbage that floods bookstores, including many D-list poems by A-list poets. Another is that if a poet aspires to be noticed—and poets, like children, want desperately to be noticed—he or she often becomes a rejectionist within a generation, publicly denouncing predecessors, rivals and younger upstarts. (Paloff 2010)

Whether one agrees totally or in part with this statement, there is no denying that the last twenty years have produced a vibrant and varied poetry scene in a country which, for the most part of over two hundred years, suffered the kind of political and psycho-cultural turmoil that shapes and hardens strong poetic voices. In the last decade, a new generation of names has appeared on the poetry scene, blogging, "slamming" and publishing independently of literary cliques and establishments, each one creating poetry within its own separate niche, engaged, in the words of critic and poet Karol Maliszewski (b. 1960)—himself nominated for the 2007 Nike Prize for his volume of critical essays, *Dispersed Voices,* 2006)—in "a tryst between language and the world" (Maliszewski 2009, 8). Maybe it will be these solitary voices who will replace the masters of the 20th century in longer-term assessments of poetry written in Poland.

Bibliography

Individual volumes in Polish[4]

Bargielska, Justyna. 2003. *Dating sessions*. Kraków: Zielona Sowa.

—. 2009. *Dwa fiaty*. Poznań: Wojewódzka Biblioteka Publiczna i Centrum Animacji Kultury.

Biedrzycki, Miłosz. 2007. *Sofostrofa i inne wiersze*. Kraków: Wydawnictow a5.

—. 2009. *69 Poems*, translated Frank L. Vigoda. Brookline, MA: Zephyr Press.

Bonowicz, Wojciech. 2006. *Pełne morze*. Wrocław: Biuro Literackie.

—. 2010. *Polskie znaki*. Wrocław: Biuro Literackie.

Dąbrowski, Tadeusz. 2011. *Black Square*, translated by Antonia Lloyd-Jones. Brookline, MA: Zephyr Press.

Dehnel, Jacek. 2004. *Żywoty równoległe*. Kraków: Zielona Sowa.

—. 2007. *Brzytwa okamgnienia*. Wrocław: Biuro Literackie.

—. 2009. *Ekran kontrolny*. Wrocław: Biuro Literackie.

Fiedorczuk, Julia. 2000. *Listopad nad Narwią*. Legnica: Biuro Literackie Port Legnica.

—. 2004. *Bio*. Wrocław: Biuro Literackie.

—. 2006. *Planeta rzeczy zagubionych*. Wrocław: Biuro Literackie.

—. 2009. *Tlen*. Wrocław: Biuro Literackie.

Grzebalski, Mariusz. 1994. *Negatyw*. Ostrołęka: Pracownia.

—. 1997. *Ulica gnostycka*. Poznań: Obserwator.

—. 2001. *Drugie dotknięcie*. Legnica: Biuro Literackie Port Legnica.

—. 2004. *Słynne i świetne*. Wrocław: Biuro Literackie.

—. 2009. *Niepiosenki*. Wrocław: Biuro Literackie.

Gutorow, Jacek. 2001. *X*. Legnica: Biuro Literackie Port Legnica.

—. 2008. *Inne tempo*. Wrocław: Biuro Literackie.

Honet, Roman. 1998. *Pójdziesz synu do piekła*. Kraków: Zielona Sowa.

—. 2002. *Serce*. Kraków: Zielona Sowa.

—. 2008. *Baw się i kilka innycy wierszy o rzeczach ważnych*. Wrocław: Biuro Literackie.

Jakubowska-Fijałkowska, Genowefa. 2006. *Czuły nóż*. Mikołów: Instytut Mikołowski.

—. 2009. *Ostateczny smak truskawek*. Mikołów: Instytut Mikołowski.

—. 2012. *Ze mnie robak i z robaka wiersze / Of me a worm and the worm poems*, translated by Marek Kazmierski. London: OFF_PRESS.

Jarniewicz, Jerzy. 2003. *Dowód z tożsamości*. Legnica: Biuro Literackie Port Legnica.

—. 2005. *Oranżada*. Wrocław: Biuro Literackie.

—. 2009. *Makijaż* Wrocław: Biuro Literackie.

Kuciak, Agnieszka. 2001. *Retardacja*. Kraków: Zielona Sowa.

—. 2005. *Dalekie Kraje*. Kraków: Znak.

Lipińska, Elżbieta. 2007. *Pożegnanie z czerwienią*. Nowa Ruda: Mamiko.

[4] Items included in this introductory list have been selected by the authors of the current chapter as being representative—and not all are mentioned in the text of the chapter. The bibliography covers—like the chapter—poetry produced in Poland rather than in emigration, and reflects the authors' (one a poet, the other a translator and publisher) choices as to which works have been influential, and is not intended to be comprehensive.

—. 2008. *Maj to łagodny miesiąc*. Gdańsk: Wydawnictwo Oskar.
—. 2011. *Rejestry*. Tychy: Mały Teatr.
Macierzyński, Piotr. 2001. *Danse macabre i inne sposoby spędzania wolnego czasu*. Kraków: Zielona Sowa.
—. 2004. *Tfu, tfu*. Kraków: Fundacja Krakowska Alternatywa.
—. 2009. *Zbiór zadań z chemii i metafizyki*. Kraków: Korporacja Ha!art.
Majzel, Bartłomiej. 2001. *Bieg zjazdowy*. Kraków: Zielona Sowa.
—. 2006. *Biała Afryka*. Wrocław: Biuro Literackie.
Maliszewski, Karol. 1996. *Rocznik sześćdziesiąty grzebie w papierach. Wiersze z przełomu i nowe*. Warsaw: Przedświt.
—. 2012. *Ody odbite*. Wrocław: Fundacja na Rzecz Kultury i Edukacji im. Tymoteusza Karpińskiego.
Melecki, Maciej. 2008. *Zawsze wszędzie indziej. Wybór wierszy*. Olsztyn: Stowarzyszenie Artystyczno-Kulturalne "Portret."
Miłobędzka, Krystyna. 2004. *Po krzyku*. Wrocław: Biuro Literackie.
—. 2008. *Zbierane, gubione 1960-2010*. Wrocław: Biuro Literackie.
Mueller, Joanna. 2003. *Somnambóle fantomowe*. Kraków: Zielona Sowa.
—. 2007. *Zagniazdowniki/Gniazdowniki*. Kraków: Zielona Sowa.
Pasewicz, Edward. 2002. *Dolna Wilda,* Łódź: Fundacja Anima "Tygiel Kultury."
—. 2004. *Wiersze dla Róży Filipowicz*. Wrocław: Biuro Literackie.
—. 2007. *Śmierć w darkroomie*. Kraków: Wydawnictwo EMG.
Podgórnik, Marta. 1996. *Próby negocjacji*. Łódź: Stowarzyszenie Pisarzy Polskich.
—. 2000. *Paradiso*. Legnica: Biuro Literackie Port Legnica.
—. 2008. *Pięć Opakowań. Wybór wierszy 1993-2008*. Wrocław: Biuro Literackie.
Podsiadło, Jacek. 1990. *W lunaparkach smutny, w lupanarach śmieszny*. Warsaw: Staromiejski Dom Kultury.
—. 1999. *Wychwyt Grahama*. Warsaw: Lampa i Iskra Boża.
—. 2003. *Wiersze zebrane*. 2nd ed. Warsaw: Lampa i Iskra Boża.
—. 2000. *I ja pobiegłem w tę mgłę*. Kraków: Znak.
Radczyńska, Justyna. 2005. *Podmiana Joli Grosz*. Kraków: Zielona Sowa.
Różycki, Tomasz. 1999. *Anima*. Kraków: Zielona Sowa.
—. 2003. *Świat i Antyświat*. Warsaw: Lampa i Iskra Boża.
—. 2004. *Dwanaście stacji*. Kraków: Znak.
—. 2006. *Kolonie*. Kraków: Znak.
—. 2010. *Księga obrotów*. Kraków: Znak.
Siwczyk, Krzysztof. 1995. *Dzikie dzieci*. Bydgoszcz: Instytut Wydawniczy "Świadectwo."
—. 1999. *Emil i my*. Wołowiec: Wydawnictwo Czarne.
Sosnowski, Andrzej. 1992. *Życie na Korei*. Warsaw: Przedświt.
—. 1994. *Sezon na Helu*. Lublin: Stowarzyszenie Literackie "Kresy."
—. 2007. *Po tęczy*. Wrocław: Biuro Literackie.
—. 2006. *Dożynki*. Wrocław: Biuro Literackie.
Sommer, Piotr. 2009. *Dni i noce*. Wrocław: Biuro Literackie.
—. 1999. *Piosenka pasterska*. Legnica: Centrum Sztuki – Teatr Dramatyczny.
Szychowiak, Julia. 2008. *Po sobie*. Wrocław: Biuro Literackie.

Szychowiak, Mirka. 2005. *Człap story*. Strzelin: Strzeliński Ośrodek Kultury.
—. 2010. *Jeszcze się pokręcę*. Mikołów: Instytut Mikołowski.
—. 2010. *Proszę nie płakać*. Szczecinek: Samorządna Agencja Promocji i Kultury.
Świetlicki, Marcin. 2002. *Zimne kraje. Wiersze 1980-1990*. 2nd ed. Warsaw: Lampa i Iskra Boża.
—. 1999. *Schizma*. Wołowiec: Wydawnictwo Czarne.
—. 1998. *Pieśni profana*. Wołowiec: Wydawnictwo Czarne.
—. 2011. *Wiersze*. Kraków: Wydawnictwo EMG.
Tkaczyszyn-Dycki, Eugeniusz. 1990. *Nenia i inne wiersze*. Lublin: Związek Literatów Polskich.
—. 2009. *Piosenki o zależnościach i uzależnieniach*. Wrocław: Biuro Literackie.
Tomaszewska, Anna A. 2005. *Wiersze do czytania*. Kraków: Wydawnictwo Literackie.
—. 2006. *Lokomotywy, wagony, sukienki*. Tychy: Mały Teatr.
Wajs, Joanna. 2004. *Sprzedawcy kieszonkowych lusterek*. Kraków: Zielona Sowa.
Wiedemann, Adam. 2004. *Kalipso*. Warsaw: Prószyński i S-ka.
—. 2007. *Pensum*. Poznań: Wojewódzka Biblioteka Publiczna i Centrum Animacji Kultury.
—. 2010. *Dywan*. Poznań: Wojewódzka Biblioteka Publiczna i Centrum Animacji Kultury.
Wolny-Hamkało, Agnieszka. 1999. *Mocno poszukiwana*. Wrocław: Oficyna Wydawnicza Atut.
—. 2007. *Spamy miłosne*. Kraków: Wydawnictwo a5.
—. 2010. *Nikon i leica*. Poznań: Wojewódzka Biblioteka Publiczna i Centrum Animacji Kultury.
Woźniak Maciej. 2008. *Iluzjon*. Kraków: Wydawnictwo Literackie.
—. 2010. *Ucieczka z Elei*. Poznań: Wojewódzka Biblioteka Publiczna i Centrum Animacji Kultury.
Zadura, Bogdan. 2002. *Ptasia grypa i inne wierszy dla kobiet i mężczyzn*. Legnica: Biuro Literackie Port Legnica.
—. 2004. *Kopiec kreta*. Wrocław: Biuro Literackie.
—. 2008. *Wszystko*. Wrocław: Biuro Literackie.

Collections in Polish

Borowczyk, Jerzy and Michał Larek, eds. 2011. *Powiedzieć inaczej. Polska liryka nowoczesna. Antologia*. Poznań: Wojewódzka Biblioteka Publiczna i Centrum Animacji Kultury.
Czyżewski, Mariusz and Roman Honet, eds. 2004. *Antologia nowej poezji polskiej 1990–2000*. 3rd ed. Kraków: Zielona Sowa.
Cyranowicz, Maria and Paweł Kozioł, eds. 2005. *Gada!zabić? [P]antologia neolingwizmu*. Warsaw: Staromiejski Dom Kultury.
Cyranowicz, Maria, JoannaMueller and Justyna Radczyńska, eds. 2009. *Solistki. Antologia poezji kobiet (1989-2009)*. Warsaw: Staromiejski Dom Kultury.
Dąbrowski, Tadeusz, ed. 2006. *Poza słowa: antologia wierszy 1976-2006*. Gdańsk: słowo/obraz terytoria.

Dunin-Wąsowicz, Paweł, Jarosław Klejnocki and Krzysztof Varga, eds. 1997. *Macie swoich poetów. Liryka polska urodzona po 1960 roku.* Warsaw: Lampa i Iskra Boża.
Honet, Roman, ed. 2010. *Poeci na nowy wiek.* Wrocław: Biuro Literackie.
Pawelec, Dariusz, ed. 2004. *Martwe punkty. Antologia poezji "Na dziko" (1994–2003).* Katowice: Instytucja Kultury "Ars Cameralis Silesiae Superiosis."
Świetlicki, Marcin and Paweł Filas, eds. 1991. *Przyszli barbarzyńcy.* Kraków: Oficyna Literacka.

Translations into English mentioned in this chapter[5]

Skucińska, Anna and Elżbieta Wójcik-Leese, eds. 2004. *Carnivorous Boy Carnivorous Bird: Poetry from Poland,* selected by Marcin Baran. Brookline, MA: Zephyr Press.
Dehnel, Jacek, ed. 2009. *Six Polish Poets.* Todmorden: Arc Publications.
Jung, Dawid and Marcin Orliński, eds. 2011. *Free Over Blood,* translated by Marek Kazmierski et al. London: OFF_PRESS.

Secondary sources

Bartczak, Kacper. 2005. "The Hazards and Hopes of New Polish Poetry." In *New Polish Poetry in Translation,* edited by Mira Rosenthal. [Special issue of] *Lyric* 8: 82-95.
—. 2009. *Świat nie scalony.* Wrocław: Biuro Literackie.
Burkot, Stanisław. 1996. *Literatura polska w latach 1986-1995.* Kraków: Wydawnictwo edukacyjne.
Dunin-Wąsowicz, Paweł and Krzysztof Varga. 1995. *Parnas bis. Słownik literatury polskiej urodzonej po 1960 roku.* Warsaw: Lampa i Iskra Boża.
Dunin-Wąsowicz, Paweł. 2000a. "Brulion," translated by Elżbieta Kotkowska-Atkinson. *Chicago Review* 46(3-4): 368-370.
—. 2000b. *Oko smoka. Literatura tzw. Pokolenia "bruLionu" wobec rzeczywistości III RP.* Warsaw: Lampa i Iskra Boża.
—. 2002. *Xerofeeria 2.0. Antologia artzinów. Polskie alternatywne pisma literackie 1980-2000.* Warsaw: Lampa i Iskra Boża.
Gałuszka, Jacek, Grażyna Maroszczuk and Agnieszka Nęcka, eds. 2010. *Pisma kulturalne w Polsce po roku 1988. Leksykon.* Katowice: Wydawnictwo "Śląsk."
Gutorow, Jacek. 2003. *Niepodległość głosu. Szkice o poezji polskiej po 1968 roku.* Kraków: Znak.
—. 2011. *Księga zakładek.* Wrocław: Biuro Literackie.
Janowska, Katarzyna. 2005. "Federacja niepodległych nisz." *Polityka,* 25 June: 35-40.
Kałuża, Anna. 2009. "Stracone złudzenia." *Tygodnik Powszechny,* 8 December. Accessed 8 February, 2013. http://tygodnik.onet.pl/1,37701,druk.html
Klejnocki, Jarosław and Sosnowski, Jerzy. 1996. *Chwilowe zawieszenie broni. O twórczości tzw. pokolenia "bruLionu" (1986-1996).* Warsaw: Sic!
Mackiewicz, Paweł. 2010. *Pisanie osobno. O poezji polskiej lat pierwszych.* Poznań: Wojewódzka Biblioteka Publiczna i Centrum Animacji Kultury.

[5] For a more complete list of English-languages anthologies of Polish poetry, see Elżbieta Wójcik-Leese's chapter in the current volume.

Maliszewski, Karol. 1999. *Nasi klasycyści, nasi barbarzyńcy. Szkice o nowej poezji*. Bydgoszcz: Instytut Wydawniczy "Świadectwo."

—. 2001. *Zwierzę na J. Szkice o wierszach i ludziach*. Wrocław: Wydawnictwo Dolnośląskie.

—. 2006. *Rozproszone głosy. Notatki krytyk.* Warsaw: Proszyński i S-ka.

—. 2007. *www.ylęgarnia.talentów* [= title of article—Ed.]. *Tygodnik Powszechny* 50. Accessed 15 March, 2013. http://tygodnik2003-2007.onet.pl/1548,1458406,0,557350, dzial.html

—. 2009. "Przesunięcie, przesilenie, powrót." *Gazeta Nagrody Literackiej Gdynia. Dodatek Literacki* 4 (5): 1 and 8. Accessed 15 March, 2013. http:// nagrodaliterackagdynia.pl/wp-content/uploads/2011/05/dodatek_literacki_nr_5.pdf

Marecki, Piotr, Igor Stokfiszewski and Michał Witkowski, eds. 2002. *Tekstylia. O rocznikach siedemdziesiątych*. Kraków: Rabid.

Marecki, Piotr. 2005. *Pospolite ruszenie. Czasopisma kulturno-literackie w Polsce po 1989 roku*. Kraków: Korporacja Ha!art.

Mikołajewski, Jarosław. 2004. "Posłowie do tomu *Sprzedawcy kieszonkowych lusterek*." Accessed 15 March, 2013. http://biuroliterackie.pl/przystan/czytaj.php?site=260co= txt_3088

Niżyńska, Joanna. 2007. "The Impossibility of Shrugging One's Shoulders: O'Harists, O'Hara and Post-1989 Polish Poetry." *Slavic Review* 66: 463-484.

Nowaczewski, Artur. 2003. "Roczniki siedemdziesiąte odbębniają wartę." *Topos* 1-3: 58-70.

Paloff, Benjamin. 2010. "More Than Has Met the Eye." *The Nation* [online], 18 October. Accessed 9 February, 2013. http://www.thenation.com/art\-icle/155086/more-has-met-eye

Pawelec, Dariusz. 2004. *Lingwiści i inni. Przewodnik po interpretacjach wierszy współczesnych*. Katowice: Uniwersytet Śląski.

Pawluś, Kamila. 2009. "Lista (nie)obecności i sztuka uważnego czytania. Poezja tworzona przez kobiety po roku 1989." Accessed 8 February, 2013. http://www. feminoteka.pl/readart\-icle.php?art\-icle_id=682

Śliwiński, Piotr. 2002. *Przygody z wolnością. Uwagi o poezji współczesnej*. Kraków: Znak.

—. 2007. *Świat na brudno. Szkice o poezji i krytyce*. Warsaw: Prószyński i Sk-a.

Sobolewski, Tadeusz. 2009. "Nike 2009 dla Eugeniusza Tkaczyszyna-Dyckiego." Accessed 15 March, 2013. http://wyborcza.pl/2029020,99517,7109103.html

Stala, Marian. 1997. *Druga strona. Notatki o poezji współczesnej*. Kraków: Znak.

—. 2011. *Niepojęte jest*. Wrocław: Biuro Literackie.

Wieczorek, Marcin. 2005. *bruLion. Instrukcja obsługi*. Kraków: Korporacja Ha!art.

Rewritten Presences: Anthologies of Polish Poetry in English 1989-2011

Elżbieta WÓJCIK-LEESE

The "sudden fascination with the East European soul" prompted by the dissident movements in that part of the world serves as the inspiration for *Between Fire and Sleep,* a 2009 collection of essays on Polish poetry (and prose) composed between 1918 and 1989. Its author, Jarosław Anders (b. 1950), a Polish émigré who landed in New York in 1981, the year of the Solidarity uprising, has since felt compelled to explain to American readers the workings of Polish writing, and of the Polish spirit. His self-presentation in the preface (Anders 2009, vii-xvii) deserves thought, as the collection was published almost thirty years after the critical moment in Anders's and Poland's biographies. Moreover, it was released exactly twenty years after another historic landmark: 1989. The historical anchoring of the nine Polish literary figures selected by Anders for Americans should not be underestimated—it signals a recognizable pattern in anthologizing Polish literature in translation.

We cannot underestimate the significance of such a historical framing if, inspired by André Lefevere's influential *Translation, Rewriting and the Manipulation of Literary Fame*, which examines anthologizing African poetry (1992, 124-137), we acknowledge that the major strategy for promoting English translations of literatures composed in lesser-known languages is to coordinate their publication with a historical moment: "when Africa is in the news outside Africa" (1992, 126). In 2000 I borrowed Lefevere's ideas to discuss eight Polish poetry anthologies assembled between 1944 and 1993 (Wójcik-Leese 2000). In the present chapter I revisit these publications and discuss more recent anthologies. In other words, I investigate attempts at "anthologizing Poland" in order to consider the question whether the two decades that separate us from the landmark of 1989—the focus of this book—and from the 1993 anthology have allowed any distancing, and thus encouraged modifications of the strategy identified by the French translation scholar.

In this context, Jarosław Anders's 2009 collection seems to me an intriguing starting point, because it does not query the accepted mode of presenting Polish literature in the so-called West, even twenty years on. Contrary to my expectations, it seeks to further mythologize Polish literary presences, also for personal reasons. Although the book does not anthologize Polish poetry in English, but analyses instead four poets and five prose writers, it confirms the pattern identified by Lefevere in *Translation, Rewriting and the Manipulation of Literary Fame*. I would like to claim that, as a literary commentator, Anders joins other "rewriters":

> Whether they produce translations, literary histories or their more compact spin-offs, reference works, anthologies, criticism or editions, rewriters adapt, manipulate the originals they work with to some extent, usually to make them fit in with the dominant, or one of the dominant ideological and poetological currents of their time. (Lefevere 1992, 8)

Interestingly for our discussion of post-1989 Polish literature as it is perceived outside Poland, Anders's "rewriting" focuses on the last three decades while probing an even earlier past, the interwar period, in a gesture he himself considers to be ambivalent: both a nostalgic return and "a long Polish good-bye to a certain way of reading, of living with literature, that was predominant in the Eastern Europe of my youth and that is no more largely owing to the bloodless revolution of 1989, which changed not only the political but also cultural and moral landscape of my native realm." (Anders 2009, vii)

Apart from Anders's evocation of this Polish historical landmark twenty years on, another element of his preface draws my attention: the fact that it opens with references to both Czesław Miłosz and to Raymond Chandler. As an anthologist and translator of contemporary Polish poetry into English, I cannot help but notice that Anders chooses to elaborate on Miłosz, Zbigniew Herbert, Wisława Szymborska and Adam Zagajewski, poets already familiar to American readers, whereas he mentions—once—Eugeniusz Tkaczyszyn-Dycki (b. 1962) as the single and sole representative of younger poets, although he admits his admiration for "their cocky disdain for their elders' *Angst* and *Drang*," which he interprets as "a new form of freedom and a new brand of courage" (2009, xvii). Tkaczyszyn-Dycki has already been translated into English, as have others, including Marcin Świetlicki (b. 1961), Marcin Baran (b. 1963) and Marcin Sendecki (b. 1967), who together published in 1997 a poetry anthology entitled *The Long Goodbye: Tribute to Chandler* (*Długie pożegnanie. Tribute to Chandler*) followed in 2010 by *Farewell, My Lovely: Poems Noir* (*Żegnaj laleczko. Wiersze noir*), another tribute to the detective fiction master. As a rewriter myself, I would like to account for these two decades by tracing the time loop drawn by Anders in his preface, marking his signposts and adding my own.

In discussing anthologies of Polish poetry translated into English, published between 1989 and 2011, I focus on the paratext—prefaces, introductions, afterwords, cover blurbs—where the "rewriters," who frequently triple as anthologists, translators and literary commentators, reveal their poetics. I consider two questions: how the "rewriters" explain their acts of anthologizing and translating (seen by Lefevere as forms of rewriting); and how the various anthologies profit from the canonization achieved by their earlier counterparts.

When we examine English-language anthologies of Polish poetry published after 1989, we can easily observe how Lefevere's criterion of "an historical moment" comes to the fore. *Polish Poetry of the Last Two Decades of Communist Rule: Spoiling Cannibals' Fun,* edited by Stanisław Barańczak and Clare Cavanagh (1991), explicitly claims the significance of the chosen time span. The blurb promises "work from virtually every major Polish poet active during these critical decades, drawing from both 'official' and underground/émigré sources. The reader will gain a new appreciation of figures like Miłosz and Zagajewski within the total context of Polish history." Indeed, on the back cover, twenty-seven authors are listed to prove the totality of the context, which includes many less-known authors, though not yet the ones paying tribute to Chandler. Barańczak's Introduction identifies Zbigniew Herbert's *Report from the Besieged City* (1983) as "the greatest poetic sensation" of the 1980s (Barańczak and Cavanagh 1991, 8) and claims that Herbert's "complex blend of irony and moralism" typifies Polish poetry in general (1991, 9). Moreover, the eminent American critic Helen Vendler warns in her Foreword that the translated (i.e. rewritten) poems will "be read first of all as poems of witness to their cultural moment" and concludes with predictable parabolic allusions:

> The Mr. Cogitos of Poland will not lack for things to write about with respect to their own past and future; and the old and distinguished resources of the Polish literary tradition, from folk ballads to historical epics, will surely not fail them. As this collection proves, they have an astonishingly gifted set of forebears to live up to. (Barańczak and Cavanagh 1991, xxi)

Two years later, Donald Pirie's collection *Young Poets of a Young Poland: An Anthology* stresses the dilemmas of younger poets (born mostly in the 1950s and 1960s) "torn between the traditions of civic poetry, speaking for the national cause (so well represented by the master of Polish poetry, Zbigniew Herbert, much of whose verse is widely available in English), and the recent resurgence of a poetry of personal vision." (Pirie 1993, xxi) Pirie focuses on "the New Privacy" movement—paradoxically, according to this rewriter, its insistence on the private makes the poets more universal, and therefore translatable. To quote just one example of Pirie's argument:

> [Krystyna] Lars' poetry replaces the codes of allusion to Poland's historic struggles with the Freudian technique of free association, and so is more accessible than the conventional Polish imagery. Instead of collective aspirations and resentments, here is a voyage through personal obsessions and anxieties using archetypes and images familiar to

all Western readers: trains, uniforms, illicit meetings, and suppressed feelings of guilt, clothed in arrogance and cynicism. (1993, xv)

Pirie sees post-1989 developments as promising, since "authentic, convincing poetry is always located in the transitional and unstable, rather than confined by the predictable." (1993: xxvi) He optimistically emphasizes his choice of "the authentic voices of real 'singularities' and their very sensual experience of what is more than a New Poland – it is a New World." (1993: xxvi)

In 2004, eleven years after Pirie's selection, his aesthetic decisions are reinforced by Zbigniew Joachimiak, David Malcolm and Georgia Scott, who also concentrate on the "New Privacy" and on the Gdańsk area, since it "reflects the dynamics of Polish literature and history in the death throes of the People's Republic." (2004, 9) As readers of *Dreams of Fires: 100 Polish Poems 1970-1989*, another attempt at "anthologizing Poland," we are thrown back to the pre-1989 period. The three rewriters clarify in their Acknowledgments that "Many of these poems were translated many years ago for another anthology in another time in another world. Before 1989." (2004, 9) So encapsulated, the poems, composed by poets who "could not know that the end of the existing dispensation was at hand" (2004: 15), require reassurance that their validity will transcend the fateful 1989—and indeed such a confirmation comes at the end of the introduction.

An even more hopeful validation is offered in the Preface commissioned from Daniel Weissbort, himself a translator and editor of an anthology tellingly entitled *The Poetry of Survival: Post-War Poets of Central and Eastern Europe* (1991). Weissbort evokes Miłosz as a rewriter who "invented Polish poetry for us, as Pound invented Chinese, although far more reliably than the latter" (Joachimiak, Malcolm and Scott 2004, 17), thus referring not only to Miłosz as a poet but also to Miłosz as a translator and anthologist whose seminal 1965 *Postwar Polish Poetry* founded a canon of Polish poetry in English translation. Moreover, Weissbort names Pirie as the one "who drew my almost mesmerized gaze away from the first generation of post-War poetry, from what has been called the 'poetry of survival'" (2004, 21). Noticing that *Dreams of Fires* foregrounds the same period as *Cannibals' Fun*, Weissbort identifies one important difference: "hindsight" (2004, 21). He also maintains that the particularity of the Polish experience is—thanks to the skill of the poets who write about it—accessible, hence translatable. He singles out Tadeusz Różewicz, Zbigniew Herbert and Piotr Sommer, whose poem entitled "What It Might Be" ("Czym mógłby być") is "a fine example of this peculiarly Central European genre" (2004, 23). Safely categorized as recognizable, the selection confirms the canon of the Polish poetry already known outside Poland.

But we should return to the 1990s and to the anthology which seeks to enlarge the canon by drawing our attention to women writers. While *Cannibals'*

Fun boasted the presence of five women, *Ambers Aglow* (1996) collects thirty-one women poets. This *Anthology of Contemporary Polish Women's Poetry* is lucky to be ushered in by Wisława Szymborska's Nobel Prize (1996). As Eva Hoffman argues in the blurb, Szymborska's prize demonstrates that "Polish women's poetry constitutes a powerful body of literature, which deserves to be better known in the West." Regina Grol has a mission to carry out as a rewriter, and she is very clear about her mission statement: "to crumble the walls of ignorance about Polish women's poetry, make the poetry known outside Poland, and provide a doorway to the understanding of Poland and its culture." (1996, xxi) She realizes that now is the time, because "Poland has often been in the headlines since the collapse of its Communist regime, and the steady flow of media reports on the status of Polish women continues." (1996, xxii)

Grol arranges her poets alphabetically to avoid favouritism or thematic groupings. She includes the Polish versions of the poems (all written between 1981 and 1995) to account for what she identifies as the unavoidable loss in translation:

> Little known in the West and written in a language with minority status, Polish poetry is very difficult to translate. [...] Dominant in this volume are poems which foreground the semantic content, are likely to be accessible to American readers, and in which greater emphasis is placed on the lexical rather than phonetic aspect. (1996: xxxiv-xxxv)

She stresses not only the external transformations, but also the inner ones:

> Even when Polish women do choose the conventional roles of mothers and housewives, recently their motives have changed. Now they do so not as obeisance to the traditional values, but to reclaim the private realm and distance themselves from the corrupt public domain in which they were forced to participate under Communism. (1996: xxviii)

I would argue that *Ambers Aglow* testifies to the canonized activities of survival and subversion, even as it sets out to modify the canon.[1]

Here, a short aside about my own contribution to "rewriting Poland." Around this time I started publishing my own translations of contemporary Polish poetry: in 1998 my English versions of Marcin Świetlicki, one of the three Marcins associated with the tribute to Raymond Chandler, appeared. In 2000, I completed the editing of an anthology of recent Polish poetry selected by Marcin Baran, another "Chandler Marcin." However, because of the financial difficulties of the two publishers, the book only appeared four years later. In the meantime three other volumes were published; to a lesser or greater extent I was involved in their preparation.

1 Another substantial anthology of translations of Polish women's poetry, mostly post-1989, is forthcoming (Kovacik 2014).

In 2000 William Martin edited a special issue of *Chicago Review* devoted to *New Polish Writing*. The Introduction's opening sentence highlights *the* historical moment: "In 1989-1990, Poland experienced a sea-change in every area of public life" (Martin 2000, 7). Its significance is strengthened by the editorial claim to another momentous occasion coupled with another fifteen-minute attention span: "Given that Poland is the featured country at the Frankfurt Book Fair this year, now seems an especially opportune, if not overdue, moment for publishing this issue." (2000: 8) The selection—a well thought-out cross between "the closed form of the anthology" and "the more open, improvisational form of the quarterly"—has a very ambitious task to perform, therefore Martin as the guest editor ventures a strong opinion: since the change, "Polish literature and literary culture have shown themselves to be the richest and most vibrant in Europe." (2000, 8) In order to prove his point, Martin features not only poetry and fiction (work written or published after 1989, from Czesław Miłosz to Marzanna Kielar), but also essays, interviews, reportage, reviews—by seventy-five contributors. The issue features Krzysztof Koehler's essay "O'Harism" and Marcin Świetlicki's "Koehlerism" to better situate younger poets, less known in English, because the emergence of the "New Barbarians" is considered "the defining moment of Polish literature in the 1990s" (2000, 7). In his contribution, "Are Things Worse or Is This Normal? Polish Poetry in the 1990s," literary historian Piotr Śliwiński questions the artistic significance of the "barbarism vs classicism" opposition and criticizes the poetry which, in aspiring to normalcy, becomes instead "enslaved by freedom" (Martin 2000, 340). Śliwiński quotes poet and critic Piotr Kępiński's diagnosis about post-1989 Polish poetry, which forces us to reconsider Helen Vendler's optimistic predictions (expressed in the *Spoiling Cannibals' Fun* anthology) about the future of Poland's Mr Cogitos: "Here, in contemporary poetry, an assertive author has appeared, an author who, at times consciously, at times purely mechanically, carries on his back a romantic burden. And he does not know what to do with it." (Martin 2000, 341)

One year after Martin's special issue, a Polish issue of *Przekładaniec: A Literary Translation Journal* appears. It is "special also in the way it presents work in progress: namely, pieces of contemporary Polish writing that are being translated at the moment" (2001, 10). As its guest editor, I wished to showcase translators—rewriters who are responsible for the recognizable status of "their" writers. In my editorial, I list the names familiar to English-speaking readers: Miłosz, Szymborska, Lem, Konwicki, Kapuściński; then Herbert, Różewicz, Zagajewski, Gombrowicz, Mrożek, Krall, Herling-Grudziński, and provide the names of their translators. As a former Fulbright scholar, I had had a chance to meet translators-members of the American Literary Translators' Association and was impressed by the Association's efforts to make translators visible. I therefore include, for example, selections from Wiesiek Powaga's translation of Natasza Goerke's story, which was first published in the 1996 collection *The Eagle and the Crow: Modern Polish Stories,* edited by Teresa Halikowska and George Hyde. To justify the reprinting, I quote Powaga's comment: "Such publications do not become bestsellers, and authors featured, though they merit attention, need to reappear in print frequently enough to have their presence acknowledged" (2001, 10). Re-reading the introductory material now, I am surprised to notice Lefevere's "historical moment": the then Director of the Polish Cultural Institute in London (the issue's sponsor) mentions Polish preparations for joining the European Union in her letter to *Przekładaniec* readers. The subject of EU accession was to return in five years, when I was asked to guest edit the Polish issue of *Poetry Wales*.

Meanwhile, the "recent" Polish poetry I translated and co-edited for the delayed 2000 anthology was becoming less and less recent. Moreover, I was contacted by Tadeusz Pióro, who was working on a similar presentation of contemporary Polish poetry. We agreed that the overlap would be unfortunate, since his selection would obviously include several of the names that Marcin Baran had also chosen for our anthology. Thus, exceptionally, English-speaking readers received two selections almost simultaneously: readers in the UK could enjoy *Altered State: The New Polish Poetry* (2003), whereas readers in the USA could appreciate *Carnivorous Boy Carnivorous Bird: Poetry from Poland* (2004). I want to emphasize, however, that the impact of such a lucky coincidence is weakened by the fact that these two publishing markets and two readerships, even if united by the same language, are quite separate.

Let me discuss *Altered State* first. Edited by Rod Mengham, Tadeusz Pióro and Piotr Szymor, "[t]his anthology breaks new ground in the English-speaking world by publishing translations of poems by Polish writers all under the age of forty-five." So we are informed by the blurb and the introduction, where Mengham continues:

> Practically all work in this selection was written in the post-communist period, but in cultural historical terms it reflects the evolution of a sensibility that began to emerge in the mid 1980s, when Polish poetry was being realigned contentiously with newly visible traditions of European and American writing. (2003, 11)

The modifier "post-communist Poland" significantly frames the period. Interestingly, though, the reference is no longer to 1989, but instead to July 1986, which appears as the publication date of the so-called "blue" issue of the Polish journal *Literatura na Świecie*; the New York School is mentioned, as are the "Barbarians," the "New Classicists" and "Banalism." Unlike Vendler and Weissbort, Mengham does not see the post-era as hopeful for the future of Polish poetry:

> Post-communist Poland has willingly abandoned one of the "grand narratives" of European history, and yet its literature is haunted by the sense of evacuation, of being deprived of ideological guarantees worth writing for. [. . .] Many of the poems in this anthology reflect a determination to rediscover and re-explore the basic contours of Polish domestic space, as if attention to the basic components of everyday life should enable the reconstruction of social norms and relationships. (2003, 13)

Mengham singles out the work of Andrzej Sosnowski (b. 1959), suggesting a simile which may bring this selection of Polish poetry closer to its UK readers: "contemporary subjectivity as a condition that has been caught up in the 'dream' of Polish history, like Prince Hamlet, disabled by a legacy that is too overpowering to live up to" (2003: 14). Mengham's conclusion clarifies that "altered state" should not be understood as a perfective mood or an accomplished achievement, but as "constant alteration in a constantly altered State" (2003, 15), where the capital S insists on the political, rather than psychological, identity of this key term.

I comment on the title of Mengham and Pióro's anthology, because, when choosing a name for the selection co-edited by Anna Skucińska and myself, we wanted to avoid easy associations with Polish political and historical conditioning. *Carnivorous Boy Carnivorous Bird* features twenty-four poets and seventeen translators. Familiar with the previous anthologies, where poems were "rewritten" by only one or two translators, we wished to diversify the poetic voices much further by allowing them to speak through multiple translational dictions. Marcin Baran, who selected the poets, deliberately uses only two dates in his introduction: 1958 and 1969, indicating the earliest and latest birth dates of the anthologized poets. In his introduction, entitled "Informal, Singular Duties," Baran expresses the belief that "[t]he political, social and cultural changes of the last decade allowed young Polish poetry to cast off [the] burden" of duties usually performed by "politicians, soldiers, priests or journalists." (Skucińska 2004, i)

But perhaps the most important are two of Baran's rhetorical moves. First, he opens his introduction with the claim to normalcy: "This is an anthology of Polish poetry which is normal and ordinary; that is, if any poetry created in any country and under any circumstances can be viewed as normal and ordinary." (2004, i) Second, he decides to arrange the presented poets into eight groups of three, a very subjective classification, as he admits—and a very conscious gesture by a rewriter who deliberately plays with such risky "pigeonholing." The anthology lists preceding anthologies in the selected bibliography to suggest how large the canon of Polish poetry in English translation has already become. Indirectly, this bibliography helps us to ward off politically correct questions about the number of women presented in our anthology. There is only one, Marzanna Kielar (b. 1963); had our anthology been compiled closer to its date of publication, it would have also featured Julia Fiedorczuk (b. 1975) and Marta Podgórnik (b. 1979), as *Altered State* does. At the time we assembled it, we were not interested in including women to improve the statistics. Moreover, we felt we were allowed such freedom because there already existed *Ambers Aglow*.

A year later, in 2005, American readers could update their knowledge of Polish poets thanks to Mira Rosenthal's *New Polish Poetry*, a special issue of *Lyric*. Her presentation of twenty-four poets is assisted by nineteen translators, as well as by critics Karol Maliszewski, Kacper Bartczak and Marian Stala. Bartczak, a John Ashbery expert, dismisses the Polish O'Harists (possibly with the exception of Marcin Świetlicki), who, in his opinion, dominate *Altered State* and *Carnivorous Boy*, and tips the balance of attention towards Polish "Ashberists." Andrzej Sosnowski in particular deserves attention, as he "shows that poets can achieve originality in the age of intertextuality, and the success of his daring poetics encourages younger poets." (Rosenthal 2005, 93) Bartczak regrets that the contemporary Polish scene is "too deeply divided" and mentions a reading by Adam Zagajewski boycotted in Łódź (Rosenthal 2005, 94).

As Zagajewski has become a familiar name in the English-speaking world, thanks to systematic translation, his example may counter Stala's pessimism about attempts to rewrite Polish poetry so as to make some names (here specifically women's names) known outside Poland: "It's not a big thing to enumerate the names, but I don't know whether something comes out of such an enumeration. I also believe that some of them might have been translated into foreign languages. But, probably, nothing comes out of this too, especially since it is quite often purely accidental." (Rosenthal 2005, 106) Significantly, Stala summarizes developments of the previous fifteen years in Polish poetry suggesting that it draws more on Tadeusz Różewicz than on Czesław Miłosz. Since this particular anthology is addressed to American readers, Stala's comment indirectly invites qualification not only of the canon of Polish poetry available in the USA but also of the founder of this canon, Miłosz himself. Given Bartczak's dismissal of the Polish O'Harism, it is vital to consider another Polish model: Miron Białoszewski (1922-1983).

Białoszewski and Tymoteusz Karpowicz (1921-2005) appear in my introduction to the 2006 issue of *Poetry Wales*, which was dedicated to Polish poetry. Asked by editor Robert Minhinnick for suggestions, I could refer him to *Altered State* and *Carnivorous Boy*, by now part of the canon of Polish poetry in English translation. He selected Marzanna Kielar (whom he had already published), Dariusz Sośnicki (b. 1969), Jerzy Jarniewicz (b. 1958) and Grzegorz Wróblewski (b. 1962). He added Agnieszka Kuciak (b. 1970), Tomasz Różycki (b. 1970) and Krystyna Miłobędzka (b. 1932). I was requested to discuss Polish membership of the European Union and its implications for Polish poetry, but decided to dodge another "historical moment" or another *post*-modifier. Resisting too rigid an emphasis on the events of 1989, as well as the assumption that change began only in that specific moment, or that contemporary poets could not be influenced by much earlier poets, I begin with the summer of 1988, "because it came before the notoriously familiar 1989, with its autumn of nations, which captured and still holds the imagination of those thinking of Central Europe." (Wójcik-Leese 2006, 40) Foregrounding the aesthetic and linguistic qualities of the presented poetry, rather than the obviously unavoidable political context, the selection, entitled "Alternative Signposts," ends with a discussion of Miłobędzka:

> Miłobędzka's craft points to such Polish poetry experimenters as Tymoteusz Karpowicz, Miron Białoszewski or Bolesław Leśmian [1877-1937], whose work is almost entirely unknown in translation because of its rootedness in the peculiarities of the Polish language. And it is Białoszewski and Karpowicz who have become alternative signposts for younger Polish poets. (Wójcik-Leese 2006, 44)

As a gloss I should add that in his Acknowledgments to *Spoiling Cannibals' Fun*, Barańczak regrets not including seventeen Białoszewski translations due to copyright problems (1991, xiii).

In 2007, Brian McCabe, the editor of *Edinburgh Review*, offered a Scottish take on "rewriting Poland." He embraces both the *post*-1989 and *post*-2004 (the date of Poland's accession to the European Union), but the vantage point changes: Poles are no longer the exotic "other," they are *in* Scotland. Their experience becomes the Scottish experience—or as McCabe sums up: "'made in Poland' can sometimes also mean 'made in Scotland'" (2007, 5). Let me quote a longer passage to clarify McCabe's statement:

> In "The Bread and Meat of Life," Will Brady examines the effects of the dismantling of communism on Poland's identity and culture, and considers the implications of the new wave of Polish immigration to the UK, finding cause for hope in the vibrant Polish community now thriving in Edinburgh—a community aptly celebrated in Desirée Elfström's photographs of Polish shops in the city. Catherine Czerkowska reflects movingly on her Polish heritage, as does the narrator of Merryn Glover's short story "Broken Bread." Even Scottish poet Ian McDonough's sequence, resolutely set in some of Scotland's less glamorous locations—"Supermarket Car Park, Dalkeith"—by rolling together observation of the everyday and philosophical reflection, manages to have a strangely "Polish" feel. (2007, 5)

It would be interesting to ask McCabe for his definition of "the Polish feel." Importantly, McCabe's title for his rewriting of Poland, "Made in Poland," refers us to the title of a 2004 theatre production by the Helena Modrzejewska Theatre in Legnica, discussed by Michał Lachman in his analysis of Polish theatre after

1989. McCabe also includes an essay on Polish film, and two other photo essays: "Post-Industrial" and "Signs of Place: 1960s Neons, Warsaw."

For McCabe's project, instead of providing another overview of contemporary Polish poetry signposted by "historical moments," I decided to write about four poetry nominations for the 2007 Nike Prize: Ewa Lipska (b. 1945), Wojciech Bonowicz (b. 1967), Marcin Świetlicki and Tomasz Różycki. I felt we should feature individual poets and volumes of Polish poetry simply because they were being read and appreciated currently in Poland (although I am well aware of the "politicized" context of poetry nominations for any prestigious literary award). Reviewing only four names allowed for more detail, even though I could only include a limited number of translated snippets.

Translation features in McCabe's issue also thanks to Adam Czerniawski's essay entitled "Not Lost in Translation," which offers a very personal view on the presence of Polish literature in the UK:

> I think it safe to say that before World War II English-speaking peoples had no awareness of Polish poetry. [. . .] Thanks to [Hitler and Stalin], I and many other Polish writers found ourselves exiled in English-speaking countries; some of us acquired sufficient competence in English to attempt literary translations, often with the help of native speakers. (2007, 61)

Czerniawski concentrates on his own versions of Tadeusz Różewicz, Cyprian Kamil Norwid (1821-1883) and Jan Kochanowski (1530-1584); he mentions that one Kochanowski lament "taken from an edition limited to 400 copies of his *Treny*, published bilingually in Oxford—a remarkable achievement in itself—appears in Carol Ann Duffy's *Out of Fashion*, a Faber poetry anthology of 20,000 copies." (2007, 62) Tracing the life of the English versions of Polish poems, Czerniawski stresses the assistance they offer to translators of Polish poetry into languages of the Indian subcontinent as well as Chinese, Persian or Arabic. "But perhaps the most extraordinary example is the inclusion of a poem by Leopold Staff (1878-1957) in *Family Business*, the New Cambridge Intermediate English Course Reader comprising a selection of prose and verse. A Polish poem for students of English!" (2007, 63) This example deserves our attention also because it testifies to such rare occasions when translated poems live beyond their immediate context of "anthologizing Poland."

"New Voices from Europe and Beyond" is the name of the series of bilingual anthologies produced by Arc Publications in cooperation with Literature Across Frontiers. Significantly, the series title no longer specifies: Eastern or Central or Western Europe. Instead, it points to Europe as a whole, and suggests a possibility of transcending the geopolitical positioning. Thus, the fifth volume in the series, *Six Polish Poets* (2009), edited by Jacek Dehnel, can focus on "neo-classicist" poets and choose *not* to be representative because of the already established canon of Polish poetry in translation. The existing anthologies have allowed this rewriter freedom to select six poets, "sometimes [. . .] to their loud objection" (2009, 12). He features: Anna Piwowska (b. 1963), Dariusz Suska (b. 1968), Tomasz Różycki, Maciej Woźniak (b. 1969), Agnieszka Kuciak and Jacek Dehnel (b. 1980). The series editor, Alexandra Büchler, accounts for this narrowed-down approach in her preface, stating that the anthology "nevertheless provides an insight into today's literary scene in Poland" (2009, 9). She thus explains its shift in focus:

> Unlike the poets of the previous generation [Büchler generalizes here about the generation of Świetlicki et al., born in the 1960s; three of Dehnel's poets were also born in the 1960s—Ed.] who, in the period of new-found freedom after the fall of communism, adopted a highly individualist, anarchic, sometimes brutal style, the poets presented here re-examine and experiment with traditional poetic forms, themes and cultural references in poems that are refined and witty, moving and informed, ranging across every aspect of human existence. (Dehnel 2009, 9)

Dehnel meanwhile hopes that neo-classicist poetry "bridges some recent divisions, reconciling poetry from before 1989 with the work of the *brulion* [sic] generation, deriving influences from both these sources, and creating poetry of a completely different nature." (2009, 13)

I believe that Dehnel's anthology as well as the Welsh and Scottish presentations let us transcend the need to identify (and canonize) those poets who might be considered representative according to some collective criterion of value. I particularly appreciate the organic co-presence cultivated by *Poetry Wales* and *Edinburgh Review*, where Polish poets appear alongside other, non-Polish, poets (for example, the "Polish" issue of *Poetry Wales* introduces "Six new poets from Wales"). National identity—Polish, Central European or European—does not have to be the main criterion justifying the need for presenting good poetry. As the Americans Wayne Miller and Kevin Prufer, editors of *New European Poets*, observe: '"European" has increasingly emerged as a significant identity alongside—or in addition to—European national identities. This is aided by the fact that Europeans, and European writers, now move between countries more or less as easily as Americans move between states. Meanwhile European countries have been socioculturally diversified by the rapid growth in immigration from outside of Europe—primarily from the former colonies of European powers (2008, xxvii). *New European Poets* comes into being not only because Europe itself has changed, but also because European poetry has moved beyond the recognizable "European" territories known to North American readers. It is worth observing that a simple need to learn about something unfamiliar can also lead to new anthologizing attempts, no longer prompted primarily by "an historical moment."

Two such anthologies materialized in 2011. The first, *Six Poets: Twenty-eight Poems*, introduces writers "united" by Sopot, a town located on the Baltic Sea close to Gdańsk and Gdynia, and home of the International Literary Festival BACK2 and prestigious journal *Topos* (Kuczkowski 2011, 4). Here the local aspires to the international without the immediate historical significance that requires commemoration or the support of historical justifications. The second selection, *Free over Blood,* issued by the British publisher OFF_PRESS presents nineteen poets: from the more established, now also in English, such as Tkaczyszyn-Dycki, Sosnowski and Dehnel, to those published in translation for the first time, such as Radosław Wiśniewski (b. 1974), Justyna Bargielska (b. 1977) and Joanna Mueller (b. 1979). Although the title of the second anthology refers to the Polish national colours, it also rewrites—or subverts—their symbolism conventionalized by nearly two centuries of political strife. These anthologized presences "no longer align themselves with flags or other well-worn standards" (Jung and Orliński 2011, 9), while the selection hopes to "show just how far Poland has moved on from her tragic past, and yet just how many strong voices keep calling out in verse form" (2011, 283).

Conclusion

Free over Blood can be seen as a farewell to a certain mode of reading, defined by Jarosław Anders in *Between Fire and Sleep* as "an act of communication not only between the author and the reader but also between the reader and his [sic] fellow citizens [. . .] an act that restored a sense of togetherness in a deliberately fragmented, distrustful society." (2009, xii) Yet we cannot overlook the fact that even the rewriters of the 2011 selection of translated Polish poetry sanction their departure from the established means of "anthologizing Poland" with a recognizably ponderous cliché: "her tragic past." Be it the Solidarity uprising thirty years ago or the partitions of the Polish-Lithuanian Commonwealth over two centuries ago, the past is still reckoned with, especially that its "tragedy" seems to demand from writers some kind of testimony, still expected, according to Anders, by both Polish readers and foreign readers of Polish literature in translation. However, as the paratext of the discussed anthologies reveals, more recent selections no longer aim at protecting the national soul and language. Moreover, some anthologists want to move away from such exemplars as Herbert or Miłosz.

On the one hand, Anders's decision to "revisit the great trinity of contemporary Polish poets—Milosz, Herbert, and Szymborska" (2009, xv) well demonstrates the pull of the particular nostalgia that typifies not only one individual rewriter. We can also observe it in the reading preferences of quite a few anthologists presented in this chapter. On the other, we should not overlook the fact that

Anders, in his personal overview, acknowledges recent Polish reassessment of Herbert, just as Stala speaks about the re-positioning of Miłosz in contemporary Polish poetry. As the recognizable historical moments, the year 1989 among them, begin to be reassessed, so too the familiar literary figures. Thus the room is being prepared for alternative signposts. Significantly, Anders chooses to write also about Bruno Schulz, Witold Gombrowicz and Stanisław Ignacy Witkiewicz, whom he calls "three madmen" (2009, xiii) because they rebelled against their role as custodians. By drawing the attention of English-speaking readers to such authors in order to demonstrate "how the best in contemporary Polish writing was in fact a product of a clash between the two traditions—one collectivist, didactic, and ecstatic, the other personal, skeptical, and ironic" (2009, xiii), Anders not only manipulates their literary fame, in the manner defined by Lefevere, but also suggests other possibilities for rewriting the Polish literary presence in translation.

Bibliography

Anthologies and selections of translations (in order of editor)

Barańczak, Stanisław and Clare Cavanagh, eds. 1991. *Polish Poetry of the Last Two Decades of Communist Rule: Spoiling Cannibals' Fun,* translated by Stanisław Barańczak and Clare Cavanagh. Foreword by Helen Vendler. Evanston, IL: Northwestern University Press.

Dehnel, Jacek, ed. 2009. *Six Polish Poets.* New Voices from Europe and Beyond. Todmorden, Lancashire: Arc Publications.

Grol, Regina, ed. 1996. *Ambers Aglow: An Anthology of Contemporary Polish Women's Poetry*, compiled, translated and with a critical introduction by Regina Grol. Austin, TX: Host Publications.

Joachimiak, Zbigniew, David Malcolm and Georgia Scott, eds. 2004. *Dreams of Fires: 100 Polish Poems 1970-1989*, translated by Zbigniew Joachimiak et al. Preface by Daniel Weissbort. Salzburg: Poetry Salzburg.

Jung, Dawid and Marcin Orliński, eds. 2011. *Free Over Blood.* London: Off_PRESS.

Kovacik, Karen, ed. 2014. *Calling Out to Yeti.* Buffalo, NY: White Pine Press.

Kuczkowski, Krzysztof, ed. 2011. *Six Poets: Twenty-eight Poems.* Sopot: Biblioteka Toposu.

McCabe, Brian, ed. 2007. *Made in Poland: New Writing from Poland.* [Special issue of] *Edinburgh Review* 121.

Martin, William, ed. 2000. *New Polish Writing. Chicago Review* 46(3-4).

Mengham, Rod, Tadeusz Pióro and Piotr Szymor, eds. 2003. *Altered State: The New Polish Poetry*, translated by Rod Mengham et al. Todmorden, Lancashire: Arc Publications.

Miller, Wayne Miller and Kevin Prufer, eds. 2008. *New European Poets.* Saint Paul, MN: Graywolf Press.

Pirie, Donald, ed. 1993. *Young Poets of a Young Poland: An Anthology*, translated and introduced by Donald Pirie. UNESCO Collection of Representative Works, European Series. London: Forest Books.

Rosenthal, Mira, ed. 2005. *New Polish Poetry.* [Special issue of] *Lyric* 8.

Skucińska, Anna and Elżbieta Wójcik-Leese, eds. 2004. *Carnivorous Boy Carnivorous Bird. Poetry from Poland*, selected by Marcin Baran. Brookline, MA: Zephyr Press.

Weissbort, Daniel. 1991. *The Poetry of Survival: Post-War Poets of Central and Eastern Europe*, introduced by Daniel Weissbort. London: Anvil Press.

Wójcik-Leese, Elżbieta. 2001. *Contemporary Polish Writing*. [Special issue of] *Przekładaniec. A Journal of Literary Translation.*

Wójcik-Leese, Elżbieta, ed. 2006. *Poland*. [Special issue of] *Poetry Wales* 42(2).

Secondary sources

Anders, Jarosław. 2009. *Between Fire and Sleep: Essays on Modern Poetry and Prose.* New Haven, CT: Yale University Press.

Baran, Marcin, Marcin Sendecki and Marcin Świetlicki, eds. 1997. *Długie pożegnanie. Tribute to Chandler*. Kraków: Zebra.

—. 2010. *Żegnaj laleczko. Wiersze noir.* Kraków: EMG.

Lefevere, André. 1992. *Translation, Rewriting and the Manipulation of Literary Fame.* London: Routledge.

Wójcik-Leese, Elżbieta. 2000. "Jak zaistnieć—współczesna poezja polska w przekładzie na angielski, antologie i wybory." In *Język trzeciego tysiąclecia* [Proceedings of the First Tertium Conference], edited by Grzegorz Szpila, 507-516. Kraków: Wydawnictwo Tertium.

—. 2006. "Alternative Signposts: Selected Contemporary Polish Poets." *Poetry Wales* 42(2): 40-44.

—. 2007. "Just Did It: Four Poetry Nominations." *Edinburgh Review* 121: 112-118.

Afterword: Political Controversy since 1989

Anthony KEMP-WELCH

Prelude: 1988-1989

Seven years after banning Solidarity and interning its leaders and advisers, the same Polish generals invited them to a Round Table on the future of communist power. Few observers had anticipated the historic compromise by which the communists abandoned their attempt to "govern permanently against the determined opposition of their compatriots." (Pelczynski [1982], 30-31) The idea of inviting the "adversary" to a Round Table shocked many in the Communist Party (Polska Zjednoczona Partia Robotnicza), whose revolt was only quelled by the threat to resign of the ruling team. As Adam Michnik points out, the communist authorities did not "benevolently cede their power to the opposition the moment democracy became possible." (Michnik 1999) On the contrary, they came to the Round Table with a strong hand expecting to co-opt the opposition, but were swept away soon afterwards by an electoral avalanche which no one had anticipated (Skorzyński 2002). Their subsequent abdication was unique in history and signalled the systemic changes which abruptly, and largely peacefully, terminated the "Soviet bloc."

In summer 1980, the Polish authorities had sought to end national strikes against food-price increases by accepting the first free trade union in the communist world: Solidarity. In return, its leader Lech Wałęsa formally acknowledged the "leading role" of the Communist Party in state affairs. But Soviet leaders under Brezhnev were totally hostile to this development and made immediate plans for its reversal. Even before the Gdańsk Agreement had sanctioned Solidarity, they planned to mobilize tens of thousands of troops "in case military assistance is provided to Poland." (Kramer 1999, 11-12) Dozens of Soviet "advisers" supervised Polish preparations for martial law which was eventually imposed in December 1981. Though superficially successful by interning several thousand activists and advisers, the "self-invasion" failed in its major objective: to destroy Solidarity. The outlawed union went underground and developed an elaborate network of non-violent resistance, assisted by the Catholic Church.

The consequent impasse was eventually challenged by a new team in the Kremlin. From the mid-1980s, Gorbachev's advisers started a fresh analysis of relations with East and Central Europe. They reached the conclusion that the reasons for occupying the region in 1944-1945 had turned into their opposite

(Kemp-Welch 1991). Though intended by Stalin as a "buffer zone" to protect the Soviet Union from future invasion, Eastern Europe was incurably unstable, requiring regular military interventions to restore the status quo. Rather than providing economic reparations that Stalin had sought at Yalta and Potsdam, the "socialist commonwealth" cost the Soviet Union dearly in terms of cheap energy and other subsidies. Instead of being an area for exploitation, the purpose of an empire, the centre was financing the periphery. Lastly, the region showed scant signs of gratitude for membership in the most advanced camp in world history. Its politicians were incurably "revisionist," often challenging Moscow's doctrinal hegemony. Recognizing these realities, the Gorbachev team attempted to change the terms of the relationship.

Addressing East European leaders at Konstantin Chernenko's funeral (March 1985), Gorbachev called for a new relationship based on equality. Their initial response was sceptical: all incoming Soviet leaders had said the same and nothing really changed. An additional source of caution was political: should Gorbachev be genuine in seeking change he might be deposed by those who sought the status quo. Prudence thus suggested a "wait and see" attitude towards developments in the Kremlin. When later Gorbachev's sincerity did become clear, there was a further impediment to change—conservative and ageing leaderships in most East European states. Only Wojciech Jaruzelski in Poland and the Hungarian politicians around Kádár (though not János Kádár himself) wished to use new opportunities now opening up.

Polish promptings for political change came from Bronisław Geremek, long-term Solidarity advisor, and until 1968 a Party member. Interviewed at the end of 1987, he suggested that both sides had learned from the early eighties. Society now understood that its aspirations must be confined within political limits, while the authorities had understood that without authentic social forces there could be no turning point to rescue the economy. He proposed an "anti-crisis pact" whereby Solidarity would be re-legalized in return for helping the authorities to rebuild the economy (Geremek 1990, 9-10). Public life would be divided into two. The Party would continue to run the state, while society would be guaranteed pluralism and the rule of law. But his proposal to re-legalize Solidarity was anathema to many in the Party leadership and rank-and-file. Accustomed to consider Solidarity deceased—the interview with Geremek referred to him as "adviser to the former Solidarity"—they looked askance at the rebirth of the "adversary."

During the spring and summer of 1988, intense political debates took place behind the scenes, and Gorbachev was personally involved in these negotiations. His six-day Polish visit (July 1988) celebrated "the beginnings of achieving full mutual understandings" far beyond mere diplomatic politeness. He sought to speed up a Polish reform process that had thus far been "very slow." The visitor posed questions such as "relations with the opposition" and "the influence exerted on various parts of the social structure by so-called Solidarity" (Medvedev 1994, 82-87). In the sharpest contrast to the Brezhnev period, these references were not derogatory. During bilateral talks, Gorbachev remarked that there "is no substitute for dialogue with the nation, as a method of public opinion research." He referred to "socialist renewal" in Poland and *perestroika* as twins. At last, long-suppressed but still crucial bilateral issues were now aired. A joint commission was set up to look into the Katyń massacre of Polish citizens in 1940 and other "blank pages" in Russo-Polish relations (Medvedev 1994, 108-117; Dzienkiewicz 2010).

Underlying Soviet concerns was the dramatic increase of public unrest in Poland. On the twentieth anniversary of the "March 1968" events, Polish students again became the vanguard of political protest. Then in late April, the key player in the Polish drama, subjugated by years of martial law and economic deprivation, re-entered the political stage. First in Bydgoszcz, transport workers halted all bus and tram services. The Lenin Steelworks in Kraków began a ten-day strike next day. Protests soon reached the Baltic Coast and Silesia (Dudek and Marszałkowski 1999, 372-379). This raised what Mark Kramer has called the "Khrushchev Dilemma": "If a comparable crisis had erupted in 1989, the pressure for Soviet military intervention would have been enormous, just as it was on Khrushchev in 1956."(Kramer 1994, 182-183) To decline to use force would give his domestic opponents an ideal pretext to move against him. Alternatively, military intervention would destroy the new structure of East-West collaboration which Gorbachev had so carefully constructed. This fatal choice had to be averted.

When the Round Table convened in Warsaw on 6 February 1989 there was a tacit agreement to overcome the past. Twenty-nine delegates from the "Party-government" team, twenty-six from the Solidarity-led opposition and three Catholic observers, as mediators, negotiated in three major panels, a plethora of sub-tables and working groups. A curious osmosis took place. Instead of dominating proceedings, the "Party-government" team became ever more prone to compromise. They accepted Geremek's argument that re-legalization of Solidarity was the essential starting point for a plural political order and agreed to partially free elections in the near future, to be followed by fully free elections in four years time. Solidarity won the elections by a landslide. After a forty-minute phone call from Gorbachev, Polish leader Mieczysław Rakowski accepted the results (Kramer 2011, 1566-1570). Solidarity formed the world's first post-communist government.

1989-2011

Although the new prime minister, Tadeusz Mazowiecki, sought reconciliation, promising to draw a "thick line" under the politics of the past, others sought vengeance for crimes of the communist era. Most vehemently, his Interior Minister Antoni Macierewicz attempted to expose "agents" of the former authorities who had remained in high office. This clumsy attempt to frame former government and police officials and their collaborators, including the new President Lech Wałęsa (who succeeded General Wojciech Jaruzelski in December 1990), were condemned by the Episcopate as "slanderous" and by a parliamentary commission as "capable of destabilizing the state." Macierewicz was dismissed. However, procedures for addressing past crimes, and the highly controversial issue of justification for the imposition of martial law in 1981, remained unresolved.

The planned economy was rapidly dismantled and "shock therapy," devised and implemented by Leszek Balcerowicz, began the transition to capitalism. A joint committee of parliament (the Sejm) and the Senate was formed to draw up a new constitution, and decided Poland should have an elected presidency. Much difficulty followed in determining what role the president should play (McAvoy 2012, 207-210). As the committee, chaired by Geremek, granted more and more powers to the presidency, it became clear the incumbent would come into increasing conflict with the prime minister. Further problems arose when the committee drafted an electoral law based on an extreme form of proportional representation: fifteen citizens were sufficient to form a political party. The first elections under the new system sent twenty-nine parties to parliament.

Solidarity governments at first dominated post-communist politics, but Wałęsa abruptly dissolved parliament in May 1993. After a confused summer, during which the cabinet continued to rule without parliamentary control, former communists won a crushing victory in a general election. Afterwards, the president asserted his right to control key ministries, whilst leaving post-communists responsible for the economic reforms on which Western credits crucially depended. To bolster his authority, he proposed to head a "Non-Party Bloc to Support Reforms" (Bezpartyjny Blok Wspierania Reform, 1993-1997). But despite his prestige and unlimited access to the media, the general public showed little interest in joining a "presidential" party. Attempts to foster a Christian Democratic Alliance also failed, and the Church retreated to the margins of the political stage.

In one sense, this confirmed the new stability of Polish politics: mediators were not needed. Consequently libellous attempts by politicians of the right, such as former presidential adviser Jarosław Kaczyński, to brand President Wałęsa and his immediate entourage as "police agents" of the former communists (or even the USSR) fell on deaf ears. Having thus survived a stormy first term in office (1990-

1995), which saw three parliaments, six prime ministers and twenty-two presidential vetoes of parliamentary legislation, Wałęsa indicated his intention to seek re-election in 1995. However, Wałęsa was narrowly defeated in the first round of an acrimonious presidential campaign (33.1%). The winner was the former communist Aleksander Kwaśniewski (35.1%), a self-styled pragmatist committed to economic and security integration with Western Europe and to domestic reforms, who in the run-off a fortnight later polled 51.7% to Wałęsa's 48.3%.

Though his victory disappointed those with painful memories of communist rule, it seemed promising to those seeking continued modernization of the country under constitutional rule. During the run-off, the Catholic Church had attempted to influence the outcome through an Episcopal letter to local priests directing them to oppose Kwaśniewski from their pulpits. Wałęsa joined in with his peculiar idiom, claiming "the communist hyena is clawing back, it is spinning webs [. . .] and has wormed its way into the whole of the economy." But his continuing autocratic style and increasingly intemperate vocabulary did not improve his popularity. He lost the run-off and boycotted the swearing-in ceremony. By contrast, the victorious Kwaśniewski stressed he sought to be a president of consensus.

He allowed parliament and the prime minister scope for autonomous activity, thus helping to establish the political plurality set by NATO as a precondition for entry. When challenged on his former communism, Kwaśniewski replied that the new Polish constitution should be based on "principles of liberty, equality and tolerance" and should "make use of Christian traditions and values." Describing his political stance as that of a "social democrat or even social liberal," he accepted market competition and political democracy. He envisaged Poland as a market of 40 million consumers and a bridgehead for future investment by Western Europe in the East, but also recognized that the difficult transition to a free market economy required political stability amidst often harsh economic changes. This had a strong resonance with younger Poles (half the population being under thirty-five) most of whom saw free-market policies as providing the only realistic route to personal and national advancement.

The political legacy of communism continued to be contested in court. In spring 1996, former President Jaruzelski stood trial in Gdańsk with eleven others accused of ordering the killing of coastal workers during the disturbances of December 1970. The case collapsed when the district court ruled it had no jurisdiction over a matter that should be referred to the State Tribunal. Responsibility for overcoming the economic legacy of communism, notably state ownership, lay with the Ministry of Ownership Changes (Ministerstwo Przekształceń Własnościowych), i.e. privatization. Following much public controversy, a national referendum on privatization proved inconclusive. Since the 30% turn-out was well below the required 50%, the vote had no legal force. But privatization continued, including the proposal to sell off the government's 60% stake in the Gdańsk Shipyard, famous as the birthplace of Solidarity in 1980. Thousands of workers occupied the Shipyard and later held a protest march in Warsaw. After an acrimonious few months a reprieve was granted on condition that the Shipyard produced a credible reconstruction package.

Foreign orientation was less contended. Queen Elizabeth II told a joint session of the Polish parliament in March 1996 that the UK would support Poland's application for NATO membership. When President Kwaśniewski visited Washington in July, he was reassured by Present Clinton of US support for entry. Polish opinion endorsed such steps. Over 80% of the population favoured NATO entry, with only 2% "strongly opposed." This was partly a reflection of political uncertainty in Russia and its possible destabilizing effects on Poland's borders, particularly the powerfully-garrisoned Russian exclave of Kaliningrad. Following Polish participation in the NATO-led Implementation Force in Bosnia, joint Polish, French and Ukrainian military exercises were held in southern Poland. It was agreed that a joint Polish-Lithuanian peace-keeping battalion would be formed in 1997.

In July 1997, NATO formally invited Poland, together with the Czech Republic and Hungary, to join the alliance as full members. In February 1999, the Polish lower house ratified NATO accession by 409-7 (with four abstentions) and the Senate did likewise by 92-2. President Kwaśniewski and his Czech counterpart Václav Havel signed documents confirming this decision. A formal accession ceremony, including Hungary, took place in March just prior to NATO's fiftieth anniversary. Under a fifteen-year modernization programme, the Polish armed forces were to be reduced to 180,000 with greater reliance on professionals. Accordingly, compulsory military service was reduced from eighteen to twelve months.

As part of developing an even-handed foreign policy, President Kwaśniewski signed a declaration of reconciliation with Ukraine which condemned both the murders of Poles by Nazi Ukrainian nationalists in 1943 and the deportation of up to 100,000 Ukrainians from communist Poland in 1947. A further wartime issue was also brought to resolution. The Auschwitz synagogue, destroyed by the Nazis, was rededicated at a ceremony attended by Polish, Israeli and US officials. The government put in motion a programme to restore seized property or to compensate Poland's Jewish communities for losses suffered in the period. Post-war crimes were also condemned, including expulsions or enforced flight from Poland during an antisemitic and anti-intellectual pogrom in 1968 (Stola 1998). Kwaśniewski publicly condemned this shameful episode from the communist past, restoring citizenship to those affected and inviting them to return home.

In contrast to its predecessors, the government took a more robust approach to the communist past. Reversing earlier policies, parliament passed a resolution condemning "the communist dictatorship imposed on Poland by force and against the nation's will by the Soviet Union and Joseph Stalin." The former Communist Party was held to have been responsible for the "crimes and offences" of the communist period. The military court issued an arrest warrant for an elderly woman, by then a naturalized British citizen, who had been a Polish military prosecutor in the Stalin period. The British Home Office declined the request for extradition.

To give Polish citizens greater access to the past, an Institute of National Remembrance (Instytut Pamięci Narodowej) was established by parliament to house the Ministry of Interior files from 1939-1989. Contrary to expectations, the public showed much more interest in Soviet than German records. Files were opened to the public, enabling victims to be traced and revealing the names of agents and informers (Friszke 2008). Much recrimination and confusion ensued. The settlement of ancient political scores was far less acrimonious than that following opening of former Stasi files from Eastern Germany. However, taken with the speeding-up of privatization, they marked a defeat for the old Polish left, and indicated that the political right was regrouping for a significant comeback. The Public Interest Ombudsman was given access to IPN files, including communist security archives. Politicians shown to have lied about their previous collaboration with the security services could be disbarred from public life for ten years.

During the 2000 presidential election, candidates were subjugated, yet again, to allegations of collaboration with the communist regime. But President Kwaśniewski was acquitted when five secret police (SB) agents told a Warsaw court that he had not been an informer for their service. Similar charges against ex-President Wałęsa were shown to have been fabrications. The election resulted in a clear victory for the incumbent. President Kwaśniewski won outright, receiving 53.92% on the first ballot. In second place (17.30%) was an independent and Western-oriented economist Andrzej Olechowski whose pro-market and pro-European outlook found rapport amongst business and younger voters. Wałęsa who finished seventh, with 1.01% of the vote, declared his retirement from active politics.

The Ministry for European Integration brought forward legislation planned for 2002 to keep Poland on track for admission to the European Union in its next round of enlargement. Concern had been aroused by a recent European Commission report on candidate countries which praised Poland's overall performance of steady growth and progress towards a restructured market economy, but criticized slowness in enacting enabling legislation. It also noted that agricultural reform had not started at all. There was indeed much scepticism towards Europe in Poland's rural communities. Farmers themselves estimated that only 600,000 of the country's two million private farms would survive the accession process, leaving the rest bankrupt or dependent on subsidies. In the meantime, they argued, Polish access to Western markets would be blocked, while Polish supermarkets were swamped by cheap EU food imports, supported by a Common Agricultural Policy from which Poland was excluded.

Despite this anxiety, a national referendum in June 2003 showed a significant majority (77.5 %) in favour of European accession. 13.5 million had voted in support, with fewer than 4 million against. The result reflected a wide spectrum of support for entry, including from ex-President Jaruzelski and Pope John Paul II, who sent an openly partisan pastoral message saying that Europe needed Poland and Poland needed Europe.

Western Europe increasingly occupied Polish politicians. Discussions between the new Polish prime minister—Leszek Miller of the Democratic Left Alliance (SLD)—and German Chancellor Gerhard Schröder in September 2003 were dominated by a proposal from the German right to establish a centre of remembrance in Berlin for some 12 million ethnic Germans displaced from Eastern Europe (principally Western Poland) at the end of World War II. Their tactful joint communiqué suggested establishing a centre for all European exiles, to be overseen by the Council of Europe, in a less controversial venue: Sarajevo, Geneva or Strasbourg. However, tensions in Polish-German relations remained.

These came into the open in September 2004 when the Polish parliament voted unanimously (with one abstention) to demand "financial compensations or war damages" for losses caused by "German aggression, occupation, genocide and loss of independence" during World War II. Under Nazi occupation some 6 million Polish citizens, including most of the country's 3.1 million Jews had been killed. The parliamentary resolution, which was not legally binding, disclaimed any financial obligations towards the estimated 12.5 million German citizens displaced when Poland was moved westwards in 1945. The resolution was rejected by both the German leader and the Polish prime minister at their annual September meeting. Chancellor Schröder had already called on German courts to resist claims for lost land or compensation. The Polish prime minister stated that "the question of claims in Polish-German relations has been closed once and for all" referring to the bilateral treaty of December 1970. The two governments agreed to form a joint legal team to contest the claims of the Prussian Claims Society on behalf of ethnic Germans.

There was also renewed interest in the East. Ukraine's "Velvet Revolution" at the end of 2004 found wide resonance in Poland, whose Solidarity movement had pioneered the peaceful revolutions of the late 1980s. Wałęsa flew to Kiev in an attempt to mediate, as did President Kwaśniewski. The chosen international orientation of their largest Eastern neighbour was a Polish strategic concern. When Ukraine's outgoing President, Leonid Kuchma reversed his pro-EU stance,

Poland responded with border restrictions. Primarily aimed against smuggling, they involved several thousand newly-recruited border guards and customs officials, partly funded by 85 million euros in EU aid. At the same time, Poland sought to reduce the impact of restrictions for Ukrainian visitors by allowing minimal paperwork and issuing free visas. But Poland's tensions with its Eastern neighbour continued in 2005, when Poland backed Ukraine's pro-Western presidential candidate, Viktor Yushchenko, while Moscow supported his pro-Russian opponent.

These strains extended to Belarus, whose autocratic leader, President Aliaksandr Lukashenka began a crackdown on his country's 400,000-strong Polish ethnic minority. Fearing they could start a Ukrainian-style revolution, Belarusian police raided the headquarters of a group representing ethnic Poles in Belarus and arrested the group's two leaders. Following diplomatic expulsions from both Minsk and Warsaw, the USA expressed concern about "a continuing pattern of harassment against those seeking to peacefully express their views." A radio station was set up in Poland to transmit to Belarus. Former Solidarity activists helped Belarusian dissidents to set up printing presses. Polish universities admitted Belarusian students banned from universities at home.

At the end of August 2004, Wałęsa hosted a large gathering of world leaders to mark the 25th anniversary of the Gdańsk Agreement. The presidents of Georgia and Ukraine were greeted with standing ovations as they declared that Solidarity's example should inspire democracy activists in Belarus to topple their authoritarian president. Polish speakers called for a more muscular EU policy on democracy and human rights towards the Russian and other post-Soviet regimes. The Poles, Ukrainians, Lithuanians and Georgians present advocated a "new democratic coalition of states."

Poland continued to be concerned about the close relationship between the German and Russian governments. In particular, there was anxiety about potential "energy blackmail." The new North European Gas Pipe Line was due to cross from Russia through the Baltic Sea to Germany, thus bypassing Poland and Ukraine. Polish analysts saw the scheme as political rather than economic, enabling Moscow to exert pressure by threatening to turn off supplies to Central Europe without jeopardizing lucrative deliveries to Western Europe.

The 2003 US-led invasion of Iraq led to intense debate in Poland. Over-riding much domestic opposition, and condemnation of the war by Pope John Paul II, Poland contributed 2,500 troops to the multi-national invasion force. President Kwaśniewski told European journalists that though he had been "deceived" about the existence of weapons of mass destruction prior to the war, there would be no precipitate withdrawal. The government was further embarrassed by television coverage of its own commandos, who could only operate successfully in secrecy.

Their commander was recalled to Warsaw and a timetable was agreed whereby Polish troops would be withdrawn by the end of 2005.

A new and more troubling historical sensation was found at home. The Polish Ministry of Justice sanctioned the exhumation of the remains of Jewish victims of a pogrom in Jedwabne in July 1941 (Gross 2001). Additional research by the Institute of National Remembrance (IPN) revealed that far from being an isolated incident, numerous similar atrocities had taken place during both Nazi and Soviet occupations (Machcewicz and Persak 2002). Despite the stormy debate (Polonsky and Michlic 2003), prominent public figures sought to heal old wounds. Cardinal Józef Glemp, Primate of Poland, broke with years of silence to apologize for the part played by Catholics in the Jedwabne massacre. Unveiling a memorial at Jedwabne, President Kwaśniewski apologized for Polish crimes against Jews.

Several other statements urged national reconciliation. The Institute of National Remembrance apologized in February 2005 for leakage, via the internet, of a communist-era secret service file of agents, collaborators and their victims (the so-called Wildstein's List). The list of 240,000 names had failed to distinguish agents from victims, thus leading to the fear that the innocent would be condemned by public opinion. They included Prime Minister Marek Belka, who made his secret police file public. In a dramatic admission of past failure, (the now retired) General Jaruzelski apologized on Czech television for his role as Minister of Defence in the five-power invasion of August 1968 to crush the Prague reform movement (Garlicki and Paczkowski 1995). The 82-year-old stated the intervention had been "wrong" and "shameful." Political accord was also restored in the period of mourning for the first Polish Pope, who died on 2 April 2005. He had visited 129 countries during his pontificate and was widely remembered for his triumphant first pilgrimage to Poland in June 1979, seen as inspiring Solidarity.

The 2005 presidential elections reflected a popular feeling that Poland's decommunization was incomplete. The eventual winner Lech Kaczyński, who won 54% of the final vote (on a turnout of 51%), condemned a "Bermuda quadrangle" of corrupt politicians, police agents, business leaders and criminals for holding the country to ransom. Such populist rhetoric was accompanied by a raft of centre-right policies. Stressing "moral renewal" and Christian values, he opposed abortion and gay rights. As mayor of Warsaw he had twice tried to ban the gay pride ("Equality") parades, and when one went ahead, questioned why the police did not break up the "illegal demonstration." Two years later the European Court of Human Rights found the Polish Government guilty of violating the right to freedom of assembly guaranteed by the European Human Rights Convention. Kaczyński also supported the death penalty, despite EU policy.

There was now a centre-right in Polish politics, whose main parties agreed on most issues except the economy. The ruling Law and Justice Party (Prawo i

Sprawiedliwość), led by the president's twin brother Jaroslaw Kaczyński, using populist and nationalist language, stressed the need for state intervention and social protection. By contrast, Civic Platform (Platforma Obywatelska), led by Donald Tusk, favoured the free market. After a fractious year in which Law and Justice emphasized the need to purge public life of corruption, crime and communist residua, in a process known as *lustracja* (vetting), Law and Justice was replaced by Civic Platform, and Donald Tusk became prime minister (November 2007) on a programme to restore trust at home and abroad.

Throughout 2008, Civic Platform, in coalition with the rural Polish Peasants Party (Polskie Stronnictwo Ludowe), led by Waldemar Pawlak, enjoyed strong public support. But it lacked a sufficient majority to override frequent presidential vetoes. This had been foreshadowed earlier. On taking office, President Lech Kaczyński had declared the first task was to purge the Republic of "various pathologies in our life." These included "the great rush for unjust enrichment" poisoning society and preventing the state from providing basic social security, health services and normal conditions for family development. But there was a more positive side to his politics. He commemorated and rehabilitated Polish national heroes who had perished at the hands of the secret police (SB), the Soviet NKVD, SMERSH and other repressive organs of communist rule. On 21 December 2008, Kaczyński became the first Polish head of state to visit a Polish synagogue, attending a ceremony on the first night of Hanukkah.

In April 2010, a Russian-built plane carrying the president, his wife and ninety-four distinguished public and military figures to commemorate the Katyń massacre, crashed while trying to land at Smolensk. There were no survivors. Though Russian Prime Minister Vladimir Putin took personal charge of the investigation, the Polish public felt the lack of a satisfactory explanation for the tragedy, widely regarded as a "second Katyń." The president and his wife were buried in Kraków's Wawel Cathedral alongside the ancient monarchs and other national heroes. In a gesture of reconciliation, Russian President Dmitrii Medvedev was present at the funeral—one of the few world leaders able to attend as European airspace was closed on account of volcanic ash. Marshal of the Sejm (Speaker of Parliament) Bronisław Komorowski of Civic Platform was elected as the country's new president in July 2010.

A surprising controversy arose concerned the long-serving foreign correspondent Ryszard Kapuściński (1932-2007), famous for a series of supposedly first-hand accounts of third world dictatorships, including *The Emperor* (about Haile Selassie, 1982) and *Shah of Shahs* (1985), which many saw as allegories for Poland under communism. An initially impressed, much younger journalist started to check Kapuściński's sources and found that in significant cases they were imaginary. His highly controversial findings were published in Polish under the title "Non-Fiction" (Domosławski 2010; trans. 2012). Public opinion was further divided when it became apparent that the price paid by Kapuściński for freedom to travel—passports for the West were issued by the security authorities—was to provide secret reports on those he encountered on his travels. Kapuściński supporters replied that his style of "literary reportage," using embroidery or even the manufacture of "facts" was a skilful technique to create a reality "truer than truth itself." They also pointed to *Imperium* (1993; trans. 1994), his insightful retrospective on the Soviet Union, described by one devotee as "the most passionate, engaging and historically profound account of the Soviet empire that I have ever read." (Ignatieff 1994)

On 1 July 2011, Poland assumed the six-month rotating presidency of the European Union. Amongst other priorities, Poland sought to foster greater cooperation of the EU with its neighbours through the Eastern Partnership. Relations within the EU were furthered by the victory of the pro-market Civic Platform in the October elections, making its leader Donald Tusk the first prime minister to be re-elected since 1989. Perhaps the most impressive proposal to end controversy came from the Polish foreign minister towards the end of the EU Presidency.

Speaking in Berlin on 28 November 2011, Radek Sikorski asked: "What do I regard as the biggest threat to the security and prosperity of Poland today? It's not terrorism, it's not the Taliban, and it's certainly not German tanks. It's not even Russian missiles which President Medvedev has just threatened to deploy on the EU's border. The biggest threat to the security and prosperity of Poland would be the collapse of the Euro-zone." His conclusion was a heartfelt appeal. "I demand of Germany that, for your own sake and for ours, you help it survive and prosper. You know full well that nobody else can do it." His speech ended on an extraordinary note. "I will probably be the first Polish foreign minister in history to say so, but here it is: I fear German power *less* than I am beginning to fear German inactivity." (Sikorski 2011, 9)

Bibliography

Domosławski, Artur. 2010. *Kapuściński. Non-fiction.* Warsaw: Świat Książki.

—. 2012. *Ryszard Kapuściński: A Life,* translated by Antonia Lloyd-Jones. London: Verso.

Dudek, Antoni and Tomasz Marszałkowski. 1999. *Walki uliczne w PRL, 1956-1989.* Kraków: Wydawnictwo Geo.

Dzienkiewicz, Anna. 2010. *Rosja a Katyń.* Warsaw: Karta.

Friszke, Andrzej. 2008. "Tajni współpracownicy UB/SB. Próba typologii przypadków." In *Naznaczeni i napiętnowani. O wykluczeniu politycznym,* edited by Maria Jarosz, 78-107. Warsaw: Instytut Studiów Politycznych Polskiej Akademii Nauk.

Garlicki, Andrzej and Andrzej Paczkowski, eds. 1995. *Zaciskanie pętli. Tajne dokumenty dotyczące Czechosłowacji 1968 r.* Warsaw: Wydawnictwo Sejmowe.

Geremek, Bronisław. 1990. *Rok 1989. Bronisław Geremek opowiada, Jacek Żakowski pyta*. Warsaw: Plejada.

Gross, Jan T. 2001. *Neighbors: The Destruction of the Jewish Community in Jedwabne, Poland, 1941*. Princeton, NJ: Princeton University Press.

Ignatieff, Michael. 1994. "What about Anna Andreyevna?" *London Review of Books* 16(19): 8.

Kapuściński, Ryszard. 1993. *Imperium.* Warsaw: Czytelnik.

—. 1994. *Imperium,* translated by Klara Glowczewska. London: Granta in association with Penguin.

Kemp-Welch, Anthony. 1991. "Change in Eastern Europe." In *The Impact of Gorbachev: The First Phase, 1985-1990,* edited by D. W. Spring, 135-153. London: Pinter.

Kramer, Mark. 1999. "Soviet Deliberations during the Polish Crisis, 1980-1981." Cold War International History Project Special Working Paper 1. Washington, DC: Woodrow Wilson Center.

—. 2005. "Gorbachev and the demise of east European communism." In *Reinterpreting the End of the Cold War: Issues, Interpretations, Periodizations,* edited by Silvio Pons and Federico Romero, 179-200. London and New York: Frank Cass.

—. 2011. "The Demise of the Soviet Bloc." *Europe-Asia Studies* 63(9): 1535-1590.

Lewis, Paul G. 2001. *Party Development and Democratic Change in Post-Communist Europe: The First Decade.* London: Croom Helm.

Lewis, Paul G. and Zdenka Mansfeldová, eds. 2006. *The European Union and Party Politics in Central and Eastern Europe.* Basingstoke: Palgrave Macmillan.

Lewis, Paul. G. and Radosław Markowski, eds. 2011. *Europeanising Party Politics? Comparative Perspectives on Central and Eastern Europe.* Manchester: Manchester University Press.

McAvoy, David. 2012. *Zbigniew Pelczynski: A Life Remembered.* London: Grosvenor House Publishing.

Machcewicz, Paweł and Krzysztof Persak, eds. 2002. *Wokół Jedwabnego.* 2 vols. Warsaw: Instytut Pamięci Narodowej.

Medvedev, Vadim A. 1994. *Raspad. Kak on nazreval v "mirovoi systemie sotsializma."* Moscow: Medzhdunarodnye ostnoshenia.

Michnik, Adam. 1999. "Neither Conspiracy or Benevolence: The Miracle of the Polish Round Table." *Gazeta Wyborcza* (English version), 3 July.

Millard, Frances. 1994. *The Anatomy of the New Poland: Post-Communist Politics in its First Phase.* Aldershot: Edward Elgar.

—. 1999. *Polish Politics and Society.* London: Routledge.

—. 2010. *Democratic Elections in Poland, 1991-2007.* Abingdon, Oxon: Routledge.

Pelczynski, Z. A. [Zbigniew Andrzej]. [1982]. "The Road from Communism." Special R. B. McCallum Lecture, 29 May. Oxford: Pembroke College.

Polonsky, Antony and Joanna Michlic, eds. 2003. *The Neighbors Respond: The Controversy over the Jedwabne Massacre in Poland.* Princeton, NJ: Princeton University Press.

Sarotte, Mary. 2009. *The Struggle to Create Post-Cold War Europe.* Princeton, NJ: Princeton University Press.

Sikorski, Radosław. 2011. "Poland and the Future of the European Union." Accessed 28 March, 2013. http://www.mfa.gov.pl/resource/33ce6061-ec12-4da1-a145-01e2995c6302:JCR

Skórzyński, Jan. 2002. "'Solidarność' w drodze do Okrągłego Stołu. Strategia polityczna opozycji 1985-1989." In *Polska 1986-1989: Koniec systemu. Materiały międzynarodowej konferencji, Miedeszyn, 21-23 October,* edited by Paweł Machcewicz, 59-73. Warsaw: Wydawnictwo Trio i Instytut Studiów Politycznych Polskiej Akademii Nauk.

Stola, Dariusz. 1998. *Kampania antysyjonistyczna w Polsce 1967-1968.* Warsaw: Instytut Studiów Politycznych Polskiej Akademii Nauk.

Szczerbiak, Aleks. 2011. *Poland within the European Union: New Awkward Partner or New Heart of Europe?* Advances in European Politics 76. Abingdon, Oxon: Routledge.

Notes on Contributors

Uilleam Blacker is a Postdoctoral Research Associate of the Memory at War project, Department of Slavonic Studies, University of Cambridge. He is co-author of *Remembering Katyn* (2012), and co-editor of *Memory and Theory in Eastern Europe* (2013). He has published articles on cultural memory, urban space, gender and contemporary literature in Poland, Russia and Ukraine.

Urszula Chowaniec is Assistant Professor at Andrzej Frycz Modrzewski Kraków University, and Teaching Fellow in Polish Language at the UCL School of Slavonic and East European Studies. Her research interests focus on contemporary Polish literature and language, women's writing, migration and emigration. Author of the monograph *W poszukiwaniu kobiety. O wczesnych powieściach Ireny Krzywickiej* (2007), contributor to and joint editor of several volumes on contemporary women's writing and cultural memory (2008, 2010 and 2012).

Knut Andreas Grimstad is Associate Professor and Head of Polish Studies, University of Oslo. He has published on Polish Modernism, as well as contemporary Polish prose and poetry. Among his current research interests are popular culture and Jewish-Polish relations in Poland from 1918 to the present day.

Elwira Grossman is Stepek Lecturer in Polish Studies and Director of the Comparative Literature programme in the School of Modern Languages and Cultures at the University of Glasgow. Her research interests include contemporary Polish drama, theatre and cinema, gender studies, intercultural communication, the Polish/Jewish relationship as well as teaching Polish as a foreign language. She edited and contributed to the collection of essays *Studies in Language, Literature, and Cultural Mythology in Poland. Investigating 'The Other'* (2002). She is currently involved in an AHRC-funded international project on *Translating Russian and East European Cultures: Exchange and communication within a multidisciplinary and multicultural Area Studies context.*

Wioletta Grzegorzewska is a poet, writer and editor. Her poetry volumes include *Wyobraźnia kontrolowana* (1998), *Parantele* (2003), *Orinoko* (2008), *Inne obroty* (2010), *Smena's Memory* (2011), *Ruchy Browna* (2011) and *Notatnik z Wyspy* (2012). Her first novel *Spóźnione dokarmianie pszczół* is forthcoming in 2013. Her poems have been translated into English. In 2006, she left Poland and moved to the UK, where she currently resides in the town of Ryde on the Isle of Wight.

Jerzy Jarzębski is Professor in the Faculty of Polish Studies at the Jagiellonian University, Kraków, and at the State East European College in Przemyśl. His interests focus on Polish prose of the 20th and 21st centuries, mainly on the life and work of

Bruno Schulz, Witold Gombrowicz and Stanislaw Lem. He has published thirteen books and prepared scholarly editions of the collected works of these three writers.

Marek Kazmierski escaped communist Poland and settled in the UK as a child political refugee. Today, he runs a series of insider art initiatives, including the arts magazine *Not Shut Up*, the publishing house OFF_PRESS and Intersection, a book and new media project in Central London. *Damn the Source*, his collection of short stories on the experience of modern migration, is published in the summer of 2013.

Anthony Kemp-Welch is Reader in the School of History, University of East Anglia. His research interests include the political history of Poland, Cold War history and international relations. Author of *Poland Under Communism: A Cold War History* (2008), also published in translation as *Polska pod rządami komunistów* (2010).

Joanna Beata Michlic is a social and cultural historian, Lecturer in the Department of Historical Studies at Bristol University, and founder and Director of the HBI (Hadassah-Brandeis Institute) Project on Families, Children, and the Holocaust at Brandeis University. Her latest major publication is *Bringing the Dark to Light: The Reception of the Holocaust in Postcommunist Europe,* co-edited with John-Paul Himka (2013). She is also the editor of the forthcoming *Jewish Families in Europe, 1939-Present: History, Representation, and Memory* (2014). Her two current research topics are the history of rescuers of Jews and East European Jewish childhood, 1945-1950.

Agnieszka Mrozik is a researcher at the Institute of Literary Research, Polish Academy of Sciences. She recently published the book *Akuszerki transformacji. Kobiety, literatura i władza w Polsce po 1989 roku* (2012). Her academic interests include critical analysis of media discourse and popular culture, communism and PRL studies from the perspective of gender, contemporary women's literature and feminist discourse.

Grzegorz Niziołek is Professor of Theatre Studies at the Jagiellonian University, Kraków. His research interests focus on post-war Polish theatre and drama, the relationship between history and art, and memory and theatre. He is co-founder of the theatre magazine *Didaskalia* and its current editor-in-chief. His publications include books on Krystian Lupa, Tadeusz Różewicz and Krzysztof Warlikowski. Articles on contemporary Polish theatre have been published in various theatre magazines in Poland and abroad.

Ursula Phillips is Honorary Research Associate at the UCL School of Slavonic and East European Studies. Her research interests cover many aspects of 19th-, 20th- and 21st-century Polish literature, in particular feminism and prose by women. Author of the monograph *Narcyza Żmichowska. Feminizm i religia* (2008), joint editor of several multi-authored volumes, translator of inter alia Maria Wirtemberska, Narcyza Żmichowska and Zofia Nałkowska, and currently working on a monograph on Nałkowska.

Monika Świerkosz completed her PhD in the Department of Polish Studies at the Jagiellonian University, Kraków. Her dissertation was on feminist literary discourse as it relates to tradition, memory, history and women's intergenerational conflicts. She has published in many Polish literary magazines including *Zadra*, *Dekada Literacka*, *FA-art*, *Opcje* and *Teksty drugie*. She is also joint editor of *uni-GENDER*, a peer-reviewed internet magazine devoted to issues of gender studies.

Dirk Uffelmann is Professor of Slavic Literatures and Cultures and Vice President for Academic and Student Affairs at the University of Passau, Germany. His research interests are Polish, Russian, Czech, Slovak, and Central Asian literature, philosophy, religion, migration and internet studies. He is co-editor of *Contemporary Polish Migrant Culture and Literature in Germany, Ireland, and the UK* (2011) as well as of the book series *Postcolonial Perspectives on Eastern Europe* and *Polonistik im Kontext*.

Kris Van Heuckelom is Professor of Polish Studies at KU Leuven, Belgium. His research interests include modern Polish literature, translation studies, visual culture and film. He co-edited (together with Dieter De Bruyn) the volume *(Un)masking Bruno Schulz: New Combinations, Further Fragmentations, Ultimate Reintegrations* (2009) and is currently finishing a monograph on the representation of Polish migrants in European cinema.

Paul Vickers, a graduate of UCL, is currently completing an AHRC-funded PhD at the University of Glasgow on communist-era Polish peasant autobiography, exploring relations between academia, popular memory, censorship and dominant public history. He has used his archival research to publish on representations of experiences of abortion in communist-era competition autobiographies, while his Master's research produced a study of Polish-German relations in theatre ("Staging memoirs of forced migration: Jan Klata's Polish-German theatre project 'Transfer!'," *Polish Theatre Perspectives*, 2010: 1). Paul is also an active translator, currently collaborating with the Grotowski Institute in Wrocław.

Błażej Warkocki is Lecturer in the Department of Literary Anthropology at the Institute of Polish Philology, Adam Mickiewicz University, Poznań. Joint author (with Przemysław Czapliński, Maciej Leciński and Eliza Szybowicz) of *Kalendarium życia literackiego 1976-2000* (2003) and joint editor (with Zbyszek Sypniewski) of the collection *Homofobia po polsku* (2004). Author of the book *Homo niewiadomo. Polska proza wobec odmienności* (2007).

Elżbieta Wójcik-Leese, Centre for Internationalisation and Parallel Language Use, University of Copenhagen, works on contemporary poetry, genetic criticism, translation studies and cognitive poetics. She also translates contemporary Polish poetry. Her recent publications include: *Nothing More* (translations of Krystyna Miłobędzka, 2013) and *Cognitive Poetic Readings in Elizabeth Bishop: Portrait of a Mind Thinking* (2010).

Katarzyna Zechenter is Lecturer at the UCL School of Slavonic and East European Studies where she teaches Polish literature, culture and cinema. Research focuses on contemporary Polish-Jewish writers including Jadwiga Maurer, Michał Głowiński and Jarosław Marek Rymkiewicz. She is the author of a monograph on Tadeusz Konwicki's fiction (2007). Her poems have been translated into English, French and Spanish; her latest volume *W cieniu Drzewa. Wiersze* appeared in 2011.

Index

Mittel- und Ostmitteleuropastudien
Der Sturz der Diktatur
Opposition in Polen und der DDR
1988/89
Dominik Trutkowski
LIT

Gerhard Besier; Agnieszka Debska; Zbigniew Gluza; Katarzyna Stokłosa; Anna Zinserling (Hg.)

Deutsche und Polen während und nach dem Zweiten Weltkrieg

Gemeinsame Geschichte gemeinsam erinnern

Die Leiden, die der von Hitlerdeutschland ausgelöste Zweite Weltkrieg über die Völker Europas gebracht hat, waren ungeheuerlich. Ungeheuerlich waren auch – am Ende des Krieges – die Leiden der Deutschen. Nachkriegspolen strebte danach, die Deutschen aus den Gebieten östlich von Oder und Lausitzer Neiße zu vertreiben und wandte dabei ebenfalls brutale Methoden an. Heute kann man über diese Ereignisse offen sprechen und sie an dem gemeinsamen Kriterium der Menschenrechte messen und nicht an den vergangenen Standpunkten zweier verfeindeter Völker.

Wenn wir den Ballast dieser schweren Geschichte abwerfen, wenn wir das damals erlittene Leid überwinden wollen, dann müssen wir einander zuhören. Hierzu bedarf es nicht nur eines Willens, sondern auch einer Methode. Der Wille auf beiden Seiten ist nach wie vor deutlich vorhanden, es mangelt jedoch nach wie vor an Erfolg versprechenden Mitteln. Aus diesem Grunde stellen wir eine deutsche Ausgabe der von der polnischen Quartalschrift „Karta“ in Polen gesammelten Zeugnisse vor. ueberdenautorKatarzyna Stoklosa is Assistant Professor in the Institute of Border Region Studies at the University of Southern Denmark.

Mittel- und Ostmitteleuropastudien, Bd. 6, 2007, 304 S., 19,90 €, br., ISBN 978-3-8258-0504-3

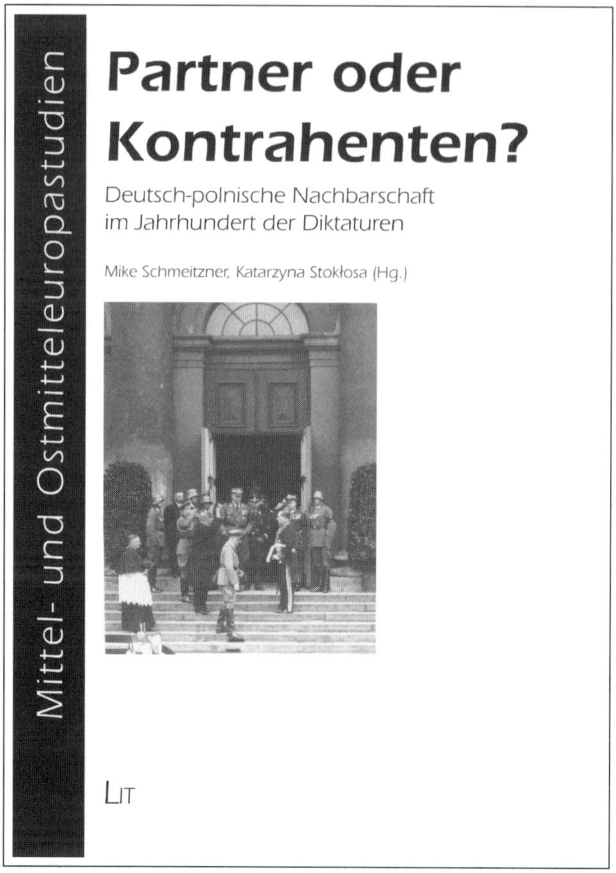

Mike Schmeitzner; Katarzyna Stokłosa (Hg..)

Partner oder Kontrahenten?

Deutsch-polnische Nachbarschaft im Jahrhundert der Diktaturen

Der Sammelband nimmt vier verschiedene Perioden deutsch-polnischer Nachbarschaft in den Blick: In einem ersten Teil werden Probleme und Chancen der Zwischenkriegszeit ausgelotet und Fragen nach einem (begrenzten) Miteinander gestellt. Der zweite Teil konzentriert sich auf die Dekade zwischen der Entfesselung des Zweiten Weltkrieges und des damit verbundenen deutschen Überfalls auf Polen im Jahre 1939 und der Gründung beider deutscher Staaten 1949. In einem dritten Teil stehen die beiden deutsch-polnischen Nachbarschaften während des Kalten Krieges und der Détente im Mittelpunkt der Betrachtungen. Die Überwindung der bisherigen politischen und ideologischen Vorgaben ist Thema des vierten Teils, der sich mit den Herausforderungen des neuen Europa und neuen Wegen eines deutsch-polnischen Miteinanders beschäftigt.

ueberdenautorKatarzyna Stoklosa is Assistant Professor in the Institute of Border Region Studies at the University of Southern Denmark.

Mittel- und Ostmitteleuropastudien, Bd. 8, 2008, 240 S., 19,90 €, br., ISBN 978-3-8258-1254-6

Rolf Reißig; Michael Thomas (Hg.)
Neue Chancen für alte Regionen?
Fallbeispiele aus Ostdeutschland und Polen
Band 1 der „Texte aus dem BISS“ bringt Untersuchungen insbesondere zu problematischen Regionen in Ostdeutschland und Polen und stellt diese in die laufende Debatte um Regionalisierung und Regionalentwicklung.
ueberdenautorMichael Thomas ist zur Zeit als wissenschaftlicher Mitarbeiter am BISS und der TU Berlin; er koordiniert sozialwissenschaftliche Forschungsprojekte in verschiedenen Regionen.
Texte aus dem Brandenburg-Berliner Institut für Sozialwissenschaftliche Studien (BISS e. V.), Bd. 1, 2005, 344 S., 29,90 €, br., ISBN 3-8258-7884-8

LIT Verlag Berlin – Münster – Wien – Zürich – London
Auslieferung Deutschland / Österreich / Schweiz: siehe Impressumsseite